THE FATHER-DAUGHTER PLOT

THE
FATHER-DAUGHTER
PLOT

Japanese Literary Women and the Law of the Father

EDITED BY

Rebecca L. Copeland

and Esperanza Ramirez-Christensen

University of Hawai'i Press, Honolulu

01 02 03 04 05 06   6 5 4 3 2 1

Library of Congress Cataloging–in-Publication Data
The father-daughter plot : Japanese literary women and the law of the father/ edited by
Rebecca L. Copeland and Esperanza Ramirez-Christensen.
p.   cm.
Includes bibliographical references and index.
ISBN 0–8248–2172–6 (cloth : alk. paper)—ISBN 0–8248–2438–5 (pbk. : alk. paper)
1. Japanese literature—Women authors—History and criticism.   2. Fathers and daughters
in literature.   I. Title: Japanese literary women and the law of the father.   II. Copeland,
Rebecca L.   III. Ramirez-Christensen, Esperanza.

PL721.F37   F38   2001
895.6'093520431—dc21   2001023555

Designed by Kenneth Miyamoto
Printed by The Maple-Vail Book Manufacturing Group

CONTENTS

PREFACE

This volume of essays on the "daughterly" experience of Japanese women writers has been a long time in the making and has been derived from a variety of sources. The first spark of inspiration for the project was lit at the Third Annual Meeting of the Midwest Association of Japanese Literary Studies, held at Purdue University in Indiana and organized by Professor Eiji Sekine around the theme "Desire for *Monogatari*." Esperanza Ramirez-Christensen presented a paper on Sugawara Takasue's Daughter and her "desire for *monogatari*," or fictional tales. In her presentation, Esperanza spoke of the bond between the daughterly author and her father, the way the oedipal tension in this bond figures in the daughter's literary production and can be said indeed to constitute a repressed subtext in much classical Japanese women's writing.

The topic that Esperanza addressed struck a chord. I had also been scheduled to present a paper at this conference on the writer Uno Chiyo and the way that "makeup" figured prominently in her texts as a metaphor for self-creation. Although I had not intended to speak on Uno's relationship with her father, I had continually confronted this relationship in my research for this and other projects. It was clear that the author's "self-creation" was intimately tied to her relationship with her father and to her positioning of herself in a literary environment largely defined by father figures. Ann Sherif was also at this conference—speaking this time on Kōda Rohan. I was aware of Ann's work on Rohan's daughter, Kōda Aya, and had just read Alan Tansman's study, *The Writings of Kōda Aya*, on the same topic. The bond between a woman writer and her father (whether biological or cultural) was profoundly significant—regardless of the era in which the woman wrote. Even women who did not have an important literary father, and even women who did not have a father, were nevertheless positioned politically, ideologically, and symbolically as "daughters" in a culture that venerates "the father."

Western feminist criticism—literary and otherwise—had already explored this issue with considerable rigor. Jacques Lacan—an "originary father" of sorts—had stimulated much discussion with his re-readings of Freud and his subsequent production of "the Name-of-the-Father," which argued that all was ordered around patriarchal law. Lacan insisted on the symbolic function of the father and revealed little interest in actual father figures. The Lacanian father as a bodiless law, an ideological construct, intrigued and entreated subsequent feminist critics. Whereas some, such as Richard Con Davis, Jacqueline Rose, and Luce Irigaray worked within Lacan's paradigm, many others struggled to break the hold of "Father Law" as a monolithic principle and to recognize the father "both as a historical product and an ideological construct."[1] An early contributor to this latter enterprise was Jane Gallop, with her 1982 study on feminist psychoanalysis, *The Daughter's Seduction,* in which she analyzed the discord between father law and father desire. Ursula Owen followed Gallop one year later with *Fathers: Reflections by Daughters,* a collection of essays by women writers about their fathers. These studies stimulated a rich outpouring of writings about the father-daughter bond—from a variety of perspectives and within a variety of disciplines. For the purposes of this present volume, the most influential works have been two collections of essays published simultaneously in 1989: *Refiguring the Father: New Feminist Readings of Patriarchy,* edited by Patricia Yaeger and Beth Kowaleski-Wallace and *Daughters and Fathers,* edited by Lynda E. Boose and Betty S. Flowers. Lynda Zwinger's study *Daughters, Fathers, and the Novel: The Sentimental Romance of Heterosexuality* and Jerry Aline Flieger's *Colette and the Phantom Father* have also proved to be inspiring. In fact, there are so many studies on this topic and related issues in English that it is impossible to single out one or two as representative.

Such is not the case when we look to Japanese-language studies or studies on Japanese literature in English. Much attention has been paid to the role of the mother in the life of the Japanese male writer and to the image of the mother in Japanese literature. In 1995 a

1. Beth Kowaleski-Wallace and Patricia Yaeger, "Introduction," in *Refiguring the Father: New Feminist Readings of Patriarchy,* ed. Yaeger and Kowaleski-Wallace (Carbondale: Southern Illinois University Press, 1989), p. xiv.

conference in British Columbia honoring Professor Kin'ya Tsuruta had as its organizing theme "the Japanese mother." Two publications resulted from the conference, *Mothers in Japanese Literature*, the English proceedings; and a volume in Japanese edited by Professors Suke-hiro Hirakawa and Takao Hagiwara and entitled *Nihon no haha*. With the exception of Alan Tansman's study on Kōda Aya, however, little was available on the father in Japanese literature.[2]

With this in mind, I organized a panel for the 1996 Association for Asian Studies with the title "In the Shadow of the Father: Literary 'Patriarchs' and Japanese Women Writers." The participants included Eileen Mikals-Adachi, Edith Sarra, Ann Sherif, and myself, and Espe-ranza Ramirez-Christensen was the discussant for the papers. Almost simultaneously, Atsuko Sakaki organized "(Un)Dutiful Daughters: Modern Japanese Female Writers and Their Cultural Fathers," a day-long conference sponsored by the Edwin O. Reischauer Institute at Harvard University. Presenters at this conference included Janice Brown, Midori McKeon, Sharalyn Orbaugh, Ann Sherif, and Atsuko Sakaki. Given our mutual interests in the father-daughter dynamics in Japanese literature, presenters at both conferences decided to come together to publish their contributions. I was able to solicit chapters from a few more scholars in an effort to round out the collection. It should be noted, however, that this volume is by no means a complete picture of father-daughterness in Japanese literature. I would have liked to have included a chapter on the Tokugawa-era writer Ema Saikō, for example, or the Meiji-era Higuchi Ichiyō. In the modern era, I regret the omission of a chapter devoted to Tsushima Yūko or Yoshimoto Banana or to the more contemporary Yū Miri or Uchida Shungiku. I hope that this volume will inspire others to look more closely at these writers and to consider them from the position of their literary daughterhood.

Edited volumes are never as easy to complete as they would seem from the outset. And this volume is no exception. It has been a long time in the making and has involved copious amounts of correspon-dence between myself and my coeditor, Esperanza Ramirez-Chris-

---

2. Since the time that this study was envisioned, two books on the topic have ap-peared in Japanese: Tanaka Takako, *Nihon fazakon bungakushi* (Tokyo: Kinokuniya shoten, 1998); and Yagawa Sumiko, *Chichi no musume-tachi—Mori Mari to Anaisu Nin* (Tokyo: Shinchōsha, 1997).

tensen, and between ourselves and our contributors. We would like to take this opportunity to thank our contributors for their patience and perseverance. Because much of this correspondence took place electronically, across oceans, and across conflicting word processing systems, I would also like to thank Dr. Rick Heimbach of Tokyo, Japan, who was tremendously helpful when I was trying to access attachments and such in my lonely *kenkyūshitsu* at Kokugakuin University. His expertise and forbearance were invaluable. Our editors at University of Hawai'i Press, Sharon Yamamoto and her successor, Pamela Kelley, must also be commended for their composure and trust. They never expressed concern that the project might not reach completion.

Rebecca L. Copeland

ABBREVIATIONS

NKBT   *Nihon koten bungaku taikei*. 102 vols. Iwanami shoten, 1956–1968.

NKBZ   *Nihon koten bungaku zenshū*. 51 vols. Shōgakkan, 1970–1976.

SNKS   *Shinchō Nihon koten shūsei*. 48 vols. Shinchōsa, 1976–1989.

Introduction

ESPERANZA RAMIREZ-CHRISTENSEN

We have gathered together the essays in this book as an exploration of writing by women and its discursive relationship to the patriarchy, an order whose continued reproduction in the family is no longer certain. The materials for the investigation are inevitably limited by the authors' literary and geographical focus on Japan and, within it, on specific works or writers, so that we cannot claim a representative coverage of the literature. Nevertheless, we offer these essays as a contribution to the study of women's writing in the West, as it opens up to the experience of women in other parts of the globe both before and after their contact with the West.

This contact with the West occurred in Japan initially with the introduction of Christianity in the sixteenth century and later with the state-sponsored adoption of Western science and institutions in the Meiji period (1868–1912). But Japanese women were already writing poetry in the seventh century, and in the Heian period (794–1185) they were the principal producers of the singular art of fiction called the poem-narrative. Its masterpiece was *The Tale of Genji* (ca. 1010), by the court lady Murasaki Shikibu, still considered the major work in the classical canon and a reference point for any discussion of it.

The father-daughter relation that is our focus has not heretofore been foregrounded in any literary study within Western Japanology itself. The specific study of women's writing is still a relatively new area for this discipline, but for other reasons, the omission is perhaps not surprising. Among the pairs of relations (husband-wife, father-son, mother-son, father-daughter, mother-daughter, siblings) in the nuclear family, the father-daughter pair is at once the most superfluous and the most revealing.[1] It is superfluous because the daughter's traditional structural role in the middle-class family has been negligible.

1

She was not expected to carry on the father's name and patrimony, which belonged to the son. At best, she was her mother's helper, a temporary family member until marriage took her away to assume her proper structural role as wife and mother in another family. And yet it is just this ambiguity of the daughter's positioning as both insider and outsider that brings into focus the nature of the family as an artificial social construction constituted by the patriarchal imperative to perpetuate itself. Through marriage with another family's son, the daughter has been the necessary link in the formation of the social alliances that structure the community.

The question of the patriarchy's beginning in Japan is still a matter of some debate. It was long the commonly held belief within Japanese historiography that the patriarchy came into being with the institution of the *ritsuryō* state and its laws in the last half of the seventh century (645–701). However, feminist historians subsequently questioned this assumption and argued that what existed during the two subsequent centuries was an incomplete patriarchy more honored in the letter than in practice, and this is now the widely accepted view. The incomplete patriarchy thesis began as a matrilineal theory in the work of the pioneering feminist historian Takamure Itsue (1894–1964) and is based primarily on her study of the family and marriage practices in the eighth and ninth centuries.[2] Using as documentary sources the ancient chronicles *Kojiki* (712), *Nihongi* (720), and the poetic anthology *Man'yōshū* (comp. ca. 759), as well as later literature and diaries, she observed that the typical ancient marriage practice was matrilocal, of the type called *tsumadoikon* (wife-visiting marriage), in which the man regularly visited the woman, who continued to reside with her parents and children in her natal home. This would later evolve into the *mukotorikon* (taking-a-son-in-law marriage), in which the husband was taken into the wife's natal household, settling with her parents, children, and siblings, or constituting a separate household with his wife and children but still within the uxorilocal and matrilineal environment. This crucial observation of the matrilocal and matrilineal character of the ancient Japanese family had long been obscured by orthodox historians' primary reliance on the early *ritsuryō* state's official household registers *(koseki)*. These records, along with the legal codes, state bureaucracy, and institutions adopted in the mid-seventh century from China, followed a Chinese patrilineal orientation, listing all household members under the name of the male "head" and therefore giving the impression that wife and children lived with the husband/father in *his* house, when actually he lived in *her* house. In other words, the ancient patriarchy that was thought to have replaced the prehistoric communal society with the formation of the *ritsuryō* state was in part an official or legal fiction maintained by the center for its own ideological ends. Scholarship after Takamure, based on archeological and literary evidence, shows that it would take more than three centuries, from the mid-seventh through the eleventh, for the letter of the Father's Law to erase the memory of prehistoric social practices and their later developments in people's daily living arrangements with regard to marriage and the evolution of the family.[3]

Ancient marriage may be said to have evolved from the type of casual and temporary visiting or cohabitation practice known as *tai-gūkon,* lasting only as long as both partners desired, and with no binding presumption of sexual exclusivity on either party. This open and temporary arrangement was made possible by the old clan system of communal organization, under which both male and female persons held property rights. It is also evidenced by the absence in ancient Japanese language of the concepts of adultery *(kantsū),* virginity, or secret lover *(misoka otoko, ma otoko);* the concepts did not exist because they were not yet an issue in a prepatriarchal society. It is not until the tenth century that the concept of illicit relations—brought into being by the husband's exclusive rights to the wife's sexuality—appears among the nobility, and not until the eleventh century among commoners. Significantly, this is the period that saw the first female-authored narratives that have survived to this day. With the establishment of a class-governed society, sexual companionship, formerly consensual and temporary, becomes invested with sociopolitical and economic significance. Where conjugal cohabitation had been the decision of the two parties, and acknowledged by the parents only after the fact, now with its imbrication into the socioeconomic system, the father begins to exercise the paternal authority to decide whom his daughter will marry. The father also holds a ritual to signify public acknowledgment of the marriage, underscoring the sociopolitical nature of paternal authority and that it is he who takes a son-in-law (thus the name for it, *mukotorikon*) before the daughter acquires a husband.

It is in this momentous shift in sexual relations, in the triangulation brought about by the intervention of the woman's father, that we must seek the key to the father-daughter relation in that new order.

It is, I believe, the implicitly patriarchal character of this relation that justifies the oedipal hermeneutic for reading even classical Japanese women's writing. As abundantly demonstrated throughout *The Tale of Genji,* the worldly destinies of a father and his daughter are intimately linked; they rise and fall together. As is well known, marriage was an instrument of power and status enhancement among the aristocracy of the Heian period; the daughter was her father's valuable investment, so to speak, in the economy of marriage politics, and the father was the daughter's key to entry into her newly prescribed roles as wife and mother. This factor renders the emotional attachment between the two of even more momentous significance. The tragedy of fatherless daughters (fatherless by virtue of his early death or his withholding of paternal protection) informs this monumental narrative right from the beginning, in the case of Genji's own mother, Kiritsubo, to the very end, with the Uji princesses, particularly Ukifune. Bridging them are the varied stories of Yūgao, Utsusemi, the Hitachi Princess, Murasaki herself, Akikonomu, and Tamakatsura. In this sense, it may be said that in the *Genji,* the female narrative is basically constructed as a father-daughter plot that tends to go well or ill, depending on the father's fortunes and political ability.

I have previously asserted that "the [Freudian] family romance is not thematized . . . in the *Sarashina nikki* or elsewhere, since it must be kept under a taboo, but as a repressed factor it willy-nilly inscribes itself everywhere, from *Kagerō nikki* to the *Genji,* and may be said to be the ubiquitous subtext of Heian women's writing."[4] This is admittedly a grand assertion to make when dealing with the literary artifacts of a history and culture that until the nineteenth century pursued a course distinct from the Anglo-American or the European. Yet how is it possible to read the female-authored *Genji* and not sense that something like the oedipal plot is variously at work in the unconscious of the text? It is not only that Genji famously plays the role of father/husband/lover to the work's much admired heroine—and dutiful daughter/wife—Murasaki. One of the most disturbing scenes in this narrative is surely the night he deflowers the still childlike girl whom he has been rearing as an adopted daughter, making her his wife.[5] This act, striking the modern reader as no different from father-daughter rape or incestuous abuse, momentarily tears apart the haze of aesthetic/erotic illusion and makes one wonder about the reality of paternal domination behind the fiction of pseudoincest. When a female author in early eleventh-century Japan describes, with such psycho-

logically compelling vividness, the effects on the girl of such an inci-
dence of sexual violence, what are we to make of it? Did Murasaki Shikibu place this singular scene early in the novel to put before her
readers the reality of paternal violence that undergirds the social institutions of her court society? Or was such conduct permissible as an
upper-class or even imperial privilege, given that Genji is in this narrative invested with the splendor of an emperor in all but name? It is
striking that the father-daughter relation similarly figures as a subtex-
tual metaphor in Genji's ties with Akikonomu, Tamakatsura, and the
Third Princess. The early loss of the mother, which among other fac-
tors motivates Genji's lifelong narcissistic pursuit of women, is significant. But perhaps even more significant, the female oedipal relation
—the psychosomatic aspect of the father-daughter plot—is crucial in
fully appreciating the story of the Lady of Akashi vis-à-vis the sociopolitical ambitions of her father, the Lay Monk, and in the destinies of
the Uji princesses, good daughters all to Prince Hachi, or trying their
best to be, in the implicit injunction to honor the Name and the Law
of the Father.

Another way of viewing the work is to note that Murasaki Shikibu
seems to have found the most potential narrativity in the person of a
woman who must find her own way in the world without her father,
only to be discovered by the Shining Prince. On one level, Genji's
attraction is indeed his figuration as the father/lover of female oedipal
fantasy, the man who is (almost) all things to all women, even, arguably, standing in place of the mother. But this work's durability has
more to do with how the fatherless daughters manage to improve
their lives by exercise of their abilities in poetry, music, calligraphy—
their mastery of the aesthetic symbolic order, certainly—and above all
through the prudent management of complex relationships within
the constricted space of a strictly rank-governed society. The subtext
of the work, what is artfully concealed beneath its decorous façade, is
an extended protest against patriarchal domination. And this silent
protest is in spite of the consolation it seeks in the utopian discourse
of the poetic exchange as a perfect communication between man and
woman, even and especially because they don't see eye to eye and
sexual relations must be negotiated by the power of the poetic word.
These imaginary tales of love may resonate gloriously in the lyric
poetry and prose, with their intricate and unparalleled shades of feeling and their minute attention to the details of daily life and human
interaction, but love is ultimately shown to be a utopian fiction un-

attainable within patriarchal society. While perhaps recalling the libidinal freedoms of the ancient *taigū* practice, the *Genji* also reveals its untenability for women in a new order that restricts their mobility, the better to foster their dependency on the father. The result, predictably, is a secondary narcissism on the part of daughters, a seeking after maternal comfort and self-confirmation from the father and later from the husband as his substitute. The narcissistic structure is, significantly, a striking trend in the modern women's narratives as well.

It is not necessary here to expand further on these statements that demand to be demonstrated at length in a rigorous psychological and political analysis. Others will surely take up the challenge of such a task. I introduce these ideas here to suggest a way of reading the essays beyond their necessarily local concerns, as a mode of theoretical self-reflection that could tie in Japanese women's texts with texts written by women elsewhere. Again, I am not necessarily asserting that a Freudian or even a Lacanian psychological reading has universal validity. What I am saying is only that, as a system of male dominance, the Japanese patriarchy seems eminently readable, using these hermeneutic tools. One could then also show their limitations when applied to literary texts, symbolic works with that peculiarly gratifying quality—that they resist any final determination. Doubtless it would be equally plausible to postulate that what appears to be the unconscious of the textual/fictional family is but a matter-of-fact inscription of the diffused emotional affects of the father–daughter/lover/wife–husband filial relations during a stage in Japanese history when the patriarchal family was just coming into its own as a sociopolitical and economic unit.

The Law of the Father in the present book's title is the Lacanian generic term for the laws—prohibitions, injunctions, rituals, institutions—that structure and give coherence to culture.[6] The Father is the figure of the agency that institutes the founding prohibition against the instinctual gratifications of the mother-child dyad and compels their sublimation into the symbolic realm of language or, more broadly, the order of the sign in all fields of human endeavor. And the father is the Law's concrete representative in the patriarchal family structure. Several of the essays in this book refer to the author's relationship with her real father, particularly his role in the daughter's accession to a family legacy of letters and, in modern times, her access to publication. The Father can also refer to the cultural fathers, which in our context means the male critical establishment that determines standards of value against which the daughter's writing performance is measured. But the focus of most of the essays is necessarily on the father as he is constructed in the daughter's literary discourse, as a signifier of patriarchal authority, the Law that defines woman's place in culture and against which she enacts her transgressions in the work of self-representation. On the other hand, he is also a ubiquitous reference point for her narratives of desire, because he is identified with the Phallus, signifier of satisfaction and guarantor of meaning in the symbolic order, what might be called the transcendental signified in a culture system.

The question of female sexuality in relation to desire and the father is indeed a major one in Japanese women's writing. As might be expected from the ambivalence of the daughter's position in the family, the issue is by no means a simple one. As Freud observed, the resolution of the male oedipal conflict is fairly straightforward; under the paternal threat of castration, the son decides to postpone his libidinal gratification until he can symbolically displace the father by marrying a mother substitute. The female oedipal conflict, on the other hand, is not amenable to a similar resolution, because the daughter is excluded from the phallic order and cannot hope to succeed to it. Thus she remains, allegedly, in a state of penis envy until she replaces the desire for the phallus with a baby.[7] This explanation is clearly unsatisfactory because it presupposes—and fails to address—the secondary social positioning that gives rise to the problem for woman in the first place and does not disappear with her accession to motherhood.[8]

Motherhood, at any rate, is not thematized in the majority of the works studied here. Particularly in the case of the Heian memoirs, this silence is remarkable in view of the fatality, for the mother, that often accompanied childbirth or its aftereffects and in view of the overriding significance of children for both her father and her husband. I would like to suggest that such scarcity of references to motherhood goes hand in hand with the virtual elision of the body in Heian women's prose and could be correlated with the abjection of the female body (the primal mother Izanami's rotting corpse) in the founding myths of the imperial court. Furthermore, classical women's writing presents us with the displacement of the tabooed body, with its libidinal drives and enjoyments and its mortal fleshly excretions, onto the order of language, particularly its highest formal sublimation in poetry and aesthetic form. And poetry, significantly, is the first language in which girls learned to write. In this sense, the elision of the mother in favor of the father in the daughter's writing represents the symbolic shift from nature to culture, from the preoedipal identification with the mother to the oedipal attachment to the father, a state that seems to have been of remarkably long duration. Perhaps this psychic retention of the father signals—paradoxically, considering his role in the daughter's marriage—a denial of motherhood as a duty that could prove fatal and could not have been invariably assumed with willingness. But finally we must ask whether the father's manifestly idealized presence in the text does not also mask the daughter's desire for the archaic jouissance in the mother-child dyad before her entry into the father's Law. In short, I suggest that the father in these women's texts, both classical and modern, does not stand only for the Father of the Law and of (female phallic) castration under the patriarchal order. In a more immediate sense, "he" is also "the imaginary father" posited by Kristeva as an intermediary loving figure, enabling the child to negotiate the otherwise traumatic separation between the haven of the maternal body and the stern, authoritarian Father of the Law.[9] In this reading, the imaginary father represents the mother's desire for the Phallus or for satisfaction. The child's identification with this maternal desire, which is here understood as love or the mother-father conglomeration, is a fantasy of the child's conception and delivers him or her safely into the realm of the symbolic associated with the paternal function. What we might call a benign resolution of female penis envy could also be one way of reading the Heian ladies' tales of love.

We commence the study then with the woman known as Michitsuna's Mother, the author of the tenth-century *Kagerō Diary,* which is the earliest title in the modern list of canonical Heian women's texts. This text is, for this woman reader and many others, no doubt, one of the rawest testaments of female anguish in the whole canon. Sonja Arntzen's essay "Of Love and Bondage in the *Kagerō Diary*" begins with the striking observation that Michitsuna's Mother "unfolds her story of a complex and insecure marriage relationship in the shadow of a father constructed as the ideal of perfect love," a move consonant with the text's privileging of descriptions of the father's care for her in contrast to her husband's neglect, and consonant also with its eloquent silence about her father's power over her, beginning with his role in the choice of that husband. The essay then examines the father's positioning in the male sociopolitical dynamics of the time and links it with his improved prospects in the case of a tie with a scion of the powerful Fujiwara clan, Kaneie, as his daughter's husband. In other words, Arntzen uncovers what has been consigned to the outside of the text but nevertheless leaves its marks on it, the eloquent traces of a political/psychological repression that has here been displaced onto a narrative—announced by Michitsuna's Mother as an exposé of romantic tales—that is itself in the thrall of the potent expectations implanted by the same female-gendered romances.

The eleventh-century *Sarashina Diary*, by the woman known as the Daughter of Sugawara Takasue, interestingly enough—because she is Michitsuna's Mother's niece—revisits and foregrounds the question of romantic tales *(monogatari)* raised in the *Kagerō's* preface as a frame for reading her own expressly disillusioned narrative. Yet, as Esperanza Ramirez-Christensen shows in "Self-Representation and the Patriarchy in the Heian Female Memoirs," the *Sarashina* text's emplotment as a Buddhist cautionary tale against the pernicious effects of the narrator's enchantment with *monogatari* and poetry is a rather unstable construction. Its narrative of self-condemnation cannot quite efface the paternal role in the failure of the daughter's fiction-engendered desire for the love of a high-ranking courtier or for a distinguished career at court. In fact, the *Sarashina Diary* is notable for its deliberate dichotomization of the religious canon, in particular the *Lotus Sutra*—here associated with the prohibition against reading *monogatari* delivered by the priest-father in a dream—and the ostensibly wayward fantasies of the matrilineal word as represented by no less than Murasaki Shikibu's *Tale of Genji*. This opposition is a defining moment in the text. It suggests a matrilineal genealogy of readers and writers around a book banned from the canonical curriculum of the Buddhist fathers. It is also instructive for the essay's problematization of the figure of abjection in Heian female narrators' self-representation.

It is not until the early fourteenth century, more than a hundred years after the Heian period, that the female memoirists' complicity with the paternal injunction to silence about sexual politics is finally broken by Lady Nijō's memoir, *Towazugatari* (covering 1271–1306). In "*Towazugatari:* Unruly Tales from a Dutiful Daughter," a fine-grained reading of the narrator's mode of self-presentation in recounting this "story that no one asked for" (the literal sense of the title), Edith Sarra lays out how, in the course of apparently fulfilling her father's deathbed injunction that she carry on the family's literary patrimony, Lady Nijō ends up producing instead an unprecedented exposé of the sexual/political intrigues at the court of Retired Emperor Gofukakusa, to whom she was a concubine and lady-in-waiting. In the process, the narrator reveals the extent to which her life was governed by the arrangements made between her father and her sexual partners, thus laying bare the material basis of the patriarchy in the traffic in female bodies. The essay is particularly noteworthy in raising the question of the narrator's apparent innocence of her father's (and surrogate fathers') designs at the time of the event. It cautiously weighs the issue of individual guilt in the context of paternal authority and sheds new light as well on the memoir's parodic allusions to the *Genji* theme of erotic surrogacy.

As we have seen, internal evidence indicates that the *Sarashina Diary* has a textual memory of *Kagerō*. The same can be said of Murasaki Shikibu, whose numerous psychological/literary projections into the minds of her characters in the *Genji* are virtually unimaginable without the precedent set by *Kagerō*'s narrative of torturous self-reflection. These works were basically written by women for women and about women. There is in fact no surviving comparable work written by a Heian man, except perhaps for the *Tosa Diary* (935), by the male poet Ki no Tsurayuki. The reason most commonly cited for Heian women's uncommon production of writing in the native tongue is that they were barred from the use of Chinese, the language of official and legal documents, of learning, of the Buddhist canon, and, in short, of the world of knowledge developed by Chinese civilization. Thus emerged the concept of a gendered dichotomy between "the woman's hand" *(onnade)*, native Japanese language written in the *kana* phonetic syllabary, and "the man's hand," Chinese language written exclusively in *kanji* ideographs.[10]

In his essay on Heian writing and gender, "Mother Tongue and Father Script," Joshua S. Mostow complicates this binary construction and chisels away at the rigid walls that the modern valuation of Heian women's writing has erected between the two. Mostow's several citations of Heian women, particularly female court officials, who read and translated Chinese or whose Japanese writing reveals that they did so, indicate what common sense would suggest, that the boundaries between Japanese and Chinese were more porous than imagined. In particular, Mostow's historicist analysis of passages about women and Chinese learning from Sei Shōnagon's *Pillow Book* and the *Murasaki Shikibu Diary* indicates that this was as much a political issue of the rivalry between the two empresses they served. It suggests that Murasaki's valuation of Japanese over a stilted Chinese redounded to the benefit of Fujiwara Michinaga's hegemony by helping to emasculate the old Chinese-learning scholars of the Academy (Daigaku) "as an oppositional source of authority." In this way, it might be said that in the political partnership of Michinaga and the talented Murasaki, the father-daughter plot redounded to the benefit of women's writing and, indeed, the first flowering of Japanese literature in the "mother tongue." Given the involvement of Heian women's writing in the politics of language use, it is not surprising that in more modern times this writing would be appropriated to the discourse of nationalism, or that in our own time it is similarly appropriated, as in various ways in this book, in the discourse of feminism. Both cases raise the issue of ideology and literary criticism and are concrete evidence of the ambiguities attending the afterlife of texts.

Hayashi Fumiko (1903–1951), possibly the most popular and best-loved among the writers of her time, surely stands out from the others discussed in this volume in that she was not privileged to transmit a family legacy of letters. She was not a "literary daughter"; quite the opposite. Her father, an itinerant peddler, refused to acknowledge his paternity and forced her and her mother out of his house when Fumiko was seven. Thus she was early and permanently liberated from the respect for patriarchal authority that a middle-class daughter might harbor. With Fumiko, paternalism seemed never to have been internalized as a psychological issue; most of her male characters are weak and feckless, and she chose to honor the lives of disenfranchised lower-class women like herself. Still, under the constraints of making a living as a writer in a society where men had control over publishing and the system of literary patronage, she could not ignore them. As a streetwise female of poor background, she possessed a keen sense of gender-based power relations and, as Janice Brown argues in her essay "De-siring the Center: Hayashi Fumiko's Hungry Heroines and the Male Literary Canon," spiritedly refused the marginal position reserved for her. Working tirelessly to carve out a place that was of equal potency to the male author's position, she succeeded as she must, by hanging out with the boys and acquiring male mentors. But as Brown demonstrates, she also attempted "to subvert, usurp, or appropriate the male texts as a means both of resistance and of survival." A great part of her early stunning success was due to her cultivation of a simultaneously subversive and vulnerable, unabashedly female poetic voice in *Hōrōki* (Diary of a vagabond, 1928–1930), whereas her enduring legacy is the unshakable authority of a woman unflinchingly record-

ing the hunger and misery that patriarchy carves on the female body.
It is significant that Fumiko's last and greatest novel, *Ukigumo* (Floating cloud, 1949–1950), remains a story of the disenfranchised, unac-
commodated woman. It follows the exhausted heroine in a journey
of exile from Tokyo to death on an island in the remote, southern-
most margins of Japan. It parallels the first opus except in being
wholly a record of female despair that reaches even beyond the ruins
of the imperial patriarchy at the end of World War II.

The family background of Mori Mari (1903–1987), in contrast to
that of Hayashi Fumiko, was definitely middle class. Daughter of the
famous Mori Ōgai (1862–1922), surgeon to the Imperial Army and
one of the intellectual patriarchs of Japan's modernization in the
Meiji period, Mari is one of numerous modern writing daughters to
writer-fathers. They carry on the line of the Heian and early medieval
court ladies who were themselves bearers of their fathers' poetic or
literary legacy but invented a feminine discourse of their own. Other
examples in this book are Enchi Fumiko and Kōda Aya. As Tomoko
Aoyama informs us in her essay on Mari, "A Room Sweet as Honey:
Father-Daughter Love in Mori Mari," the memoirs of the daughters
about their celebrated fathers are actively solicited in the publications
of the literary milieu *(bundan);* "'literary daughters' are therefore privileged and yet marginalized: they are given opportunities to write, but
they are constantly reminded of their peripheral and parasitical positions." In the popular mind, the literary and intellectual activities of
such daughters are not remarkable, given the identity of their fathers;
their achievements are not necessarily their own but the reflected
glory of a literary paternity. The daughter gets her first opportunities
to break out in print while ostensibly paying homage to the revered
father—a filial act and undoubtedly limited by the proprieties of the
daughterly memoir genre. It is easy to see the potential conflict here
between the ambitious daughter's interest in self-definition and the
self-effacement required by the genre of "memories of my father." It
will be interesting to see how she negotiates this contradiction.

The essays indicate that while not overtly disclaiming their well-
known lineages, some of these writer-daughters go to great lengths to
distinguish themselves from their erstwhile fathers in a process of self-
creation, becoming indeed the heroine in their own stories instead
of their father's.[11] Others exhibit a marked narcissistic strain already
familiar to us from the Heian memoirs, constructing the father's
desire and approval as an element in their self-identification and in

the process re-creating both themselves and their fathers. Mari's writing is a notable example of such a narcissism, but liberated from the old guilt and evasiveness. Her memoirs of Ōgai are less interested in him than in evoking in rich, sensuous detail "the room sweet as honey" of her childhood in the warm embrace of her father's love. No part of Ōgai's works or the other family members' memoirs is allowed to contradict Mari's construction of this enchanted tale, which is in effect a vital part of her own autobiography. She has taken full advantage of the unannounced opportunity offered the memorialist daughter to cut and select from the documentary evidence in order to displace the historical father into her own story, to see him from her own perspective, and to position him in her own designs. Interestingly, as Aoyama observes, this loving father-daughter relationship, a pseudo-incest theme that recalls the *Genji*, resurfaces in Mari's novels, displaced onto the male homosexual love between a powerful older man and a poor but beautiful boy in *Koibitotachi no mori* (Lovers' forest, 1961) and *Kareha no nedoko* (The bed of fallen leaves, 1962). These are reminiscent of plotlines later appearing in *shōjo manga* (girls' comic books), underscoring the narcissistic and oedipal character of young girls' desires. Mari's final opus, *Amai mitsu no heya* (Sweet honey room, 1975), a long three-part novel that took ten years to complete, also focuses on the perfection of the father-daughter love. No other men could approach it, despite the daughter's affairs and marriage, all paralleling Mari's autobiography but fictionalized. The most startling aspect of the story, and confirming Mari's design of challenging Ōgai's serious "Apollonian" world, is the portrayal of the fictional father's secret complicity with his daughter's amorousness and pleasure in rebellion against the world, and his triumphant joy at finally finding her back in his house after her failed marriage. Here the classic Heian father-daughter plot as a tale of narcissistic pseudoincest finds perhaps the fullest modern expression. If it seems self-indulgent compared with the formal sublimations of the foremothers, that is only due to the much greater freedom that even women writers can allow themselves in our own time.

Some writer-daughters, however, are unable to confront the decisive influence of their fathers directly in either their memoirs or their psyches, and they turn to fiction to explore the deeper implications of this often repressed relationship. The case of Enchi Fumiko (1905–1986) is particularly instructive in this regard. Readers of the works that have existed for some years in English translation, such as *The*

Waiting Years (Onnazaka), Masks (Onnamen), and short stories like "A Bond for Two Lifetimes—Gleanings" *(Nisei no en—shūi),* will be in no doubt that her constant theme has been the oppressiveness of the patriarchal system, and her most distinctive heroine the strong, proud, and fearfully repressed avenging figure spawned by it. Similarly, it is Enchi whose ear has been most attuned to the unarticulated yet dramatized grievances of her Heian foremothers, the one who has laid out explicitly, within the patriarchal setting of the Meiji period or the Shōwa period (1926–1989), the sexual repression and psychological debilitation entailed by it. Eileen Mikals-Adachi reveals in her essay, "Enchi Fumiko: Female Sexuality and the Absent Father," however, that Enchi, whose early exposure to the beauties of classical literature was a gift from her famous father, Ueda Mannen (or Kazutoshi, 1867–1937), a distinguished professor of the national language and literature, in effect suppressed his presence from the surface of her fiction. This is trained primarily on the heterosexual relationship rather than the father-daughter or parent-child relationship. Nevertheless, the suppression of the father in Enchi's texts leaves its mark in the hovering, disapproving shadow against whom her disobedient protagonists, involved in infidelity or affairs with younger men, enact their transgressions. Indeed it was not until Ueda Mannen was long dead and Enchi herself established as the dean of women writers that she felt sufficiently strong to confront her early sense of rivalry with his name and his censure of her "unfeminine" ways. The semi-autobiographical trilogy *Ake o ubau mono* (Stripped of crimson, 1956–1968), as Mikals-Adachi demonstrates, is the vehicle Enchi chose "to look back on the road she herself had followed" and to analyze especially that aspect of herself, female sexuality, that had long been repressed by the disapproving father. Here, the protagonist Shigeko confronts the possibility that the men in her life had been substitutes for her father, a figure at once beloved and perfect but coldly indifferent to her attributes as a woman. The successive bloody events that punctuate Shigeko's sexual existence—the loss of her virginity, a mastectomy, a hysterectomy—may be read as the daughter's masochistic self-wounding before the father's blindness, which doubtless refers to the abjection of female sexuality as pollution in the symbolic order of Shintō.

Another writer-daughter who employs the figure of the father to chart her own emerging identity as an individual and as a writer, as Rebecca L. Copeland demonstrates in "Needles, Knives, and Pens," is

Uno Chiyo (1897–1996). Copeland's analysis of *Aru hitori no onna no hanashi* (The story of a single woman, 1971), which draws on other scenes evoking the father-daughter relationship in other earlier works by Uno, reveals a subtext that is a quest for a long-absent father. Copeland reconstructs from the Uno heroine's memories of the father a tyrannical patriarch who literally binds her to his house and punishes her for any expression of narcissistic desire and, significantly, forbids her pleasure in reading novels or in writing, albeit she seems to nourish a masochistic attachment to him. Here the father's death, while liberating the daughter into the heretofore forbidden knowledge of her own sexuality, does not free her from guilt at transgressing his law. Her amorous encounters turn claustrophobic or suffocating, as if she still inhabited the closed room into which her father had confined her. However, a rift in the image of the omnipotent father begins to appear in the narratives as the heroine discovers his desire, his lack, his libidinal excesses, in short the human weakness covered over by the rigid authority of the paternal position. Feminizing the father by seeing him as a creature of desire, in effect castrating him, makes it easier for the wounded daughter to identify with him. In later Uno narratives, however, the identification assumes a different structure: the daughter succeeds to his authority through "fathering" him in her writing, becoming a son to him, and herself repeating the hidden life of debauchery that she willfully interprets as her father's final directive to her at his death. In sum, Uno's father-daughter narratives construct an imaginary father answering to the stages of the daughter's need and desire. They follow a healing trajectory of metaphors from the phallic knife the father had used to bind his daughter to the writing daughter's phallic pen that had been used to re-create him in her own design, and finally, her sewing needles as tools of creative self-expression. Copeland ends by evoking the scene in which the heroine of "Kokyō no ie" (The house where I was born, 1974) returns as the prodigal daughter to her father's house, there to take his place as family head, having tamed and domesticated his once-terrifying presence by her empowering mastery of the symbolic as a means of liberating the oppressed self.

The memoirs of Kōda Aya (1906–1990), daughter of the scholar-intellectual and novelist Kōda Rohan (1867–1947), portray the father as an exacting Confucianist mentor who does not hesitate to employ humiliation as a teaching method. But this is apparently not felt by the narrator-daughter as oppressive. In fact, Ann Sherif begins her essay, "A Confucian Utopia," by cautioning us against the tendency to villainize the father as representative of an oppressive patriarchal system, a reductive simplification that can obscure the specificity of the father-daughter relationship in each instance, and especially the one she examines here. Always paired with her famous father in the public mind, Kōda nourished, rather than rejected, the identification, an attitude that has led at least one female critic to call her a spokes-person for the patriarchy. One can sense, in Sherif's finely modulated translations from the memoirs, that Kōda deliberately conceptualized their relationship as one between a strict and exacting mentor and a somewhat slow-witted, occasionally rebellious, but grateful student. There is no doubt that Kōda's self-identification as a person was essen-tially molded by Rohan's Confucian-based philosophy of knowledge as self-cultivation: the close "investigation of things" (*kakubutsu*) as the measure of wisdom, an authentic being-in-the-world; and the training in verbal and body behavior as an expression of moral and spiritual value. In contrast to her women-writer contemporaries who rebelled against patriarchal values by rejecting marriage and a domestic role, she apparently led an utterly conventional life. Yet the public image of Kōda's self-identification with her father needs closer examination. It is, after all, the daughter who retrospectively narrates and constructs the relation to her father as a very special, nurturing, and privileged mentorship, and she who discovers herself as a writer in the process of remembering him. Moreover, in time the narrative of her mentor-ship invests her with a public identity as a teacher in her own right, as people came to look to her as an authority on morality, the family, old age, and other sociocultural issues. As distinct from Mori Mari's bold tales of an imaginary jouissance in being the father's desire, Kōda's ostensibly self-effacing story of an exacting apprenticeship is far from lending itself to eroticization and in that sense reflects the Confucian injunction against emotional indulgence. Her recollections of his tutelage, however, possess a quiet humor, leavening those scenes and interaction, and also a deep affection. When we recall that Kōda returned to her father's house after an unsatisfactory marriage, and that she resumed her both wifely and motherly care for him in his old age, it is difficult to put aside wholly the sense that theirs was a master-disciple relationship made exceptional by a daughter's love, trust, and indulgence. It is tempting to speculate that the daughter's so-called positive oedipal relation remains the ideal one for both, despite the same patriarchy's injunction to leave the father's house

and obey another man. Or to put it in another way, Rohan's particular
position as an intellectual of considerable breadth and depth ensured
him a place in his daughter's heart and mind that no other men
could rival. There is no more revealing instance of paternal power
and privilege vis-à-vis his own daughter, as distinct from a rival son.

In a signal departure from the father-daughter orientation of the
other essays here, Sharalyn Orbaugh's contribution, "Ōba Minako
and the Paternity of Maternalism," focuses on the mother role and
the mother-daughter dyad mainly left out of this book's discussion
and whose depiction is a primary concern of the texts written by Ōba
(b. 1930). In this sense, Orbaugh's essay is a necessary counterpoint
to our dyad, a reminder of the corresponding relation that would
otherwise have been, again and typically, overlooked. It is a careful
observation of the compulsion of the family—how motherliness is
constituted/compelled as a fixed subject position in the structural
dynamics of the family triad, wherein the daughter rejects identification with the mother in favor of the more powerful subject position
of the father, desiring his affection, favor, and attention. The mother's
fixed role in the middle-class bourgeois family is felt by Yuri, the protagonist of one of the stories analyzed here ("The Three Crabs"), as
oppressive, inhibiting, and nauseous. It generates a need for temporary escape through indifferent sexual encounters outside its enclosure, and an equal compulsion to return to it again and again.
Moreover, Yuri recognizes that her daughter's rejecting gaze merely
replicates her own gaze trained upon her own mother in the past,
until motherhood and the family compels her into that role and the
recognition of its unchanging cyclical nature in the patriarchal order.
Especially compelling is Orbaugh's articulation of Yuri's subjectivity
as Ōba shows it. In her principled refusal to indulge and participate
in the sanctioned rituals of social gratification for married couples
(here, a bridge party), she is akin to Franz Kafka's Hunger Artist who
starves himself for a living and has made his abhorrence of food into
his art. Her refusal to settle into the sanctioned role of mother, her
straitened need to distance herself from this enclosure even while
staying within it, constitutes a truly austere subjectivity in stories that
Ōba's male critics have described as evoking an "immeasurable ghastliness," read as a symptom of the crisis of the family in a morally bankrupt postwar Japan. In this wide-ranging essay, Orbaugh's "paternity
of maternalism" has at least three referents: motherliness as structurally compelled by or originating from the patriarchal system; Ōba's

discourse of maternalism as endorsed and culturally reproduced by
the male critics who awarded her both the Gunzō New Writers Award
and the Akutagawa Prize in 1968; and Kafka as one of the cultural
fathers whose work inspired her figuration of motherhood as a compulsion to self-starvation.

In Kurahashi Yumiko (b. 1935), we find a woman writer who began
her career in the sixties with a deliberate rejection of the conventions
of the native *shishōsetsu* (the "I"-novel), then the dominant paradigm
for modern Japanese fiction and criticism, in favor of the experimental French *nouveau roman,* among other foreign influences. Atsuko
Sakaki's essay, "Kurahashi Yumiko's Negotiations with the Fathers," is
an illuminating critical presentation of the terms of the controversy
that this "unfilial" daughter aroused among her cultural fathers, the
male critical establishment whose endorsement is necessary for
achieving a niche in the literary world. As distinct from the generally
favorable acclaim won by Ōba Minako's portrayals of a straitened
motherliness in the postwar family, Kurahashi's work met with general rejection and disapproval. There was its apparent indifference
to the real world or even to the author's own subjectivity ("I didn't
begin to write fiction because I had something to tell about myself"),
the disconcerting absence of a sense of (the "proper" Japanese) place
and names or even a discernible message in her texts, and the illogical
and abstract quality of her plots. All these marked her as not only un-
recognizable per se but also recognizably un-Japanese, an illegitimate
daughter spawned by Western literature, though, as Sakaki observes,
ignored by those same French "fathers" in the global politics of un-
equal literary exchange. Moreover, in such texts as *Kurai tabi* (1961),
this daughter chooses to write in such a way as to avoid representing
female subjectivity, instead foregrounding in her complex narrative
strategies the constructed nature of femininity itself, another disconcerting departure from the naturalization of gender implicit in the
dominant narrative. Kurahashi's irreverent parody of the cultural
fathers, whether native or Western, her provocative strategy of exposing the traces of a promiscuous paternity across her playful texts,
would seem paradoxically to signal a refusal to acknowledge any essentialist notion of literary paternity whatsoever. In sum, Kurahashi is
one of the pioneers of postmodern fiction in Japan. Her writing confronts in its very method the breakdown of the Name and the Law of
the (Japanese) Father, and consequently of the father-daughter plot
structurally embedded in the patriarchal family structure.[12]

Ogino Anna (b. 1956) is yet another daughter who writes, so to speak, after the death of the Father or, at the very least, after his "emasculation" in the breakdown of the "proper" that was formerly guaranteed by the symbolic order. As we learn in Midori McKeon's "Ogino Anna's Gargantuan Play in *Tales of Peaches*," Ogino grew up in a female-headed household marked by the absence of the father, a French-American merchant sea captain who could visit his Japanese family but rarely. Nevertheless, Ogino's upbringing in the international milieu of Yokohama, the familiarity with European cultural traditions acquired in Catholic schools there, and, surely, an incipient curiosity about her father would have nourished her fascination with the symbolic "hybridity," the pluralistic comic/cosmic universe of her first and enduring inspiration, the works of sixteenth-century French writer Rabelais. Indeed, McKeon's absorbing study of Ogino's major work to date, *Momo monogatari* (Tales of peaches, 1994), in juxtaposition with Rabelais's *Gargantua and Pantagruel* (1532–1564), is precisely a demonstration of the surrogate literary father's decisive nurturing role in forming the generously large comic spirit and iconoclastic devices of his self-proclaimed literary daughter in Japan.

In Ogino's delightful tearing down of the boundaries separating the symbolic order of the proper and the improper, her challenge to decorum and the canonical understanding of dead Japanese males, it is important to note that the new undutiful daughters apparently find fuel and strength, as well as the authority, to criticize their native fathers through an empowering detour into studies of the Western fathers—from Kafka to Joyce, Rabelais to Sterne. One of Ogino's novel genres is that of "critifiction," or "fiction critiques" (criticism in a fictional vein), which she first discovered while engaged in an essay on a native cultural father, the unorthodox male novelist Sakaguchi Ango (1906–1955). "Katayoku no pegasasu: Ango o meguru gesakuteki shihyōron no kokoromi" (One-winged Pegasus: an essay of playful, informal critique on Sakaguchi Ango, 1988) is a homage to Ango's spirit of farce. Nevertheless, it is also an acute critique of Ango's limitations as a "one-winged Pegasus" whose satiric flight is ultimately held back by an insufficient objectivity as well as the confining form of the novel. Hereafter, in writing that mixed the essay form, criticism, and full-fledged fiction, Ogino would continue to stage her critifictional parodies of the fathers, from Shiga to Kawabata, from Dazai to Mishima.

Despite her playful way with the modern era's canonical male authors, however, Ogino's literary paternity has an equally old lin-

eage in the haikai (comic linked poetry) of the Danrin school, in
Saikaku, Bashō, as well as the irreverent fiction of Edo *gesaku*. In this
comic and parodic tradition in both poetry and prose, the reversal of
sacred and profane, high and low, *ga* (elegant, serious, refined) and
zoku (vulgar, mundane, informal) had already been accomplished.
However, this comic iconoclastic tradition has remained a subterra-
nean stream in the general accounts of literary history, with their
valorization of the respectable and of "pure literature" *(junbungaku)*.
Thus the parodic handling of the grave native fathers in the works of
Kurahashi and Ogino could be construed as a provocatively incursive,
oppositional discourse by the female voice that has long been silenced
or consigned to the limiting category of "women's literature" *(joryū
bungaku)*.

Nearly a millennium separates the poetically sublimated resistance of the dutiful daughters of the Heian memoirs from the disloyal,
iconoclastic daughters of our time. To judge from their disavowal of
and spirited playfulness with the symbolic order erected by the fathers
in the intervening centuries, Japanese women are once more claiming the territory of literature once held by their foremothers. It is a
remarkable coincidence that the pioneers of writing "in the mother
tongue" should now be symbolically unraveling the Law of the Father
that instituted the father-daughter plot to begin with. We might view
with alarm the apparent demise of love from the classical feminine
repertory of writing. But that was mostly a fiction generated by the
paternal order and will doubtless continue to resurrect itself in other
forms out of the essential human need for a nurturing relation with
others. For now, we cannot underestimate the liberating power of
the denaturalized daughters' parodic laughter, or their willful destruction of fixed categories, in a world uneasily suspended between the
murderous factional strife of the fathers and the emerging "totalita-
rianism" of the technology-powered, new global order.

Notes

1. The virtual absence of critical studies of the father-daughter relation for
Japan is paralleled by a similar silence, until recent years, in Western discourses
of the family. For an analysis of the "absent daughter," see Lynda E. Boose, "The
Father's House and the Daughter in It: The Structures of Western Culture's

Daughter-Father Relationship," in *Daughters and Fathers,* ed. Boose and Flowers, pp. 19–25.

2. See Takamure, *Josei no rekishi* (1948) and *Shōseikon no kenkyū* (1953), *Takamure Itsue zenshū.* Among the numerous studies on women's history influenced by Takamure, and further illustrating and/or revising aspects of her thesis, a useful comprehensive source is Sekiguchi, *Nihon kodai kon'inshi no kenkyū.* In the United States, McCullough confirmed Takamure's observations early, using additional sources, in "Japanese Marriage Institutions"; the importance of this definitive study for Japanese scholarship was not recognized until its translation, "Heian jidai no kon'in seido," appeared in *Shakai kagaku* more than ten years later. The recent publication in English of *Women and Class in Japanese History,* ed. Tonomura et al., illustrates the recent trends in modern Japanese scholarship on gender and women's history; see "Appendix: Past Developments and Future Issues in the Study of Women's History in Japan: A Bibliographical Essay," pp. 299–313, for a capsule account of the history of Japanese research in this topic.

3. In this regard, Takamure's analysis diverges from the sociopolitical development pattern set up in her own theoretical source, Frederick Engels's *Origins of Family, Private Property, and the State.* Engels identified the formation of the state with the rise of private property and the patriarchal family. In Takamure's analysis, however, the patriarchal system comes into its full force only in the Muromachi period (1333–1568), much later than the historic establishment of the *ritsuryō* state. See Sekiguchi, 1:12–13, on this point, and 1:3–37 for a summary of her own modified dating of the shift to the patriarchy in marriage types and the formation of the family. I have used Sekiguchi in the main for my account, because it is the most widely cited authority among other recent publications on this topic. I have also consulted *Nihon joseishi no rekishi,* ed. Sōgō, pp. 14–110, as a more general source.

4. See "The Desire for *Monogatari* in *Sarashina nikki,*" in *The Desire for* Monogatari, ed. Sekine, p. 36.

5. In the "Aoi" (Heartvine) chapter of *Genji monogatari,* 2:63–65; also *Tale of Genji,* 1:180–181.

6. A good source for Jacques Lacan's principal concepts and modifications on Freud's psychoanalytic views is Bowie, *Lacan.* A more detailed, rigorous study is Ragland-Sullivan, *Jacques Lacan.*

7. Freud's 1932 essay, "Femininity," is a good summary of his views on the complexities of girls' psychosexual development, in particular on the overriding importance of their preoedipal identification with the mother, the difficulties accompanying the shift of object to the father in the oedipal phase, and the subsequent long duration of women's intense attachment to their father. See *Freud on Women,* pp. 342–362.

8. That Freud realized that his views were not yet adequate to solve "the riddle of femininity" is clear from the essay above, which ends by admitting that his explanation is "certainly incomplete and fragmentary and does not always sound friendly." He then bids his audience to inquire from their own experiences or to turn to the poets "or wait until science can give you deeper and more coherent explanations." *Freud on Women,* p. 362.

9. For a comprehensive analysis of the place of the "imaginary father" in Julia Kristeva's reading of Freud and Lacan, see Oliver, *Reading Kristeva*, pp. 69–90.

10. *Onnade* is the referent in the first collection of critical essays on Japanese women's writing, entitled *The Woman's Hand*, ed. Schalow and Walker. It raises the issue of gendered writing and includes a useful "Selected Bibliography of Japanese Women's Writing," compiled by Joan E. Ericson and Midori Y. McKeon.

11. Similar issues are discussed by Gilbert and Gubar with reference to Maria Edgeworth and Jane Austen in their book *The Madwoman in the Attic*, pp. 146–183.

12. Jardine's critique of American feminism in relation to postmodern French theory, *Gynesis*, would be instructive from a comparative perspective, in considering the French inspiration of Japanese women writers like Kurahashi and Ogino.

Works Cited

Location of Japanese publishers is Tokyo unless otherwise noted.

Akio Abe, et al., eds. *Genji monogatari*. 6 vols. Shōgakkan, 1970–1976.

Boose, Lynda E. "The Father's House and the Daughter in It: The Structures of Western Culture's Daughter-Father Relationship." In *Daughters and Fathers*, ed. Lynda E. Boose and Betty S. Flowers, pp. 19–25. Baltimore: Johns Hopkins University Press, 1989.

Bowie, Malcolm. *Lacan*. Cambridge: Harvard University Press, 1991.

Freud on Women: A Reader. Ed. Elizabeth Young-Bruehl. New York: W. W. Norton and Company, 1990.

Gilbert, Sandra M., and Susan Gubar. *The Madwoman in the Attic: The Woman Writer and the Nineteenth-Century Literary Imagination*. New Haven, Conn.: Yale University Press, 1979 and 1984.

Jardine, Alice. *Gynesis: Configurations of Woman and Modernity*. Ithaca, N.Y.: Cornell University Press, 1985.

McCullough, William H. "Japanese Marriage Institutions in the Heian Period." *Harvard Journal of Asiatic Studies* 27 (1967): 103–167. Trans. as "Heian jidai no kon'in seido," *Shakai kagaku* 24 (Kyoto: Dōshisha Daigaku Jinbunkagaku Kenkyūjo, 1978).

Oliver, Kelly. *Reading Kristeva*. Bloomington: Indiana University Press, 1993.

Ragland-Sullivan, Ellie. *Jacques Lacan and the Philosophy of Psychoanalysis*. Urbana: University of Illinois Press, 1986.

Ramirez-Christensen, Esperanza. "The Desire for *Monogatari* in *Sarashina nikki*." In *The Desire for* Monogatari: *Proceedings of the Second Midwest Research/Pedagogy Seminar on Japanese Literature*, ed. Eiji Sekine (West Lafayette, Ind.: Purdue University, 1994).

Schalow, Paul Gordon, and Janet A. Walker, eds. *The Woman's Hand: Gender and Theory in Japanese Women's Writing*. Stanford, Calif.: Stanford University Press, 1996.

Seidensticker, Edward, trans. *The Tale of Genji.* 2 vols. New York: Alfred A. Knopf, 1977.

Sekiguchi Hiroko. *Nihon kodai kon'inshi no kenkyū.* 2 vols. Hanawa shobō, 1993.

Sōgō Joseishi Kenkyūkai, ed. *Nihon joseishi no rekishi: sei, ai, kazoku.* Kadokawa shoten, 1992.

Takamure Itsue. *Takamure Itsue zenshū.* Rironsha, 1966.

Tonomura, Hitomi, Anne Walthall, and Wakita Haruko, eds. *Women and Class in Japanese History.* Ann Arbor: Center for Japanese Studies, University of Michigan, 1999.

Chapter 1

Of Love and Bondage in the *Kagerō Diary*

Michitsuna's Mother and Her Father

SONJA ARNTZEN

The *Kagerō Diary (Kagerō nikki)* commands our attention as chronologi-cally the first text in the rich and distinguished tradition of Heian women's literature.[1] This autobiographical text covers twenty years (954–974), focusing on the author's marriage with Fujiwara Kaneie, a scion of the most powerful branch of the Fujiwara family. The author is known to posterity as Michitsuna's Mother, a name derived from her position as mother of an only son, but in this essay I will reconstruct her as daughter.

The *Kagerō Diary* is generally famous as a record of female jealousy, largely because of its early, striking passages recounting the author's virulent chagrin over an affair her husband began with another woman just after the birth of the author's only child. The genius of the writing produces a vivid reenactment of this traumatic event to the point that readers experience the anguish of unfulfilled desire, hatred of her rival, and resentment toward her husband almost as though from within the author's own skin. While the exposure of such raw and negative emotions makes an indelible impression that tends to color many readers' perception of the work, there is much more to this multifaceted text. The diary may also be read as a remarkable record of the author's emotional and mental growth that culminates in a greater freedom of mind. That growth is nowhere more apparent than in the shifts that occur in the author's relationship with her father.

In reading the *Kagerō Diary* as a record of growth, one must con-sider its complex nonlinear quality. Although the text has a basically chronological order, the author indicates, particularly in Book One, that she is recalling many of the events long after their occurrence. She comments on those events from the vantage point of knowing

how things turned out in the end. It is assumed that she began com-
piling the diary around 971 when the tension in her marriage was
reaching a crisis point. The reader must also remember that this diary
is a consciously literary work intended for an audience. The diary's
introduction makes that clear.[2] I proceed with this analysis on the
assumption that the inclusion and omission of certain kinds of information were the result of literary choices on the author's part and
that, even in the passages about her youth, we are not dealing with a
naive "direct" recording of the past.

   The father of the author makes only sporadic appearances in the
diary and is never described in detail. The central story of the diary
concerns the vicissitudes of her marital relationship, which ends in
separation. The author privileges those moments in her marriage that
were interwoven with poetry. The marriage/sexual love plot must be
central because the author's primary identification as a writer is as a
female *waka* poet participating in the exchange of poetry between
lovers.[3] This is the realm of the *uta monogatari* (poem tale), which
usually takes as its subject the romantic relations between men and
women. Although the poetic exchanges in *uta monogatari* are not exclusively confined to those between lovers, the world of courtly love
is the genre's principal domain. The *Kagerō Diary*, like an *uta monogatari*, places priority on the poems the author exchanges with her
lover/husband.[4] It is noteworthy, for example, that nowhere in the
diary does the author exchange poetry with her father, perhaps because he cannot, as her father, assume the position of a potential lover.
Nonetheless, her father plays a critical and formative role in her life
and text, particularly with respect to her relationships with the other
two men in her life—her husband, Fujiwara Kaneie, and her son,
Michitsuna. The author unfolds her story of a complex and insecure
marriage in the shadow of a father constructed as the ideal of perfect
love. Two moves, at once literary and psychological, are necessary to
the construction of her father as an ideal. One is an avoidance of any
consideration of her father's real place in the sociopolitical world,
which constitutes an erasure of his role in the inception of the marriage and of his power over her. The second move is to privilege
descriptions of her father's love and care for her while implying a
contrast with her husband's insufficiency in this respect.

   Beth Kowaleski-Wallace in her essay "Reading the Father Metaphorically" argues: "In considering the father, our tendency has been
to scrutinize the individual father as the substitute for patriarchy with

its oppressive effects, and we have implied that if only we could remove
the influence of the father from his daughter's lives, we could remove
the effects of patriarchy itself." She goes on to suggest that "a project
designed to expose the father, to render him human, fallible, and real
—in short to concretize what a process of metaphoric comparison can
make obscure—begins to make him less omnipotent."[5] Michitsuna's
Mother never portrays her father as an oppressor, but I would suggest
that a metaphorical reading/writing of the father as ideal bestows
just as much omnipotence on him as one that would hold him as oppressor. In the course of the diary, the author rewrites her father from
representation of an ideal to a portrait of a real and fallible person
caught in a specific sociopolitical nexus. Interestingly, as part of the
same process, she also frees her mind from an obsession with her husband's neglect and achieves emotional independence from both her
husband and son. Exploring the shift in the author's relationship with
her father sheds light on the trajectory of her growth toward this freedom and equanimity of mind.

A Paternal Genealogy

Before tracing the arc of that trajectory through textual examples,
the author's father must be situated within the historical specificity of
family and political dynamics in Heian society. He belonged to the
zuryō kaikyū (provincial governor class), a middle rank of aristocracy
outside the innermost circle of power. Because the fathers of all the
major Heian women writers were of this class, the description and
discussion of the career of the father of Michitsuna's Mother is relevant to family backgrounds of the other women writers as well.

The father of Michitsuna's Mother, Fujiwara Tomoyasu (d. 977),
was a member of the Fujiwara family's *Hokke*, or Northern House.
Tomoyasu was thus of the same lineage as Michitsuna's Mother's husband, Fujiwara Kaneie (929–990); they shared the same forefather,
Fujiwara Fuyutsugu (775–826)—four generations removed for
Tomoyasu, five for Kaneie. The Northern House had virtually
monopolized all high positions at court since the time of Fujiwara
Yoshifusa (804–872), but it also contained collateral branches that
had fallen into decline. Tomoyasu was from one of these less fortunate branches. The family had descended into the lower ranks of the
aristocracy from the time of Tomoyasu's grandfather,[6] and Tomoyasu's father, Koretaka, ended his career with only the rank of Junior

Fifth Lower, at which the young scions of the most powerful branch of the family started their careers.[7] Koretaka was also the first in the family to have taken posts as a provincial governor, a sign of low aristocratic status.[8] More will be said shortly about the role and status of the provincial governor in mid-Heian society.

Nothing in the *Kagerō Diary* could be termed a description of Tomoyasu; his character can only be gleaned from the few accounts of his direct interaction with his daughter, most of which are cited in the body of this chapter. Such information as is available from the few other sources of information about Tomoyasu are summarized here.[9] Given that he produced a daughter with such literary skill, it is noteworthy that there are indications that he had some literary inclinations himself. He is listed in one Fujiwara genealogy as a Monjō no shō,[10] that is, someone who had taken the literature course at the court university and had passed the civil service examination, which required superior skills in literary composition. By the mid-Heian period, this kind of academic success no longer brought increase in rank or preferment in government posting, so one might conjecture that Tomoyasu's choice of such a course of study at least in part reflected talent and personal predilection.

In a record of the Iwashimizu Shrine Special Festival held in 941, he is listed as the leader of a group of ten *waka* poets involved in the festivities.[11] His most noteworthy claim to literary fame is the inclusion of one of his compositions in the *Honchō monzui*,[12] an anthology of poetry and prose in literary Chinese compiled in the late Heian period after the model of the Chinese Six Dynasties period anthology, the *Wen Xuan* (J. *Monzen*). The piece is a formal request for posting as a provincial governor. In accordance with the precedent of the *Wen Xuan*, well-composed government documents were included for their literary qualities. Tomoyasu coauthored this document with three others—Minamoto Shitagō, Fujiwara Tamemasa (Tomoyasu's son-in-law, husband of Michitsuna's Mother's elder sister), and Fujiwara Koresuke. On one hand, the coauthorship makes it difficult to assess Tomoyasu's particular contribution; on the other hand, Minamoto Shitagō (911–983) was a courtier acclaimed both as a *waka* poet and as a *kanshi* (Chinese poetry) and *kanbun* (Chinese prose) writer, indicating that Tomoyasu kept good literary company.

Regarding Tomoyasu's official career, the details are somewhat uncertain,[13] but the broad outline is clear. At first mention in contemporary documents, the occasion of the Iwashimizu Shrine Special

Festival in 941 noted above, he is listed as Lesser Assistant of the Central Affairs Ministry (Nakatsukasa Shōjō), a post normally filled by someone of the Junior Sixth Rank Upper.[14] Following Oka Kazuo's suggestion that a reasonable conjecture for Tomoyasu's age at death in 977 would have been about sixty-six,[15] Tomoyasu would have been approximately thirty years old at this first mention and still the possessor of only modest rank, a career profile in line with the relatively low status of his father. The other point of interest regarding his early posts is that he was apparently made Assistant Director of the Right Imperial Stable (Umeryō no Suke) in 949. Since Kaneie, his future son-in-law, was appointed Assistant Commander of the Right Military Guards (Uhyōe no Suke) in 951, their personal contact likely began at this time through their professional duties.

Undoubtedly the turning point in Tomoyasu's career came in 954 with his appointment to the provincial governorship of Michinoku, only a month or so after the marriage of his daughter to Kaneie. There is some debate as to whether Tomoyasu owed the chance of this appointment to his new son-in-law or to his close relations with Fujiwara Saneyori, Kaneie's paternal uncle and the most powerful senior official during most of Emperor Murakami's reign, 946–967. Matsuda Shigeo, for example, questions the extent of Kaneie's political influence at this early stage in his career when his two elder brothers were still alive.[16] However, the close timing of the appointment with that of the marriage certainly suggests a connection between the two events. Whichever relationship may have been the determining factor, and perhaps both were important, the opportunity to serve as Provincial Governor of Michinoku was certainly a boon to Tomoyasu.

A word is in order about the role and status of the provincial governor class *(zuryō)* in mid-Heian society. Actually to go to a province and fulfill the duties of a provincial governor carried a social stigma and precluded that person's ever rising to the highest levels of aristocratic society. Nevertheless, since the provinces were the site of the production of real wealth, the provincial governor's post provided significant opportunities for material enrichment. Thus, it was a desirable consolation prize for those who had given up competition for preferment within the inner circle of power. Moreover, the post of provincial governor gave much more scope for the exercise of administrative expertise than any post in the capital within Tomoyasu's reach. Tomoyasu's first appointment, Michinoku, was one of the largest provinces, comprising most of northeastern Honshū. The post entailed the hardship of being far removed from the capital but certainly offered opportunity for ingenuity in management. Tomoyasu did prove to be a very able administrator, particularly in the way most appreciated by the central court, the production of tax income. The proof is in a report in Saneyori's diary that Tomoyasu was able to send more than three thousand *ryō* of gold dust as part of the tax income for each of the five years he served as Michinoku's governor.[17] It may well have been this meritorious service that prompted Saneyori to employ Tomoyasu as his own household manager. Because such private employment is not part of the official record, it is difficult to know when his service for Saneyori began, but it was likely after he retired from the post in Michinoku in 960.

His next appointments as provincial governor, Kawachi in 963 and Tanba in 967, also indicate some link with the Saneyori employment. Both were highly developed and wealthy provinces within a day's travel of the capital. With postings so close by, he could manage Saneyori's financial affairs as well as serve as governor.[18] Thus, Michinoku was indeed an important proving ground for Tomoyasu. Moreover, it may be assumed that his subsequent career, both as private household manager and as governor, must have resulted in a considerable personal fortune for Tomoyasu himself.

By 971, however, Tomoyasu found himself out of office. Saneyori had died in 970, and Tomoyasu's governorship of Tanba ended in 971. In the next two years, the marriage between his daughter and Kaneie began to show signs of breaking down, which must have made it difficult for Tomoyasu to petition Kaneie. Around this time, Kaneie himself was having his career frustrated at every turn by his elder brother, Kanemichi, and therefore may not have been in position to grant favors. Tomoyasu's formal request for posting as a provincial governor, which he composed with Minamoto Shitagō and the others, dates from 974, during this period of career hiatus. The document's eloquence may have worked, because about a year later he was made Governor of Ise and died in 977 while serving in this position. His official court rank at his death was Senior Fourth Rank Lower, more than one full rank above his father's highest rank, a difficult accomplishment.

I have dealt with Tomoyasu's career at some length to provide a context for the political and economic importance to Tomoyasu of the marriage between his daughter and Kaneie and also to give some historical background for the diary excerpts that follow. What effect would such a career and place in the world have had on Tomoyasu's relationship with his daughter? A career as provincial governor, however lucrative, was hardly distinguished so far as the society of the time was concerned. The desire to regain social position—if not for oneself, then for one's heirs—must have been a motivating force for men such as Tomoyasu.[19] Such hopes would have to be pinned more on the future of one's daughters than of one's sons. In the Heian period, the status of a son was much more closely tied to the rank of his father. The mother's status also played a role in the children's opportunities but could never lift a son beyond his father's rank. In contrast, a daughter had more possibility for social mobility through marriage upward in the social scale. The extreme case of this scenario for the provincial governor class is played out fictionally in *The Tale of Genji* through the character of the Akashi Lay Monk who stakes his whole life of religious devotions on the hope that his daughter will marry into the first circle of power in the capital and give birth to a daughter who will become an imperial consort and in her turn give birth to a future emperor. This is, of course, the pattern of marriage politics played by the main branch of the Fujiwara family for decades to maintain power at court.

It was probably not with such grandiose dreams that Tomoyasu entertained the overtures of Kaneie regarding his daughter, but the distant chance of his daughter's giving birth to a future empress may not have been lost on him. Indeed, had Michitsuna's Mother borne a daughter instead of a son, such a destiny for the daughter would not have been impossible. All of the daughters by Kaneie's other wife, Tokihime, became imperial consorts. One of them, Senshi, became an empress and wielded great political influence for many years.

Father-Daughter Dynamics

So then how would this situation affect Tomoyasu's attitude toward his daughters and his contribution to their rearing? All his daughters would have provided precious opportunities for him. He must have been alert to any possibility that he might have a daughter of exceptional qualities. What would such qualities be? Physical beauty would be important but not sufficient. She must have the potential for becoming a woman capable of fascinating a man through a charm based on intelligence and wit. Since poetry was so much part of the courtship ritual, she must have the talent to become a skilled poet. More intangibly, she must be someone with a sense of pride and self-worth, able to participate in the exchange of *waka* on equal terms. Although this society paid careful attention to minute differences in rank, within a *waka* there was no room for the marking of rank through the use of honorific or humilific language. In the exchange of *waka,* one was on an equal and intimate footing with one's partner. This is particularly interesting with regard to the relations between men and women. It is no exaggeration to say that to produce a daughter able to compete in marriage politics, one had to raise a self-confident artist. I do not assert that fathers like Tomoyasu raised their daughters this way as a conscious stratagem but rather suggest that such a rearing issued out of the cultural complex of the time.

Daughter-father relationships in Heian society had two interlocking facets. One was the sociopolitical dimension in which daughters were a valued commodity whose strategic marriage or placement at court was the key means for securing political advantage for an individual father and his patrilineal clan. The other was the personal dimension of love between daughter and father, nurtured within a domestic world to which the father usually came as a longed-for visitor. Important to both these dimensions was the daughter's access to a language of self-expression, primarily *waka* poetry. In order to be desirable and therefore valuable capital in the game of marriage politics, a daughter had to be cultivated as a writer. To become a good writer, the daughter had to be raised to value herself and her own feelings.

There is very little record of childrearing practices in the Heian period. The most detailed treatment of the rearing of a daughter is in *The Tale of Genji,* with its extended descriptions of Genji's rearing of young Murasaki. Admittedly, it is a fictional account and presents the extreme case of a man raising a child not of his own blood with the ultimate intention of making her his lover/wife. Is it not reasonable, however, that the very possibility and appeal of this as a fictional situation might have been based on an unconscious eroticism that underlay the relations between Heian fathers and daughters? The intimacy and playfulness in Genji's relation to the child Murasaki was likely present in the usual relations between fathers and daughters in the Heian period. One can imagine how much the combination of the potential value of the daughter to the prospects for one's family, and the sanctioned pleasure of allowing or encouraging a small girl to grow up into a talented, spirited, and desirable woman, would have resulted in doting fathers. Moreover, the relation between father and daughter was not severed by the daughter's marriage.[20] The father could anticipate having a close relationship with his daughter for as long as his relationship with her mother remained close. Because the daughter stayed in her mother's house to which both her husband and father usually came as visitors, the visit of the father would tend to be a treasured event for both daughter and father. There would have been no opportunity for familiarity, on the one hand, to breed indifference or, on the other, to produce a "realistic" perception of the father.

The above is an imagined reconstruction of the sort of relationship that Tomoyasu might have had with his daughter. Admittedly, there is very little in the way of sources to confirm it, but such a father-daughter relationship would explain the depth of Michitsuna's Mother's attachment to her father and her tendency to idealize him.

The Father Ideal

In the first part of the diary, Michitsuna's Mother presents her father as the provider of unconditional love and caring. Given that her relationship with her husband is the central story of the diary, the first mention of her father is not surprisingly in connection with her marriage:

Well then, for this ultimately disappointing affair, there was, of course, the exchange of love letters; from about the time that he became "a tall tree among oak trees" [that is, Captain of the Right Military Guards], it seems that he made his intentions known. An ordinary person would have sent a discreet letter using a serving maid or someone like that as a go-between to make his feelings known, but this man goes right to my father, half-joking, half-serious, hinting at the idea, and even though I told my father that it did not suit me at all, just as if he [Kaneie] did not know, one day, he sends a retainer riding on a horse to pound on our gate. Who was bringing whose messages, we had not a hint, so there is a big commotion, we were quite perplexed, and accepting the message brings on another commotion. When I look at it, the paper and so on are not what you would expect in such a letter; I had heard from of old, that in such a case the hand would be perfect, but the writing in this is so bad that I feel it couldn't be that sort of letter; it is so very strange.[21]

Michitsuna's Mother's disappointment in this match arises from frustrated expectations based on the paradigm of "romantic" or courtly love as constructed within the *waka* poetry and *uta monogatari* tradition.[22] To begin with, her would-be lover should have approached her first through a female intermediary, giving her a sense of real choice regarding the match. When the suit is initiated through her father, it already has vexing complications arising from the power differences among the players. Now, if she were to refuse the match, she must also refuse her father, and his relationship with Kaneie is such that he cannot refuse the suit no matter what his daughter says. Second, a private approach would have given her a chance to "fall in love," which within the Heian literary context involved nurturing a love in secret fueled by poetic imagination. A whole segment of the love cycle in *waka* poetry anthologies is devoted to just such longing in secret. And finally, even the choice of paper and the handwriting did not live up to the ideal of romance. She has after all been raised in an atmosphere that would foster expectations of becoming a heroine in her own *uta monogatari,* and this beginning to her own love tale is not auspicious.

Particularly conspicuous by its absence in this account is any reference to the possible political or economic significance that this match may have for her father and family. It seems inconceivable that she would be utterly ignorant of political reality. She hints later in the diary that she is aware of her father's status in political life and what it means. Thus, we must suppose that she consciously omits reference to the political implications of this proposed match. What would be the source of that discretion? Was it that it would have been unseemly for a woman to admit that kind of knowledge? Was it that it would destroy the atmosphere of courtly romance that she felt drawn to create in language? Or was it, at least in part, that she could not allow consideration of the social reality of marriage into the account without diminishing her father's status as an ideal of unconditional love. I do not mean to imply that Michitsuna's Mother shaped her diary with abstract concepts like "ideal" and "unconditional love" in mind. Rather, these concepts help us as readers in this age to uncover an aesthetic and psychological process that manifests itself in the diary only within concrete description of events and emotions.

Although Kaneie approaches her father first, thus forestalling a refusal of the suit, she writes as though she still has free choice in the matter. She flatly refuses her father at first mention of the possibility, but Kaneie does not take no for an answer. In the exchange of poems that follows, she resists his protestation of love and yet appears in the end to be reluctantly "won," falling instantly into a melancholic mood of worry and complaint the moment the marriage is consummated. It appears that she was allowed to resist the match for two to three months, but given the power relations between father-daughter and father-suitor, it is unlikely the final result of the courtship was ever in question.

Most interestingly, at no point in the account of the proposal above, nor in the ensuing exchange of courtship poems, does she give any indication of pressure from her father to entertain and accept the suit. The only words of admonishment to her are from her mother, who tells her, "How awful, hadn't you better be a bit more mature about this and send him a reply."[23] In this interaction, Michitsuna's Mother refers to her mother as *kodai naru hito* (the person from the older generation),[24] and one can sense a tone of light disdain in the address—"Silly old Mom insisted I reply to that tiresome man." Yet it seems inconceivable that her father would not have pressured her. What is clear is that she holds her father utterly free of blame with respect to the inception of marriage. Moreover, her father's potential gain from the match is kept outside her account and perhaps even outside her consciousness. Thus, he can stand as an ideal of love and caring, even though he is unattainable or unthinkable as an actual lover (or a partner in poetry).

In fact, this tendency to hold the father as an ideal divorced from the real situation of his position as a low-ranking aristocrat anxious for advancement is even more pronounced in the first extended treatment of her interaction with her father, the account of his departure for his first post as Provincial Governor in Michinoku.

> With things going on in this way, there came a time when the person I relied on most, my father, was to leave for Michinoku province.
>
> The season, late autumn, is such a sad time itself, and I still cannot say that I am really used to seeing my husband; every time I see him now, I just burst into tears, and feel so sad and uneasy, there is nothing to which I can compare it. My husband expresses sympathy for me and although he keeps saying he will never forget me, as I wonder if his heart will really be true to his words, I only feel even more sad and anxious.
>
> Now the day has come for them all to leave; the one who is to go cannot restrain his tears, and I, the one who is to stay, am

sadder than I can say. "We are way behind schedule,"—even though urged thus by his attendants, he cannot leave, rolling up a letter and pushing it into an inkstone box beside him, once again breaking into tears that sprinkled down, he left the room. For awhile, I have not the heart to look at what he has left. Having watched until he went out of sight, pulling myself together, I approach and when I look at what sort of thing was there, this poem is what I see,

kimi wo nomi	Only on you
tanomu tabi naru	I rely at this time, setting out;
kokoro ni ha	in my heart,
yukusuwe tohoku	thoughts of the long road ahead—
omohoyuru kana	may your life with her be as long.

Thinking that he intended to have this seen by my husband, I feel so sad, and place it back just as he had left it; it was not long before my husband came to visit. As I was lost in my own thoughts and did not meet him with my eyes, he consoles me by saying, "Come now, this is a perfectly ordinary occurrence in the world. Your persisting in going on like this must mean you do not trust me." Noticing the letter in the inkstone box, "Ah, how touching," he says, and sent off after my father this,

ware wo nomi	Since you say you
tanomu to iheba	rely only on me, at the end
yuku suwe no	of the road ahead,
matsu no chigiri mo	Sue pines will betoken our vows;
kite koso ha mime	return and see us unchanged.

In this way, the days passed. Imagining my father travelling under strange skies brought sadness, and my husband's heart did not appear to be something I could rely on that much.[25]

Once again, the absence in this account of any mention of the potential benefit of this appointment for her father's advancement is conspicuous. Rather, she chooses to foreground his grief at parting from her. The extremity of both their reactions indicates that this is the first time they have ever faced a long-term separation.[26] This is also the first passage in which the contrast between her father and her husband is made explicit. Her father is the one she can trust and rely on; her husband is unfamiliar and an uncertain repository of trust. Her husband's attempts at consolation move from admonishment of her to be realistic to mild chagrin concerning his own reputation in the situation. On the other hand, her father empathizes with her pain and gives full rein to the expression of his own matching feelings. In fact, it is her father's expression of emotion in the poem to her husband that moves Kaneie to enter into the emotion of the event and respond through poetry. Although the poignancy of this passage lies in the link of sympathy within this family triangle, it also reveals that the structure of Michitsuna's Mother's relationship to her husband is established in the shadow of the father as the ideal of unconditional love.

The relationship among the three of them—father, daughter, and husband—is a triangle of love and power. Through the father, Kaneie obtains access to the daughter. He accomplishes and maintains his relationship with the daughter through his skills as a lover and poet. Yet, this relationship is only a small part of his life, and he invests only so much energy in it. For the rest, he can depend on his power relationship with the father to keep the marriage going. In her text, Michitsuna's Mother gives no indication that she is bound to her husband by the expectations of her father and family. That would be to assume the position of family servant or pawn. Instead, she adopts the position of a heroine in a poem tale and holds her father as outside concerns of self-interest.

The second passage in Book One that reveals the continuing depth of Michitsuna's Mother's relationship with her father occurs within the description of the crisis in her health precipitated by her mother's death in 964, about ten years into the author's marriage. There is curiously little mention of the mother in the diary, yet the degree of Michitsuna's Mother's emotional reliance on her mother can be inferred from the extremity of her reaction to her mother's death. Shortly after this traumatic event, Michitsuna's Mother lapses into a seemingly psychosomatically produced paralysis. She stops eating and loses the movement of her limbs, much to the consternation of her other family members, who fear they may have to prepare for a second death in the family. At this juncture, her father appears. He is serving as Governor of Kawachi, one of the capital-area provinces, so he is able to come to her side.

> Even though I was unable to speak, I was still conscious and could see. My father, *the person most concerned about my welfare,* came, and said, "Have you only one parent? How could you have come to this?" He urged me to swallow some broth, and drinking things such as this, my body began to mend. (Emphasis added.)

Here, her father symbolically assumes the role of mother as well by bringing her to life again through the personal provision of nourishment. Her physical health is restored through his ministrations, so important is he to her even after ten years of her marriage to Kaneie. Thus, her father is still the ideal of unconditional love, and her husband the forever inadequate emotional provider.

Marital Reality

Of course, Kaneie had already proved himself unreliable as a husband in the first year of their marriage by starting an affair with the Machi Alley woman immediately after the birth of Michitsuna, the author's only child. This affair sparked a violent reaction in Michitsuna's Mother and nearly resulted in an early end of the marriage. It may be argued that within the social context of the Heian period, when polygynous marriage was the norm, her expectations were unreasonable from the start. Kaneie already had one wife at the time of his marriage. The author hints she was aware of this at the time of the affair when she prefaces a poem of mutual commiseration addressed to the first wife, Tokihime, by saying she had corresponded with the lady several times before. She appeared to accept the existence of Tokihime but absolutely to reject the notion that Kaneie should take another wife after herself. Her own father had two wives and eventually a third, yet she never expresses chagrin concerning that. She seems simply not concerned with the social context of the time and the contrariness of her own attitude within that context, instead concentrating on her own feelings about her particular circumstances. In a playful poem at the beginning of Book Two, intended magically to bring good fortune at the New Year by speaking auspiciously, she articulates her "impossible" expectations: "Thirty days and thirty nights of every month, let him be by my side."

This unreasonable desire dovetails with the construction of her father as the ideal of love. It is not that her father is literally with her every minute of every day, but her certainty of his love for her is constant. Much of Books One and Two of the diary are animated by her struggle to have her relationship with her husband comply with her ideal, and her resistance to satisfaction with anything less.

The Son

All the while, Michitsuna's Mother's relationship with her son develops in the shadow of her despair over the inability or refusal of her husband to fulfill her expectations. It is as though she ties her son to her with fierce bonds of dependency to compensate for her dissatisfaction. Again, given the focus of the diary on the marriage relationship, there are few appearances of the son. In his early years, he is mentioned only in connection with his father and, more significantly, in underscoring the absence of his father.

> My little one here has just begun to say a few words. Whenever his father takes leave of us, he always says, "See you soon," and the little one hearing this goes around imitating him.[27]

She reprises this description in a long poem of complaint to her husband, emphasizing how the boy's mimicking of his father serves only to remind her of his absence.

> [. . .] parting you said, "See you soon"
> thinking these words
> must be true our young pine
> waits endlessly
> mimicking your voice,
> each time I hear it,
> I think ill of you, tears just fall.[28]

As the boy matures, two striking passages reveal an emotional closeness and mutual dependency between mother and son. One is the account of a domestic quarrel that erupts between Kaneie and Michitsuna's Mother when Michitsuna is about twelve years old. In a fit of anger, Kaneie calls the boy out to observe his departure and tells him, "I will no longer be coming here."[29] Michitsuna is reduced to tears and runs to his mother in distress. Kaneie inflicts this emotional pain on the son in order to punish the mother. His treatment of mother and son as a unit here seems to recognize the deep bond between the two.

The second passage is later in Book Two when Michitsuna is about fourteen years old and the author, unable to stop dwelling on her dissatisfaction with the marriage, considers becoming a nun. One thing that impedes her from pursuing the thought seriously is concern for her son's welfare. She reaches the point of broaching the subject with Michitsuna:

> I continued to sink deeper into a depression; all I could think about was if only I could die as my heart desired, but when I think about my only child, I get very sad. If only he would grow up and I could leave him in the care of some dependable wife, then I could die in peace, but failing that, how bereft he would be; thinking

about that, it seems very difficult to die. When I said to him one day, "How would it be, if I were to take the tonsure and try separating myself from the suffering of this world," even though he is still not capable of deeply understanding things, he began to sob piteously. "If you were to do that, I would surely become a monk myself. How could I involve myself in the affairs of the world after that?" And as he broke out sobbing again, I too could no longer hold back my tears, but in the midst of our misery, I tried to make a joke out of it. "Well then, if you became a monk, how could you possibly manage without your hawks," at which, he got up quietly, ran to his tethered hawks, untied them and let them all go. Even the attendants looking on couldn't help crying, and I was sad the whole day long.[30]

It is one of the more dramatic scenes in the diary. Michitsuna appears to demonstrate a passionate identification with his mother that, however, only has the effect of increasing her melancholy. He has been bound to her as a compensation for the neglect of the husband, but such a dependent relationship is also a burden. Thus, Michitsuna's Mother's relationship to both her husband and her son can be seen as interlocked with and originating from the primary relationship with her father, in which he is constructed as the provider of a perfect love. But neither her father nor her son can be the perfect lover/husband she craves, just as neither of them is a fitting partner in poetry.

In the above web of relationships, Michitsuna's Mother has virtually no sense of agency and freedom of mind. She can only resist through refusal and complaint. The culmination of her resistance occurs in Book Two with her retreat to Narutaki, where she contemplates severing all her relationships with men by becoming a nun. Significantly, all three men in her life act in concert to bring her down from the mountain, with her father giving the crucial word to initiate the move.

Thinking that this time, he [Kaneie] will not take no for an answer, my mind was in an uproar when the one I rely on most, my father, having just come back to the capital from a tour of duty came right away to see me. Telling me what was going on, he said, "I thought it would be all right for you to stay here for awhile and continue your devotions, but it has been a most regrettable thing for our young master here. Return as quickly as possible to the capital. If today is as good a day as any, we could go back together. Today or tomorrow, I will escort you." To be spoken to thus in no uncertain terms, my strength left me and I agonized inwardly. He said, "Well then, tomorrow it is," and left.[31]

Shortly after this, her husband arrives and marshals the support of his son for the move. During the period of retreat at Narutaki, her son had already declared his independence from her and allegiance with his father by stating that he was going home with his father and never coming back, when Kaneie first attempted to bring Michitsuna's Mother down from the mountain.[32] Although he was forced to stay with his mother then, this time he acts as an ally of his father and is the one to take his mother finally by the hand and lead her into his father's carriage. With her own father, son, and husband all acting against her, her resistance broken, she is forced back into the norm of her marriage as it had been established by her father and husband, yet she returns subtly transformed rather than defeated.

Freedom of Mind

Book Three, which begins about six months after the return from Narutaki, starts thus:

> In this way, another New Year dawns; it seems it is the Third year of Tenroku. Feeling my gloom and pain have quite cleared away, I help dress our young Lord and send him on his way to court. As I watch him run down into the garden and straight away give a cere- monial bow, he looks so terribly splendid, I want to cry. I think, "Shall I hold a sutra reading service tonight?" but then my period is likely to come. That is the sort of thing people usually consider inauspicious, and I wonder in my own heart once more how will things turn out for me. However, this year, having resolved firmly in my own mind that regardless of whether he [Kaneie] might be the most annoying person in the world, I will not lament over things, my heart is very much at peace.[33]

This attitude is maintained throughout Book Three as Michitsuna's Mother assumes more agency in her affairs through the adoption of a daughter, lets go of her husband without dwelling in bitterness, and grants her son independence while at the same time taking the oppor- tunity to appropriate a male voice vicariously by participating in the composition of her son's courtship poems.[34] Her relationship with her father exhibits a change as well. Although she is still economically dependent on him, she starts to view her father and his place in the world with a sense of irony and objectivity.

Actually, the beginning of the transformation in her view of her
father may be seen earlier in the diary. In Book Two before the retreat
to Narutaki, Michitsuna's Mother makes a pilgrimage to Ishiyama in
an attempt to find some peace of mind. On the way there, she and
her small party are overtaken by a much larger entourage. She describes the encounter thus:

> . . . a large number of mounted guardsmen with a caravan of two or
> three carriages came up making a big commotion. Someone says,
> "It's the carriage of the Governor of Wakasa." They pass by with-
> out stopping and I feel relieved. *How poignant,* I think to myself,
> *just like someone of that status to drive along with great pride and abandon,*
> *while, back in the capital, morning to dusk, he has been bowing and scrap-*
> *ing. Just so, he would drive along with a great commotion the moment he is*
> *out of the city limits.* It occasions heart-rending feelings.[35]

The reason this encounter occasions such emotion is, I suggest, because she is thinking of her father, who is in the same position as the
Governor of Wakasa. Here she reveals an awareness of her father's
place in the objective world. At this point, she still finds it painful to
accept the reality of her father's position.

Another critical passage where the difference in her attitude to her
father manifests itself is in the latter part of Book Three. By this point,
Michitsuna's Mother has moved to a house owned by her father in the
suburbs of the capital, an acknowledgment that her relationship with
her husband, at least in terms of his physical visits, is over. The author
in this particular passage has come to stay for a period at her father's
residence in the capital to avoid a directional taboo. While she is there,
a letter arrives for her from Kanemichi [Lord Horikawa], her husband's elder brother.

> Then, in the evening, when the torches had been lit and I was just
> about to eat, my brother drew near and took out from his pocket,
> a letter on thick white mulberry paper that had been tied into a
> knot and attached to a spray of withered pampas grass. When I say,
> "My, how odd. Whose is this?" he says, "Just have a look at it." I open
> it and, looking at it in the lamplight, see that it is in a hand resem-
> bling that of the person I am estranged from. This is what was
> written. "What ever happened to 'What colt'?"

shimokare no	Frost withered myself,
kusa no yukari zo	the bond I feel with the dry grass
aware naru	is sad and moving,
koma gaherite mo	becoming a colt again
natsukete shigana	I would want to draw near you.

"Ah, what a pity." Since it contained those syllables from the poem I had regretted sending to my husband, it was so strange. When I asked, "What is this?" and "Did it come from his Lordship Horikawa?" I was told, "Yes, it is a letter from the Grand Minister. One of his attendants came with it and when told, 'Her Ladyship is not in,' said, 'Please make sure she receives this,' and gave it to me." Although I thought and thought, it was so strange; I could not figure out how he could have heard of that poem. When I talked this over with others, my rather old fashioned father hearing of it admonished me, "This is a very serious matter. Write a reply quickly and it must be sent back with his Lordship's servant." Well, I did not intend to write such a silly poem, but it was just tossed off:

sasa wakeba	Parting scrub bamboo,
are koso masame	you approach but the grass is
kusa kare no	more withered and distant,
koma natsuku beki	is it really beneath these trees
mori no shita ka ha	that a colt would want to draw near?

This is what I wrote and sent. I heard later from an attendant, "His Lordship intended to write a reply to your poem, but after getting it half done, he said, 'I haven't quite got an ending yet,'" and since indeed a long time had passed without an answer, I found it most amusing.[36]

Kanemichi's letter refers to a poem the author had sent to her husband when he had accused her of entertaining a suitor of her adopted daughter so warmly as to cause gossip that the suitor was actually a lover of the author. In her poem of rebuke, she compared herself to withered grass and said, "what colt would think to draw near this abandoned grass." She is puzzled how knowledge of the poem came into Kanemichi's hands, but she had accidentally shown this poem to the suitor Tōnori, who happened to be the younger half-brother of both Kanemichi and Kaneie, so it was presumably through Tōnori that the poem came to Kanemichi. Kanemichi and Kaneie were not on good terms at this time. Kanemichi was in a superior position and doing everything in his power to frustrate the advance of his younger brother. Moreover, her father was out of office at that time and clearly desirous of a posting—hence his anxious urging of his daughter to reply to this missive from someone in a position to favor him.

Michitsuna's Mother's description of this hints at an awareness of the political dynamics behind this situation, yet her general attitude is one of amusement. She does answer the poem at her father's insistence but only in a spirit of play and is much amused when Kanemichi is bested in the exchange. Is not the ability to laugh with compassion at oneself and others a hallmark of freedom of mind? She exhibits a tolerant acceptance of her father's ambition but no personal entanglement with it. She refers to her father here as *furumekashiki hito* (old-fashioned person), a term of address curiously similar to the one she used years ago for her mother in a similar situation. Significantly, her father does not stand here as an absolute, whether as an ideal or as an ultimate authority.

This portrayal of her father as an ordinary, vulnerable person also occurs in a passage close to the end of the diary that serves as the diary's culminating scene. The occasion is the Kamo Special Festival held in the eleventh month of 974. In the author's description of this event, all three of the important men in her life—husband, son, and father—are assembled as though in a tableau. The scene is a rest break in the procession.

> On the day of the Festival, no matter what, I had to go and have a look. As I set out, I noticed on the north side of the street an unremarkable palmwork carriage parked with its blinds both in back and front pulled down. Sleeves of purple brocade layered over lustrous red silk spilled out from underneath the bamboo blind in front. Just as I was looking at this thinking it must be a woman's carriage, a man of the sixth rank with a sword at his waist approached from the gate of the house behind the carriage and with great dignity knelt with one knee on the ground to say something. With some surprise, when I looked more closely, I could see that beside the carriage that man had come out of, there were all sorts of men in costumes of red and black standing there all crammed together, so many I couldn't count them all. One of my attendants said, "If one looks carefully, there are some men there we have seen before." Things had got underway a little earlier than usual. The high nobility and their followers as well, all seemed to notice him; they stopped and parked their carriages in the same place with the fronts of their carriages facing his [Kaneie's]. The one I care deeply about [Michitsuna] and his attendants too, looked magnificent even though they had had little time to prepare. When the high nobility offered him snacks with their own hands and spoke to him, I felt proud. My old fashioned father not permitted to be in the audience was mingling among the musicians with blossom festooned caps. When he was sought out in the crowd

and offered a cup of sake brought forth from the other house, just for that moment of time, I seemed to feel content.[37]

Her father was not permitted to be in the official audience because he was currently out of office. It is assumed the mark of favor betokened by the cup of sake was bestowed on her father by Kaneie. What is remarkable about this account is that the author is able to look at all three men with affection and equanimity. The equanimity is particularly noteworthy with respect to Kaneie, because apparently he is there with another woman. She is proud of her son and thankful for the kindness shown her father by Kaneie. Her father is the focal point of this tableau, but he no longer bears the weight of being an ideal. It is characteristic of the psychological acuity of the author that she recognizes the fleeting quality of contentment. She pulls back at the moment of perception to view her own feelings objectively so that it "seemed" she was content "just for that moment of time."

One might argue that nothing has changed in Michitsuna's Mother's circumstances that would constitute a liberation. Certainly this is true of her material and social circumstances. She is still dependent on her father. She still obeys him when he tells her she must correspond with Kanemichi. She has lost her lover/husband, and she has given up what may be considered a wonderfully transgressive resistance to settle for less in terms of her desire. And yet she writes from a position of feeling free. She is no longer at the mercy of her circumstances. She can be at ease in her life and love her father as a fallible human being in a vulnerable social position. Simultaneously, it appears that she is no longer in the thrall of the romance myth that made the relationship with her husband so vexing.[38] By rendering her father as a "real" individual, she also achieved a mental freedom for herself.

Notes

1. There is some debate as to whether the *Tōnomine Shōshō monogatari* preceded the *Kagerō nikki* as the first work of Heian women's prose. See Miyake, "*Tōnomine Shōshō monogatari*," pp. 57–61. Nonetheless, so far as the canon of Heian women's literature is presently constructed, the *Kagerō nikki* is considered the first major work. An earlier English translation of this text by Edward Seidensticker renders the title *The Gossamer Years*.

2. For a detailed analysis of the introduction, see Arntzen, *Kagerō Diary*, pp. 1–8.

3. Shinozuka Sumiko in her essay "*Kagerō nikki* no shudai o megutte" has written comprehensively about Michitsuna's Mother's desire for and identification with the *uta monogatari.*

4. The next most numerous kind of poetic exchange issues from the author's relations with female friends and relatives, the language of which is almost indistinguishable from love poetry. Then there are her self-reflective *dokugin* (monologue poems), few in number but some of the most interesting and unusual poems in the text. Finally, in the last book of the diary, when her marriage has ended, she records the courting poems of her son and their responses, thus reasserting the atmosphere of the *uta monogatari.*

5. Kowaleski-Wallace, "Reading the Father," p. 297.

6. *Kagerō nikki,* p. 83.

7. McCullough and McCullough, *A Tale of Flowering Fortunes,* p. 794. The highest rank is number one. It should also be remembered that emolument went with rank and not office in the Heian period.

8. *Kagerō nikki,* p. 83.

9. This summary is indebted to the detective work done on Tomoyasu's career by Oka Kazuo for his biography of the *Kagerō nikki* author, *Michitsuna Bo.*

10. The Maeda manuscript of *The Fujiwara Clan Genealogy.* Oka, *Michitsuna Bo,* p. 13.

11. In the *Honchō seiki,* a chronicle of court activities covering 935–1153. Ibid.

12. Ibid.

13. The uncertainty issues from errors and omissions in the *Sompi bunmyaku,* the fourteenth-century compilation of genealogical and biographical information on the principal aristocratic families that is usually consulted on such matters. Ibid.

14. Ono, *Kogo jiten,* pp. 1476–1477.

15. Oka, *Michitsuna Bo,* p. 21.

16. Matsuda, "*Kagerō nikki,*" p. 17.

17. The citation of Saneyori's diary is made in Fujiwara Sanesuke's voluminous *Shōyūki.* Oka, *Michitsuna Bo,* p. 16.

18. Ibid., pp. 18–19.

19. Matsuda, pp. 16–17.

20. This aspect of Heian daughter-father relations is dealt with in some detail by Shinozuka, *Kagerō nikki,* p. 180.

21. *Kagerō nikki,* p. 126; Arntzen, *Kagerō Diary,* p. 57.

22. Michitsuna's Mother makes direct reference to an implicit comparison between her actual life and the fantasy world of tales in the opening passage of the diary: ". . . when she looks at the odds and ends of the old tales, of which there are so many, they are just so much fantasy, that she thinks perhaps if she were to make a record of a life like her own, being really nobody, it might actually be novel, and could even serve to answer, should anyone ask, what is it like, the life of a woman married to a highly placed man." *Kagerō nikki,* p. 125; Arntzen, *Kagerō Diary,* p. 57.

23. *Kagerō nikki,* p. 127; Arntzen, *Kagerō Diary,* p. 59.

24. *Kagerō nikki,* p. 126.

25. *Kagerō nikki*, pp. 132–134; Arntzen, *Kagerō Diary*, pp. 65–67.

26. Oka makes this observation (p. 15) as part of an argument to support the assumption that Michinoku was indeed Tomoyasu's first appointment as a provincial governor.

27. *Kagerō nikki*, p. 150; Arntzen, *Kagerō Diary*, p. 89.

28. *Kagerō nikki*, p. 153; Arntzen, *Kagerō Diary*, p. 93.

29. *Kagerō nikki*, p. 183; Arntzen, *Kagerō Diary*, p. 135.

30. *Kagerō nikki*, p. 235; Arntzen, *Kagerō Diary*, p. 205.

31. *Kagerō nikki*, p. 282; Arntzen, *Kagerō Diary*, p. 253.

32. *Kagerō nikki*, p. 263; Arntzen, *Kagerō Diary*, p. 235. In fact, Kaneie refused to have Michitsuna come back with him at that point. He held the young man responsible for his mother's misbehavior. Nonetheless, an important watershed was reached in terms of Michitsuna's sense of identification that was quickly perceived by his mother. She began to refer to him from that point on with his official title of court rank rather than as "young one."

33. *Kagerō nikki*, p. 301; Arntzen, *Kagerō Diary*, p. 277.

34. There is some debate about whether the author wrote all of her son's courtship poems that are cited in the diary. In the diary itself, she does not state that she wrote them. However, in the collection of the author's poems that is appended to all the manuscripts of the diary, the compiler of the collection notes: "When the Imperial Tutor [Michitsuna] was first beginning to court women with letters, she [Michitsuna's Mother] wrote this in his place." *Kagerō nikki*, p. 399; Arntzen, *Kagerō Diary*, p. 389. It seems that we are to assume that she wrote all the following poems in the collection related to Michitsuna's courtship of women. By extension, it seems that her inclusion of so many of Michitsuna's courtship poems in her own diary must be because she had a hand in writing them.

35. *Kagerō nikki*, p. 238; Arntzen, *Kagerō Diary*, p. 209.

36. *Kagerō nikki*, pp. 385–386; Arntzen, *Kagerō Diary*, p. 365.

37. *Kagerō nikki*, pp. 387–388; Arntzen, *Kagerō Diary*, p. 371.

38. It is not that she repudiates the romantic world of the *uta monogatari*. She still enjoys participating in it through the exchange of poems with her adopted daughter's suitor and through being a ghostwriter for her son, but she is no longer personally fettered by it.

Works Cited

Location of Japanese publishers is Tokyo unless otherwise noted.

Arntzen, Sonja, trans. *The Kagerō Diary: A Woman's Autobiographical Text from Tenth-Century Japan*. Ann Arbor: Center for Japanese Studies, University of Michigan, 1997.

Kagerō nikki. Ed. Kimura Masanori and Imuta Tsunehisa. In *Tosa nikki, Kagerō nikki*, pp. 125–409. *NKBZ* 9. Shōgakkan, 1973.

Kowaleski-Wallace, Beth. "Reading the Father Metaphorically." In *Refiguring the Father: New Feminist Readings of the Patriarchy,* ed. Patricia Yaeger and Beth Kowaleski-Wallace. Carbondale: Southern Illinois University Press, 1989.

Matsuda Shigeo. "*Kagerō nikki:* sakusha no shōzō." In *Ochō joryū nikki hikkei,* ed. Akiyama Ken. Gakutōsha, 1989.

McCullough, Helen C., and William H. McCullough, trans. *A Tale of Flowering Fortunes: Annals of Japanese Aristocratic Life in the Heian Period.* 2 vols. Stanford, Calif.: Stanford University Press, 1980.

Miyake, Lynn. "*Tōnomine Shōshō monogatari:* A Translation and Critical Study." Ph.D. dissertation, University of California at Berkeley, 1985.

Oka Kazuo. *Michitsuna Bo.* Rev. ed. Yūseidō, 1970.

Ono Susumu. *Kogo jiten.* Iwanami shoten, 1974.

Shinozuka Sumiko. *Kagerō nikki no kokoro to hyōgen.* Benseisha, 1995.

———. "*Kagerō nikki* no shudai o megutte." In *Joryū nikki bungaku kōza,* vol. 2, *Kagerō nikki,* pp. 97–117. Benseisha, 1990.

Chapter 2

Self-Representation and the Patriarchy in the Heian Female Memoirs

ESPERANZA RAMIREZ-CHRISTENSEN

It is by now axiomatic to assume, when reading the genre known as Heian women's diary literature *(Heian joryū nikki bungaku)*, that we are dealing with artistic narratives of female self-representation rather than the unstructured series of disparate entries commonly understood by the term "diary." These "diaries" are the creative products of a highly selective process of sifting through the memory, aided by notebooks of poems sent and received, with brief indications of their occasion and circumstance, and other sketches of events and personal encounters recorded close to the time of their occurrence. There is reason therefore to approve the trend in recent studies to refer to them as "memoirs," a term that could apply equally well to Michitsuna's Mother's *Kagerō Diary (Kagerō nikki;* also translated as *Gossamer Diary)* as to Sei Shōnagon's *Pillow Book (Makura sōshi).*[1] On the other hand, it is also instructive to regard these writings as what would be called autobiography in the Western tradition. This is a genre whose ever more ambiguous definition has not discouraged its ongoing production since St. Augustine's *Confessions* and Rousseau's and Montaigne's *Essays,* to cite only the classic titles.[2] Are not the Heian memoirs the works of women writing about their own lives, and therefore admissible to the dignity of the term "autobiography," indeed antedating the classic Western examples (barring Augustine) by some five hundred years?

In the critical essay "Conditions and Limits of Autobiography," Georges Gusdorf finds it necessary to point out "that the genre of autobiography . . . has not always existed nor does it exist everywhere," for it expresses "a concern peculiar to Western man"—the concern, that is, "to turn back on one's own past, to recollect one's life in order to narrate it," which is grounded on "the conscious awareness of the singularity of each individual life [and] is the late product of a specific civilization."[3] Gusdorf sees the autobiographical impulse as arising, in the Western world, from the emergence of a sense of self apart from the structure of predetermined roles such as are seen in so-called primitive communities. He also presupposes the emergence, from belief in the timeless repetition of mythic structures in ancient cultures, of a concept of history as a sequence of unrepeatable events enacted by individual men at specific points in time. Autobiography then belongs to the post-Copernican history of humanism in the West.

If we nevertheless claim that the Heian women's memoirs are precisely the textual manifestations of an early autobiographical impulse outside the history of Western humanism, it then behooves us to inquire what sociohistorical conditions, and in particular what discursive formations, compelled it. Here it would be necessary to observe, first of all, the dominance of lyric poetry as the ritual language of the Heian cultural elite for communicating feeling, whether publicly during occasions of celebration and mourning, or privately during the course of a love affair. The early emergence of the genre called poem tales *(uta monogatari)* illustrates how even nameless characters can assume depths of sensibility, a heart *(kokoro),* by the mere recitation of a poem that distills the affect of a situation through the agency of the metaphor. It will be argued, no doubt, that such a nameless poet can hardly count as an individual person, particularly when we consider that Ki no Tsurayuki (ca. 868–945), the pioneering legislator on these matters, declared Japanese poetry to be the universal response of the human heart to the experience of being in the world.[4] In other words, the lyrical "I" can by no means be equated with the sense of self of Western humanism precisely because "the heart" was understood to be, ideally at least, what binds everyone in a common humanity rather than setting them apart. On the other hand, the very introduction of poetry spoken by specific characters in prose narratives has the effect of endowing those persons with an interiority and a psychology within the network of external events, actions, and encounters in which they are inscribed. As a universal expression of the heart-mind, poetry transcended class boundaries, as evident in the absence in it of linguistic markers of social hierarchy required in ordinary language. And perhaps most important of all, Tsurayuki's poetics of *kokoro* entailed sincerity or truthfulness *(makoto)* as a necessary value of the poetic voice.[5] In poetry, then, we have a highly developed discursive formation in current use and with its own archives (anthologies, treatises, poem tales), which a literate person could adopt to signify a kind of self-understanding in the course of a life.

It was, however, apparently women who took the first steps in narrating their own lives by using the language of the poem-narrative and the covenant of sincerity implicit in it.[6] The question is why. Why is it the women who felt the autobiographic impulse so keenly as to inaugurate the earliest tradition of self-referential writing, as far as we know, in East Asia? And in so doing to contribute directly to the production of what is loosely termed "the world's first novel," Murasaki Shikibu's *Tale of Genji* (ca. 1010), as if the modern reader sensed, in the density of the characters' interiority, a territory not unfamiliar to the West after Freud? Many answers have been offered to resolve these questions, mainly having to do with women's use of native Japanese rather than the Chinese used by men for official records, laws, and proclamations, as well as poetry and diaries. That answer implies that if women indeed pioneered the art of autobiography, it was only by default—not a wholly satisfying explanation. Here, however, I would like to examine the question from a sociopolitical angle and will propose that it was women's ambiguous positioning in the Heian patriarchal system that paradoxically motivated them to that quest for the self and for the meaning of a life that we sense in these memoirs.

The Position of Women in the Heian Patriarchy

It is now accepted historical opinion that Japanese women suffered a major loss of power and status when they were excluded in the main from holding positions in the local and central governing structures established by the *ritsuryō* legal reforms in the mid-seventh century. Adopted from China, these reforms also instituted the patrilineal order by identifying the male as head of household *(koshu)* in the official registers. The full effect of the new system of male dominance, what in current critical usage is called phallocentrism, was not fully felt until later. The right of women to own and administer property was maintained until the medieval period, and the sexual equality that obtained in the ancient communal system was not easily erased from actual practice.[7] Nevertheless, by the tenth century among the court aristocracy and the late eleventh century among commoners, the process that would establish the patriarchal family *(kafuchōsei kazoku)* as the basic social unit was well on its way.[8] And it is this period that saw the production of the two memoirs to be discussed here, as well as *The Pillow Book* and *The Tale of Genji.* Gender inequality was already established with the practice of *ippu tazai* (one husband, several wives), which permitted polygamy for men but not for women. The systematic exclusion of women from public office was also crucial, because public office guaranteed a secure income and, more importantly, access to new property rights. Thus women could not enlarge whatever holdings they owned through inheritance, and their dependency on their menfolk increased. It is true that a few positions were reserved for women at court in the Handmaids' Office (Naishidokoro) and that the emperors' consorts, female kin, and ladies-in-waiting could and did exercise a degree of hidden power by their proximity to it. However, the overriding importance of actual rank and office in Heian aristocratic society, and of women's decisive exclusion from acquiring them, is attested to by that lady of keen social observations who made her acuity acceptable by the device of wit, Sei Shōnagon (ca. 965–after 1000):

> High office is, after all, a most splendid thing. . . . After all, women really have the worse time of it. There are, to be sure, cases where the nurse of an Emperor is appointed Assistant Attendant [*Naishi no Suke*] or given the Third Rank and thus acquires great dignity. Yet it does her little good since she is already an old woman. Besides, how many women ever attain such honors? Those who are reasonably well born consider themselves lucky if they can marry a governor and go down to the provinces. Of course it does happen that the daughter of a commoner becomes the principal consort of a High Court Noble and that the daughter of a High Court Noble becomes an Empress. Yet even this is not as splendid as when a man rises by means of promotions. How pleased such a man looks with himself![9]

When Sei Shōnagon, a lady-in-waiting to Empress Teishi (977–1000), thinks that not even her mistress's position is as splendid as when a man rises by his own being as a male *(saredo, naho otoko wa, waga mi no nariizuru koso medetaku),* surely the implication is that a woman does not attain to rank on her own but through her male kin: her father, brother, husband, and sons. Sei's observation is confirmed by the fact that a woman lacked a proper name or singular personal identity in herself in the everyday practice of nomenclature. She was formally registered simply as a "daughter," "wife," or "mother" under the male head of household's clan name in the patrilineal genealogical system. Thus, the names by which the authors of the memoirs are known, such as Sugawara Takasue's Daughter or Michitsuna's Mother, confirm the woman's secondary status as ultimately a dependent, an appendage, or a virtual possession of a male relative. So does the Heian aristocracy's practice of marriage politics, whereby the daughter functions as a resource for the betterment or at least the maintenance of her father's position, a kind of human currency in the Heian economy of status and power exchange. This is of course to put the matter in stark economic terms; in practice, family relations were understood in terms of the prevailing Confucian ethos of filial piety. But in understanding Heian women's literacy, literary productivity, and high aesthetic culture, it helps to know that such endowments were appreciated currency in their time and place. And it is equally important to know that they also employed their abilities for their own cause.

To put the matter succinctly, I believe that the introspection that drove the feminine autobiographic desire was both a specular reflection of and a resistance to woman's secondary—and ultimately false—positioning in the patriarchy, whose primary representative was the father. Spatially, that positioning may be understood—and only in part figuratively, based on Murasaki's representation of it in *The Tale of Genji*—as one of confinement: seclusion in the women's apartments and within those rooms, behind blinds, curtains, and screens, and, further, within several layers of robes. So many-layered were these enclosures—and these are only the physical ones—that the woman's self risked disappearance within them, unless she took up her writing brush to inscribe her autograph, so to speak, the physical mark that she existed, albeit that existence had, as she frequently wrote, a dream-like quality about it.

But is it sound to rely on the *Genji*'s representation of woman's positioning? I believe it is necessary, given the dearth of any other so-called objective historical record of sufficient density to represent her. But my gesture also deliberately acknowledges the claim to truth of literary works and what Jameson calls the "political unconscious" that inscribes itself in the textual representation.[10] In this view, a literary figure, such as the figure of confinement I read in the *Genji* text, is no mere aesthetic invention but speaks, sometimes despite itself, of the sociopolitical conditions of its time. We can further read the woman's autobiographic impulse, along with her well-known practice of the arts and letters, as in part a defensive response to her positioning as the immobilized object of the male gaze. The enclosures were solid enough to confine her but were yet of sufficient porosity to enable the man's gaze to glimpse and eventually to possess her. As principal object of male exogamous exchange, it may be said that her first experience of the larger society occurred when a man penetrated her virginal enclosures as a lover or husband. In other words, figuratively speaking, the male gaze constituted women's first experience of their ambiguous place, at once fixed—in their familial roles —and tenuous (a role is not a proper identity), in the sociopolitical hierarchy and all the dangerous complications entailed by it. It is when a man's gaze is trained upon her that a woman becomes self-conscious, that is, conscious of the self that must be mirrored in the man's, and eventually society's, gaze. Being thus objectified, the woman sees herself as an other for the first time and in self-defense begins the process of self-questioning that will produce the autographic text, a discursive double that will mark her presence and will be immune to any sort of final appropriation, because what it inscribes is also, I will propose, the shape of her absence—her lack of a proper name.

Ambivalence and Self-Abjection in the *Kagerō Diary*

We now come to the issue of subjectivity in the Heian female autographic text. This difficult issue, rife with paradox, is well illustrated by the opening passage of the *Kagerō Diary,* translated below. The diary covers the years 954–974 in the life of the woman known as Michitsuna's Mother (ca. 936–995). She was one of the wives (not the principal one) of Kaneie, scion of the powerful Fujiwara clan who would eventually reach the loftiest position of Regent and Chancellor and ensure his posterity through his sons by his principal wife. Three of these sons succeeded in their turn to the same position, the most famous being Michinaga (966–1027), patron of Murasaki Shikibu, Izumi Shikibu, and other women producers of the cultural splendor of the Heian court. The *Kagerō Diary* details the vicissitudes—inception, brief flowering, and protracted breakdown—of the author's marriage to Kaneie.

> Such as they were, these times have passed. There was someone who drifted through them in deep uncertainty, unable to grasp anything at all [*yononaka ni ito monohakanaku, tonimo kakunimo tsukade*]. Plainer than most in appearance and not possessed of any great understanding, she inevitably ended up of no use to anyone. Such thoughts assail her as she passes the uneventful days and nights,

occasionally looking into some of the old tales circulating in great numbers. Where such fabrications abound, surely even her own inconsequential life, written down as a journal, would be of unique interest? Let it be an example [*tameshi*] too for those who would inquire about [marriage to] one of the highest-ranking in the land. But her memory of what went on months and years in the past is vague, and there are many places where she simply makes do with what she can.[11]

The first notable aspect of this prefatory passage is the narrator's reference to the protagonist in the third person (as *hito,* "a person," "someone," or "she"), whereas the rest of the diary is implicitly in the first person. But by explicitly using the third person in the preface, the author draws a boundary between herself and the woman whose past she is about to recount, a gesture announcing that she is both writer and reader of her story. This signal of self-objectification, or what we might call the splitting of the self into the subject and object of the autobiographical text, underlines its reflexive character. The one who writes and reads the life is also the one who is written and read in a specular relation of "I" and "other" as understood in the Lacanian postulate of the split subject. Furthermore, the narrator claims no omniscience in this writing; the disclaimer about her uncertain memory of the past reveals its unreliability, that this record of a life is incomplete and fragmented, shot through with gaps and inconsistencies perhaps, which she will nevertheless try to connect into a coherent narrative. The second feature to notice is the setting up of a distinction between "tales" or fiction *(monogatari),* which she judges to be empty fabrications *(soragoto)* lacking in substance, and her diary *(niki),* which is then implied to be truthful and real. In other words, the writer is claiming authority for her story as real, insofar as she is witness to it, while simultaneously disclaiming any mastery or domination over it, as if to say that reality, or that part of it that is sedimented in the memory, is ultimately inexplicable. Going further, one could read the disclaimer as precisely a claim for its absence of design or calculation and, consequently, a claim for its truth, its sincerity.

A third notable feature is the profession of how insignificant this woman's life has been and how lacking she was in beauty and brains. This low self-valuation, which cannot be dismissed as a conventional rhetoric of female self-abjection, is in the meanwhile belied by her proceeding to write a rambling text that is almost 300 pages long in the Shōgakkan edition. Is an insignificant life worth writing so many pages about? Or is not the writing precisely an act of resistance to preclude the public judgment of herself as insignificant because of her failed marriage? I would suggest that writing for this woman is no less than an act of self-recuperation against the erasure threatened by her erstwhile husband's abandonment. Where female identity is socially determined by the male, his absence demands that she reconstitute herself through the graphic presence of her autograph.

And finally we should note that she offers the journal as no less than an illustration of how it is to be married to "one of the highest-ranking in the land," namely, her now practically estranged husband, Kaneie. Given his high public position, to write about such a man is surely a bold move, a challenge to his right, or privilege, against exposure of his private life. What we have here then is a woman, object of the masterful male gaze, who reverses gender roles and subjects the male to female scrutiny. We would expect endless recrimination and illustrations of Kaneie's fecklessness, infidelity, and cruelty—in short, a denigration of his character. But amazingly, Kaneie emerges from this narrative relatively unscathed. He is shown to have his fair share of flaws, such as preferring the company of several other women besides the protagonist and becoming so caught up in them that he neglects his fatherly duties to her child. She is portrayed in a state of such sexual and emotional frustration that she falls into depression and neurosis and, finally lapsing into indifference from the sheer necessity of survival, ceases either to wait for him or to upbraid him. Indeed, if anything, the protagonist herself appears to be a rather unattractive character in her nearly constant state of offended dignity, resentful and even vindictive anger, and seemingly insatiable craving for attention. In short, she emerges as a simultaneously tragic and demanding female, and he as an attractive but feckless male. There is no resolution of the issue of who is right and who is wrong; the relationship simply peters out as Kaneie rises in the official hierarchy and the protagonist gets older and turns her concerns to her children: Michitsuna, her son and only child by Kaneie; and a girl she adopts, who is Kaneie's daughter by another woman.

For a modern reader, the most dissatisfying aspect of the narrative is its lack of closure, of a sense of poetic justice, an ending that rationalizes the story on a moral or ideological plane. Seen from a classic Western humanistic perspective as an autobiography, it lacks the sense of a subject with clear rights and responsibilities according to the law. There is no appeal to a moral order, no teleological center on whose basis actions could be condemned or praised, no formal coherence to the randomness of events. Significantly, there is only the appeal to feeling, to the kindness and consideration due the protagonist as one of Kaneie's publicly recognized wives. In other words, the narration relies on the pact of *makoto* (sincerity and truthfulness) implicit in the practice of *waka* (the classic five-line, 5-7-5-7-7-syllable poem; also known as *tanka*) discourse. As inscribed in the *Kokinshū Kana* Preface, *waka* is also said to "move heaven and earth without the application of force, ... *harmonize the relations between men and women,* and pacify the hearts of raging men of arms" (emphasis added). We observe this in the protagonist's acute sensitivity to whether or not her husband responds in kind to her poems, and on those occasions when he appears in person instead of replying to her letters, his presence does not mitigate her disappointment at this lack of verbal response. It is as if the body could not signify as (poetic) words do, precisely because of the pact of sincerity embedded in speaking/writing them.[12]

Possibly the most eloquent example of how the pact of sincerity can be violated is the husband's response to the poem sent by the narrator after she discovers his affair with the woman in Machi Alley. On the night of his next visit, Michitsuna's Mother ignores his knocking at her door, and he goes instead to the other woman. And then,

the following morning, thinking that things couldn't remain like this between us, [I wrote]

nagekitsutsu	Do you know
hitori nuru yo no	how interminably long it feels—
akuru ma wa	a night when one lies alone
ikani hisashiki	beset by a grief that turns again
mono to ka wa shiru	and yet again until the dawn?

Writing it out more carefully than usual, I attached the letter to the stem of a faded chrysanthemum. He replied: "I intended to wait patiently until the dawn, but a messenger came with a hasty summons, you see. What you say is just.

genigeni	True, all too true,
fuyu no yo naranu	though it is not a winter night,
maki no to mo	the cedar wood door
osoku akuru wa	that laggard took till dawn
wabishikarikeri	to open, was quite miserable.

> This was bad enough. Afterward, his continued pretense that
> nothing at all was wrong grew quite incredible. It would have been
> appropriate at least for a while longer to try to conceal the situation
> by some such excuse as court business. This blandness was more
> and more galling, it was beyond endurance.[13]

Kaneie's reply here is a blatant evasion, in fact a lie, because the
reader knows that her husband did not wait till dawn but repaired to
the other woman's house instead. Yet the protagonist's emotional investment in poetic discourse is so great, she prefers that he maintain
the illusion of love even as a formality, for it shows consideration for
what they had shared, instead of this humiliatingly indifferent, in-
sincere, and bare-faced lie. Again, later, she attempts to break through
his armor of serene guilelessness by writing a long poem *(chōka)* to
make him understand in detail how she felt. His response, in the same
form, seems reasonably well intentioned, in that he carefully takes
up her points one by one, even as he denies that she has any just cause
to suspect his devotion to her.[14] His profession of having only sincere
intentions this time puts her on the defensive—such is the power of
poetic language—and lends new lease to the relationship. But this
period proves to be only a lull before the text returns to Kaneie's ever-
dwindling responsiveness to her poetic overtures. And it is this contradiction between the narrator's great investment in the truth of the
poetic word and Kaneie's sociopolitical power to empty it of all meaning and significance that underscores the burden of the diary as a
narrative of female abjection. The *Kagerō Diary* is, above all, a story of
the impotence of female speech, of the impossibility of achieving,
within the phallocratic order, the blissful male-female "harmony"
promised by the *waka* poetics of *makoto* as a signifying act transcend-
ing social boundaries. Poetry that moves the powerful "without the
application of force" *(chikara o irezu)* here proves to be a fiction. And
yet, such is the ambivalence of this text that, directed toward the
reader, it nevertheless retains the power of drawing sympathy for the
protagonist.

On the level of story, the narrative adheres to the ideology of
waka's truth and function as defined in the *Kokinshū Kana* Preface
for the field of heterosexual relations. Poetic discourse, the discursive
exchange par excellence, is that which harmonizes and pacifies *(yawa-
ragu)* differences between husband and wife. And this would include
the class difference between "one of the highest-ranking in the land"
and a middle-class daughter of the *zuryō*. But as the story develops,

it becomes clearer that the utopian intersubjective communication promised by the ideology of *waka* discourse is impotent against the reality of a marriage system that sanctions polygamy by men. Consequently, the narrator's promise of offering something more real than the fabrications of *monogatari* or fiction would imply that reality is this amorphous, unintelligible sequence of events with neither rhyme nor reason. It is only the irrational and arbitrary rhythms of whim and desire, the waxing hot and cold of emotion—whether of passion or anger, cruelty or kindness, attention or indifference. The perception of an utter lack of an order of meaning or reason in this autographic discourse is represented in fact by the narrator's statement at the end of Book One, after recounting the first fifteen years of a waxing and waning marriage:

> So pass the years and months, but lamenting a life that does not accord with my desire, I find no pleasure in the voices of the New Year. Thinking how empty everything here is, you might well call it, for it seems so unreal, a gossamer diary [*nao monohakanaki o omoeba, aru ka naki ka no kokochi suru kagerō no niki toiu beshi*].[15]

Indeed, by this negative example of the real as unreal, the author inadvertently reveals why *monogatari*, or fiction—the narrative of the imaginary, and particularly poem stories—was such a deep object of desire for Heian women. Ironically, the initial appeal in the preface to deal in the real ends in the narrator/reader's discovery of the pervasive slipperiness of the real. And it is in this sense that the "gossamer diary" inscribes the experience of an absence of self for even this aristocratic woman of substance. The emptiness is not primarily the effect of an absence of a teleology that would confirm the individual's identity, regardless of sex and gender. It is rather the failure of the self-confirmation that the narrator had invested in the poetic exchange. Her rage lies in Kaneie's evasiveness in his responses to her poems, his general refusal to match her seriousness with one of his own. The text thus confirms the secondary character of female speech already narrated in the myth of the first marriage, when the firstborn of Izanagi and Izanami was judged illegitimate and discarded because she, the female, spoke first. It is instructive to recall, in this regard, that its source, the *Kojiki* (712), was compiled precisely during the institution of the laws that would eventually eat away at women's prehistoric status.

But how are we to take the *Kagerō Diary*'s negative evaluation on the plane of the real? No doubt, we are to take it as a wholly subjective construction of the author's experience of marriage with Kaneie. After all, from a mundane point of view, her situation was far from abject and miserable. She was certainly affluent in comparison with many others, and marriage to a very important man entitled her to various privileges and marks of honor. More important, shortly after her marriage, her father was appointed to the governorship of a great and rich province known for its gold mines, Michinoku, and went up from sixth to fifth rank, and he would indeed ascend yet another rung by the end of his career. Similarly, her son, Michitsuna, would attain to the position of Dainagon (Major Counselor), which carried with it the third rank and put him on the highest level, among the senior nobles. In short, by her marriage to Kaneie, she had acted as a good daughter and mother in assuring the advancement of both her father and her son. What more could she want? But is that not the point? All the substance of her wealth and social prestige, her carrying out of her roles as daughter, wife, and mother, could not make up for her sense of lack as a person in her own right. She needed confirmation of her own worth in the eyes and heart of the man who mattered most, the same man for whom marriage to her was a political arrangement with her father and an occasional source of sexual and emotional gratification when he needed it.

But what does a woman want? As modern readers, we might conclude that the author of the *Kagerō Diary* desired a monogamous relationship in a society in which male polygamy was the norm, or that she was temperamentally unsuited for the then current practice of *kayoi kekkon,* in which the husband visited the wife instead of living with her. These conclusions are both possible but by no means certain. Further, and here we are on surer ground, she desired a sincere and durable emotional and intellectual bond with a man at a time when a woman was a mere appendage to her husband. To put it bluntly, she desired the impossible. Moreover, lacking a language of resistance based on rational grounds, she could only protest her positioning in an inarticulate way that inevitably appears hysterical, neurotic, childish, and, to put it harshly, mad. She is a woman of pride and accomplishment whose desires and behavior tested the limits of what was possible in her time. Her text is her testimony that a woman's initiation to adulthood in such a society means the open-eyed recognition of and resignation to the abject female self. For outside of resignation, there is only madness, a state of hysteria compellingly depicted at least once in the narrative.

Deconstructing *Sarashina Diary*'s Cautionary Tale

In contrast to the *Kagerō Diary,* we may examine the *Sarashina Diary* (*Sarashina nikki*, ca. 1059), by none other than Michitsuna's Mother's niece, who was known as Sugawara Takasue's Daughter (1008–after 1059). (It is disturbing that we should have to bear the awkward intrusion of the patrilineal names where I wish to focus on the matrilinear nature of the autographic text.) This latter memoir virtually eschews any interest of the protagonist in her husband until he dies, and then only in the context of her grief for the reduced prospects of her son. The *Sarashina Diary* is also much shorter; although it covers some forty years (1020–ca. 1059) of the author's existence, whereas the *Kagerō Diary* spanned twenty years, it comes to barely one hundred pages of text in the Shinchōsha edition. This laconic autobiography relies on the eloquent silence of strategically deployed ellipses and the spatial contiguity of passages in order to induce the shape of the narrator's desire. Nevertheless, its end point is the same as that figured in the *Kagerō Diary*'s preface: the narrator's encounter with abandonment and the abject self. The final passage of self-examination near the end of the text is in effect a synoptic account of the events laid out in all the preceding pages that apparently led to this woeful conclusion—a husband dead before the children are properly settled, and a woman widowed and eventually abandoned by her closest kin, awaiting only the end:

> If, from long ago, my mind had not been wholly absorbed in unprofitable tales and poems [*yoshinaki monogatari, uta no koto*] but in practicing piety day and night, surely I would not now be leading such a dreamlike existence [*ito kakaru yume no yo o ba mizu mo ya aramashi*]. That first time in Hatsuse, when a cedar branch was cast in my direction and a voice said, "It is the cedar-token of the favor bestowed by Inari," had I left directly to worship at Inari, perhaps things would not have turned out so for me [*kakarazu ya aramashi*]. In those years, when I dreamed that someone was telling me, "Pray to the August Deity Amaterasu," my only thought was that I would become the honored nurse of an imperial child and live at the Palace, basking in the protection of the emperor and empress, and I even consulted a dream-interpreter about it. But not a single one of these signs was ever fulfilled. Only the sad-looking image in the mirror proved no lie—so pathetic and depressing. A creature whose life has run its course with nothing ever conforming to her heart's desire, I only drift, not even striving to earn merit for the life to come.[16]

There is in this unembellished self-appraisal an abjectness from which we would rather cast aside our eyes. Expressing self-condemnation and bitter regret, it empties out the weight of a whole life by suggesting that it should have been lived otherwise. And the matter is not improved by the final disclaimer of any religious aspiration. It speaks no desire for redemption. True, this passage is immediately followed by another that reveals that the narrator had, in fact, seen a vision of the Amida Buddha in her garden three years previous. He had promised to come back later to welcome her to the Amidist Paradise, and on this alone she pins her hopes for the afterlife. But this vision, even while it echoes the popular Amidist teaching that salvation is assured as long as one desires it with all one's heart, is unsupported by any special efforts at piety on her part and remains an isolated one. The thread of the sacred remains suspended in a void in this narrative of a failed life. The profane world returns to inscribe the abject female self in the allusion to the Obasuteyama (abandoned-hag mountain) legend in the poem that follows the vision.

> I have been used to seeing my nephews and others together in the same house from morning till evening, but following this sorrowful event [her husband's death], they all went their separate ways. It is rare now that I meet anyone at all. One dark night, a nephew who is sixth among his brothers appeared. It had been so long, I was moved to say these words without thinking.

tsuki mo idede	There is no moon and
yami ni kuretaru	Obasute the abandoned hag
obasute ni	is engulfed in darkness
nani tote koyoi	so why have you come
tazunekitsuran	to seek her out this night?[17]

The allusion here to the legendary image of the stooped old woman, left by her nephew to die on the summit of a mountain in Sarashina (Shinano Province; modern Nagano), is very pointed indeed, for the narrator had reared her sister's children after their mother's untimely death. Moreover, her husband's death is the immediate occasion for the final construction of her life as useless. Although it is not clear whether the author or later readers named her work the *Sarashina Diary,* the striking citation of Obasuteyama in this passage is indeed the sole locus of the title and indicates that she or they understood the work as a classic story of female abandonment.

That is not, however, its modern claim to fame. Lady Sarashina (and from here on I shall call the narrator/protagonist by the name of her text) is, as far as we can tell from the surviving literature, the very earliest memoirist to confess her addiction to reading tales *(monogatari)* and especially *The Tale of Genji*. Indeed the desire for these tales that her own aunt had earlier dismissed as sheer fabrication is a major thematic structuring the narrative and announces itself from the very start of her text:

> Brought up in a country so remote it was even beyond the reach of the Azuma Highway, wild, uncouth child that I must have been, however did it start, this longing for the tales whose existence I could just barely imagine? At idle hours of the day or evening, as I listened to my sister and stepmother talking about this or that tale, or discussing episodes from the life of the Shining Genji, my fascination increased the more [*yukashisa masaredo*], but how could they recount from memory enough to satisfy me? So great was my need that I had a statue of the Yakushi Buddha built in my size and would steal into the chapel when people were not around. There, after washing my hands in ritual ablution, I would solemnly prostrate myself and pray, "Grant that we may leave for the capital soon. They say there are many tales there—please let me read all of them!"[18]

Framed between this foregrounding of the desire for tales in the beginning, and its apparently complete rejection in the end in favor of religious piety, Lady Sarashina's autobiography is about the failure of reality to live up to the desires engendered by fiction. According to the narrator's final self-reflection, her failure in life—her sense of the unreality, or "dreamlike" quality of her existence near the end—is due to her absorption in "unprofitable tales and poems" and her simultaneous neglect of religious practice. That is to say, if she had abandoned her romances earlier and turned her attention to proper reading of the divine signs (the cedar branch from Inari) and admonitions (prayer to the deity Amaterasu) vouchsafed her in dreams, then reality would have turned out according to her heart's desire *(kokoro ni mono no kanau)*. This final realization, or end point, is in fact the psychological beginning of her story, because it is from this perspective that past events fall into a certain pattern. She looks backward, retrospectively, and rereads (recounts, rewrites, reevaluates) dreams that had come to her at certain points in her life, for the first time seeing in them a meaning they had not had when they occurred.

This logic, which is instructive on the futility of regret, is surely circular. She is blaming herself for failing to read signs that do not in fact become readable until they are constituted as signs to be read, and that happens only in the end, retrospectively. That is to say, since it is the end that constitutes the beginning and everything else between, the narrator could be accused of artificially imposing a kind of retrospective intelligibility upon her past. Another blind spot is the claim that had she abandoned her mental and emotional investment in *monogatari* and prayed instead, then reality would have fulfilled her heart's desire. The illogic here is that had she indeed devoted her life to pious practices, she would not even have conceived the fiction-generated desires for which she needed to enlist the help of Amaterasu or the Buddha. There is also the blatant contradiction that a memoir censuring tales and poems is itself recounted by means of them; the text is replete with allusions to the *Genji*, retellings of provincial legends, dreams, and visions and, of course, includes ninety poems in all, the last four occurring after the final passage of self-examination cited above.

In brief, Lady Sarashina's story as her narrator ostensibly wishes it interpreted is about the failure of reality to live up to *monogatari;* it is a moral or cautionary tale and easily deconstructs itself on that level. No doubt, it bears the imprint of admonitions like that given to Princess Sonshi by Minamoto Tamenori in *The Three Jewels* (*Sanbōe,* comp. 984), where *monogatari* are seen as idle and empty inventions with pernicious effects on women's hearts, in clear contrast to the salutary effects of the volumes of Buddhist stories collected for the Princess's edification.[19] One could hazard, furthermore, that in thus thematizing her desire for tales, she is drawing on the Buddhist literature of *zange,* the public confession of one's past misdeeds as a sign of an awakening to faith.[20] The fact remains, however, that even the several pilgrimages undertaken by the protagonist are depicted more as sightseeing excursions, and as mentioned earlier, she either ignores the divine signs given her in dreams or they are placed within a context related to her worldly desires. Consequently, despite her avowed regret in the end for her past waywardness, the narration of that past remains more eloquent for what it reveals of the tension between two kinds of reading of the meaning of a life: the vicissitudes of desire and its self-repression in the patriarchal system as revealed by the text despite itself, and the religious reading belatedly professed by the narrator at the end of the text.

A Father's Love, A Daughter's Confinement

It is possible to detect in the memoir traces of other stories that are suppressed and not thematized but nevertheless inscribe themselves through the very repression. Important for this preliminary exploration of the issue of female self-representation in the Heian patriarchy is the incontrovertible fact that the text shows the protagonist's strongest and most durable emotional bond to be with her father, Takasue. He is the other party in the most moving scene of parting and reunion in the narrative, when he, at sixty years of age, departs for his last appointment as Governor of Hitachi (Ibaragi Prefecture), leaving his family behind in the capital. She is then already twenty-five.

On the thirteenth of the Seventh Month, Father departed. During the five days preceding, he would not come inside, as the prospect of parting was apparently more than he could bear. It was even worse on the very day amidst all the bustle. When the time came, he raised the blinds, and as our eyes met, the tears were streaming down his face. And then he turned and left. Watching him go, everything grew dark before my eyes, and I collapsed from grief. A servant who had seen his entourage off, staying with them through the night, came back with this on note paper.

omou koto	Were I so situated
kokoro ni kanau mi	that my heart could follow
nariseba	my desire,
aki no wakare o	I would plumb the depths
fukaku shiramashi	of this parting in autumn.

This was all he wrote, yet I couldn't read it through. On better occasions, I might have fussed no end about the syntax of my response. Words failed me; I could not think what to say.

kakete koso	Never until now
omowazarishika	had it ever crossed my mind
kono yo nite	that in this very life
shibashi mo kimi ni	I should be parted from my lord
wakarubeshi to wa	even for a little while.

So I seem to have written.

Fewer people came to see us. In loneliness and uncertainty, I fell to brooding, spending whole days wondering whereabouts he would be by now. Since I knew the way, my longing followed him until far away; my desolation knew no bounds. From morning till dusk, I stared vacantly at the outline of the eastern hills.[21]

And this parting is followed shortly thereafter by the citation of the father's letter, brought by a messenger from Hitachi, detailing how, while paying homage to the shrine deities of Hitachi Province, he notices the beautiful landscape of meadow with a river running through it, and his first thought is regret that he could not show it to her. Learning that the adjoining grove of trees is called Child-Yearning Woods (Koshinobi no Mori),

> "Just like myself, I thought, and getting off my horse, I stood and was lost in reflection for a long, long time.

> | todomeokite | Leaving someone behind, |
> | waga goto mono ya | did it feel as I the ache of |
> | omoikemu | a thought in the mind? |
> | miru ni kanashiki | There is sorrow in the sight |
> | Koshinobi no mori | Of the Child-Yearning Woods. |

> This is how I felt." You can imagine my own feelings reading it. In reply, I sent,

> | koshinobi o | When I that he left behind |
> | kiku ni tsukete mo | hear the name Child-Yearning, |
> | todomeokishi | I must find it cruel, |
> | chichibu no yama no | Chichibu, the father mountain |
> | tsuraki azumaji | along the Eastern highway.[22] |

On the face of it, such instances among others are clearly intended to portray an extraordinarily loving father-daughter relationship. The poem exchanges evince a mutuality of care and affection, two voices in ideal filial accord. Yet the reader must wonder if the emotional dependence also revealed here was not responsible for the protagonist's late marriage—for that time—at the advanced age of thirty-three. It is also eloquent that the parting scene quoted above is preceded by an incredibly long speech by the father whose sheer volubility and indirection merely point up the exigency (she is already twenty-five) of its unspoken subject, namely, the matter of her marriage before his departure for Hitachi, a province even more remote than Kazusa (his first posting) and hardly what he had expected. Positioned before the parting scene above, the speech silently suggests that the protagonist's utter sense of desolation at her father's departure is accompanied by thoughts of her uncertain future during his four-years' absence from the city.

> As I passed the time filled with such vain thoughts as how I would surely become quite a noble lady with Father's promotion, he

ended up getting an assignment to the remote eastern region. [This is what he said to me:]

> Until now, I had thought that once appointed, as I desired, to a province close by, I could take care of you as much as I wished. I would take you with me, show you the sight of mountains and seas, to be sure, but certainly strive to set you out in a manner grander than that to which you were born. But we have a miserable karma, you and I, for the end of all the waiting has turned out to be this distant province. Even back when you were but a child and I took you with me to the Azuma region, I worried about how helpless you would be in such a place were I to pass away there. Not even the fearsome ways of those people would have bothered me if it were only myself. But it was torture to imagine how wretched it was for you, living among so many in such a constricting place where one could not do or say what one would. And it is even worse now that you are all grown up. To take you down there without knowing what might happen to me—even in the capital, doubtless, it could happen that people became homeless —but that you should end up a helpless rustic in Azuma, that would be too terrible. Even here in the capital, we might not have relations whom I could trust to care for you. Still and all, it would not be proper to reject the appointment so recently offered me [and stay]. So it looks like we have to resign ourselves to an everlasting separation. I do not even see how I could make suitable arrangements for you in the capital.

> Listening to his laments night and day, I abandoned all my dreams of flowers and crimson leaves. It was sad, I could not help lamenting myself, but what was there to do?[23]

Did Lady Sarashina remember that whole long 1032 speech in 1059, when it is presumed she started writing her memoirs? Or did she reconstitute it under the final knowledge of how her life subsequently turned out? As various commentators have observed, it is not a very flattering image of her father.[24] Doting and anxious, complaining and apologetic, all at the same time, he strikes the reader as lacking the courage, initiative, and certainly the wherewithal to find her a suitable husband. The speech exaggerates the dangers for an unmarried daughter of life in the provinces and even in the capital. And the bald statement of their common misfortune, "we have a miserable karma, you and I" *(ware mo hito mo sukuse no tsutanakarikereba)*, while certainly revealing that the Heian daughter's destiny is wholly in her father's hands, is not bound to strike any confidence in his abilities. Indeed the amazing speech is most striking for the absence of any reference to any positive efforts he might have undertaken to find her a husband. Instead, it seems intended to impress upon the protagonist her father's infinite care and concern for her, in a way that fosters her dependency upon him, as if, at twenty-five, she were still a child who would be lost without her father. It might even be wondered if he is at all interested in giving her away to another.

In this connection, it is significant that Lady Sarashina's mother (a sister of the author of the *Kagerō Diary*) remained back in the capital during Takasue's first posting in Kazusa Province (Chiba Prefecture). There is no indication in the memoir that she harbored any strong emotional ties to her husband. It was the daughter of Takashina Shigeyuki (also read Nariyuki), the one the narrator calls "stepmother" in the opening passage, who went down and kept house for them as the Provincial Governor's wife. Sadly, however, this stepmother leaves Takasue not long after their return to the capital from Kazusa. Lamenting the separation from the woman who had opened her mind to tales of court life, the narrator writes, "My stepmother, who had been serving at court before going down to the provinces, apparently experienced all sorts of disappointments and was dissatisfied with the world"[25] (which is to say with the relationship with her father). This stepmother had been a lady-in-waiting before her marriage to Takasue and after their divorce resumes that service at the court of Emperor Goichijō (1008–1036; r. 1016–1028), using the name Kazusa no Tayu. Takasue's resentment of her continued use of his name at court even after she remarries is duly noted by the narrator; indeed she composes a poem on his behalf, chiding her for it.[26] It is another example of the problems women experienced from not having a proper name. But the point here is the inescapable conclusion that Takasue, abandoned by his lover for a more rewarding life at court, had every reason to find satisfaction in his daughter's continued devotion and emotional attachment to himself. He would not have been very motivated to find her a husband.[27]

But was he indeed without the resources to do so? Let us consider the external evidence of his biography. Sugawara Takasue (973–ca. 1040) was the descendant in the fifth generation of a famous Minister of the Right and scholar-poet of Chinese, Sugawara Michizane (845–903). In 993, at twenty-one, he had been appointed Chamberlain (Kurōdo) in the household of Prince Okisada (later Emperor Sanjō, r. 1012–1017), and in 1000, at twenty-eight, also Chamberlain at the imperial household during the reign of Emperor Ichijō (980–1011; r. 986–1011), concomitant with the positions of Lieutenant in the Right Bodyguards (Uemon no Dai'i) and in the Imperial Police. As such he would have been a colleague of men like the Chamberlain Tadataka and Michikata, who appear in the pages of Sei Shōnagon's *Pillow Book*. They served under the direction of then Head Chamberlain Fujiwara Yukinari (972–1027), in whose diary, *Gonki*, Takasue's name is mentioned twenty-two times in the course of the year 1000.[28] He appears to have been a diligent chamberlain and officer, kept busy transmitting messages from Yukinari to Michinaga, delivering imperial edicts, representing the court at ritual prayers for rain or good weather, and reporting on trouble among the chamberlains; he was even entrusted with the preparation of the furnishings for the lying in of Empress Teishi. As the scion of the Sugawara family of Chinese scholars, he is also noted as participating at a Chinese poetry session on 9.24.1000, in the presence of Emperor Ichijō and Michinaga, among others.

It is surprising that, subsequent to his accession to the sixth rank in 1001, no further reference is made to the diligent Takasue in the *Gonki* until 1011, raising the possibility that he did not hold office in the interval and that his membership among the followers of the late Empress Teishi did not sit well with Michinaga and his daughter, Empress Shōshi (988–1074). The date of his marriage to the sister of Michitsuna's Mother is not clearly known, but one can hazard that it was around 1005 or 1006. The *Gonki* lists Takasue among the Chamberlains of the Fifth Rank assisting at the funeral of Emperor Ichijō on 6.25.1011. He is also listed among the participants at the initiation ceremony of Michitsuna's son, which was held at the Tsuchimikado Mansion on 8.23.1011. Because Michitsuna was then Major Counselor and, as such, a member of the senior nobles, in addition to being Michinaga's patrilineal cousin, surely Takasue's marriage to his aunt was of political significance. Nevertheless, there is again a gap of several years before his appointment as Governor of Kazusa on 1.24.1017, during the first year of the reign of Emperor Goichijō. He seems to have returned from Kazusa in 1020 as a very prosperous man, rich enough, some scholars now believe, to have purchased the former palace of Retired Emperor Sanjō, the Sanjōin.[29] This is the property the narrator, who had been so excited at finally arriving at the capital after the three-month journey from Kazusa, describes with some dis-appointment as "a vast, deteriorating place, looking no different from the hills we had just passed, filled with great, fearful-looking trees as in the remote mountains, so that it did not feel at all like being in the capital."[30] Possibly Takasue spent another period without office; his last appointment was to the governorship of Hitachi in 2.8.1032, at which time he was already sixty, with the rank Senior Fifth Lower. Back from Hitachi in 1036, he announces his retirement, apparently plunging the narrator into as much desolation as when he set out.

The image of Takasue in the *Sarashina* text, particularly the long speech quoted earlier, is such that readers have tended to dismiss him as lacking in courage, ambition, and the worldly skills to employ his undoubtedly high connections to further his career. Unlike his ancestors, including his father, Suketada, or even his own son Sada-yoshi and other descendants, he did not attain to the traditional posi-tion of Doctor of Letters (Monjō Hakase) and Head of the University (Daigaku no Kami) expected of the Sugawara heirs. Given his ancestry, connections, and apparent diligent competence as chamberlain, his inability to rise higher in the court hierarchy is somewhat inexplic-able and raises the possibility that he refused to exert positive efforts to cultivate his standing with Michinaga. His appearance, after a long interval, at Emperor Ichijō's funeral seems telling. Ichijō was never reconciled to Teishi's death and Michinaga's power. Also telling is that when Lady Sarashina goes into service as lady-in-waiting, it is at the household of Princess Yūshi, whose mother, Empress Genshi, was Teishi's granddaughter. That is to say, Genshi's father was the ill-fated Prince Atsuyasu, who would have been Emperor had Michi-naga's daughter, Empress Shōshi, not given birth to Prince Atsuhira (later Emperor Goichijō), the celebrated event recorded at length in the *Murasaki Shikibu Diary*.[31]

Nevertheless, it can by no means be said that Takasue was as help-less as he is made out to be by the amazingly unrestrained speech imputed to him in his daughter's memoirs. It is striking, moreover, that he had not been so helpless in the matter of the narrator's older sister; we know from the text that she was married, since her death postpartum is recounted as a deep loss to the narrator, who becomes the surrogate mother of her sister's two children. The narrator's simple and quiet resignation in response to her father's self-indulgent speech, one whose burden marks the end, as she hints, of her illusions about marriage to the high-ranking courtier of her dreams, emerges all the more eloquently by its brevity. Is the pointed juxtaposition meant only as an implicit recognition of her impotence or as a criticism of the one he professes in that speech? The narration of their reunion on his return from Hitachi in 1036 ends with a similarly brief allusion to her own feelings, not further elaborated.

> Father, who had gone down to the East, returned and was staying for a while in Nishiyama. We all proceeded there and in our happiness talked all night long.

kakaru yo mo	To think that
arikeru mono o	such a time should come!
kagiri tote	Where now the autumn
kimi ni wakareshi	when I parted from my lord
aki wa ikani zo	thinking it would be the last?

So I said, and overcome with tears, he replied,

omou koto	Hope thwarted,
kanawazu nazo to	why go on, I thought, and
itoikoshi	hated this life
inochi no hodo mo	that lingered on till this
ima zo ureshiki	very now, filled with gladness!

> I was so sad then when he informed me that this is it, here at the gate of departure the time has come for the final parting. Compared to that sorrow, my happiness at his long-awaited and safe return knew no bounds. But then he continued, "I have observed it with other people, seen how foolish it looks to still go out and mix in society into a feeble old age. Therefore I intend to go into seclusion from here on." It seems he desired nothing more from the world. And I was overcome with a sense of helplessness.[32]

It would seem that the decision of the newly returned Takasue to retire at sixty-four had the force of plunging his daughter from extreme happiness to desolation. Although the narration in the passage above is devoted as before to celebrating their oneness of heart, the brief reference to the narrator's feelings at the end is notable. With Takasue's retirement, his daughter's marriage prospects were virtually foreclosed. He might "desire nothing more from the world," but what of her?

The desire for *monogatari* in the *Sarashina Diary* also springs from its discursive value as a signifier for the splendor of life at court and for the opportunity that a middle-class lady-in-waiting there would

have of meeting high-ranking courtiers. There is no question that
the narrator included among her early role models young women
whose fathers belonged to the senior nobility ranks *(kugyō)*, rather
than the provincial governor *(zuryō)* class. The early death, at sixteen,
of Major Counselor Fujiwara Yukinari's daughter (who was married
to Michinaga's son) affected her as deeply as the loss of her wet-nurse.
She clearly identified with this young woman, whose calligraphy had
been given her as a model for her own writing practice and whose
poems she would later weep over. Another one of her imaginary
exalted surrogates was the Princess of the First Order, Imperial Princess Teishi (later Go-Suzaku's Empress), who figures in one of her
dreams and whose position she figuratively appropriates in the immediately following poem: "I gaze upon her flowers / as if it were my own
home [*waga yado-gao ni*]."[33] Finally, the dreams admonishing her to
pray to the goddess Amaterasu, and her persistent interest in this
deity, signify a wish for affiliation with the imperial family, of which
Amaterasu is the divine progenitress. This is confirmed in the final
passage of self-reflection cited earlier, which states that she had aspired
to be the wet-nurse—that is to say, the surrogate mother—of an imperial prince and live in the palace, honored and secure in the favor of
the Emperor and Empress.

This aspiration is certainly not unrealistic; Tachibana Tokushi, who
was the aunt of Tachibana Toshimichi (1002–1058), later Lady Sarashina's husband, had been conferred the Junior Third Rank as the
emperor's nurse in 1000.[34] Indeed, leaving her father's house to serve
at court might have rescued the protagonist from the persistent angst
generated by her ambiguous status as a still unmarried daughter past
thirty years of age. Unfortunately, her career ambitions, like her earlier romantic aspirations, are thwarted by her father, who claims that
service at court is "a terrible misfortune" *(miyatsukaebito wa ito ukikoto
nari)*:

> Mother had become a nun, and though she remained in the same
> house, she lived in a separate section apart from us. Father then
> installed me as the head of the household, and he did not go out
> and socialize but lived, as it were, hidden in my shadow. Seeing
> myself cut off thus, I was feeling anxious and helpless, when, from
> a place that had heard of my plight, there came an invitation to
> serve as lady-in-waiting "instead," so they said, "of whiling away the
> days in vague anxiety, with nothing to do." My conservative father
> was of the belief that it was a terrible misfortune for people to

serve at court and bade me to refuse. But there were others who told him, "These days people think all the world of going out to serve at court; what is more, something good has been known to turn up in the course of it. So do give it a try." And so with the utmost reluctance, Father permitted me to go.[35]

Although he is reluctantly persuaded by others to let her go, her father manages by what we would now characterize as emotional blackmail to distract her from her newly launched career,[36] and within a year recalls her from Princess Yūshi's service to stay at home permanently. The passage narrating this event is quite singular; it is the first and only time that the text overtly records her resistance to her father:

Once I had come out, I should have become accustomed to court service and, despite the distractions at home, as long as I took care to avoid being regarded as an eccentric, would in time have been accepted among the other ladies-in-waiting. But for some reason that strains my understanding, only a short while later, my parents decided to keep me confined at home [*oyatachi mo, ito kokoroezu, hodo mo naku komesuetsu*]. Even so, it did not seem that this change in circumstance would suddenly bring a new vibrancy into my life, and exasperatingly thoughtless though I was, it was a condition that was shockingly far from my expectations [*ito yoshinakarikeru suzuro-gokoro nite mo, koto no hoka ni tagainuru arisama narikashi*].

ikuchitabi	How many times
mizu no tazeri o	have I reaped the marsh parsley
tsumishi ka wa	for my pain—
omoishi koto no	still all that I have desired
tsuyu mo kanawanu	have brought nothing of reward.

Letting fall such words only to myself, I was resigned.[37]

"But for some reason that strains my understanding, my parents decided to keep me confined at home." The expression *komesuetsu*, with its connotations of imprisonment, is quite emphatic. It infects the following statement, which clarifies in its very reticence the fact of her marriage, "a condition," she writes, "that was shockingly far from my expectations," as is confirmed by the poem that follows.

Lady Sarashina apparently remained filial enough to obey her father in the matter of marrying at her advanced age against her own wishes, instead of being allowed to pursue a career of service at Imperial Princess Yūshi's, whose salon was one of the artistic centers of the time and nurtured several women poets. Lady Sarashina remained the good daughter, caring for her aged parents till the end, chaperoning her nieces to court when they in their turn were invited into service. But the price for her obedience must have been a kind of permanent breach between them, for we hear no more about her father throughout the rest of the diary. This is a remarkable silence in the text, given his previous centrality to her existence as emotional anchor and the one person who could have acted to support her dreams of a fine marriage or distinguished service at court. (We know from the Sugawara genealogical records that her brother attained to the position of Head of the University, so his career was not similarly thwarted. As a man he could, as Sei Shōnagon would say, rise by his own efforts.) And we cannot say that her father's place was taken by her husband, for the latter is barely mentioned until the decisive event of his death, which at a single stroke apparently renders the narrator's existence superfluous. As a family story, the *Sarashina Diary* is testimony to the necessarily strong bond linking father and daughter in the Heian court family, because they stand and fall together in the sociopolitical structure. Additionally, the protagonist's emotional dependence on her father is here amply portrayed in his participation in the largely feminine circle of poetic exchanges of love that oddly enough excludes her mother.[38] We may even detect it in the childlike quality of the narrating voice in several places in the text. In this way, while Takasue's role in the frustration of his daughter's ambitions is mainly repressed beneath the images of the loving father and the devoted and obedient filial daughter, the narrator's unspoken complaint leaks between the lines of the narrative. Despite the text's endeavor to suppress the reality of her situation as one whose destiny was to care for her father and, belatedly, her husband, Takasue emerges as an ineffectual patriarch in the reader's eyes, his image irresistibly drawn into the daughter's own abject self-image at the end. What the concluding passage of self-blame must conceal, in other words, is the hand of the father in the daughter's confinement within the space defined by him, as well as the strict social sanction against any open censure of his authority to do so.

Matrilineal Discourse and the Law of the Father

What were those illusions that ended with the father's virtual foreclosure of the narrator's marriage when she was still in her twenties, before he departed for Hitachi? Let us examine the passage immediately preceding the father's amazing speech, discussed above.

It being my main activity to fritter my mind in pursuit of such trivi-
alities, even on those rare occasions when I went on pilgrimages, I
could not bring myself to pray earnestly to be as other people. In
those days, by seventeen or eighteen, people began to learn the
sutras and engage in pious practices, but they held no interest for
me. What did finally hold my mind was this: that a splendid man
of the highest rank, someone like the Shining Genji of the tale
in looks and manners, would come even once a year to visit me. I
would be like the Lady Ukifune, secretly installed in a mountain village [*yamazato ni kakushisuerarete*], gazing at the flowers and the
crimson leaves, the moon and the snow, looking vulnerably lonely,
and once in a while reading his long-awaited, wonderful letters.
Such was my persistent desire, my fantasy of the future.[39]

The narrator's seduction by tales—or what might be called the matrilineal text, given that the *Genji* is clearly the one among others that
grips her—is a process that began back in the governor's mansion at
Kazusa, when listening to others recounting them. It is instructive that
the protagonist would have been reaching puberty at the time and
that her longing is associated with the circle of feminine figures—her
stepmother and older sister, perhaps also her sister's nurse and her
own—for whom she clearly feels a warm, uncomplicated love. The
feminine bonding that is enacted and nourished by the mutual sharing of what the narrator would later judge as "unprofitable tales and
poems" constitutes a thread of solace that securely weaves its way
through the vicissitudes of this narrative of a failed life. Again, it is not
thematized but inscribes itself everywhere, so that the reader could
not fail to appreciate its value for the lonely protagonist. Her first
poetic exchange on reaching the capital is with her stepmother, as the
latter is about to leave their house.[40] She mourns the death of her
nurse, her surrogate mother, in the same year with a poem.[41] She and
her sister create a fantasy tale in which the late daughter of Yukinari,
the protagonist's calligraphy model, comes to live with them, reincar-
nated as an affectionate cat of refined tastes ("I have come here for a
while due to some affinity in the previous life that has made your sister
feel such an abiding sympathy for me.")[42] Again, hearing the sounds
of a carriage with escorts arriving in the middle of the night at the
neighboring residence, the two sisters enact an imagined poem exchange between the lovers that is simultaneously a witty criticism of
the man's want of persistence.[43] When her sister dies in childbirth soon
thereafter, the narrator cites a series of multiple poem exchanges between her (sister's) nurse and herself, with rejoinders by her step-

mother, by yet another woman who had been charged by her sister to find a certain tale she wanted to read, and by their brother, who had attended their sister's body to the cremation grounds.[44]

And so on throughout the narrative, the protagonist's correspondence with women relatives, fellow ladies-in-waiting, and nuns, variously punctuated by a sharing of mutual stories, the borrowing and lending of books of tales, and the exchange of poems, shows that this discursive feminine milieu is what sustained her to the end. This incontrovertible textual witness to their real life- and self-sustaining value, directly contradicting the narrator's final appraisal of them as "unprofitable tales and poems," manifests the unspoken conflict between the matrilineal discourse and the Law of the Father as represented by the Buddhist doctrine of the emptiness of desire and the need to seek enlightenment by its repression. The reader might even go so far as to wonder whether it is not indeed the author's resistance to the paternal discourse that is the repressed subtext of the narrative rather than its confirmation in the self-abjecting conclusion. The resistance had been revealed earlier in possibly the most famous passage in *Sarashina,* the scene of reading after the narrator receives from an aunt "the more than fifty books of the *Genji* in a chest" and other tales besides:

> I came home with all this bounty, deliriously happy [*ureshisa zo imi-jiki*]. The *Genji,* of which I had seen only parts before and always in a rush so that I despaired of understanding it all—now as I took out the books one by one, I could read it at my leisure from the very start, lying behind my curtains, avoiding others' company. Before this bliss, what was the rank of an Empress to me? All day long and far into the night as long as I could stay awake, I kept the lamp burning close, and since there was nothing to distract me, soon I could remember it from memory and was thinking how marvelous that was, when in a dream a very handsome-looking priest, wearing an unfigured yellow surplice, came and said, "Learn the fifth scroll of the *Lotus Sutra* at once." Yet I told no one of it, nor did I bother to learn the sutra. My mind wholly absorbed in tales, I was at this time unspeakably plain. When I grow up, I thought, I shall be boundlessly lovely in looks, my hair gracefully long. Then I should truly be as the Shining Genji's Yūgao or the Uji Captain's Ukifune—my heart that desired it to be so was, it is now clear, shockingly ignorant.[45]

The most notable aspect of this scene of the bliss of reading the *Genji*'s narrative of desire is its interruption by the authoritative paternal figure, the setting into conflict of feminine jouissance and paternal prohibition, of the romantic heroine against the stern priest, the *Genji* against the *Lotus Sutra,* the matrilineal text of the Imaginary against the patrilineal Symbolic, here the prescribed texts for devotional practice. We might say that the clear oppositional structure in the design of this scene was possible only because writing/reading was not a male prerogative in Heian court society. Women had access to literacy, and the feminine milieu was the locus of the cultural production, dissemination, and consumption of the matrilineal discourse, including the *Genji.* It is compelling evidence of its influence that in the following medieval period, the Buddhist clergy would find it necessary to either devalue the work and its author or appropriate both to their own ideological purposes.[46] Indeed we already see the seeds of this appropriative discursive formation right here in the ambivalence and doubleness of the *Sarashina* text itself, in its manifest need to overlay the narrative of desire with a Buddhist interpretation. It is a movement reflected also in the Buddhist popular tales *(setsuwa)* subsequently told about other Heian women writers and poets like Ono no Komachi and Izumi Shikibu, whose lives were constructed as revelatory tales of religious awakening *(zangemono)* or of reincarnation *(ōjōden),* and thereby made Buddhist doctrine, with its phallocentrism and even misogyny, more accessible and appealing to women.

The inescapable conclusion is that women-authored texts, the feminine discourse of the Imaginary, were regarded as wayward and seductive stories that must be proscribed in favor of canonical sutras like the *Lotus Sutra,* in particular. Its fifth scroll recounts how the great piety of the Dragon King's daughter enabled her to attain buddhahood by becoming transformed into a man, the gender that, as Sei Shōnagon said, could attain to rank and position in its own right and, here, to religious enlightenment as well. Both worldly and spiritual advancement are obviously gendered male, superior to the female, and a more direct route to salvation.[47] Is it any wonder that Lady Sarashina's ecstatic reader, recognizing in the *Genji* her own feminine desires, ignores the priestly admonition and continues to let the maternal Imaginary have its way with her heart? The narrator's expressed identification with Ukifune is usually explained by their common upbringing in the eastern region and Ukifune's association with the *zuryō* (provincial governor class) through her stepfather, the Governor of Hitachi. There is also a similarity to Ukifune in the protagonist's turn away from desire and toward religion in the end. These homologies are undeniable, and they undoubtedly influenced the structural design of the memoir as well. Not to be ignored, however, is the narrator's willful (with the willfulness of desire) misreading of Ukifune's story, which is hardly a happy one. As we know, she is not depicted as taking delight in Kaoru's letters, and those rare visits by Kaoru or Niou to Uji were often quite threatening to her physical and psychological well-being. It is their male phallocentric rivalry, set in conflict with the good daughter's duty to make a fine marriage, that eventually drives her to suicide.

Matrilineal Discourse and the Semiotic *Chora*

There is reason, I believe, in the *Sarashina* reader-protagonist's misprision. She has chosen to take Ukifune's situation as the model of a heroine loved for herself alone, outside the unpalatable complications of marriage politics. She desires to be "secretly installed" *(kakushisuerarete)* in the mountain village, safely insulated from the trafficking in daughters as currency in the power plays in the capital. "Gazing at the flowers and the crimson leaves, the moon and the snow, looking vulnerably lonely, and once in a while reading his long-awaited, wonderful letters." How are we to take this passage but as answering to a desire to be cherished and loved by a man but only from a distance, without the troubling physical and intimate presence of the lover? It hints, furthermore, of a childlike desire to be hidden and safe in the maternal bosom of nature, a desire for tranquil intimacy with the beautiful, drifting tides of the seasons, punctuated only by the inscription of these same images in the figuration of feeling represented by the lover's letters.

And here I would like to return to the subject of the maternal discourse in order to propose that its compelling power lies in its poeticity, in the utopian vision of perfect communication or communion implicit in the *waka* poetics of affect and response. This is splendidly conjured best of all by the *Izumi Shikibu Diary*, that seductive text that is wholly focused on the workings of the poetic Imaginary, the ebb and flow of the seasons as figured in the drifting (dis)course of the lovers' relationship. I call the poem tale, from the *Ise* to the *Genji*, maternal because as a discursive formation it enacts an imaginary dissolution of borders—between the two subjects of a poem exchange, between the prose of the framing narrative and the poem that resolves it into an imagistic figure, between the seasons and human activity, between the protagonist and the reader identifying with him or her

—a doubling or reciprocal movement that harks back to the relationship between infant and mother before the child's entry into the realm of the Symbolic through the intervention of the paternal prohibition, the Law of the Father. Here I am reading the Heian poem tale through the thought of Julia Kristeva, who holds that the body has an archaic memory of the presymbolic or semiotic realm of a nurturing love within the dyadic unity of the mother-child relation, and that this material trace of a oneness that is also two finds its way into the Symbolic realm, particularly through the agency of the Imaginary and its artistic signifying practices.[48]

In the Lacanian theory of psychic development, the realm of the Imaginary refers, first of all, to the infant's identification with the image of its primary caregiver, usually the mother, and with its own image in the mirror as a unified integral body.[49] Following upon the pre-mirror stage, in which the infant identifies with the discrete objects in his milieu (and perceives himself as discrete body parts), the mirror stage inaugurates the process of self-formation. But it also marks the beginnings of alienation in that the self comes into view—discovers itself, paradoxically, as separate from itself, as an "other" that is a specular image in the mirror. This mirror phase, initiating the infant's consciousness of itself as separate from the mother, is immediately succeeded by early language acquisition. This enables the child to compensate through words for the loss of the earlier identificatory objects. The process of differentiation is reinforced by the intervention of the father in the later oedipal stage, when, under threat of castration, the child learns that the mother's body is forbidden to him and consequently begins to identify with the father. The paternal prohibition facilitates the child's entry into the realm of the Symbolic— the order of language or the sign and all the sociopolitical structures erected upon it, the world of culture in general as opposed to "nature" —through which the child becomes socialized as a bona fide "autonomous" subject.

The subject's inscription into the Symbolic order, however, can never heal the self-splitting that occurred in the mirror stage of its psychic development, the fatal miscognition that would henceforth constitute the self as a lack and set it on the path of desire for the other in the mirror, which is to say, desire for persons or objects in which it seeks (self-)recognition or self-confirmation in the mechanism of cathexis. And since the mother is the first object in which it sees itself mirrored, as well as the body from which it was torn in order to become one, the desire for the other is also ultimately the desire for the (m)other.

> As the addressee of every demand, the mother occupies the place of alterity. Her replete body, the receptacle and guarantor of demands, takes the place of all narcissistic, hence imaginary, effects and gratifications; she is, in other words, the phallus. The discovery of castration, however, detaches the subject from his dependence on the mother, and the perception of this lack [*manque*] makes the phallic function a symbolic function—the symbolic function. This is a decisive moment fraught with consequences: the subject, finding his identity in the symbolic, *separates* from his fusion with the mother, *confines* his jouissance to the genital, and *transfers semiotic motility onto the symbolic order.* (Final emphasis mine.)[50]

I would like to propose that the semiotic motility characterizing the preoedipal, mother-child dyad, the maternal receptacle that Kristeva calls the *chora,* enters the Symbolic of Heian literature transposed onto the sights, sounds, and textures of seasonal objects in the *waka* poetic language. "Gazing at the flowers and the crimson leaves, the moon and the snow," with its images typifying spring, autumn, and winter evokes a desire to drift with the flow of the seasons, which in turn can be read as a metaphorical figure for the *chora,* "a nonexpressive totality formed by the drives and their stases in a motility that is as full of movement as it is regulated."[51] The *chora,* "which is analogous only to vocal or kinetic rhythm," also refers to the dynamic state of connections between the infant's body and the objects of its milieu, the ecosystem that includes members of the family structure. We can posit that in Heian women's writing, the *chora* is evoked among others in the poetic exchange as the coming and going of affects (feelings mediated by the material qualities of the seasonal objects) within the enclosure of the maternal family or kinship unit, where, in keeping with the practice of *kayoi kekkon,* children were actually reared despite their registration under the paternal genealogy. In this regard, it is also noteworthy that both the *Genji* and the memoirs structure time not according to the days of the calendar (as in the *kanbun* male diaries) but according to the rhythm of the seasons. The cycle of repetition with variation—trees coming into leaf and flower and scattering, snow that forms and melts away—evokes a continuum analogous to the course of the oral and anal drives' energy discharges through the preoedipal body.

Indeed, the very activity of reading itself evokes the maternal imaginary not only on the Symbolic order, the level of story and meaning, but also as a material sequence of graphic marks on the page. In the premodern West, the dearth of women's writing has led scholars to conclude that writing here was traditionally a male activity, that artistic creation was reserved for the masculine sphere, and that consequently the very fact that women dared to write at all—to take hold of the pen, or "metaphorical penis," as Gilbert and Gubar put it—constituted a challenge to the distinct role assigned them in the patriarchal system.[52] This fear of wielding the phallus did not, I would venture to say, apply to Heian women, or if it did, it was on the level of the necessary suppression of explicit reference to proper names and inhibition of open criticism of real male persons in the memoirs, as I have indicated in the discussion above. At any rate, it is not clear that the metaphor itself of pen as phallus—signifier of mastery and power, of the male dominance over the realm of the Symbolic and consequently of culture—is immediately applicable to Heian women or, if relevant, would need further elaboration, for two reasons. First, women were not kept from writing and, second, they were indeed encouraged to write as part of their education, along with training in poetry and music, and so writing cannot be the distinguishing feature separating the sexes. For the woman, writing as such was not necessarily a transgression of the Law of the Father. Rather, one could hypothesize it first as a receptacle of the maternal semiotic within the order of the Symbolic, aided by the rhythms and imagery of poetry and music. (In this regard, some of the most splendid passages in the *Genji* are precisely scenes of poetry, music, and dance.) Women's writing could thus be regarded as a paternal instrument for containing female desires safely within cultural bounds. If, nevertheless, writing for Heian women could also be characterized as a transgressive act, that is so because, as a signifying practice, it involves the historically positioned subject in the reflexive quest for the self through a reading of a life that inevitably leaves traces of the sociopolitical contradictions in it. Ironically, such gaps and inconsistencies that the poetic word cannot cover over become constituted as such precisely because of the paternal poetic ideology's promise of "universal" intersubjective communication and the imaginary experience of jouissance taught by the maternal text. Thus it could be said that in Heian female writing, women left a durable record of that which cannot be assimilated into the patriarchal order and continues to expose the lie in it.

The Japanese brush is not a pen. Formed from animal hair, it could be soft or stiff, thick or thin, moist or dry, applied with a heavy or a light touch, depending on the needs of the occasion—in short an infinitely more flexible tool than the rigid point of a pen. The inked brush applied to paper belongs to a poetics of touching and caressing, of the tactile as much as the visual, and so has a maternal aspect unsuited to the insertive, aggressive, or transgressive act figured by the penile pen. And so a woman at calligraphy practice, whiling away the time copying old poems or stories, a recurrent scene in *The Tale of Genji,* could easily be seduced into a state of reverie, losing herself in the twists and turns of the story as she follows the beguiling flow of the calligraphy until she begins to identify with the heroine in a process facilitated by the notorious ellipsis of personal pronouns in the Japanese language or by the habit of the narrator herself of moving in and out of her character's minds without any warning. And this apparent freedom in Murasaki Shikibu's narrative style of merging the boundaries of third and first persons, of passages of narrating and of interior speech, can also be claimed as a feature of the maternal body in which the fetus is nurtured and sustained as separate, yet part of the whole.

In sum, the nostalgia for maternal solace that is unconsciously invested in the narrator's remembered pleasure in the poetic language of the *Genji* is generated by the series of losses that she suffers, whether by death—of her beloved nurse, of Yukinari's daughter, of her sister, and finally, of her husband—or by parting from her childhood home in Kazusa or from her stepmother, her father, her putative lover, and others. In an important sense, and paradoxically, the text accomplishes the work of mourning by tapping into the semiotic *chora* to sustain her in the face of unfulfilled desires originally raised by the *Genji* but impossible to explore under the patriarchal order. Tales here are not only associated with the capital and the *Genji.* The place-names and provincial legends told in the long travel account from Kazusa that immediately follows the opening passage may also be read as identificatory objects. They mark the narrator's retrospective emotional investment in those places along her childhood journey to the capital city that would in the end disappoint her. Along with her travels on pilgrimages, they are signifiers of movement and motility against the immobilization that holds her within the abject circle of grief, aging, and death at the end of the text.

Conclusion

This chapter has been an initial exploration of the issue of self-representation in Heian women's life narratives in an attempt to answer the question of whether they are autobiographies in the classic Western humanist tradition. The answer to this question must be both yes and no: yes, because they are retrospective quests for the meaning of a life, and no, because in place of finding reasons for that life's substance and significance against the certitude of death, what they discover is the abject female self confronting a past that seems no more than a dream. Such a self-dissolution, the discovery that the specular "I" in the mirror is but an illusion, is salutary in its way. It indicates that these texts are less projects in self-explanation than meditations on the insubstantiality of desire. On the manifest level of story, however, that insubstantiality is primarily a function of the woman's tenuous position when she desires something other than the roles of daughter, wife, and mother as the patriarchal social order has defined them for her. In an implicit move to clarify a matrilineal genealogy for Heian literature, I have used the examples of the *Kagerō Diary* and the *Sarashina Diary* with reference to *The Tale of Genji*, a text whose long passages of reflexive interiority are unmistakably descended from the *Kagerō Diary* and impossible without it, and which is in turn explicitly foregrounded as both the receptacle of maternal love and the bitter seed of desire in the *Sarashina Diary*. I have tried to show that the figure of female confinement under the Heian patriarchal order that recurs throughout the *Genji* resonates with the *Kagerō* protagonist's vigorous yet ultimately helpless straining against the limits of the marriage system of her time, and that these walls are the very same that thwarted the *Sarashina* protagonist's desire to leave her father's house in pursuit of a career. Finally, I have indicated that the maternal discourse of the Imaginary, in the form of narratives couched in the soothing yet hypnotic rhythms and seasonal objects of *waka* poetic language, provided self- and life-sustaining comfort for Heian women long after their entry into the patriarchal order that would only disappoint them. Coming at the intersection of the tenth and eleventh centuries in Japan, these pioneering works of the female hand still touch us, and both comfort and distress us, at the start of a new millennium. The question is why they still do.

Notes

This essay is a revised and expanded version of two lectures: "The Desire for *Monogatari* in *Sarashina nikki*" at a conference at Purdue University in 1993 and

"Genre/Gender and Heian Women's Diaries" at the University of Michigan's Center for Japanese Studies in 1996.

1. For instance, "memoirs" is the term used in the latest critical study of these diaries by Edith Sarra, *Fictions of Femininity.* See this excellent book for a detailed treatment of gender and intertextuality in the women's memoirs, including the two discussed here.

2. For a good and useful introduction to the state of autobiography criticism in our time, see Olney, ed., *Autobiography,* particularly the essay by Olney, "Autobiography and the Cultural Moment: A Thematic, Historical, and Bibliographical Introduction," pp. 3–27.

3. Gusdorf, "Conditions and Limits," pp. 28–29.

4. The poet Ki no Tsurayuki was the main compiler of the *Kokinshū* (Anthology of early and modern poems; comp. ca. 905), the very first of a total of twenty-one *waka* anthologies regularly commissioned by imperial order until the early fifteenth century. Tsurayuki also wrote the *Kana* Preface that has exerted a permanent influence on the Japanese understanding of the nature and function of poetry. Its opening lines, which follow, are famous.

> Japanese poetry has its seed in the human heart, which sprouts into a myriad leaves of words. The man who lives in this world, faced with a density of event and circumstance, expresses what he feels in his heart through things visible and audible. Listen to the warbler crying among the flowers, the croaking of the frog that dwells on the waters—is there any among creatures vital and alive that does not give vent to song? It is poetry that moves heaven and earth without application of force, stirs to compassion the unseen demons and deities, harmonizes relations between men and women, and pacifies the heart of raging warriors. (*Kokin wakashū*, ed. Ozawa, p. 49)

5. In the *Kokinshū Kana* Preface, Tsurayuki evaluates Henjō's poetry as "having an understanding of form but lacking in truth [*makoto*] . . . as if one were looking at a woman in a painting and became uselessly stirred by her" (*Kokin wakashū*, ed. Ozawa, p. 57). There is also his negative valuation of the poetry of his time as given to surface "color," showing that "people's hearts have turned to flowers," producing only "vain and ephemeral words" (p. 54). The use of *kokoro* as signifier of sincerity and truth is fairly consistent in the history of *waka* criticism.

6. For the moment, I am counting Tsurayuki's *Tosa Diary* (ca. 935) outside this genealogy because my sense is that he meant it to be less a memoir than a pedagogical exemplar of how people in various walks of life naturally respond to moving situations through the language of poetry. I think that his motive for adopting the open disguise of a female narrator, which is belied by his Sinified parallel prose, is his consciousness of writing something other than "the thing called diary that men are said to write." Most of all, there is no problem here of the quest for the self that seems peculiar to the Heian women's memoirs. For an illuminating analysis of the issue of gender in this work, see Miyake, *"Tosa Diary."*

7. For a summary, based on archeology and literary evidence, of the posited gender equality in ancient Japan, see *Nihon josei no rekishi,* pp. 14–62.

8. Fukutō, "[Chūsei] jidai o miru," p. 64.

9. Morris, trans., *The Pillow Book*, pp. 192–193; *Makura sōshi*, pp. 337–338, where the corresponding line in this passage mentions only "the daughter of an ordinary High Court Noble" *(tadabito no kandachime no musume)* becoming empress, not the daughter of a commoner becoming the principal consort of a High Court Noble.

10. The "political unconscious" refers, first, to the founding Marxist narrative of history as a record of the human struggle to win a space of freedom from socioeconomic and political oppression. "It is in detecting the traces of that uninterrupted narrative, in restoring to the surface of the text the repressed and buried reality of this fundamental history, that the doctrine of a political unconscious finds its function and necessity." Jameson, *Political Unconscious*, p. 20; see also pp. 48–49.

11. *Kagerō nikki*, p. 125. Unless otherwise specified, translations are mine. Complete translations of the diary are available in Seidensticker, trans., *Gossamer Years*, and Arntzen, trans., *Kagerō Diary*. See also Arntzen's essay in this volume for an analysis of the father's presence in this text.

12. In this regard, the depiction of Kaneie's courtship of the protagonist is also significant. It develops from her formally replying to his poems only by proxy, through one of her ladies, to her directly replying to him herself, signifying a new, more intimate and "truer" level. Eventually, we discover that the marriage has taken place only through the burden of their poems to each other. In this way, the poetic exchange seems to signify a displacement of physical intimacy into language that is nevertheless more intimate than the body. See *Kagerō nikki*, p. 130.

13. *Kagerō nikki*, pp. 136–137.

14. Ibid., pp. 151–155.

15. Ibid., p. 202.

16. *Sarashina nikki*, pp. 107–108. Unless otherwise specified, translations are mine. A complete translation is available in Morris, *As I Crossed a Bridge of Dreams*.

17. *Sarashina nikki*, pp. 109–110.

18. Ibid., p. 13.

19. See Kamens, trans., *The Three Jewels*, p. 93.

20. For examples of *zangemono* (revelatory tales), see Childs, trans., *Rethinking Sorrow*. Although the stories translated by Childs come from a later period, it is evident here that the concept of confessing the error of one's ways as a sign of repentance and religious awakening was in dissemination earlier.

21. *Sarashina nikki*, pp. 58–59.

22. Ibid., pp. 61–62. The narrator's reply poem embeds the homonym *chichi* (father) in the place-name Chichibu in response to her father's reference to the place-name Child-Yearning Woods (Koshinobi no Mori).

23. Ibid., pp. 57–58.

24. See, for example, Akiyama Ken's commentary, which, while admitting the father's weakness as portrayed by the narrator, attempts to redress the balance by citing from external sources instances of his energy and resourcefulness; Akiyama, "Kaisetsu," in ibid., pp. 118–119. Male critics are apparently made uncomfortable by the abject portrait of the man as painted by his daughter.

25. Ibid., p. 31.

26. Ibid., p. 55.

27. Tsumoto Nobuhiro, in his *Sarashina nikki no kenkyū*, pp. 20–25, proposes that the person the narrator calls Mother *(haha)* may actually be her grandmother *(baba)*, that is, Takasue's mother. This would account for her staying behind when the family goes to Kazusa; she would have been too old to make the trip. It would also explain the protagonist's sense of her "mother" as "an old-fashioned person" *(kodainaru hito)*. Tsumoto posits that the mother who was the sister of Michitsuna's Mother had either died or divorced Takasue and he had subsequently married Takashina Shigeyuki's daughter, the narrator's stepmother *(mamahaha, keibo)*, two years before the family went to Kazusa. This would account for the stepmother's having a "five-year-old child" (*itsutsu bakari naru chigo; Sarashina nikki*, pp. 31–32) when she left Takasue. The hypothesis accounts for some puzzling aspects of the narrative, in particular the apparent lack of an emotional tie between the narrator and her mother, as well as the sense of loss and seeking after maternal solace that threads through the narration. On the other hand, the hypothesis raises other inconsistencies in the text, and not all of the arguments are persuasive. Thus, while taking it into consideration in my interpretation of the text, I regard it as a provisional hypothesis needing further investigation.

28. See Tsumoto, *Sarashina nikki no kenkyū*, pp. 9–13, for the relevant *Gonki* entries and pp. 1–18 for an account of Takasue's career.

29. Kadota Bun'ei, "Sugawara Takasue no teitaku," in *Kodai bunka* (August 1966); also included in *Ōchō no eizō—Heian jidaishi no kenkyū* (Tōkyōdō shuppan, 1970); as cited in Akiyama, "Kaisetsu," *Sarashina nikki*, p. 119.

30. *Sarashina nikki*, pp. 30–31.

31. It does not help Takasue's posthumous reputation that a compendium of historical documents and anecdotes, *Fusō ryakki* (comp. after 1094; cited in Tsumoto, *Sarashina nikki no kenkyō*, p. 5), records an incident showing Michinaga's low valuation of Takasue's common sense. On 10.19.1023, when Michinaga was on pilgrimage to Mount Kōya, he also visited the Ryūmonji in Yoshino. There, he and his party discovered the calligraphy of Sugawara Michizane and Miyako no Yoshika preserved on the door panels of a room. The whole company was much moved, and they composed Chinese verses to that effect. But they also notice, alongside the ancient calligraphy, "writing in *kana*" *(kanade no bun)* inscribed by Takasue and, thinking it utterly lacking in common sense, had the offending lines whitened over. Other poems by Confucianists likewise received the scorn of Michinaga's group. Since neither the offending lines nor the poems are quoted, however, it is difficult to judge whether Michinaga was scandalized at the inappropriate use of the native phonetic syllabary beside Michizane's Chinese writing or at Takasue's audacity in matching his writing with his illustrious ancestor's. In any case, the incident reveals that Takasue was not in Michinaga's good graces.

32. *Sarashina nikki*, pp. 66–67.

33. Ibid., pp. 37–38.

34. As recorded in the *Gonki* entry for 1.27.1000; cited in Tsumoto, *Sarashina nikki no kenkyō*, pp. 9, 572. It is possible that Sei Shōnagon was referring to this event in the *Pillow Book* passage quoted earlier.

35. *Sarashina nikki*, pp. 68–69.

36. Ibid., pp. 71–72.

37. Ibid., p. 74.

38. See note 27 for Tsumoto's suggestion that Lady Sarashina had lost her mother by either death or divorce before the family went down to Kazusa Province when she was ten.

39. *Sarashina nikki*, p. 56.

40. Ibid., p. 32.

41. Ibid., p. 33.

42. Ibid., pp. 39–40.

43. Ibid., p. 42.

44. Ibid., pp. 45–47.

45. Ibid., pp. 35–36.

46. For an account of the formation of the Buddhist critique of the *Genji* as "wild words and fine phrases" *(kyōgen kigo)*, see Teramoto, *Genji monogatari juyōshi ronkō*, pp. 493–534.

47. For the scriptural account of the wisdom and speedy attainment of buddha-hood by the daughter of the Dragon King Sagara despite her sex, see Hurvitz, trans., *Scripture of the Lotus Blossom*, pp. 199–201. Sariputra, skeptical about the girl's claim to enlightenment, states that "a woman's body is filthy, it is not a Dharma-receptacle." Consequently the sutra narrative's demonstration to the contrary necessitates that "the assembled multitude all saw the dragon girl in the space of an instant turn into a man" (pp. 200–201). And it is as a male bodhisattva seated on the jeweled lotus blossom that the daughter achieves the authority that Sariputra earlier denied her.

48. For the concepts of the semiotic and the *chora*, see Kristeva, *Revolution in Poetic Language*, pp. 25–30, 46–51.

49. For the mirror stage and desire in Lacanian psychoanalytical theory, outlined below, see Ragland-Sullivan, *Jacques Lacan*, pp. 24–30, 68–89.

50. Kristeva, *Revolution in Poetic Language*, p. 47.

51. Kristeva, *Revolution in Poetic Language*, p. 25.

52. Gilbert and Gubar, *The Madwoman in the Attic*, pp. 3–92.

Works Cited

Location of Japanese publishers is Tokyo unless otherwise noted.

Arntzen, Sonja, trans. *The Kagerō Diary: A Woman's Autobiographical Text from Tenth-Century Japan.* Ann Arbor: Center for Japanese Studies, University of Michigan, 1997.

Childs, Margaret Helen, trans. *Rethinking Sorrow: Revelatory Tales of Late Medieval Japan.* Ann Arbor: Center for Japanese Studies, University of Michigan, 1991.

Fukutō Sanae. "[Chūsei] jidai o miru," in *Nihon josei no rekishi*, ed. Sōgō Joseishi Kenkyūkai. Kadokawa shoten, 1992.

Gilbert, Sandra M., and Susan Gubar. *The Madwoman in the Attic: The Woman Writer and the Nineteenth-Century Literary Imagination.* New Haven, Conn.: Yale University Press, 1979 and 1984.

Gusdorf, Georges. "Conditions and Limits of Autobiography," in *Autobiography: Essays Theoretical and Critical,* ed. James Olney, pp. 28–48. Princeton, N.J.: Princeton University Press, 1980.

Hurvitz, Leon, trans. *Scripture of the Lotus Blossom of the Fine Dharma (The Lotus Sutra).* New York: Columbia University Press, 1976.

Jameson, Fredric. *The Political Unconscious: Narrative as a Socially Symbolic Act.* New York: Cornell University Press, 1981.

Kagerō nikki. Ed. Kimura Masanori and Imuta Tsunehisa. In *Tosa nikki, Kagerō nikki,* pp. 125–409. *NKBZ* 9. Shōgakkan, 1973.

Kamens, Edward, trans. *The Three Jewels: A Study and Translation of Minamoto Tamenori's Sanbōe.* Ann Arbor: Center for Japanese Studies, University of Michigan, 1988.

Kokin wakashū. Ed. Ozawa Masao. *NKBZ* 7. Shōgakkan, 1971.

Kristeva, Julia. *Revolution in Poetic Language.* Trans. Margaret Waller. New York: Columbia University Press, 1984.

Makura sōshi. Ed. Matsuo Satoshi and Nagai Kazuko. *NKBZ* 11. Shōgakkan, 1974.

Miyake, Lynne. "*The Tosa Diary:* In the Interstices of Gender and Criticism." In *The Woman's Hand: Gender and Theory in Japanese Women's Writing,* ed. Paul Gordon Schalow and Janet A. Walker, pp. 41–73. Stanford, Calif.: Stanford University Press, 1996.

Morris, Ivan, trans. *As I Crossed a Bridge of Dreams: Recollections of a Woman in Eleventh-Century Japan.* Middlesex, England: Penguin Books, 1975.

————, trans. *The Pillow Book of Sei Shōnagon.* New York: Penguin Books, 1971.

Nihon josei no rekishi: sei, ai, kazoku. Ed. Sōgō Joseishi Kenkyūkai. Kadokawa shoten, 1992.

Olney, James, ed. *Autobiography: Essays Theoretical and Critical.* Princeton, N.J.: Princeton University Press, 1980.

Ragland-Sullivan, Ellie. *Jacques Lacan and the Philosophy of Psychoanalysis.* Urbana: University of Illinois Press, 1986.

Sarashina nikki. Ed. Akiyama Ken. *Nihon koten shūsei,* vol. 39. Shinchōsha, 1980.

Sarra, Edith. *Fictions of Femininity: Literary Inventions of Gender in Japanese Court Memoirs.* Stanford, Calif.: Stanford University Press, 1999.

Seidensticker, Edward, trans. *The Gossamer Years (Kagerō Nikki): The Diary of a Noblewoman of Heian Japan.* Rutland, Vt.: Tuttle, 1964.

Teramoto Naohiko. *Genji monogatari juyōshi ronkō.* Vol. 2. Kazama shobō, 1984.

Tsumoto Nobuhiro. *Sarashina nikki no kenkyū.* Waseda Daigaku Shuppanbu, 1982.

Chapter 3
Towazugatari
Unruly Tales from a Dutiful Daughter

Edith Sarra

The memoir *Towazugatari* of the late Kamakura period (after 1306) is best known to readers of English through Karen Brazell's translation, *The Confessions of Lady Nijō*.[1] A more literal, if less elegant, rendering of the title is *A Tale No One Asked For.* For reasons that will become clear later in this essay, I prefer the more literal translation, though I believe both titles have their own merits as evocative commentaries on the kinds of interpretation this text invites. I will return to this matter below.

The memoir was written by an aristocratic woman who served as a high-ranking concubine to Retired Emperor Gofukakusa (1243–1304; r. 1246–1259), and it recounts a period of thirty-six years (1271–1306), a chronological sweep that distinguishes it as one of the most sustained autobiographical narratives in the court tradition. Writing more than a century after the close of the Heian period (794–1185) but deeply influenced by the literature of the Heian court, Lady Nijō (1258–after 1306) describes a life self-consciously lived and deliberately represented in relation to the plots and rhetoric of earlier classics of court narrative and poetry by women writers, especially *The Tale of Genji* (*Genji monogatari,* ca. 1010).

The strong, premodern tradition of female writers in Japanese literature originated some four centuries earlier at the Heian court, within the physical and discursive confines of a largely patriarchal society in which the strategic marriage and pregnancy of an upper-class daughter could contribute to or even secure the success of her father's career at court. To this end, promising young ladies were assiduously educated in the arts of music, dyeing, painting, calligraphy, and composition of *waka* (poetry in Japanese). The two latter of these arts in particular played crucial roles in the literature and rituals of courtship and seduction. Thus, the relationship between women and writing in the upper levels of Heian court culture generated arrangements quite different from those that predominated in both the West and other eras of Japanese history before the nineteenth century. Not only were elite women allowed access to written culture, but they also were actively educated and encouraged to participate in the creation of it, even if that meant that they often merely performed as dutiful daughters, literary accomplices to regimes that were ultimately more interested in the literary and sociopolitical destinies of fathers, husbands, and sons.

But writing being what it so often is in the hands of skilled writers and strong readers, many of the texts these women produced resist the role of simple accessory to patriarchal plots. Some of them can be and have been read as sites for the deconstruction as well as the construction of cultural norms. Let us take it as a given that any writer who shows an awareness of writing as a medium for generating meaning and pleasure possesses the potential to create intellectually productive kinds of ambiguity. During the Heian period, aristocratic women serving at the imperial court and in the mansions of the politically powerful established a tradition of prose narrative that was in its more sophisticated moments concerned with questions about the nature of language itself, the power of words not only to beguile the tedium of the upper-class woman's sedentary existence but also to persuade, deceive, or seduce others, to conjure up a past that might justify or subtly critique the present, or to construct and carry on a family name or personal image as cultural icon. Although much of classical court women's literature represents a thematically and rhetorically conservative tradition, it is also tense with contradictions and incoherences, moments when we sense a deft hand fidgeting with the loose seams of old discourses. A number of these writers proved themselves capable of making that tradition over into something that, while not entirely new, was not quite the same old thing either. Nijō inherits this tradition but employs the thematic and rhetorical repertoire of her skilled predecessors to create something that is strikingly new.

At the imperial court in Nijō's belated day, though not for much longer, aristocratic women were still expected to write, and to write well—in Nijō's case, even admonished to do so. As she reminds us late in her narrative, her father with his dying words had charged her with advice not only about obeying the retired emperor whose child she

was carrying at the time but also about carrying on the literary reputation of her family.[2] He continues to admonish her on this score even
from beyond the grave. Visiting her father's grave in 1304, thirty-three
years after his death, Nijō is angry that—perhaps because she is no
longer serving at court and thus is not easily able to make requests
on his behalf—none of her father's poems has been included in the
most recent imperially commissioned anthology, though they had
been regularly included in past years, beginning with the *Shokukokinshū*
(1251). In the dreamed conversation she reports having with him that
night, her dead father makes a speech that further enumerates specific
poetic achievements of their family, going back for generations to
Prince Tomohira (964–1009), and closes with final instructions to her
in *waka* form:

nao mo tada	Still continue to
kakitometemiyo	sow all the words you can
moshiogusa	for in a better age
hito o mo wakazu	men shall judge the harvest
nasake aru you ni	by its intrinsic worth.[3]

In Nijō's own reckoning then, her father authorizes her text by
exhorting her to promote the literary reputation of the family. She
also portrays him as having had a certain plot in mind—at least for
her extraliterary activities: serve the emperor faithfully; should he for-
sake you and you then try serving another master, consider yourself
disowned by me; better, at that point, to become a nun.[4] She frames
the story of her life as a text that follows the letter, at least, of her
father's wishes for her, but the spirit of her own desires emerges with
unusual force—our first clue is her very protestations that, in all that
she did (especially in writing about what she did), she was only trying to follow through on what her father (or father surrogates)
asked of her.

As in *The Tale of Genji* and certain other Heian tales and memoirs,
an eroticized imagery of the father-daughter relationship informs
many of the anecdotes told in *A Tale No One Asked For*, as well as the
daughterly conceptualization of writing that underlies it. This chapter
will explore how and why the memoir presents itself (and has been
understood) as both a filial tale and as something more unruly, "a
tale no one asked for." I will focus in particular on what this double-
edged mode of self-presentation has to do with the memoirist's relationship to the figure of the father and to writing itself.

On Confessions, Bidden and Unbidden

There was no clear convention regarding the titling of Heian and Kamakura memoirs—especially memoirs left by female memoirists. *Kagerō nikki* (Kagerō diary, also translated as Gossamer diary; after 974) takes its name from a passage toward the end of the first volume in which the memoirist suggests a name for her text herself, but such cases are not the rule. *Sarashina nikki* (Sarashina diary, after 1059) seems to have been named by Fujiwara Teika (1162–1241) or some earlier copyist, who drew on an *utamakura* (poetic pillow-word; in this case, a toponym) that occurs in one of the memoir's final poems. Sarashina is a place-name associated in the *waka* tradition with brilliant moonlight and the legend of an old woman abandoned by her child in the mountains, a story whose themes and imagery resonate in various ways with those of the memoir. It is not clear who titled Nijō's memoir *A Tale No One Asked For*. It may not have been Nijō herself; it could have been a later reader or copyist, though most Japanese commentators are inclined to read it as her title.

Titles have historically functioned as telling commentaries on the memoirs they name, and this seems profoundly so for *A Tale No One Asked For*. Regardless of who ultimately named it, the title of Nijō's memoir has something emphatic and complicated to say about the text it names. It prompts the reader to enter the narrative with a certain set of expectations, with certain assertions and caveats borne in mind. Obviously, the idea that the memoir we are about to read might be something no one asked for undercuts the memoirist's own counterinsistence that in fact she was fully authorized to write, not simply asked but commanded by her father's ghost to "sow all the words" she could. The title sounds like an apology then, or a warning that the kind of words she actually did sow amounted to a tale her father might not have wanted to hear.

The term *"towazugatari"* itself has a rich history in Heian literature. A glance at its usage there reveals that it is also a strongly gendered term, typically denoting a type of speech that women and/or victims of possessing spirits make in moments of crisis. The author of the *Kagerō Diary* uses it memorably in a letter she writes to her husband at a critical juncture in the story of their troubled marriage. Fed up with his neglect of her and contemplating Buddhist nunhood as an alternative to the frustration of waiting for a man who seldom visits, she is about to rush off on an ill-considered retreat to a temple in the hills west of the capital: "You will say this [letter in which she hints at these intentions] is a weird, unasked-for tale *(ayashiki towazugatari)*."[5] In other words, it will be considered a strange outburst, uncalled for and unbecoming, and therefore susceptible to being trivialized as a passing fit of passion.

A survey of the term's appearance in *The Tale of Genji* uncovers its connection there with two interrelated strands of signification. One is the irrepressible reminiscing of old women, often former ladies-in-waiting who have seen all there is to see and know about their mistresses or masters (Kashiwagi's wet-nurse Ben no Kimi, for example, who finally reveals to Kaoru the mystery of his parentage). Second, the term harbors associations with the involuntary speech of Buddhist mediums and victims of possessing spirits (almost all of whom are female, at least in *The Tale of Genji*). This latter nuance suggests both psychological urgency as well as a kind of scary emotional authenticity: the unbidden outbursts of the possessed convey the otherwise unvoiceable grievances of the dead or the intense resentments of the living. *"Towazugatari"* (unasked-for tales) of this sort represent a dire means of communicating things that cannot be communicated in any other way.[6]

In court women's memoirs of the Kamakura period and later, the term *"towazugatari"* is often coupled with words expressing triviality and irksomeness. In both *Kenshūmon'in Chūnagon nikki* (ca. 1219) and *Takemukigaki* (after 1349), it appears as a self-deprecating description for the memoirs themselves. *Takemukigaki* styles itself *"itazura no towazugatari"* (a bothersome tale that no one asked for).[7] The shift in designation from oral outbursts to written records suggests a claim of spontaneity that has an almost defensive ring to it. It implies that these texts were not premeditated and finely threshed over years of writing and revising. They simply poured forth, the scribal ranting of old women who could no longer bear to keep it to themselves. The usage hints at perennial anxieties about women and written records. In the Kamakura period, aristocratic women are still educated to express themselves in writing—but what they write may be no more controllable than what they might say. Those tales that come forth unbidden give voice to what perhaps ought to have remained unwritten. But if post-Heian usage suggests a trivialization of women's discourse, a falling away from the melodramatic seriousness of the *Genji* (dark family secrets) and the *Kagerō Diary* (freakish female passion), Nijō's memoir seems to stand somewhere in between the two traditions. It is a tale told by an older woman, filled with family secrets and female passion, but there is very little about it that partakes of the tiresome ramblings of a crone or the eerily portentous speech of the possessed. Indeed a remarkable self-possession seems everywhere apparent, even if the narrator sometimes portrays herself as having behaved without full command of her own actions.

In titling her translation *The Confessions of Lady Nijō,* Karen Brazell highlights a set of thematic and structural features in the text that have long been focal points for much of the commentary written in modern Japanese. Some few years after 1283, when Nijō was struck from the official list of Gofukakusa's ladies-in-waiting, she took Buddhist vows. Thus the first three books of her memoir chronicle the years of her service at court (1271–1283, plus a passage on events from 1285), whereas the last two detail her travels and experiences as a Buddhist nun (1289–1306). The six-year hiatus between these two distinct phases of Nijō's life is dramatized textually by an abrupt movement from one to the other in the narrative. Book Three ends soon after the account of Nijō's removal from court; Book Four opens abruptly with her setting out on a journey in a nun's habit four years after the last event described in Book Three. The absence of transitional passages explaining or describing her taking of the tonsure is so conspicuous as to have inspired some readers to speculate a volume is missing, while others, citing similar chronological leaps in Heian and Kamakura fiction and memoirs, argue that the gap was intentional. Thematically and rhetorically as well, there are dramatic differences between the first three and the final two volumes of the memoir, and I have written elsewhere on the preoccupation with guilt and blame in *A Tale No One Asked For,* suggesting connections between that preoccupation and similar themes in (and modes of reading invited by) narratives in the post-Augustinian confessional tradition in the West.[8]

I would add here only that Brazell's evocation of the tradition of confessional literature in the title of her translation resonates with the strong tendency in Japanese scholarship to treat Nijō's taking of Buddhist vows as the pivotal (non)event of the narrative. Like the moment of conversion in spiritual autobiographies of the Christian tradition, the turn toward religion is understood as the moment in both text and life that determines the basic significance of both. Imazeki Toshiko has also noted the tendency of scholars to read the first three and final two volumes as two opposing halves of a career radically split between the pull of worldly romance and secular affairs, and the spiritual freedom of religious pursuits. Imazeki, however, suggests that such a division is not so clearly drawn by Nijō herself. Arguing against the received view of Nijō's nunhood as a willful, positive choice, Imazeki questions Nijō's freedom to choose at all, her view being that Nijō intentionally presented her nunhood as a long-sought-after alternative in order to put a better face on events that were in fact out of her control.[9] I would merely point out that neither case is entirely clear, nor is the truth fully recoverable. Certainly Nijō presents herself as banished from court and forsaken by Gofukakusa at the end of Book Three (at which point, taking the tonsure merely fulfills her father's deathbed instructions). But she also claims to have yearned since childhood to one day write her own version of *Saigyō ga shūgyō no ki* (The record of the religious pilgrimages of Saigyō), the wandering poet-monk.[10] And yet the text also (whether by design or by loss of a volume) leaves her personal motives for becoming a nun in doubt because it contains no account of the actual time surrounding that ritual. The ambiguity both invites and resists interpretation, but its importance as a critical juncture in the narrative remains, no matter what view a reader may take.

The memoirist's shift in identity from concubine to nun suggests a dramatic shift in her view of her own past. Like the writer of a confession, Nijō reads and interprets the events of her youth from an epistemological position other than the one she once maintained. As modes of discourse, both confessions and *towazugatari* insist on a certain authenticity—spiritual, psychological, emotional. With confessions written in the Judeo-Christian tradition, the guarantor of authenticity is God himself, the ultimate addressee of the discourse. To create a text for human readers, confessing sin and faith, is a secondary act, a form of bearing witness to the mysterious ways God has worked in the writer's life. In *towazugatari,* the claim to authenticity is bolstered by the strong implication that the discourse is highly spontaneous and therefore uncalculating. And yet precisely because of this implication, the term *"towazugatari"* suggests an anxiety about distinctions between spontaneous and calculated actions or speech. In designating a written text as an unbidden outburst, the writer is making an assertion about sincerity while at the same time seeking in the reader some sort of affirmation of content. Some wrong has been done; something that was hidden (either from the writer herself or from others or both) now comes to light. The reader is called upon to listen, to judge, to learn. From beginning to end, *A Tale No One Asked*

For is concerned with clarifying distinctions between deeds committed
in ignorance and a present level of experience that has transformed
her understanding of her own deeds and their relationship to the
paternal figures who presided over her past. She writes from the stand-
point of one who sees and understands things that had been hidden
from view when she experienced them. Her retelling of the past highlights precisely those places where issues of innocence and knowledge
play dramatic roles. What is it she was once blind to? What is it she
now sees and wishes to reveal? The answers are not hard to find. This
is a powerful memoir, but its power does not lie in its subtlety.

The Poetics of the Father-Daughter Bond

Spring mist is rising among the black bamboo. It is dawn on a New
Year's Day at retired emperor Gofukakusa's court. His ladies-in-waiting, competing with one another in their radiance, are seated in a line
together, and "I too took my place among them."[11] So opens *A Tale
No One Asked For,* the story beginning with the moment at which its
narrator-heroine—one radiant girl among many—is about to be singled out by Gofukakusa himself. She remembers exactly what she was
wearing. We get an elaborate description of her seven layers of gowns,
their color schemes, the patterns of embroidery on them, followed
by an equally vivid though briefer detailing of the ritual rounds of
medicinal sake (rice wine) her father the Major Counselor offers to
Gofukakusa and the drinking party that ensues at the retired emperor's behest in an inner chamber after the formal ceremonies.
Finally, the climax of the passage is presented: Gofukakusa importunes
the Major Counselor for fulfillment of a pledge made to him before
Nijō was born—that she should be given to him as a concubine in compensation for the loss of her mother, Sukedai (d. 1259), who had become the Major Counselor's wife years ago. Nothing of this fateful
transposition of daughter for mother is mentioned here, however;
Gofukakusa's request of the Major Counselor is made by means of a
poetic allusion. Having proposed a somewhat excessive three rounds
of sake, with nine cups per round, he hands the cup to Nijō's father
and says simply, "Let 'the wild goose of the fields' come to me this
spring" (a reference to a tenth-century poem in which the image of
the wild goose serves as metaphor for a girl who has been offered in
marriage by her mother to the hero).

Accepting this proposal with great deference, my father drank the cups of *sake* offered to him and retired. What did it all mean? I had seen them speaking confidentially, but I had no way of knowing what was afoot.[12]

Nijō's mother, Sukedai, had served in the bedchamber of Emperor Gofukakusa before her marriage to Nijō's father, Koga Masatada (1223–1272), the Major Counselor of the opening passage. There her duties had included "teaching [the emperor] the secret arts of the bedroom," as one commentator quaintly puts it.[13] Naturally, Sukedai's involvement with Gofukakusa predated the formal entrance at court of his empress Higashi-Nijō (1232–1304). Besides thus being his first lover, Sukedai also apparently left an empty space in his heart. Significantly, Gofukakusa confesses to Nijō later in the narrative: "I was secretly very fond of her." Women of Sukedai's station, however, were not ordinarily destined for the imperial harem. When she was later courted by Omikado Fuyutada and Koga Masatada, and finally married to the latter, Gofukakusa did not resist. He was only fifteen years old at the time ("still an adolescent timid in the ways of the world," he protests to Nijō, as if by way of explanation). And so Sukedai passed entirely out of his hands, first by her marriage, then by her death when Nijō was only two.[14] At the opening of *A Tale No One Asked For,* Gofukakusa has been waiting (we learn later) fourteen years for Sukedai's daughter to become one of his ladies-in-waiting.[15]

Like a number of the *Genji* heroines, Nijō has been raised without knowing her biological mother and has been, like some of the great Heian memoirists, the favorite daughter of a doting father: "I have lavished on you alone the 'love due three thousand,'" he will tell her on his deathbed.[16] Unlike her literary predecessors, however, Nijō has also been destined since birth—not by karma but by matter-of-fact parental design—to replace her own mother in a former emperor's affections. This revelation is not made until late in the narrative, at a moment when in fact Gofukakusa's affections for Nijō seem to be on the wane. Thus it colors in retrospect the tale of her girlhood, giving the lie to the language of poetic allusion in which the narrative of that period is conveyed, even as it makes an almost desperate gesture toward the lovely fictions of the Heian romances. Experiences that had appeared to duplicate those of the Heian fictional heroines are exposed as strangely flawed repetitions. Hidden realities, when eventually revealed, always appear more mundane and sometimes less benign than what had originally been supposed. Illusions, many of them modeled deliberately upon scenes and themes from *The Tale of Genji*, are repeatedly overturned to reveal a banality that impinges almost vengefully upon those whose vision of things would render the world into something more aesthetically and emotionally pleasing than it actually is (not only for Nijō but also for Gofukakusa himself).

The fourteen-year-old Nijō is still unaware of these details of her own background, details characteristic of the world *A Tale No One Asked For* constructs: a world of man-made arrangements dressed up in, but ill-adapted to, the themes of Heian court tales and memoirs. What we are shown as the memoir begins is the older Nijō's recollection of how she saw things at age fourteen: the splendor of her own gowns and of the other women, the elegant drunkenness, her father conferring with the retired emperor in a highly encoded poetic idiom, her innocence, and their indifference to her perceptions. In order to begin to appreciate the power of this text, a couple of things should be borne in mind. If the girl portrayed in the opening passage is unable to fathom the import of the retired emperor's request, her contemporary reader would not have been. The scene depicted is entirely comprehensible in terms of the repertoire of classical *monogatari:* a daughter is about to be formally given in marriage or concubinage to a powerful suitor. What is extraordinary here is not the subject but the unusual fitting of subject to mode of discourse.

A Tale No One Asked For is written from the limited, more or less first-person perspective characteristic of the genre of *nikki* (memoir). Yet it boldly narrates, from that particularly constrained and limited generic perspective, scenarios that are usually conveyed, when conveyed at all, in the context of *monogatari* (fictional tales), in which the narration proceeds from multiple perspectives. This memoir departs radically from the thematic conventions of its genre by spelling out her father's marriage plot so explicitly. *A Tale No One Asked For* reverts again and again to narratives about its heroine's involvement in arrangements that include her centrally but whose implications remain unclear to her until it is too late for her to respond appropriately. Yet the memoir does not simply present her as having been unaware of the arrangements being made for her future. Nothing separates Nijō more from the earlier memoirists than the particular emphases she uses to portray her father's, and later her father surrogates', plots. What sets *A Tale No One Asked For* apart is the way it repeatedly makes

the differences between her perceptions and those of her "fathers"
into the main subjects of recollection.

A Tale No One Asked For brings into the foreground at least two
other issues that earlier memoirists either deliberately ignore or unconsciously mask. The first of these, as already suggested, is the extent
to which the memoirist's life (and hence the story of her life) is under-
lain and governed by explicit arrangements made between her father
and the other men in her life. Such arrangements were commonplace
enough, and depiction of them in tale literature was not new; marriage deliberations are treated at length in *The Tale of Genji* (we will
return to this below). Depiction of them is new, however, in the context of memoir literature. In contrast to the *Genji,* whose focalization
shifts back and forth between worried fathers, passionate men yearning for a lost ideal woman, and the often (though not always) unwit-
ting women who become the objects of that commemorative yearning and those worries, *A Tale No One Asked For* presents paternally
authored sexual arrangements exclusively from the heroine's viewpoint. What emerges is a perspective on masculine desire that is at
different times critical, uncomprehending, or sympathetic, but usually
less concerned with making something aesthetically or romantically
pleasing out of the portrayal of relations between desiring men and
desirable women. It is also a perspective far less given to the kind of
idealization of the father that can be seen in works like the *Kagerō
Diary* and the *Sarashina Diary.*

In those earlier memoirs, not only is focalization limited to the
heroine's perspective, but the memoirist's range of vision is also
(consciously or unconsciously) restricted to a comparatively demure,
feminine-gendered array of topics and situations—most noticeably
so when it comes to representation of the father. The *Kagerō* memoirist
may allow herself a contemptuous (or perhaps covertly proud) backward glance at her husband's direct and unmannerly way of impor-
tuning her father (dispensing with a go-between), but her handling of
perceived collusions between father, husband, and even son (when
they rise to the surface of the text) are couched in the sentimentalized
rhetoric of *waka* and filial piety.[17] The *Sarashina* memoirist is even
more discreet. The matter of her marriage arrangements is passed
over lightly with a single reference that is so indirect that its connection to her marriage remains in some doubt. Conflict with or resistance to the father, when expressed at all, is masked. The *Sarashina*
memoirist resists, not by self-assertion but by constructing a persona,

which, prone to girlish enthusiasms, prevents her from following a more ordinarily filial path through life. The *Kagerō* memoirist directs her resistance elsewhere, assuming toward her husband the passive-aggressive pose of the *matsu onna* (the woman who waits) as long as she can, and, when she can wait no longer, complains bitterly about his mistreatment of her, but never about her father's role in these unsatisfying arrangements.

The conspicuous idealization of the fathers in the *Kagerō Diary* and the *Sarashina Diary* brings us to a second broad area distinguishing Nijō's memoir: its depiction of her relationship to her father. Esperanza Ramirez-Christensen has argued that "the family romance between father and daughter . . . may be said to be the ubiquitous subtext of Heian women's writing, the strength of the incest taboo precluding an overt treatment of the theme, at the same time that it insures its reappearance, like the return of the repressed, over and over again . . . in tales and memoirs primarily concerned with other kinds of relationships."[18] Again, one can point to some generic differences in the handling of the father-daughter romance in Heian women's writing. Memoirs written by daughters typically sublimate the father-daughter romance in various ways, whereas the *monogatari* tradition finds ways of flirting more overtly with the incest taboo. Biological fathers and daughters do not couple sexually in Heian *monogatari* any more than they do in Heian memoirs, but *The Tale of Genji* is notorious for making much of romance between men and girl-like women whose relationships mimic the father-daughter bond.

In the earlier memoirs, on the other hand, while strong father-daughter dyads are represented, distinctions between sentiments accorded to fathers and those that husbands or lovers excite are clear-cut. The *Kagerō* memoirist appears less concerned with her father than with detailing her relationship with her husband and her son. The *Sarashina* memoirist, for all her outright sentimentalization of her father in the early and middle sections of the memoir (it is not for nothing that she is known to posterity as Takasue's Daughter), neglects to mention his death—an omission that might seem odd (perhaps another form of subtle resistance to the father?), given the heroine's earlier intensely emotional concern for him. Husbands are portrayed as a different sort of animal altogether. There is nothing fatherly about the *Kagerō* memoirist's outrageously insensitive husband. The *Sarashina* memoirist hardly mentions her husband at all until he dies (and potential lovers appear primarily as fantasy figures in fictional tales). Fathers, in these memoirs, receive by contrast a disproportionate amount of whatever positive sentiment the writers express toward real men. Yet the exact nature of their involvement with their daughters' lives and texts seems vague indeed compared with the word-by-word, day-by-day detail we are provided in *A Tale No One Asked For.* What we are shown instead are scenes of intense emotional attachment, typically showcased at moments of parting. Both earlier memoirists were daughters of men who served as provincial governors, and both memoirs contain extended passages detailing highly charged farewells between daughters and fathers as the latter depart for posts in distant provinces.

When it comes to the *monogatari* tradition, things get more complicated, both thematically and structurally. *The Tale of Genji* capitalizes on the erotic potential of the incest taboo in many of the major love affairs it depicts. Its use of the narrative strategy of shifting focalization allows the tale to serve as a forum for thinking through different perspectives on an erotic, quasi-father-daughter dyad: the yearning of a hero for a daughterlike lover who can replace his lost (motherlike) ideal love, and the longing of a heroine for a fatherlike lover who can replace her lost father or fatherly ideal. The working out of this dyad in *The Tale of Genji* has been discussed under various rubrics, ranging from the Freudian oedipal to philologically inspired meditations on the poetic image of the *yukari* (link, or erotic surrogate). The lineaments of the *yukari* theme will be familiar to any reader of *Genji.* It has been usually presented in the secondary literature, however, from the basically masculine perspective foregrounded in the opening chapters of *Genji.* To summarize: the erotic longing of an adult male for a particular woman is foreshadowed and to some extent dictated by the story of his prior longing as a boy for an unattainable or dead parent or lover. The hero bent on seeking fulfillment for such a longing—to the extent that fulfillment may be won or at least pursued—will seek his object in someone who closely resembles the original beloved in all important respects except this one: she is daughterly. Her youth and inexperience commend her to his shaping hands. If all goes smoothly, he will be able to discover in her (or more actively, make her into) someone as near his ideal as possible. In the story of Genji's discovery and abduction of the young Murasaki, Murasaki's powerful appeal for Genji has to do with her identity as an erotic surrogate for Fujitsubo, her own aunt and Genji's forbidden but desired stepmother.[19]

Genji provides numerous examples of the way this eroticized quasi-father-daughter romance theme informs plots that circulate around the romantic and political careers of its heroines. Idealized in the early chapters, the father-daughter dyad undergoes a subtle process of questioning as the tale proceeds. In the scene of young Murasaki's sexual initiation, Genji is represented as an ideal father-husband to his child-bride, an ideal only slightly undercut by the narration's glance at young Murasaki's passive discomfort at Genji's caresses and her nurse's admonishments the morning after. The theme takes on an unmistakably ironic tone in the Tamakazura chapters, with the depiction of the middle-aged Genji's relationship to his foster-daughter Tamakazura. Here, finally, the heroine is herself allowed to voice sly criticism of the would-be romantic hero—without at any point undermining her own status as a desirable, nubile female.

Of course, if everything went smoothly, there would be no tale to tell. In the story of Genji's love for young Murasaki, as long as one sticks with Genji's perspective all seems to be going well enough. Murasaki grows up, under his tutelage, to become an ideal wife, and their marriage becomes the envy of the world. But the *Genji* complicates its own thematic weave by constantly introducing competing perspectives on the idyll of quasi-incestuous romance. The original idyll shows signs of unraveling, and new erotic surrogates and new idylls are brought into the forefront of the narrative, only to repeat the process of frustration, disappointment, and deferment. All that might be wrong with the Murasaki idyll is only hinted at in the early chapters and does not emerge clearly until much later in the narrative. As we read on, Murasaki remains childless, she suffers spirit possession and falls into a brooding silence when Genji marries the Third Princess and briefly renews his affair with Oborozukiyo, and finally she dies. What is "wrong" is that Murasaki's perspective on Genji's passion(s) has always been marginalized. While Genji is at times sensitive to her unvoiced suffering, it has had little effect on his behavior, while his behavior has had a disproportionate effect on hers: an effect that resembles the disproportion that might obtain between a father with a daughter who is dependent on him in all areas, sexual, as well as practical and emotional.

A Tale No One Asked For, savvy as it is about the interlocking themes of the *Genji* and earlier memoir literature, picks up on this "ubiquitous subtext" and spells out in new ways the story of how the father's pedagogical, political, and erotic desiderata operate in and with Nijō's own unbidden tale—a "tale" that is at once her life (her career at court and her travels as a nun), and her textualization of that life. Her life and her writing of her life become almost interchangeable at times, given the nature of Nijō's "work" at court and in the provinces, which took place as often as not in the realm of the literary as it did in that of the erotic. Its strategies, however, do not include subtle questioning. What is wrong with the idyll is almost immediately exposed. The exposure is simply a matter of viewpoint. We see a shabbily belated version of the world of *Genji,* and we see it initially through the eyes of Nijō as a latter-day young Murasaki.

Compared with the laconic narration of Genji's sexual initiation of young Murasaki, and the sharp, but still seductive wittiness of Genji's flirtation with Tamakazura, the scene of Nijō's sexual initiation by Gofukakusa reads like a bald narrative of discomfort and active resistance, both physical and psychological, presented exclusively from a raw girl's outraged perspective. In the few days that follow between Gofukakusa's New Year's request to the Major Counselor about the "young goose" and the consummation of the marriage, neither her father nor her women take pains to enlighten Nijō further about her impending destiny, though her room, the stage for the retired emperor's nuptial visits, is conscientiously prepared by her father himself ahead of time. Gofukakusa is no stranger to her. She has passed much of her childhood at the imperial palace and has known him as a playmate. So his sexual advances come as a total shock. We are immediately put in mind of the story of young Murasaki's deflowering by Genji, but the version we are reading is written not from Genji's perspective or the perspective of Murasaki's nurse but from that of the girl herself.[20]

The effect is stunning. What is conspicuously lacking in this tale of sexual initiation is eroticism. What is conspicuously foregrounded are the linkages between Nijō's relation to her father and her new relationship to Gofukakusa. The interactions between Gofukakusa and Nijō echo and amplify the verbal exchanges between Nijō and her father that have just preceded them in the narrative. The sexual implications of her father's plans had been completely lost on Nijō prior to Gofukakusa's wedding visits—or so Nijō as memoirist asserts, though she remembers recognizing at the time the existence of an open secret between her father and her own attendants. What is striking in this scene is the narrative attention to the father's patronizing trickery and to Nijō's prompt, apparently guileless resistance to his

wishes and instructions, as well as her insistence on her general incomprehension of their real import:

> . . . my father came in, hung several gowns about the room for
> their decorative effect, and said to me, "*Don't fall asleep* before His
> Majesty arrives. Serve him well. A lady-in-waiting should never be
> stubborn, but should do exactly as she's told." Without the least
> idea what these instructions were all about and feeling bewildered
> by all the commotion, I leaned against the brazier and *fell asleep.*
> (Emphasis added.)[21]

Nijō handles the grand themes of courtly romance with a comic
and deflationary directness that has the effect of reducing them from
pathos to humor and criticism: the romantic ideals of the world of
Genji come off as immediately questionable, as do those individuals
who attempt to live their lives by them, Gofukakusa in particular, but
also Nijō herself.

Consider her treatment of the theme of erotic surrogacy. This
theme, while strong in *The Tale of Genji,* is elegantly indirect. On one
level, the indirection is worked out in terms of the kinship ties between original and substitute (Murasaki is Fujitsubo's niece, not her
daughter; Ukifune is Oigimi's half-sister). An exception to this pattern
is the example of Yūgao, whose daughter Tamakazura was sought as
her substitute. Tamakazura was in other ways, however, as one of
the narrators in *Mumyōzōshi* puts it, "no substitute *(yukari)* for her
ephemeral mother."[22] Not only are the kinship ties between original
and substitute typically indirect, but often the manner in which
the substitute enters the hero's orbit is also elegantly indirect. Genji
stumbles on Murasaki out in the country while convalescing; Ukifune
first enters Kaoru's orbit as the subject of rumor. Tamakazura surfaced
unexpectedly years after her mother's death, her parentage was not
immediately understood by her biological father, Tō no Chūjō, and
Genji exploited this ambiguity, while Tō no Chūjō remained duped
in part by dint of his own prior neglect of both mother and child. In
contrast, the relationship between original and substitute in *A Tale
No One Asked For* is flatly matter of fact. It had been agreed between
Nijō's father and Gofukakusa that Nijō would be exchanged between
the two men as a replacement for her own mother, Sukedai, among
Gofukakusa's ladies. The reasoning, like the exchange itself, is quite
straightforward.

The notion that Nijō was destined to be a replacement for her own mother is mentioned twice in *A Tale No One Asked For,* both times in speeches made by Gofukakusa.[23] In both instances it is apparent that, despite Nijō's position as lady-in-waiting, she has not lived up to expectations. The hope for another Sukedai has been little more than an unfulfilled fantasy on Gofukakusa's part. From Nijō's point of view, the intelligence that Gofukakusa had wanted her to replace her own mother in his affections serves as a negative reminder of what she has failed to become in her relationship with him. Yet, ironically, it is precisely because she fails to fulfill Gofukakusa's wishes that their relationship in fact succeeds in amplifying the pathos of Sukedai and Gofukakusa. In effect, Nijō "wins" by losing (if losing can also be understood here as her resistance, whether conscious or not, to Gofukakusa's designs). I am tempted to say there would have been no tale to tell had Nijō simply become her own mother. Or at least no tale so provocative as *A Tale No One Asked For.* Her failure to replace her own mother (as her father and Gofukakusa had hoped) keeps her tale from being simply a daughterly one. But paradoxically, it also allows her to create a tale that carries on the *monogatari* tradition of the *yukari* (the story about the substitute who can never really replace the lost original but generates a good tale about the hero's frustrations finding that out). Had Nijō simply become a successful substitute for her mother, there would be no story, and she would have nothing in common with the Heian *monogatari* heroines. What happens to Nijō as the heroine of her own memoir parallels her career in the "real world" of sexual/political intrigues in the court at the former Heian capital. She loses her position at court and gets shunted aside into the margins. Yet her memoir carries on this tradition of aestheticizing suffering and loss, with some unique twists.

The Tale of Genji is very much attuned to the ways in which women who are the objects of the Heian family romance and its peculiar dynamics of erotic surrogacy suffer. It is also attuned to the ways in which men who obsessively seek a replacement for a lost ideal lover suffer. What *Genji* fails to explore as a thematic possibility is the idea that women too might suffer from the same impulse to seek erotic surrogates actively or to try to discover in the current lover the shadow of an unattainable former love. *Izumi Shikibu Diary* represents a tentative venture in this direction. At the inception of that narrative, the romance between its heroine and Prince Atsumichi is framed by the heroine's memories of her love for Atsumichi's brother, dead when the narrative begins but very much alive still in her reverie.

The figure of the woman who receives two or more lovers concurrently or successively is a type explored in *Genji* chiefly along the lines of the Unai maiden plot. Both Yūgao and Ukifune are pursued by two men, and both, unable to choose between the two, or indeed to exercise much agency in the matter, meet tragic or pathetic ends.

One of the distinct contributions *A Tale No One Asked For* makes to the thematic repertoire of classical court women's narrative is its almost offhand reversing of gender roles in the scenario of erotic surrogacy. The memoir works out at length the narrative possibilities of a woman who—herself failing to fulfill the role of erotic surrogate for her first lover—finds or is presented with multiple replacements for him (and for the unavailable father the original replacement, Gofukakusa, had been intended to replace). This is not the whole story, of course. A number of the affairs delineated in *A Tale No One Asked For* involve Nijō with men she would have preferred not to have been involved with (Kameyama, Kanehira, and Ariake to some extent). But the image of Nijō as a woman who was able, if only covertly, to pursue her own desires in the realm of romance and sex comes across quite clearly at times.

Nijō's compliance with her father's wishes, and the wishes of her fatherly husband, Gofukakusa, are compromised from the start by her expressed desire for a third man, Akebono (Saionji Sanekane, 1249–1322), who stands, at least by her account, outside the frame of the fatherly plot entirely, and prior to it in her affections. *A Tale No One Asked For* presents Akebono's pursuit of Nijō as beginning before she is given as concubine to Gofukakusa. Her first betrayal of her father's wishes in fact revolves around this yet unconsummated affair. A set of robes—a gift from Akebono—is delivered to her room at court the very day of Gofukakusa's conversation with her father. The gift sets in motion an exchange of *waka* between Nijō and Akebono that is couched in the language of courtship. When her father asks her if she received the robes from the retired emperor, Nijō lies boldly in order to hide her incipient romance with Akebono:

> My heart throbbed, but somehow I replied calmly, "They are from Her Highness, Lady Kitayama."[24]

Her fragmentary depictions of Akebono's relations with her (entered into voluntarily on her part and whose beginnings predate her sexual initiation by Gofukakusa) suggest a discursive alternative to the father-daughter plot and its development in her betrothal to Gofukakusa. It will remain a minor subplot in the memoir, never significantly to disturb the hegemony of the more conventional attachments in her life (to her father, to Gofukakusa). This is testimony to the strength those paternally authored attachments borrow from their identification with the mainstream themes of courtly narrative. Nonetheless, the intermittent accounts of Akebono's presence suggest the existence of viable alternatives—viable at least in the *life* of a woman in Nijō's position, if not so prominent in the *story* she writes about that life.[25]

Generally speaking, the problem of other men is repressed in the *Genji* romance plots. Genji himself typically couples with fatherless women or women whose fathers, patrons, or lovers are weak, indifferent, or swayed by other women (their principal wives, their mothers, their in-laws). Murasaki's father, Prince Hyōbu, is ruled by his principal wife in the matter of his daughter (this is why she has been left in the care of her grandmother, where Genji discovers her); Tō no Chūjō is similarly unassertive with his jealous principal wife when it comes to his relations with Yūgao and Tamakazura, the daughter she bears him. In a similar vein, men are seldom depicted as overtly colluding to cooperate with each other in their sharing of desirable women as pawns or gifts. When they are depicted that way—and typically the theme is confined to collusion between fathers and potential husbands —things inevitably run amok. Consider the disastrous outcomes of Suzaku's conferring of the Third Princess on Genji, or the Eighth Prince's involved but equivocal conversations with Kaoru concerning the Uji princesses. Genji and Tō no Chūjō's friendly rivalry over Gen no Naishi and Suetsumuhana are burlesque parodies of male rivalry. The stakes are not high enough to render the competition serious— neither Gen no Naishi nor Suetsumuhana is desirable. Where male rivalry is serious and does impinge on the hero's coupling with a particular heroine, betrayal and secrecy are involved (Genji and his father, the Kiritsubo Emperor; Kashiwagi and Genji; Kaoru and Niou over Ukifune).

Again, Nijō's approach to the topic reflects one of the central differences between her tale and the tales told in *Genji*. Romances in the latter are typically concerned with male-female-female triangles. *A Tale No One Asked For* reverses these proportions. Nijō's triangles are emphatically male-male-female. Thus, *A Tale No One Asked For* manages to get at the problem of male rivalry from the perspective of the woman who is its object. Arguably there are adumbrations of this theme in the stories of Yūgao, the Third Princess, and Ukifune, but these heroines are passive and inarticulate compared with Nijō.

A Tale No One Asked For carries forward its variations on the theme of erotic surrogacy boldly, yet without losing sight of the complex dynamics of the heroine's situation. She may have been manipulated as a gift between Gofukakusa and his brother, and her sexual favors exchanged by Gofukakusa for political ones that benefited him but not her, but the complexity of her rendering of these exchanges ensures she cannot be convincingly interpreted as a simple victim. She loses out in the long run at court, but this does not preclude her from exercising agency and desire, nor indeed if you take an even longer view, from having the final word on the subject. It would be going too far to paint Nijō as simply a passive pawn in the hands of her father and Gofukakusa. Yet neither does she appear as simply a carefree, self-assertive female variant of Genji or Prince Niou.

Figurations of the Father, Figurations of the Text

How then has Nijō constructed the figure of the father in her life (and life story)? As portrayed in the person of her biological father, he is the source of a central contradiction in her life, the setter of impossible standards and goals, which Nijō implicitly critiques by presenting them as unreasonable and flawed, even when their ostensible goal is her protection. The father is thus the originator of the daughter's guilty dilemmas and at the same time the instigator of a memoir that largely revolves around dilemmas in which it is necessary but difficult to assign blame fairly. In many of these, the figure of the father emerges as the guilty party. But he also thus becomes, flawed as he is in her depiction of him, the means by which she implies again and again that she should be absolved from the guilty implications of her own story.

Even in his efforts to safeguard her best interests, her father winds up undermining her position inadvertently, as Nijō pointedly implies in her report of the talk occasioned by his extraordinary fussing over her return to Gofukakusa's palace after their wedding:

> "The major counselor certainly treasures her," they said. "He's sent her with all the ceremony due an official consort [*nyōgo*]." The gossip spread, and before long Empress Higashi-Nijō began to be unpleasant.[26]

Throughout Books One through Three, Nijō's simultaneous compliance with the letter of her father's explicit instructions and implicit, covert resistance to the spirit of his wishes becomes a recurring feature of the story of her career as a lady-in-waiting. In fact, I would argue that it comprises the thematic mainspring of the memoir as a whole. One of the central "problems" her narrative revolves around is precisely this tension between the contradictory desire both to comply with and to resist the desire of the father. The reason for this is simple, and strongly implied by the kinds of anecdotes the memoirist chooses to recall. One of the consequences of the memoir's scrutiny of paternal desire is the revelation of contradictions at the heart of that desire. Nijō demonstrates repeatedly that to obey the wishes of her master often also serves as a means of displeasing him. At times, obedience is as sure a way to disappoint him as resistance is at other times.

The figure of the father as a self-interested but self-defeating authority gets amplified in the characterizations of Gofukakusa. "A lady-in-waiting should never be stubborn," her father had advised her on the night of Gofukakusa's first wedding visit, "but should do exactly as she's told." Apart from the several striking instances recounted in which Nijō is stubborn or assertively refuses to do as she is told and suffers for it (her refusal to play the secondary role of the Akashi lady in the *Genji*-inspired concert at court comes to mind), the memoir also portrays her suffering from her own compliance with this advice. Doing what Gofukakusa tells her to do lands her in some of the most complicated and ultimately damaging intrigues of all, notably her affair with Ariake (identified variously as Gofukakusa's half-brother, Priest Shōjo [d. 1281], abbot of the Ninnaji Temple, or as Hōjo, Shōjō's teacher). The affair with Ariake is first urged on Nijō and abetted by Gofukakusa, who then becomes sulky and hostile to her as the affair deepens. Gofukakusa is also the authority who sanctions—even insists upon—a sexual liaison between Nijō and the regent Takatsukasa Kanehira (1228–1295), an affair that Nijō herself clearly presents as unwelcome to her.

Nothing Succeeds Like Failure

It is helpful to remember here Michele Marra's argument that the pose of the literary recluse in premodern Japanese tradition often provided the ground from which a writer might safely express political discontent. A position on the losing side—or at least the margins of intrigues at court—is a conventionally (and paradoxically) strong one in classical court narrative. In the case of *A Tale No One Asked For,* political marginality positions the writer to take a kind of aesthetic revenge on the center—but the degree of her continuing dependence on the center compromises that "revenge" and suggests her complicity as well as her resistance.[27] The survival of Nijō's memoir secures the literary reputation of her family after all (or at least, after 1940, when the seventeenth-century Katsura manuscript was belatedly rediscovered in the Imperial Household Library).[28] She paradoxically secures the reputation of her house by chronicling the demise of their own political fortunes. And this she does through the medium of an unprecedentedly desentimentalized account of fathers, daughters, and fatherly lovers, in short, an exposé of sexual intrigues at court in the late Kamakura period.

My argument differs, therefore, with readings that would paint Nijō as a woman who remained unaware of the important political roles she played out for the men with whom she was sexually involved.[29] In this regard, I would underscore two issues in particular, neither of which Marra addresses: Nijō's relatively brief and understated feelings for the fates of her several children, and her frequent references to the malevolent machinations of Empress Higashi-Nijō. Gofukakusa's persistent favoring of Nijō, even in the face of protests from his empress, suggests that Nijō posed a threat to the latter. The danger of attracting the further malice of the empress may have had much to do with Nijō's downplaying of her grief over her own children when writing her memoir years later (when she is still anxious to present herself as having been undeserving of the empress's ire). Marra's reading offers a corrective to earlier depoliticized readings of the memoir by resituating it within the framework of the power relationships among Nijō's men. But his reading assigns too much power to those men, and by the same token, in suggesting that Nijō herself remained more or less unaware of the way she was being manipulated, it implies that she was not only apolitical but also profoundly innocent of the workings of a world in which she spent most of her childhood and adult life. A posture of innocence is often quite difficult to carry off convincingly. The more skillful the pose, the less susceptible it is to detection *as a pose.* Reading Nijō at face value, Marra, whose other essays are so alert to the potential political readings of the apolitical poses that writers sometimes assume, stumbles past the possibility of its presence here.

If Nijō had indeed presented herself as a victim who was so victimized that she sympathized with her oppressors and could blame only herself for her misfortunes, why write *A Tale No One Asked For* in the first place? I think the memoir was produced by a writer who was not only aware of the injustice of her situation but also intensely interested in distinguishing her own guilty deeds from those of the people around her. The memoir has little interest in the construction of simple victim-victimizer dichotomies, nor does it bury its discontent in a seamless rhetoric of sorrow. *A Tale No One Asked For* exposes the father(s) because it renders them as strikingly human, not as heroes. They are not above trickery and deceit, even of those most dear to them, but neither are they reducible to villains. Good intentions go awry, innocence and affection go unrecognized and unrespected, bad deeds are left unpunished, and the blame for them is unfairly placed. But none is entirely blameless, least of all the principals: neither father nor daughter, much less the enigmatic figure of the retired emperor, both cuckolded and consciously pandering to the desires of other men from whom he needs political support.

Does Nijō's writing fulfill or subvert her father's wishes for it? I think the answer is that it does both. As we have seen, *A Tale No One Asked For* is very explicit about the kind of writing and literary recognition Nijō's father *did* ask for. What we actually get, however, is far more than a collection of Nijō's *waka* and reminiscences in prose about her life at court and her travels as a Buddhist nun. Anecdotes illustrating issues of guilt and responsibility—her own as well as those of the men she serves—recur repeatedly in the account of the years leading up to her expulsion from the court and from the list of Gofukakusa's ladies-in-waiting. Her memoir is—regardless of whether or not she titled it so—precisely what "no one asked for," a narrative that exposes not simply Nijō's failure to fully satisfy her father's hopes for her (in literature and in her career at court) but also the fallibility of the father *as* figure of authority, in the person of her biological father as well as the father surrogates who people her account of service at court. What we are left with is a very unruly set of tales, told by a daughter who had been groomed to tell something far more bland and undisturbing. *A Tale No One Asked For* is a memoir that reflects the necessity of writing both for and in spite of the father, and the impossibility (for Nijō) of writing simply as her father's dutiful daughter.[30]

Notes

1. Brazell, trans., *Confessions of Lady Nijō*. References to the original will cite the edition of *Towazugatari* edited by Fukuda Hideichi.

2. Brazell, *Confessions*, p. 251; *Towazugatari*, p. 314.

3. Brazell, *Confessions*, p. 252; *Towazugatari*, p. 314.

4. Brazell, *Confessions*, p. 25; *Towazugatari*, p. 40.

5. *Kagerō nikki*, p. 259.

6. See Matsumoto, *Chūsei joryū nikki bungaku no kenkyū*, pp. 323–325.

7. See *Takemukigaki*, p. 133.

8. See my "GoFukakusa'in Nijō," pp. 80–85.

9. Imazeki, *Chūsei joryū nikki bungaku no ronkō*, pp. 220–240.

10. Brazell, *Confessions*, p. 52; *Towazugatari*, p. 73.

11. Brazell, *Confessions*, p. 1; *Towazugatari*, p. 11.

12. Brazell, *Confessions*, pp. 1–2; *Towazugatari*, pp. 11–12.

13. Matsumoto, "Gofukakusa'in Nijō," p. 144.

14. Brazell, *Confessions*, p. 124; *Towazugatari*, p. 161.

15. Nijō became one of retired emperor Gofukakusa's *nyōbō*, a category designating female attendants whose duties (and whose rank) were various. In Nijō's case, it was clear from the beginning that she was sought by Gofukakusa as a concubine as well as a lady-in-waiting.

16. Brazell, *Confessions*, pp. 24–25; *Towazugatari*, p. 40.

17. See, for example, my discussion of the denouement of the *Kagerō* heroine's retreat to the western hills in *Fictions of Femininity*, pp. 73–75.

18. Ramirez-Christensen, "Desire for *Monogatari*," p. 36.

19. For extensive analysis in English of the theme of erotic surrogacy as it is played out in *The Tale of Genji*, see Field, *The Splendor of Longing*, and Shirane, *The Bridge of Dreams*, especially chapters 10 and 11.

20. Margaret Childs reads the scene as a description of rape. See her "Genji, At Least, Was Not a Rapist," p. 147.

21. Brazell, *Confessions*, p. 4; *Towazugatari*, p. 15.

22. *Mumyōzōshi*, pp. 31–32.

23. Brazell, *Confessions*, pp. 62–64; *Towazugatari*, pp. 85–88; and Brazell, *Confessions*, pp. 122–124; *Towazugatari*, pp. 159–161.

24. Brazell, *Confessions*, p. 3; *Towazugatari*, p. 13.

25. Some scholars have suggested that Akebono (assuming that this figure is indeed identifiable with Saionji Sanekane, a powerful ally of Gofukakusa and whose daughter became the empress of Gofukakusa's son Gofushimi) was from the beginning a patron of Nijō's, and their relationship was thus known and sanctioned at court. If this was indeed the case, Nijō's painting of the relationship in the language of clandestine romance is itself somewhat misleading, though not, perhaps, deliberately disingenuous. Nijō's language may be best understood as partaking of the limits of her own discourse as a woman, writing in the tradition of court ladies' memoirs. In that tradition, the writer's knowledge of the mechanics of bedroom politics is seldom explicitly flaunted.

26. Brazell, *Confessions*, p. 12; *Towazugatari*, p. 24.

27. See Marra, "Images from the Past: The Politics of Intertextuality," chapter 5 in *The Aesthetics of Discontent.*

28. Karen Brazell gives a brief account of Yamagishi Tokuhei's discovery of the Katsura manuscript in the Imperial Household Library in 1940. See her "*Towazugatari:* Autobiography of a Kamakura Court Lady," pp. 220–221. For a more detailed meditation on the work's textual history, see Matsumoto, "*Towazugatari* denbon kō," pp. 41–49.

29. See Marra, especially pp. 120, 126.

30. We need more supple definitions of terms like "patriarchy" and even "father" and "daughter" when it comes to the literature of the classical Japanese court. These are issues I hope to develop in a longer essay exploring the representation of patronage in the context of texts which, like *Towazugatari,* locate the writer at positions in the center of unstable and shifting networks of power and influence, both literary and political.

Works Cited

Location of Japanese publishers is Tokyo unless otherwise noted.

Brazell, Karen. "*Towazugatari:* Autobiography of a Kamakura Court Lady." *Harvard Journal of Asiatic Studies* 31 (1971): 220–221.

——, trans. *The Confessions of Lady Nijō.* Stanford, Calif.: Stanford University Press, 1973.

Childs, Margaret. "Genji, At Least, Was Not a Rapist: The Nature of Love and the Parameters of Sexual Coercion in the Literature of the Heian Court." In *The New Historicism and Japanese Literary Studies,* ed. Eiji Sekine, *PMAJLS* 4 (Summer 1998), pp. 138–152.

Field, Norma. *The Splendor of Longing in* The Tale of Genji. Princeton, N.J.: Princeton University Press, 1987.

Imazeki Toshiko. *Chūsei joryū nikki bungaku no ronkō.* Izumi shoin, 1987.

Kagerō nikki. Ed. Kimura Masanori and Imuta Tsunehisa. In *Tosa nikki, Kagerō nikki,* pp. 125–409. NKBZ 9. Shōgakkan, 1973.

Marra, Michele. *The Aesthetics of Discontent: Politics and Reclusion in Medieval Japanese Literature.* Honolulu: University of Hawai'i Press, 1991.

Matsumoto Yasushi. *Chūsei joryū nikki bungaku no kenkyū.* Meiji shoin, 1983.

——. "Gofukakusa'in Nijō." *Kokubungaku* 24 (August 1979): 143–151.

——. "*Towazugatari* denbon kō," *Kokubungaku tōsa* 8 (February 1968): 41–49.

Mumyōzōshi. Ed. Kuwabara Hiroshi. *Shinchō Nihon koten shūsei,* vol. 7. Shinchōsha, 1976.

Ramirez-Christensen, Esperanza. "The Desire for *Monogatari* in *Sarashina nikki.*" In *The Desire for Monogatari: Proceedings of the Second Midwest Research/Pedagogy Seminar on Japanese Literature,* ed. Eiji Sekine, pp. 31–41. West Lafayette, Ind.: Purdue University, 1994.

Sarra, Edith. "GoFukakusa'in Nijō." In *Japanese Women Writers: A Bio-Critical Source-book*, ed. Chieko Mulhern, pp. 77–85. Westport, Conn.: Greenwood Press, 1994.
————. *Fictions of Femininity: Literary Inventions of Gender in Japanese Court Women's Memoirs*. Stanford, Calif.: Stanford University Press, 1999.
Shirane, Haruo. *The Bridge of Dreams: A Poetics of* The Tale of Genji. Stanford, Calif.: Stanford University Press, 1987.
Takemukigaki. Ed. Watanabe Shizuko. Kasama shoin, 1975.
Towazugatari. Ed. Fukuda Hideichi. *Shinchō Nihon koten shūsei*, vol. 20. Shin-chōsha, 1978.

Chapter 4

Mother Tongue and Father Script

The Relationship of Sei Shōnagon and Murasaki Shikibu to Their Fathers and Chinese Letters

JOSHUA S. MOSTOW

The term "literary paternity" was coined by Sandra M. Gilbert in 1979 in reference to nineteenth-century English female writers. Tracing her argument as far back as the mimetic theory of Plato and the story of creation in *Genesis,* she declared: "In patriarchal Western culture, . . . the text's author is a father, a progenitor, a procreator, an aesthetic patriarch whose pen is an instrument of generative power like his penis."[1] Writing is seen as an exclusively male prerogative, which has "caused enormous anxiety in generations of women who were 'presumptuous' enough to dare"[2] to pick up the pen to write. A woman writing bore the emasculating threat of castration. Like Derrida in *Of Grammatology,* Gilbert is careful to limit her assertions to "patriarchal Western culture." But, to paraphrase one of her own questions: Where does such an implicitly Western patriarchal theory of literature leave literary women from non-Western traditions?

The recognition of the ubiquity of the male-gendered metaphor of creative writing in the Western tradition led Gilbert and Susan Gubar, as well as other feminist theoreticians, to a dream of not only "a distinctively female literary tradition" but of even a separate female language and script. Gilbert and Gubar first treated this subject in "Ceremonies of the Alphabet: Female Grandmatologies and the Female Authorgraph,"[3] which brings up several points germane to issues we will consider below. The authors first point out the patriarchal basis of the very alphabet itself:

> . . . our Roman letters preserve in themselves the archaic traces of
> the patriarchal glyphs and graphs from which they evolved, as if to
> remind us that they themselves are relics of a society in which
> women were as much chattels as cattle were. Our *A,* philologists
> tell us, is originally the Phoenician pictographic symbol 𐤀 (*aleph,*
> meaning "ox") turned on its side.[4]

Obviously the same can be said, and even more clearly, for Chinese
graphs, in which the woman radical appears in characters with meanings that range from "slave" (奴) to "legitimate child" (嫡), and the
graph for "woman" itself is thought to represent a woman kneeling
with her arms held up in supplication or offering (女).[5]

Gilbert and Gubar also quote Henry David Thoreau, who in *Walden*
(1854) made a distinction between speech and writing:

> . . . by defining, on the one hand, a "transitory . . . almost brutish"
> dialect that "we learn . . . unconsciously, like brutes, of our mother"
> —"a mother tongue"—and by describing, on the other hand, a
> "reserved and select expression, *too significant to be heard by the ear,*
> which he called "our father tongue."[6] (Emphasis added.)

Curiously, however, in their own theorizing, Gilbert and Gubar reverse
these terms and see "especially alphabetic writing, with its phono-
graphic flexibility," as "associated with hierarchization," while associating more pictorial representations of thought with "the truth of
woman's condition,"[7] a visual or pictorial cultural prejudice (men =
words; women = pictures) that, as we shall see, the Japanese tradition
—at least in terms of language—will belie.

Kana Bungaku as "Grandmatology"

Yet, one could argue that the reality of these fantasies of a "grandma-
tology" were to be found in tenth- and eleventh-century Japan. Here,
we are typically told, women had their own script, *onnade* (or "woman's
hand"; related to modern-day *hiragana*), and, for writing, even their
own "tongue"— vernacular Japanese, which the men had ceded to
them by limiting their own literary production largely to Chinese,
written of course in Chinese graphs.

In what follows, I shall attempt to complicate this picture. But it
can be said at the outset that, in regard to writing in Japanese, the
brush was indeed no pen, nor penis either, and there is very little
indication that Heian woman writers felt the kind of anxiety over

usurping a male prerogative that their European sisters did. In fact, in regard to Japanese poetry, which both men and women wrote, women could be the teachers of men, as well as the transmitters of the poetic lineage of a house, which in some cases was largely matrilineal. At one level, then, in terms of writing in the vernacular, there was in Heian Japan no "nom/non de père."

Modern characterizations of women's writing in this period, however, have portrayed it not just as a "room of their own" but as an entire country, with border defenses reminiscent of the now-fallen Berlin Wall. For a man to write prose in the vernacular, we are told, was déclassé, virtually slumming, and he was likely to hide behind a female persona when doing it (as we shall see, this has also been called "literary cross-dressing"); or such writing by men was done for pedagogic purposes, and their intended audience was not other men but girls and women in need of educating. More important, we are told that women were virtually forbidden to learn that "father script," Chinese—that those few who did were thought unfeminine, and the smarter of them did their best to hide their knowledge.

In English this view of women and Chinese letters was presented most memorably by Arthur Waley, in his introduction to the third volume ("A Wreath of Cloud") of his translation of *The Tale of Genji* (1927), in which he gives a brief biography of the author. The very first anecdote he relates comes from her *Diary (Murasaki Shikibu nikki)*:

> "When my brother Nobunori (the one who is now in the Board of Rites) was a boy my father was very anxious to make a good Chinese scholar of him, and often came himself to hear Nobunori read his lessons. On these occasions I was always present, and so quick was I at picking up the language that I was soon able to prompt my brother whenever he got stuck. At this my father used to sigh and say to me: 'If only you were a boy how proud and happy I should be.' But it was not long before I repented of having thus distinguished myself; for person after person assured me that even boys generally become very unpopular if it is discovered that they are fond of their books. For a girl, of course, it would be even worse; and after this I was careful to conceal the fact that I could write a single Chinese character."[8]

Yet, Waley tells us, "The Empress had a secret desire to learn Chinese." It is here that Waley gives a characterization of Chinese that sounds like something out of a Wild West show:

The study of this language was considered at the time far too rough and strenuous an occupation for women. There were no grammars or dictionaries [there were, as we shall see], and each horny sentence had to be grappled and mastered like an untamed steer. That Akiko [the Empress] should wish to learn Chinese must have been as shocking to Michinaga [her father, and Regent] as it would have been to Gladstone if one of his daughters had wanted to learn boxing.[9]

I am at a loss to explain where Waley got such imagery: I know of no text from the Heian period, in Japanese or Chinese, that compares the learning of Chinese, whether by men or women, to cattle wrangling—one is reminded of the "muscular Christians" of the nineteenth century, which is the source, of course, along with Gladstone and boxing, for most of Waley's imagery and preconceptions.

The *Tosa nikki* as a "Bisexual" Text

We shall return to Murasaki Shikibu's *Diary* at the end of this essay. For the present, our concern is with how nineteenth- and twentieth-century European notions of gender distinctions have been overlaid onto the Heian court. The topic is a complicated one, having to do with the gendering in modern thought of the entire Heian period as "feminine," and I must postpone much of the discussion until another time. For our purposes here, we can turn our attention to another text that is used, along with the passage from Murasaki Shikibu's *Diary* just quoted, as the *locus classicus* for establishing the near-total exclusion of Heian women from Chinese letters. This text is the *Tosa Diary* of Ki no Tsurayuki, written in 936. The well-known first sentence of this text reads:

wotoko mo su niki to ifu mono wo womuna mo shite mimu tote suru nari.

[I intend to see what happens when a woman does one of those "day-records" such as men are said to do.]

This sentence would seem to imply that women in 936 did not "do diaries *(niki su),*" which were written by men in Chinese. In fact, however, we know this to be false. The oldest extant evidence of a Japanese woman's *nikki* is passages from a work called the *Taikō nikki,* or *Tenryaku taikō gyo-nikki* (The Tenryaku Empress's diary), of Fujiwara Onshi, the chief consort of Emperor Daigo (r. 897–930). The fragmentary passages appear in a fourteenth-century commentary to *The Tale of Genji*, the *Kakaishō*. In fact, the passages exist in both a *kana* form in the *Kakaishō* and a Chinese form in the virtually contemporaneous *Saikyūki*, the diary of Daigo's son, Minamoto Taka'akira (914–982).[10] At one time it was believed that the Chinese represented the record of a later hand, while the *kana* version was by the empress herself. But as Kawaguchi Hisao has argued, because these entries record the birth of a prince to the empress, and the gifts received on that occasion, we must expect that someone of the empress's station had people who would record these things for her. Kawaguchi points out that two (male) clerks, or secretaries *(shijō)*, were attached to the Empress's Office, and it would have been such men who would have made the Chinese record at the time. Kawaguchi continues:

> Moreover, there were also ladies-in-waiting similar to female archives-keepers *(jo-kurando)* or female scholars *(hakase no myōbu [joshi])* in the Empress's Office and, like the female scribes *(jokan no funzukasa)* who waited upon the Emperor, it is thought that they took charge of the brushes and ink. So, we can imagine that there were cases where they would have re-written in *kana* the diaries of daily events recorded by the (male) secretaries, and there were also probably occasions when an *Empress's Diary (Taikō nikki)* was written in *kana* by such ladies-in-waiting independently [of any previous Chinese record].[11]

In other words, there were female members of the bureaucracy who would translate Chinese documents into Japanese, as well as keep factual records in Japanese. The situation in regard to Chinese, then, might be seen as analogous to that of property: just as women could receive and transmit property but not amass it or acquire new property, so too some women could read and transmit, that is, translate, Chinese. But as will become evident in more detail below, there seem to be fewer cases of their composing new documents in Chinese.

The earliest extant entries from Onshi's *nikki* are dated 928. However, even earlier *nikki* written by women—though in Japanese—exist, specifically, accounts by Lady Ise (Ise no Go) of poetry contests in 913 and 921. These accounts are called *nikki* in the late Heian compendium of poetry contests, the *Nijikkan-bon*, edited by Minamoto Masazane (d. 1127). As Katagiri Yōichi has noted, *"nikki"* here means *tōjitsu no kiroku*[12] (a record of the day), which of course is the same usage as in the *Taikō nikki*. In any event, Ise's record of the two poetry contests details who attended, what costumes the participants wore, who served in what function, and, of course, what poems were presented and which won in each round. Despite the basic reportage format, however, a clear sense of the recorder herself is found in occasional comments and asides, such as:

> The *suhama* of the Right team was carried in by four women. They looked graceful enough, but I thought that as a team they were less interesting than the other. Their poems were engraved on the floating leaves of lotus flowers, which were made of silver.[13]

We have, then, at least two examples of *nikki* prior to the pronouncement of Tsurayuki's fictional female narrator. What are we to make of the contradiction? Recent readings by Anglophone scholars of this text describe it as "bisexual," "transvestite," and "cross-dressing" in its mixture of Japanese and Chinese linguistic forms—for comic ends, according to one,[14] and for revolutionary (i.e., protofeminist) purposes, according to the other.[15] That is, these scholars identify genre not only with gender but with language as well, and they assume that in 936 the *nikki* genre was defined by the exclusively male sex of its authors and the Chinese language in which it was written. Under these conditions, the *Tosa Diary* represents a "transvestite" act not just in the male Tsurayuki's assumption of a female persona but also in the writing of a *nikki* in Japanese rather than Chinese. Consequently, both scholars precede their discussion of Tsurayuki's text with a reaffirmation of the near-total separation of Chinese and Japanese writing based on gender distinctions. In Thomas Harper's words: "Women were supposed *not* to write Chinese, or even to know Chinese."[16] It is, of course, only with such firmly delineated distinctions between "male" and "female" writing that one can then speak of a text as "gender-bending," "bisexual," or "transvestite."

It is not my purpose here to offer an interpretation of the *Tosa Diary* as a whole. I would simply remark that modern scholars are too quick to read all distinctions as based on gender rather than class. Tsurayuki's fictional narrator is clearly not a woman of the class to serve in the court of an emperor or empress, and it is unlikely that someone of her rank would know of the diaries kept by the ladies-in-waiting there. In judging the accuracy of this narrator's statements, then, we must take into account the limitations imposed on her not only by her supposed gender but also by her indicated class.

Heian Women's Knowledge of Chinese

Some women, then, did in fact keep *nikki*. I would also argue that, far from being discouraged to learn Chinese, in certain conditions some women were positively required to know Chinese, and many did. Below are a few examples I have stumbled upon over the years.

• We can start with the Kamo Priestess Princess Uchiko (807–847), who composed a Chinese poem when her father, Emperor Saga, visited the shrine in 823. The poem is included in both the *Zoku Nihon kōki* and the *Nihon shiki*.[17]

• In the early tenth century we have Lady Ise again, a contemporary of Tsurayuki. Lady-in-waiting to Empress Onshi and sometime lesser consort to Emperor Uda, she was the most famous female poet of her day. Among her *Collected Poems* is a set of ten written for an illustrated version of Po Chü-i's "Song of Never-ending Sorrow" (Chinese, *Ch'ang-hen ko*; Japanese, *Chōgonka*). The pictures appear to have been painted on a set of screens, with the words of the Chinese poem inscribed on cartouches affixed to the screens. Ise's poems would also have been attached to the screen.[18] Her poems are not based solely on the pictures, however; each of the ten verses is related to specific lines of the original Chinese poem. This is hardly surprising, as such *kudai waka,* or Japanese poems composed on lines of Chinese verse, were popular in Uda's day—we also have compositions in this genre by Ōe Chisato.[19] The first five of Ise's poems are, additionally, composed in a male persona, that is, in the voice of the bereaved Emperor Hsüan Tsung. The first poem reads:

momiji-ba ni	They fall so that they
iro mie-wakazu	cannot be distinguished from
chiru mono ha	the scarlet leaves—
mono-omofu aki no	my autumn tears, blood-red
namida narikeri	with thoughts of you.[20]

This poem is clearly meant to respond to the following words of the original poem that it was no doubt inscribed next to:

廻看涙血相和流 [21]

[When he looked back, it was with tears of blood that mingled in their flow.][22]

Obviously the picture would not have visualized the blood-red tears/ autumn leaves metaphor.

Poem Three, as follows,

kaherikite	Coming back,
kimi omohoyuru	longing for you
hachisuba ni	—on the lotus leaves,
namida no tama to	just like my tears—
okiwite zo miru	I gaze at the dewdrops.

corresponds to

帰来池苑皆依旧
太液芙蓉未央柳

[Returned home now, and the ponds, the pools, all were as before—
The lotuses of Grand Ichor Pool, the willows by the Night-is-Young
    Palace.]

with the first words of the poem providing a Japanese reading for the
first two characters of the first line (that is, *kaherikite*). Poem Four, as
follows,

kurenawi ni	The unswept garden
harahanu niha ha	has become completely
narinikeri	crimson
kanashiki koto no	It is only my sad words,
ha nomi tsumorite	like leaves, that accumulate.

clearly corresponds to the lines:

西宮南内多秋草
落葉階満紅不掃

[The West Palace and the Southern Interior were rife with autumn
    grasses,
And fallen leaves covered the steps, their red not swept away.]

In all these cases, the poems seem linguistically close enough to the
wording of the Chinese, and sufficiently independent of any probable
pictorialization to suggest that Ise was literate to some extent in
Chinese.

• The *Takamura monogatari*, whose first section is thought to be contemporaneous with Sei Shōnagon, starts with a mother and father who
employ the man's son by a different wife to teach their daughter Chinese.
The text explains: "her parents hoped that she would become an imperial Handmaid, so they taught her Chinese."[23]

• Indeed, it is apparent that some ability in Chinese writing was necessary for a woman who wished for certain official positions at court. We have already read about women who served in the Empress's Office. Likewise, there was the Handmaid's Office (Naishi no Tsukasa), which served the emperor. The three principal offices were Principal Handmaid (Naishi no Kami), Assistant Handmaid (Naishi no Suke), and Handmaid (Naishi no Jō, or simply Naishi).[24] While the first two of these offices became no more than positions for concubines early in the Heian period, Naishi no Jō continued to execute the principal responsibilities of the office, which included conveying imperial edicts *(shōsho)* and rescripts *(chokusho)* to the officers of the court. When such imperial commands were conveyed in writing, they were known as *naishi-sen* and were written in Chinese by the Handmaids. These documents did not come to be written in Japanese (when they were then known as *nyōbō sōsho*) until the *insei* period of Retired Emperor Gotoba (1180–1239).[25] In fact, the office of the Handmaid and its duties had been adopted from the Chinese, and such female functionaries performed the same office in the Tang court.[26] Before the invention of *kana* in the late 800s, all writing was in Chinese graphs, and examples of Chinese holographs by women such as Empress Kōmyō (701–760) are still extant.[27]

• In the historical *Tale of Flowering Fortunes (Eiga monogatari),* we read the following about Fujiwara Michitaka's wife, Kishi: "For one of her sex, she handled Chinese characters with remarkable facility, and thus she had become a Handmaid in the Handmaid's Office. . . ."[28] Note that although it is clear that the degree of Kishi's skill is considered unusual for a woman, it is also what qualifies her for a position at court that was reserved for women. And *The Great Mirror (Ōkagami,* ca. 1119), another historical work written in Japanese, gives the following succinct biography of her: "Even the women in Naritada's family are learned. Kishi, the mother of Michitaka's daughters, is the lady everyone knows as Kō no naishi . . . She is a serious Chinese poet. She participated in Emperor Ichijō's Chinese poetry parties, and her compositions outshone the perfunctory efforts of certain gentlemen."[29] In fact, Kishi was the mother of Emperor Ichijō's first empress, Sadako (Teishi), who was in turn Sei Shōnagon's mistress.

• Likewise, in the *Pillow Book* of Sei Shōnagon itself we read of the following episode:

On the last day of the Second Month, . . . a man from the Office of Grounds came to the Black Door and asked to speak to me. He then approached and gave me a note which he said was from Kintō, the Imperial Adviser. It consisted of a sheet of pocket-paper on which was written,

| [*sukoshi haru aru*] | And for a moment in my heart |
| [*kokochi koso sure*] | I feel that spring has come. |

The words were most appropriate for the weather; but what concerned me was that I was bound to produce the opening lines. . . . The man from the Office of Grounds urged me to hurry; and I realized that if, in addition to bungling my reply, I was slow about it, I should really disgrace myself. "It can't be helped," I thought and, trembling with emotion, wrote the following lines:

[*sora samumi*]	As though pretending to be blooms
[*hana ni magahete*]	The snow flakes scatter in the
[*chiru yuki ni*]	wintry sky.

I handed my poem to the messenger and anxiously wondered how Kintō and the others would receive it. If their verdict was unfavourable I would rather not hear it, I thought as I eagerly awaited the news.

It turned out that the Captain of the Middle Palace Guards (who at the time held the rank of Middle Captain of the Inner Palace Guards) was present when my answer arrived, and he told me that Toshikata, the Imperial Adviser, gave the following judgement: "After this she deserves to be appointed to the Palace Attendants' Office."[30]

What Ivan Morris's translation fails to make clear is that both Kintō's lines and Sei's are based on a poem by Po Chü-i, "Snow in Southern Shenshi," with the lines:

> At three o'clock the clouds are chilly and let fly
> much snow;
> In the Second Month, the mountains are cold and
> Spring scarce;
> I think about the past, and still regret my
> disappointments.[31]

In other words, Sei immediately recognizes the Chinese poem that Kintō is paraphrasing in Japanese and caps the verse of his Japanese poem based on the same Chinese verse. It is due to this demonstration of her erudition in Chinese that Toshikata declares that she should be appointed to the Handmaids' Office.

• Another example from the *Pillow Book:* "Towards the end of the

Second Month it rained a great deal and time hung on my hands . . . by the time I went to the Empress's apartments I found that she had already retired for the night. The ladies-in-waiting on duty were in a group near the veranda; they had drawn up a lamp and were playing a game of parts."[32] "Parts" *(hen-tsugi)* seems to have been played in two ways. One was to give a *tsukuri,* or phonetic, element and then compete to see who could add the most radicals to come up with legitimate words. The other method was to choose an ideograph within a Chinese poem, to cover the radical, and to have people try to guess the correct radical based on context.[33] In other words, in this latter case, the women were reading Chinese poems, and at the least they were playing a guessing game based on Chinese characters. There is nothing in Sei's description of this scene that suggests that it was in any way unusual or exceptional. Indeed, the game is also mentioned as played by women in the late Heian–early Kamakura romance, the *Ariake no wakare monogatari.*

• Finally, there is the whole area of women and religion. The Buddhist scriptures were in Chinese, and common forms of devotion entailed chanting these sutras, as well as copying them out—practices that women fully participated in. As added evidence, we have the religious poetry of Senshi, Daisai'in, or the "Great Kamo Priestess" (964–1035). Her *Hosshin wakashū* (Collection of Japanese poems for the awakening of faith, 1012), is another example of *kudai waka,* in which she has composed fifty-five poems on specific lines of the *Lotus Sutra.* As Edward Kamens writes: "Senshi's treatment of the quotations used as *dai* for the *Hosshin wakashū* poems does suggest that she read Chinese well, so perhaps she (like her forerunner Uchiko, skilled in both Chinese and Japanese) had been trained to write it, too."[34]

• We might also mention the visual evidence of the somewhat later *Heike nōkyō* (1164). It is widely recognized that the *Lotus Sutra* was felt to be especially meaningful to women in the period, promising as it did the possibility of enlightenment without, for all intents and purposes, having to be reborn first as a man. The graphic ecstasy of this promise is movingly portrayed in "The Previous Lives of Medicine King Bodhisattva" *(Yakuō-bon)* frontispiece, where a woman's upturned face is illumined by the beneficent rays of the Buddha, while between them the words of the *Lotus Sutra* are inscribed (in a mixture of *kanji* and *kana*):

The woman who hears this sutra and acts according to the teachings of it . . . will [immediately] be able to be reborn, after her life

in this world . . . on the jewelled seat in the lotus flower bloom-
ing in the World of Happiness where Amitāyus Buddha lives surrounded by great Bodhisattvas.[35]

Such an image is hard to imagine if we suppose that all the women of
the day were unable to read the words of the sutra itself.

This, then, is some of the evidence we have to weigh against the
Tosa Diary and a cursory reading of Murasaki Shikibu's *Diary.* Clearly,
the injunction against women's reading Chinese was nowhere as strong
or explicit as modern scholars would have it. In fact, it appears that
literacy in Chinese was actually expected of some women, such as the
women who held official positions at court.

This is not meant to deny, however, that women were less than full
participants in the world of Chinese letters. After Uchiko, there seems
to have been a slow erosion and a gradual disenfranchisement of
women from Chinese at court. This is hardly surprising and is based
on the more fundamental disenfranchisement of women from direct
political power, itself based on the thoroughly patriarchal nature of
imported Chinese political philosophy, especially Confucianism. With
the establishment of the *ritsuryō* state, women were excluded from all
political office, except for a very few specific positions, as we have seen.
And as Wakita Haruko has pointed out, although women in the Heian
period could inherit property and even bequeath it to their daughters,
this was essentially a holding action, because women, excluded from
political office, could not accrue new property.[36] As I have suggested,
the situation seems to have been somewhat analogous in Chinese
letters, where women could read and translate but seem to have less
commonly written new Chinese compositions, at least of the belles
lettres variety. Chinese was, undeniably, the language of government,
used by men holding posts and positions to which no woman could
apply. In other words, Chinese was without a doubt "the Law of the
Father," the language tied to the Symbolic, and thoroughly phallocentric (if not phallogocentric). It was something given by the Father,
and its recognized appropriate recipient was the Son. How, then, did
Sei and Murasaki respond to *this* "literary paternity," that is, the paternity of Chinese?

This disenfranchisement was not, of course, solely a linguistic matter,
for with Chinese came an entire culture of historiography, philosophy,
and literature. Women writers of the Heian period faced the danger

of being denied any but the most mediated and diluted access to this rich body of knowledge, and the explicit resistance to this disenfranchisement is a dominant leitmotif in Sei's *Pillow Book.*

The Function of Chinese Letters in Sei's *Pillow Book*

Sei Shōnagon is believed to have been the daughter of Kiyowara Motosuke (908–990). He held a number of governmental appointments in the Treasury and Home Office, as well as serving as the Provisional Governor of Kawachi, and Governor of Suō and, later, Higo. More important, he was one of the Five Gentlemen of the Pear Chamber *(Nashitsubo no gonin),* a group of scholars working under Fujiwara Koremasa, who both compiled the second imperially commissioned anthology of Japanese poetry, the *Gosenshū,* and attempted to work out readings for the eighth-century Japanese poetry collection, the *Man'yōshū,* the complicated orthography of which was no longer fully understood. His colleagues were Minamoto Shitagō, Ōnakatomi Yoshinobu, Ki no Tokifumi, and Sakanoe Mochiki, all recognized men of learning, especially Shitagō, who compiled one of the first Chinese-Japanese dictionaries in Japan, the *Wamyōshō* (ca. 931–937; we will recall that Waley denied the existence of such works).

In her *Pillow Book,* Sei never mentions her mother, and she refers to her father, Motosuke, only once, when she uses his literary fame as an excuse not to write herself. Yet, interestingly, it is not Motosuke's fame in Chinese to which she is referring but his reputation as a *waka* poet. Sei is talking to the Empress:

"I have decided to give up writing poetry for good and all. If each time there is a poem to be composed you call on me to do it, I don't see how I can remain in Your Majesty's service. After all, I don't even know how to count the syllables correctly. How can I be expected to write winter poems in the spring and spring poems in the autumn and poems about chrysanthemums when the plum blossoms are in bloom? I realize that there have been many poets in my family, and of course it's a great satisfaction if one of my verses turns out well and people say, 'Of everything written on that day Shōnagon's was the best. But that's what one would expect considering who her father was.' The trouble is that I have no particular talent and, if I push myself forward and turn out some doggerel as though I thought it were a masterpiece, I feel I am disgracing the memory of my ancestors."

I was speaking quite seriously, but the Empress laughed and said, "In that case you must do exactly as you wish. I shan't ask you to write any more poems."

Late one evening, not long after this incident, His Excellency the Minister of the Centre, Korechika, who was making elaborate preparations for the Night of the Monkey, gave out subjects on which the Empress's ladies-in-waiting were to write poems. They were all very excited and eagerly set themselves to the task. Meanwhile I stayed with the Empress and talked to her about various things. Presently Korechika caught sight of me. "Why don't you join the others and write a poem?" he asked. "Pick your subject."

"Her Majesty has excused me from poetry," I said, "and I don't have to worry about such things any more."

"How odd!" said Korechika. "I can hardly believe that she would allow that. Very well, you may do as you like at other times, but please write something tonight."

But I did not pay the slightest attention. When the poems of the other women were being judged, the Empress handed me the following little note:

> Surely it is not you—
> You whom we know as Motosuke's heir—
> That will be missing from this evening's round of verse.

I laughed delightedly and, when Korechika asked me what had happened, I replied with this verse:

> Were I not known to be the daughter of that man,
> I should have been the very first
> To pen a poem for this night of verse.

And I added to Her Majesty that, if my father were anyone else, I should have written a thousand poems for her without even waiting to be asked.[37]

And in fact, very little of Sei's Japanese verse survives—her literary reputation rests on her prose.

Even in this passage, Sei's supposedly competitive nature would seem to shine forth: rather than being judged with the other ladies-in-waiting, she seeks the higher recognition that a private joke with the Empress affords. She is also clearly reluctant to compete with her father and yields the field to him when it comes to Japanese verse (Motosuke is in fact counted among the Thirty-six Poetic Immortals).

But if Sei shies away from competing with her father over *waka,* she positively goes out of her way to compete with other men in their knowledge of Chinese. Early in her work we are presented with the following incident between Sei and Senior Steward Taira Narimasa:

> "Well, well," said I, "you really are a disgraceful man! Why do you live in a house with such narrow gates?"
>
> "I have built my house to suit my station in life," he laughingly replied.
>
> "That's all very well," I said, "but I seem to have heard of someone who built his gate extremely high, out of all proportion to the rest of his house."
>
> "Good heavens!" exclaimed Narimasa. "How remarkable! You must be referring to Yü Ting-kuo. I thought it was only veteran scholars who had heard about such things. Even I, Madam, should not have understood you except that I happen to have strayed in these paths myself."[38]

(A similar situation was chosen for illustration in the *hakubyō Makura no sōshi emaki,* captioned by Morris as "Shōnagon Makes an Impressive Allusion to Chinese Literature.")

Sei's Chinese references can be divided into three types, based on who her interlocutor is. First, there are those references she makes "to herself," that is, when her display is only for the sake of her readers. These references most often appear in her famous lists, and we can subdivide them into those that depend on the knowledge of some historical or literary Chinese incident (which might not depend on Sei's knowing how to read Chinese) and those that depend on the knowledge of Chinese graphs. An example of the former would be an episode when Sei visited Bodai Temple, which concludes: "I had been truly moved by the ceremony and felt that I could remain forever in the temple. So must Hsiang Chung have felt when he forgot about the people who were impatiently awaiting him at home."[39] An example of the latter would be the list on "Words That Look Commonplace but That Become Impressive When Written in Chinese Characters."[40]

The second type of Chinese references are those such as the one with Narimasa given above, where Sei seems intent on displaying her knowledge to the men about her, insisting that such knowledge is not the sole prerogative of their sex. It is tempting to see this display as part of Sei's somewhat aggressive nature; indeed Morris remarks that "[h]er attitude to men, even to those of a somewhat higher class than hers, was competitive to the point of overt hostility."[41] This is the same passage in which he remarks that "her adoration of the Imperial family w[as] so pronounced as to seem almost pathological." In fact, I believe that both these observations are mistaken and derive equally from the common misreading of Sei's work as first and foremost a personal testament, rather than as primarily a work of political propaganda.

The Yōrō Code adopted from China specified that an emperor was to have only one empress. As McCullough and McCullough note, this "rule survived until 1000 A.D., when it became a casualty of the rivalry between Michitaka's house and Michinaga's,"[42] that is, between Michinaga's daughter Shōshi (Akiko) and Michitaka's Teishi (Sadako). Shōshi entered court on 11.1.999 and Teishi died in childbirth on 12.16.1000. In other words, there must have been intense competition between the two salons for almost fourteen months. Yet even before this, after Michitaka's death on 4.10.995, Michinaga engineered the exile of Michitaka's son Korechika the following year. Competition between brothers of the Regents' House was deadly earnest.

Yet, as I have attempted to show in a number of articles,[43] following the work of Yamaguchi Hiroshi and others, Sei's *Pillow Book* and Murasaki Shikibu's *Genji* were only the greatest works in a longish line of literary projects sponsored by the Regents' House, with its competing siblings, starting arguably with the second imperial anthology, the *Gosenshū,* and taking more obvious form with the posthumous poetry collection of Morosuke. The longest entry in the *Pillow Book* is an account of the Full Reading of the Canon at Shakuzen Temple in the Second Month of 994[44] suggesting very much that Sei was commissioned to record this event. As if to confirm this, some time after the Eighth Month of the same year Sei tells us that she was given a great deal of paper from the Empress—paper left over from the Emperor's commissioning of a copy of *The Records of the Grand Historian.* As I have suggested previously, it takes little stretch of the imagination to see Sei's work as designed to be the contemporary, Japanese, and "feminine" pendant to the famous Chinese historical work.[45] In other words, her task was to record the splendors of Michitaka's daughter-empress. This task would have taken on only greater poignancy when Sei rewrote her memoirs after Teishi's death, now as a memorial to her deceased mistress.

We can see Sei's *Pillow Book,* then, as part record of cultural splendor (realizing that such splendor was understood as the result of proper governing), part propaganda against the rival claims of Michi-naga and Shōshi, and part memorial for the vanquished and deceased Michitaka and Teishi. And it is within this context that we should return to the examples of women literate in Chinese that I gave earlier. For among them we can point out the particular prominence of Michitaka's wife, Kishi, the mother of Teishi. Michitaka was obviously proud of his wife's learning, and this learning was clearly passed on to their empress-daughter: the third type of episode in which Sei displays her own Chinese learning is where her primary interlocutor is Teishi, and these episodes serve to show off Teishi's knowledge of Chinese as well. The most famous of such incidents comes near the end of the *Pillow Book:*

> One day, when the snow lay thick on the ground and it was so cold that the lattices had all been closed, I and the other ladies were sitting with Her Majesty, chatting and poking the embers in the brazier.
>
> "Tell me, Shōnagon," said the Empress, "how is the snow on Hsiang-lu peak?"
>
> I told the maid to raise one of the lattices and then rolled up the blind all the way. Her Majesty smiled. I was not alone in recognizing the Chinese poem she had quoted; in fact all the ladies knew the lines and had even rewritten them in Japanese. Yet no one but me had managed to think of it instantly.
>
> "Yes indeed," people said when they heard the story. "She was born to serve an Empress like ours."[46]

The point is that to Michitaka's camp, their ladies' knowledge of Chinese was just further evidence that they were the proper custodians of the imperial power, providing such a qualified empress as Teishi and such learned ladies-in-waiting as Sei Shōnagon. In fact, the very reason Shōshi, Teishi's competitor, wanted Murasaki Shikibu to teach her Po Chü-i's poetry was as a means of "educating the womb" *(taikyō),* in the apparently common belief that her fetus (the future Emperor Goichijō) would absorb her learning.[47] At the same time, such knowledge could not appear bookish and was balanced, indeed set off, by the erotic tension that surrounded it. There is little one-upsmanship among the women in regard to their knowledge of Chinese—the opponent is always a member of the opposite sex. Sei demonstrates her knowledge of the Chinese classics but always uses this knowledge for the seeming purpose of coquetry, thus preserving her "femininity."

It is, in turn, against this backdrop that we must understand Murasaki Shikibu's pronouncements on both Sei and women's knowledge of Chinese. One could imagine that the skillful combination of erudition and sexual allure that Sei had devised would have been hard to compete with on its own terms. And indeed, Murasaki does not try. Rather, she denigrates the display of that knowledge, avows her own ignorance, and all the while subtly leaves no doubt about her command of Chinese.

Murasaki and the Aristocratic Denigration of Chinese Learning

Murasaki's attack on Sei is well known, but it is necessary to see it in context. First, Murasaki's criticism flows from her praise for another woman, Akazome Emon, called here Masahira Emon. Let us take the whole passage:

> The wife of the Governor of Tanba is known to everyone in the service of Her Majesty and His Excellency [Michinaga] as Masahira Emon. She may not be a genius but she has great poise and does not feel that she has to compose a poem on everything she sees merely because she is a poet. From what I have seen, her work is most accomplished, even her occasional verse. People who think so much of themselves that, at the drop of a hat, they compose lame verses that only just hang together or produce the most pretentious compositions imaginable are quite odious and rather pathetic.
>
> Sei Shōnagon, for instance, was dreadfully conceited. She thought herself so clever, and littered her writings with Chinese characters, but if you examined them closely, they left a great deal to be desired. Those who think of themselves as being superior to everyone else in this way will inevitably suffer and come to a bad end, and people who have become so precious that they go out of their way to be sensitive in the most unpromising situations, trying to capture every moment of interest, however slight, are bound to look ridiculous and superficial.[48]

And yet Sei is the one—and not Murasaki Shikibu—who is accused by scholars of being competitive![49] The first thing to note is that Akazome Emon is best known as the reputed author of the majority of the vernacular history *Eiga monogatari* (A tale of flowering fortunes), a point to which I will return below. Regarding Sei, it is perhaps too obvious to require remarking that Murasaki Shikibu's criticism of Sei's

Chinese presupposes a greater knowledge of the subject than Sei herself had. Finally, while we know that Sei in fact avoided writing poetry to some extent, Murasaki's criticism can be seen as rejection not only of Sei but of the entire "genre" that her *Pillow Book* represents.

It is immediately after this entry that Murasaki returns to the auto-biographical mode, still following a Chinese thread:

> I remember how in the cool of the evening I used to play the koto to myself, rather badly. . . . There is also a pair of large cupboards crammed full to bursting point. One is full of old poems and tales . . . the other is full of Chinese books which have lain unattended ever since he who carefully collected them passed away [i.e., her father]. Whenever my loneliness threatens to overwhelm me, I take out one or two of them to look at. But my women gather together behind my back. "It's because she goes on like this that she is so miserable. What kind of lady is it who reads Chinese books?" they whisper. "In the past it was not even the done thing to read the sutras!" "Yes," I feel like replying, "but I've never seen anyone who lived longer just because they obeyed a prohibition!"[50]

Here we should note that Murasaki has provided herself a filial excuse for reading Chinese—it reminds her of her father. And again, we should take note of the class difference between a lady-in-waiting like Murasaki, and her own ladies-in-waiting at home: the latter did not read Chinese, but neither did they show their faces to unrelated men, as women in service were required to do. There was a large gulf between the acceptable behavior of court women *(nyōbō)* and that of sequestered "house women" *(ie no onna)*.

Murasaki's final reference to Chinese letters immediately precedes her reminiscence about her brother's lessons that we quoted earlier:

> There is a woman called Saemon no Naishi, who, for some strange reason, took a dislike to me, I cannot think why. I heard all sorts of malicious rumors about myself.
>
> His Majesty was listening to someone reading the *Tale of Genji* aloud. "She must have read the *Chronicles of Japan!*" he said. "She seems very learned." Saemon no Naishi heard this and apparently jumped to conclusions, spreading it abroad among the senior courtiers that I was flaunting my learning. She gave me the nickname Our Lady of the Chronicles. How utterly ridiculous! Would I, who hesitate to reveal my learning in front of my women at home, ever think of doing so at court?[51]

It is, as I mentioned above, immediately after this that Murasaki relates the incident about her brother's lessons, and then that she was tutoring the Empress in the poetry of Po Chü-i.

How are we to explain this seemingly conflicted attitude of Murasaki Shikibu toward Chinese learning? The common explanation, as we have seen, is to attribute this ambivalence to her gender, suggesting a conflict between her intellect and her sex. But I believe the explanation lies largely elsewhere. We could also suggest, of course, that Murasaki's hostility toward women displaying their knowledge of Chinese was in direct reaction to Sei Shōnagon. But I believe the hostility toward Chinese learning runs deeper, permeating Shōshi's salon, and is by no means limited to women.

Scholars of Chinese had once been a force to be reckoned with. Under Emperor Uda there had been two serious political crises, the Akō Incident of 888 and the exile of Sugawara Michizane in 901, both pitting members of the Chinese-trained bureaucracy against the Fujiwara and their control of the imperial family. The latter of these two events signaled the complete rout of this alternative power base for members of the imperial family, but the residual sense of threat that the academy represented to the Fujiwara seems to have lingered. Scholars of Chinese learning were now ridiculed and represented as old, fusty, and hidebound. This new image appears as early as the *Utsuho monogatari,* in sections believed to have been written before 967. In that work, Suefusa, an impoverished scholar, is taunted by one of his better-born schoolmates: "I dare say even General Masayori cannot make a fine man like you his son-in-law," and at one point Suefusa attempts to go to the general's mansion in "a shabby old dress uniform . . . and a shabby hat and worn-out straw sandals."[52] Such descriptions are echoed in the *Takamura monogatari,* dating, as suggested earlier, from Sei's time. And of course there is the representation of such doctors of learning in Murasaki's *Tale of Genji,* where they are consistently portrayed as out-of-date, sticklers for details, and out of touch with the real world.

What stands in contrast to such sterile learning is what in the *Ōkagami* will be called *yamato-damashii* (Japanese spirit). These days there seems considerable misunderstanding about the meaning of this term, but in Murasaki's day it indicated a kind of political savvy and almost ruthless common sense that could cut through fusty learning and inconvenient precedents.[53] In fact, it is in *The Tale of Genji* that *yamato-damashii* is presented as the contrastive term to "Chinese learning *(zae),*" where Genji says, in relation to the education of his son Yūgiri: "It is when there is a fund of Chinese learning that the Japanese spirit is respected by the world." In the *Ōkagami* it is Michinaga who is the embodiment of this *yamato-damashii* ideal.[54]

Yet scholars such as Helen McCullough see, on one hand, Genji as the unique combination and balancing of *zae* and *yamato-damashii* while, on the other hand, seeing the celebration of *yamato-damashii* as limited to such male-authored works as the *Ōkagami* and largely missing in such "feminine" texts as the *Genji*.[55] Although Genji no doubt represents an ideal combination of traits (just as he combines imperial lineage with Fujiwara marriage politics, that is, ability with birth), and although we are given no examples of Michinaga's political acumen in Murasaki Shikibu's *Diary,* nonetheless, I believe that it is clear that the Michinaga portrayed in that latter work is still meant to represent an aristocratic ideal. And that ideal, being aristocratic, is antiprofessional, antimeritocratic, and, to some extent, anti-intellectual. McCullough mentions an incident in the *Ōkagami* in which

> Michitaka demonstrates *tamashii* [equivalent to *yamato-damashii*] in another way when, after having fallen into a drunken stupor while en route from one Kamo Shrine to the other, he shows himself "perfectly prepared for that very contingency" by producing grooming aids at his destination, "tidying himself, and stepping down, composed and fresh."[56]

Such behavior is essentially the same as we see in Michinaga through Murasaki's eyes:

> I realized that it was bound to be a terribly drunken affair this evening, so, once the formal celebrations were over, Lady Saishō and I decided to return. We were just about to do so when His Excellency's two sons, Yorimichi and Norimichi, Adviser of the Right Kanetaka, and some other gentlemen started creating a commotion in the eastern gallery. We hid behind the dais, but His Excellency pulled back the curtains and we were both caught.
> "A poem for the Prince!" he cried. "Then I'll let you go!"
> Being in such a quandary, I recited:

ika ni ikaga	How, ah how
kazoeyarubeki	on the fiftieth day
yachitose no	can we possibly count
amari hisashiki	the countless years
kimi ga miyo oba	of our Prince's reign?

"Splendid!" he said, and reciting it twice over to himself, gave a very quick reply:

ashitazu no	If I could live
yowai shi araba	As long as the crane
kimi ga yo no	Then might I count
chitose no kazu mo	How many thousand years
kazoetoritemu	His eternal reign would be.

Even in his inebriated state, he could still think in such terms; I was very impressed.[57]

In her *Diary*—no doubt like Sei's *Pillow Book,* partly a commissioned work (to record the birth of Michinaga's first grandson, the future Emperor Goichijō)—Murasaki portrays Michinaga as an aristocratic ideal, manifesting what in Italian courtly society would have been called *sprezzatura.* As Count Ludovico de Canossa says in Castiglione'*s Book of the Courtier:*

> . . . I have found quite a universal rule which in this matter seems to me valid above all others, and in all human affairs whether in word or deed: and that is to avoid affectation in every way possible as though it were some very rough and dangerous reef; and (to pronounce a new word perhaps) to practice in all things a certain *sprezzatura* [nonchalance], so as to conceal all art and make whatever is done or said appear to be without effort and almost without any thought about it.[58]

In Heian Japan, such an attitude was bound to hold the scholars of Chinese learning in little regard.

The Heian period provides a constantly changing balancing act between a variety of elements. During the *Kokinshū* era, poetry was largely the province of professionals such as Tsurayuki, and those professionals were almost entirely male—Ise no Go is the only female poet of note at the time. The situation changed dramatically in the next generation, when statesmen such as Koremasa were seen to be able to hold their own against essentially professional female poets such as Hon'in no Jijū. Kaneie, too, was an accomplished poet, as we see from the great amount of his poetry included in the *Kagerō Diary,* as well as in imperial anthologies. Yet by Michinaga's day the Fujiwara Regents had returned to a position of being mostly patrons rather than practitioners.

At the same time, there was an ever-changing emphasis on the genres that the powerful patronized. Emperor Uda had promoted poetry contests, whereas almost none seem to have taken place under Michinaga. Official histories, written in Chinese, were also a source of cultural legitimation, but the office responsible for preparing them had been disbanded in 969. In McCullough and McCullough's words: "The cessation of the National History series coincided approximately with the final subordination of the Emperor and his governmental apparatus to the control of the Fujiwara Regents, and one can scarcely doubt that the two developments were related."[59] Instead, by Michinaga's day, a number of vernacular historiographic projects were attempted. These are best exemplified by Akazome Emon's *Tale of Flowering Fortunes* but include Murasaki's *Diary* (part of which is quoted verbatim in *Flowering Fortunes*), as well as Sei's *Pillow Book*. Finally, Saemon no Naishi's nickname for Murasaki as Our Lady of the Chronicles was not far from the mark, as the *Genji* shows a wide knowledge of the Chinese and Japanese historiographic tradition. It was no doubt the very accuracy of the sobriquet that caused Murasaki to react so violently against it.

What we see in Murasaki, then, is not a rejection of Chinese learning, but a way of utilizing and incorporating it that differed from Sei's. Rather than the ostentatious display of learning and the active confrontation with the educated members of the opposite sex, Murasaki, taking her cue to some extent from her patron Michinaga, valorized precisely the discreet use of knowledge and the subtle inclusion of it as subtext rather than as explicit topic.[60]

Thus, there was tension in both Sei and Murasaki in their relationship to the Law of the Father, Chinese. Although Sei was more obviously combative, resisting women's exclusion from what was viewed as the only legitimate source of formal learning, Murasaki Shikibu found a way to, in a sense, domesticate Chinese learning and use it, in Genji's words, as the ground and foundation *(moto)* with which to set off the "Japanese spirit." Her purpose in this was not, it should be added, domestication for the sake of domestication—as art historians used to speak of the "return" to "Japanese" taste in the Heian period, following the massive importation of Chinese culture in the Nara period. Rather, the silent incorporation of Chinese learning into her Japanese work not only deepened her work, but aided her masters by encouraging the disparagement of professional scholars, thus preventing the academy from ever serving again as an oppositional source of authority.

Conclusion

I have tried to demonstrate that in some periods of the Heian era a certain group of women, far from discouraged to learn Chinese, were actually expected to be able at least to read Chinese and that certain positions at court required it. Nonetheless, there does seem to be a gradual disenfranchisement of women from Chinese learning over the course of the Heian period and beyond. But women who read and wrote Chinese can be found throughout Japanese history, such as the Zen abbess Mugai Nyodai (1223–1298),[61] or the female literati *(bunjin)* of the Edo period (1600–1868), such as Ema Saikō.[62] Women's access to and command of Chinese letters varied from period to period, and within single periods according to class and locale. The too-quick application of the metaphor of gender difference to this issue obscures the rich variety of the historical record.

Notes

I was fortunate enough to be able to present working versions of this paper at a number of venues and would like to take this opportunity to thank those institutions and some of the individuals from whose advice and encouragement I have benefited: Prof. G. Cameron Hurst and Ayako Kano of the University of Pennsylvania; Profs. Ivo Smits and Wim Boot, and Ms. Lee Bruschke-Johnson of Leiden University; Profs. Wolfgang Schamoni and Lothar Ledderose of Heidelberg University; Prof. Thomas Harper; and Prof. Timon Screech of SOAS. This essay is dedicated to Tineke Hellwig, with whom I team-taught a course many years ago now entitled "Feminist Literary Criticism and the Eastern 'Other' "— the context in which I first dealt with several of the issues treated here.

1. First published in the *Cornell Review* (1979). An extended and revised version forms the first chapter of *The Madwoman in the Attic,* by Gilbert and Gubar. My source is *Critical Theory since 1965,* ed. Adams and Searle, p. 488.

2. Adams and Searle, *Critical Theory,* p. 489.

3. In Stanton, ed., *The Female Autograph.* Much the same arguments are made in Gilbert and Gubar's "Sexual Linguistics."

4. Gilbert and Gubar, "Ceremonies," p. 22.

5. Katō, *Kanji no Kigen,* p. 253.

6. Gilbert and Gubar, "Ceremonies," p. 23.

7. Ibid., pp. 23, 37.

8. Waley, trans., *Tale of Genji,* p. vii. Hagitani Boku notes that boys started studying the Chinese classics at home around the age of seven; *Murasaki Shikibu nikki zenchūsaku,* vol. 2, p. 299. Nobunori apparently did not graduate from the university *(daigaku)* but entered the bureaucracy in 999 as Lesser Private Secretary (Shōnaiki); Namba, *Murasaki Shikibu shū,* p. 216.

9. Waley, *Tale of Genji*, p. ix.

10. On the *Saikyūki*, see Hérail, *La cour du Japon*, pp. 48–49, 254.

11. Kawaguchi, *Nihon koten bungaku taikei geppō*, p. 8.

12. Katagiri, *Ise, Nihon no sakka* 7, p. 226.

13. "The Kyōgoku Lady Hōshi's Contest of 921" *(Kyōgoku no miyasudokoro no uta-awase),* trans. Itoh, "The Muse in Competition," p. 213.

14. Harper, "Tweetaligheid en bisexualiteit." I am indebted to Prof. Harper for a manuscript of the English translation of this Dutch article, "Bilingualism as Bisexualism." Page references here refer to the published Dutch version.

15. Miyake, *"Tosa Diary."* Note, however, Miyake's qualifying comment on this "much too simplistic model" on p. 69.

16. Harper, "Tweetaligheid en bisexualiteit," p. 191.

17. See Watson, *Japanese Literature*, p. 46.

18. The Heian period screen paintings do not survive. For an example of a later pictorialization, whose relationship to earlier models is unknown, see the picture scroll by Kano Sansetsu (1589–1651), reproduced in Kawaguchi, ed., *Chōgonka emaki.*

19. On Ōe Chisato and *kudai waka*, see McCullough, *Brocade by Night*, pp. 254–256.

20. Sekine and Yamashita, eds., *Ise shū zenshaku*, p. 141.

21. Ishida and Shimizu, eds., *Genji monogatari*, vol. 1, pp. 325–331.

22. Trans. Paul W. Kroll, in Mair, ed., *Columbia Anthology*, pp. 478–485.

23. Hirano, ed., *Ono Takamura shū zenshaku*, pp. 99–101. Trans. Mostow, in *At the House of Gathered Leaves: Shorter Biographical and Autobiographical Narratives from Tenth-Century Japan* (in prep.)

24. McCullough and McCullough, trans., *Flowering Fortunes*, vol. 1, pp. 821–822.

25. Wakita, *Nihon chūsei josei shi no kenkyū*, pp. 246–248. See also Satō, *Komonjogaku nyūmon*, pp. 77–83.

26. Wakita, *Nihon chūsei josei shi no kenkyū*, pp. 16–17.

27. See Maeda, *Nyonin no sho*, pp. 6–12.

28. McCullough and McCullough, *Flowering Fortunes*, vol. 1, p. 137.

29. McCullough, trans., *Ōkagami*, p. 170.

30. Morris, trans., *Pillow Book*, vol. 1, pp. 120–121/135–136. The second page number is from the one-volume abridged edition (Penguin, 1971).

31. Tanaka, ed., *Makura no sōshi*, p. 216. Note that one of Sei's first reactions (deleted from the quotation given) upon receiving Kintō's challenge is to consult with Empress Teishi, an action whose significance will be made clear later in this article.

32. Morris, *Pillow Book*, vol. 1, p. 71/89.

33. Ōno et al., eds., *Iwanami kogo jiten*, s.v. *hen-tsugi.*

34. Kamens, *Buddhist Poetry*, p. 66. See also my review of this work in the *Journal of Asian Studies.*

35. Murano, trans., *Sutra*, p. 278. Quoted by Meech-Pekarik, in "Disguised Scripts," p. 74.

36. Wakita, "Marriage and Property," p. 80.

37. Morris, *Pillow Book*, vol. 1, pp. 110–111/123–125.

38. Ibid., p. 7/27.

39. Ibid., p. 36/55.
40. Ibid., p. 159.
41. Ibid., p. xiv.
42. McCullough and McCullough, vol. 2, pp. 818–819.
43. Mostow, "Japanese *Nikki*," "'Sword-Envy,'" and "The Amorous Statesman."
44. Morris, *Pillow Book,* pp. 219–233/220–235.
45. Mostow, "Political Memoir," p. 113.
46. Morris, *Pillow Book,* p. 243/241–242.
47. Bowring, trans., *Murasaki Shikibu,* p. 138.
48. Ibid., pp. 131–133.
49. For the continual pairing of Murasaki and Sei, see Miyazaki, *Sei Shōnagon to Murasaki Shikibu.* This comparison takes on a particular cast in the modern period, when Sei becomes the classical antecedent for the "new woman" *(atarashii onna)* in Umezawa's *Sei Shōnagon to Murasaki Shikibu.*
50. Bowring, *Murasaki Shikibu,* p. 133. This scene is illustrated in the twelfth-century *Murasaki Shikibu nikki emaki.*
51. Bowring, *Murasaki Shikibu,* pp. 137–139.
52. Kōno, ed., *Utsuho monogatari,* pp. 423–433; Uraki, trans., *Tale of the Cavern,* pp. 159–160.
53. Yamaguchi, *Ōchō kadan no kenkyū,* p. 372.
54. Seidensticker, trans., *Tale of Genji,* p. 362. McCullough (*Ōkagami,* pp. 43–53) gives the Japanese as *zae o moto to shite koso, yamatodamashii no yo ni mochiiraruru kata mo tsuyō haberame.*
55. "This aspect of Heian life [*yamato-damashii* as political savvy] is virtually ignored in *The Tale of Genji, Eiga monogatari,* and other works by female writers, who are notable for their lack of interest in politics." McCullough, *Ōkagami,* p. 45.
56. Ibid., p. 44.
57. Bowring, *Murasaki Shikibu,* pp. 91–93.
58. Castiglione, *Book of the Courtier,* trans. Singleton, p. 43.
59. McCullough and McCullough, vol. 1, p. 6.
60. On the Chinese subtexts of *The Tale of Genji,* see, for example, Tanaka, "Hikaru Genji no Kitayama-kō."
61. On Mugai Nyodai, see Ruch, "The other side of culture," pp. 502–511.
62. Sato, trans., *Breeze through Bamboo.*

Works Cited
Location of Japanese publishers is Tokyo unless otherwise noted.

Adams, Hazard, and Leroy Searle, eds. *Critical Theory since 1965.* Tallahassee: Florida State University Press, 1986.

Bowring, Richard, trans. *Murasaki Shikibu: Her Diary and Poetic Memoirs.* Princeton, N.J.: Princeton University Press, 1982.

Castiglione, Baldassarre. *The Book of the Courtier.* Trans. Charles S. Singleton. New York: Anchor Books, 1959.

Gilbert, Sandra M. "Literary Paternity." In *Critical Theory since 1965,* ed. Hazard

Adams and Leroy Searle, pp. 485–496. Tallahassee: Florida State University Press, 1986.

Gilbert, Sandra M., and Susan Gubar. "Ceremonies of the Alphabet: Female Grandmatologies and the Female Authorgraph." In *The Female Autograph*, ed. Domna C. Stanton, pp. 21–48. Chicago: University of Chicago Press, 1987.

———. *The Madwoman in the Attic: The Woman Writer and the Nineteenth-Century Literary Imagination*. New Haven, Conn.: Yale University Press, 1979.

———. "Sexual Linguistics: Gender Language, Sexuality." *New Literary History* 16 (1985): 515–543.

Hagitani Boku. *Murasaki Shikibu nikki zenchūsaku*. 2 vols. Kadokawa shoten, 1971.

Harper, T. J. "Tweetaligheid en bisexualiteit." In *Literatuur en Tweetaligheid*, ed. W. J. Boot. Leiden, Netherlands: Onderzoekschool CNWS, 1994.

Hérail, Francine. *La cour du Japon à l'époque de Heian aux Xe et XIe siècles*. Paris: Hachette, 1995.

Hirano Yukiko, ed. *Ono Takamura shū zenshaku*. Kazama shobō, 1998.

Ishida Yōji and Shimizu Yoshiko, eds. *Genji monogatari*. 4 vols. *SNKS*. Shinchōsha, 1976.

Itoh, Setsuko. "The Muse in Competition." *Monumenta Nipponica* 37.2 (1982): 201–222.

Kamens, Edward. *The Buddhist Poetry of the Great Kamo Priestess: Daisaiin Senshi and Hosshin Wakashū*. Michigan Monograph Series in Japanese Studies, no. 5. Ann Arbor: Center for Japanese Studies, University of Michigan, 1990.

Katagiri Yōichi. *Ise. Nihon no sakka* 7. Shintensha, 1975.

Katō Jōken. *Kanji no kigen*. Kadokawa shoten, 1970.

Kawaguchi Hisao. *Nihon koten bungaku taikei geppō*. Iwanami shoten, 1957.

———, ed. *Chōgonka emaki*. Taishūkan shoten, 1982.

Kōno Tama, ed. *Utsuho monogatari*. *NKBT* 10. Iwanami shoten, 1959.

Maeda Toshiko. *Nyonin no sho*. Kōdansha, 1974.

Mair, Victor, ed. *The Columbia Anthology of Traditional Chinese Literature*. New York: Columbia University Press, 1994.

McCullough, Helen C., trans. *Brocade by Night: "Kokin wakashū" and the Court Style in Japanese Classical Poetry*. Stanford, Calif.: Stanford University Press, 1985.

———, trans. *Ōkagami, The Great Mirror: Fujiwara Michinaga (966–1027) and His Times*. Princeton, N.J.: Princeton University Press, 1980.

McCullough, Helen C., and William H. McCullough, trans. *A Tale of Flowering Fortunes: Annals of Japanese Aristocratic Life in the Heian Period*. 2 vols. Stanford, Calif.: Stanford University Press, 1980.

Meech-Pekarik, Julia. "Disguised Scripts and Hidden Poems in an Illustrated Heian Sutra: Ashide and Uta-e in the Heike Nōgyō [sic]." *Archives of Asian Art* 31 (1977–1978): 53–78.

Miyake, Lynne K. "*The Tosa Diary:* In the Interstices of Gender and Criticism." In *The Woman's Hand: Gender and Theory in Japanese Women's Writing*, ed. Paul Gordon Schalow and Janet A. Walker, pp. 41–73. Stanford, Calif.: Stanford University Press, 1996.

Miyazaki Sōhei. *Sei Shōnagon to Murasaki Shikibu: sono taihiron josetsu*. Chōbunsha, 1993.

Morris, Ivan, trans. *The Pillow Book of Sei Shōnagon*. 2 vols. New York: Columbia University Press, 1967.

————. *The Pillow Book of Sei Shōnagon.* Abridged ed. Harmondsworth, Middle-sex, England: Penguin Books, 1971.

Mostow, Joshua S. "The Amorous Statesman and the Poetess: The Politics of Autobiography and the *Kagerō nikki.*" *Japan Forum* (Oxford) 4.2 (October 1992): 305–315.

————. "Japanese *Nikki* as Political Memoirs." In *Political Memoir: Essays on the Politics of Memory,* ed. George Egerton, pp. 106–120. London: Frank Cass, 1994.

————. Review of *The Buddhist Poetry of the Great Kamo Priestess: Daisaiin Senshi and Hosshin Wakashū,* by Edward Kamens. *Journal of Asian Studies* 50.1 (August 1991): 691–692.

————. " 'Sword-Envy' in the *Takamitsu nikki* and Its Influence on the *Kagerō nikki.*" Selected Papers in Asian Studies, n.s. 37, Western Conference of the Association for Asian Studies. 1990.

Murano, Senchū, trans. *The Sutra of the Lotus Flower of the Wonderful Law.* Nichiren Shū Headquarters, 1974.

Namba Hiroshi. *Murasaki Shikibu shū.* Iwanami shoten, 1973.

Ōno Susumu et al., eds. *Iwanami kogo jiten.* Iwanami shoten, 1974.

Ruch, Barbara. "The Other Side of Culture in Medieval Japan." In *The Cambridge History of Japan,* ed. Kozo Yamamura, vol. 3, pp. 500–543. Cambridge: Cambridge University Press, 1990.

Sato, Hiroaki, trans. *Breeze through Bamboo: Kanshi of Ema Saikō.* New York: Columbia University Press, 1998.

Satō Shin'ichi. *Komonjo-gaku nyūmon.* Hōsei Daigaku shuppankai, 1971.

Schalow, Paul Gordon, and Janet A. Walker, eds. *The Woman's Hand: Gender and Theory in Japanese Women's Writing.* Stanford, Calif.: Stanford University Press, 1996.

Seidensticker, Edward, trans. *The Tale of Genji.* New York: Knopf, 1976.

Sekine Yoshiko and Yamashita Michiyo, eds. *Ise shū zenshaku.* Kasama shobō, 1996.

Singleton, Charles S., trans. *The Book of the Courtier.* New York: Anchor Books, 1959.

Stanton, Domna C., ed. *The Female Autograph.* Chicago: University of Chicago Press, 1987.

Tanaka Jūtarō, ed. *Makura no sōshi, Nihon koten zensho.* Asahi shinbunsha, 1947.

Tanaka Takaaki, "Hikaru Genji no Kitayama-kō: Wakamurasaki no maki no tōgen-kyō-teki sekai." In *Genji monogatari shii to hyōgen,* pp. 92–112. Shintensha, 1997.

Umezawa K. *Sei Shōnagon to Murasaki Shikibu.* Jitsugyō no Nipponsha, 1913.

Uraki, Ziro, trans. *The Tale of the Cavern.* Shinozaki shoten, 1984.

Wakita Haruko. *Nihon chūsei josei shi no kenkyū.* Tōkyō Daigaku shuppankai, 1992.

————. "Marriage and Property in Premodern Japan from the Perspective of Women's History." Trans. Suzanne Gay. *Journal of Japanese Studies* 10.1 (1984): 73–99.

Waley, Arthur, trans. *The Tale of Genji.* New York: Modern Library, 1960.

Watson, Burton. *Japanese Literature in Chinese.* Vol. 1, *Poetry and Prose in Chinese by Japanese Writers of the Early Period.* New York: Columbia University Press, 1975.

Yamaguchi Hiroshi. *Ōchō kadan no kenkyū: Uda, Daigo, Suzaku-chō Hen.* Ōfūsha, 1978.

Chapter 5

De-siring the Center
Hayashi Fumiko's Hungry Heroines and the Male Literary Canon

JANICE BROWN

I have no teachers. I read, and those writers I like I allow into my heart. Inadvertently they become my teachers.

Hayashi Fumiko, "Itaru tokoro Aoyama ari" (Destination Aoyama)

For a writer who openly denied the traditional teacher-disciple relationship and relied almost completely upon her own experiences as well as those of other lower working-class women to provide the themes and subject matter of her writings, it comes as somewhat of a surprise to find throughout the texts of Hayashi Fumiko (1903–1951) a steady stream of references to and critiques of male writers. In fact, Fumiko's sensitivity to male writers and male texts far outweighs any corresponding regard for female writers and texts. Certainly such bias is observable in the careers of many literary women writing within hegemonic patriarchal social systems. In Japan, however, with its great classical tradition of female writers, such preference might seem less understandable. One might expect most modern women writers, especially those like Fumiko[1] who were instrumental in bringing women's writing to the forefront of modern Japanese letters, to have followed in the footsteps of their illustrious literary foremothers. For Fumiko, however, as for many modern Japanese writing women of the lower social classes, such was not the case.

The works of classical Japanese female writers, obfuscated by generations of male-authored criticism and interpretation, did not speak to women of Fumiko's class or background. Representing an elitist literary order, such texts tended to offer little inspiration to poor and/or working-class women who sought to express the realities of their own experience. Hence, would-be women writers, like Fumiko, often looked not to the classical past but to the contemporary literary scene for their models. In Fumiko's day, this milieu was all but closed to women. Still in the process of assimilating and adapting Western literary modes, methods, and texts, the 1920s Japanese literary establishment was exclusively male-oriented. Male-authored texts dominated contemporary life and thought, whether from Japan or the West, and it is not too surprising that many of Fumiko's early writings were inspired by her reading of these male writers rather than other female models.

At the same time, however, the *extent* of Fumiko's devotion to male writers is surprising, given her unabashed determination to write from the female position. Her reading, moreover, was not limited to Japanese texts but ranged over a great deal of European literature, including works by both major and minor male literary figures. In many instances, Fumiko openly declared her desire to "write like" a number of these male writers. Such admiration apparently continued throughout her life, even after she had become a major Japanese literary figure known for her writing of and about women. Fumiko's desire for the male-authored text can be read as something more than an exercise in apprenticeship to those writers who constituted the male literary canon. She had, in my view, an exceptionally powerful urge not simply to "write like" the male writers but, more important, to write *from their position,* which Fumiko intended to make her own. Impatient with tradition and with entrenched attitudes toward literature and female writers, Fumiko actively and repeatedly worked to place herself, as a woman, and her writings of and about women in a central, commanding position that had hitherto been occupied only by men.

With a view to evaluating Fumiko's keen regard for male writers and their texts as well as the significance of these texts as "models" for Fumiko in her own writings, this chapter will examine those writers who seemed to have had more than ordinary import for Fumiko and who may be said to have "influenced" her work. I will focus first on the anarcho-dadaist male poets; second on *Hunger,* by Knut Hamsun, which Fumiko herself cites as inspirational; and finally on the relationship between Fumiko and one of her mentors, the naturalist writer Tokuda Shūsei. In an attempt to determine how dutiful or undutiful a literary daughter Fumiko may have been, I will include discussion of Fumiko's own writings as they pertain to the male model(s).

I will argue also that much of Fumiko's literary desire connected with male-authored texts has, at its core, a potent awareness of gender and gender-based power relations and, further, that Fumiko, forced to mediate between her femaleness and the literary "male-stream" in which she found herself, frequently attempted to subvert, usurp, or in some way appropriate the dominant male texts, as a means both of resistance and of survival.

Down and Out in Tokyo: Fumiko, the Anarcho-dadaist Poets, and Knut Hamsun

With her diffuse, sprawling *Diary of a Vagabond* (*Hōrōki*, 1928–1930),[2] Fumiko freewheeled her way to fame and fortune, writing of her life as a poverty-stricken poet adrift on the streets of 1920s Tokyo. A mixture of prose and poetry, *Diary of a Vagabond* became one of the most successful best-sellers in Japanese literary history, selling 600,000 copies when it first appeared in a single-volume edition in 1930. The lifestyle extolled by Fumiko in this text seemed to grow naturally from her own life experience: the illegitimate daughter of itinerant peddlers, Fumiko had seldom lived a settled existence. Indeed, her wandering days in Tokyo can certainly be read as an extension of her young life as a peddler girl. At the same time, we still might want to ask, How did this disadvantaged young woman of no background and little education come to produce, at the age of twenty-five, a work of the magnitude of *Diary of a Vagabond,* which appealed equally to the general reader as well as to the literary elite? The answer to this question is complex, but if we limit ourselves to a brief examination of the literary milieu in which Fumiko found herself as well as to one particular text that Fumiko cites as pivotal to her construction of her poetic diary, then we may find some indication of how Fumiko came to write as she did—as a female outsider fascinated by the male text.

Although Fumiko did not come to Tokyo with the intention of starting a literary career (she had her sights set on, among other things, getting married or becoming an actress), she had in fact been writing poetry since about the age of fifteen. Finally, through an introduction from a male actor and sometime poet with whom she lived during her early years in Tokyo, Fumiko, at age 20, came into contact with modernist poetry circles. Her new associates were members of the anarchist and dadaist fringe who gathered in a French restaurant in the Hongō section of Tokyo. Anarchism, one of the dominant sociopolitical theories of Taishō Japan (1912–1925), attracted a wide variety of writers and intellectuals, among them the poets Hagiwara Kyō- jirō (1899–1938), Tsuji Jun (1884–1944), Takahashi Shinkichi (1901– 1986), Okamoto Jun (1901–1978), and Tsuboi Shigeji (1897–1975). By the time of Fumiko's appearance in Tokyo in 1922, these poets had begun to make a name for themselves as innovative and experimental Japanese modernist poets. The designation "anarchist," however, seems to have been applied somewhat loosely, for not all of these poets openly espoused anarchist ideas. Hagiwara Kyōjirō, for example, was a great admirer of the early modernist poet Hagiwara Sakutarō (1886– 1942) and came late to anarchism, whereas Takahashi Shinkichi was a dadaist who turned later to Zen. Tsuboi Shigeji, on the other hand, was instrumental in launching revolutionary diatribes that proclaimed the superiority of anarchist poetry, as in the following exhortation from the anarchist magazine *The Red and the Black (Aka to kuro):* "Be negative! Be negative! Be negative! We shall devote all our energy to negativity!"[3] However, Shigeji would eventually forgo his anarchist con- victions in favor of Marxism. Nonetheless, in the early 1920s these poets saw themselves as engaged in a common task, that is, the remak- ing and revising of poetic language. Hagiwara Kyōjirō, for example, attempted to kill off what he deemed to be old and antiquated in modern Japanese poetry by a decimation of language itself. Kyōjirō's *Death Sentence* (*Shikei senkoku,* 1925), his most acclaimed work, is a monument to linguistic mayhem. Making use of erratic arrangements of letters, words, and phrases, *Death Sentence* sounded the knell for poetic standards as it disintegrated into a bewildering conglomeration of signs and shapes. Resisting reading as well as translation, a brief example from one of the numerous sections of this lengthy poem will give some indication of Kyōjirō's anarchist literary agenda. In the section entitled *Life (Seikatsu),* Kyōjirō declares:

> It's man! It's woman! It's death! It's life!
> ————————— It's a parlor! • • • It's a cemetery!
>   + + + It's a playing card!
> It's an abortion! It's nature! It's a funeral!
> Cogwheel . . . cogwheel . . . cogwheel . . . cogwheel
>   . . . cogwheel . . . cogwheel . . . cogwheel
> a pig sucking its mother's tits!
> Dance! Dance!
> Ahahaha................hahahahaha
> Glory with a woman! Ahahahaha! Ha! Ha!

> Strike hard ——————— əsdɹoɔ corpse!
> It's the destruction of the power of procreation!
> White mask!
> Dance! Dance! Dance![4]

Eventually succumbing to his own verbal barrage, Kyōjirō concludes *Death Sentence* by leaving language behind. With a series of Chinese characters, alphabetic symbols, and typographical marks, *Death Sentence* proclaims its own end, even as it remains a triumph of anarchist poetic assemblage:

> skysky əɔɐɟɹns ——————— P jingle jingle PPPP
>   green light light
>   wireless telegraph sound strength P air
>   splash • jingle
> flower seller • green light
>   - - - -solid body............heavy P snow snow snow
>   • light light
>   jingle car purple light
>   • • • • • pressure PVVV lamp • • • • jingle bell despair[5]

The anarchist poets were Fumiko's first exposure to the modern avant-garde. Through these encounters, particularly with Kyōjirō and Shigeji, she acquired a new poetic perspective and, encouraged by her new confrères, began to read widely in Japanese and foreign literatures. Writing almost every day in her journal, which eventually expanded to include six large notebooks, Fumiko kept a voluminous record of her daily life, including her impressions, thoughts, feelings, and of course, her poems. Making full use of a free-flowing, stream-of-consciousness technique, Fumiko allowed her pen to roam at will. From these notebooks came *Diary of a Vagabond,* a paean to the wild and chaotic literary experiment advocated so ardently by the anarchist poets. Fumiko, however, was to outwrite her mentors. Her seemingly random and haphazard text was never as disjointed as Kyōjirō's poetry and instead gave birth to a powerful female persona that, unlike the narrow, introverted male subjects favored by the anarcho-dadaist poets, shone with vitality, originality, and humor. The following excerpts, in which Fumiko awakes one morning and decides to go for a walk, provide an example:

> The sliding door opened a crack. A young man peeps in. Who are *you?* In confusion he closes the door. This isn't the post office, you know. If you want to sleep with me, just crawl right in.[6]

Here, Fumiko adopts the nihilistic assertiveness espoused by the anar-
chists, yet rather than identifying herself as a revolutionary, she asserts
herself as female and further extends a mock invitation that points
to her body as potential object of male desire. Yet almost at once this
objectification is refused, as Fumiko presents a female body that is
soiled, unclean. She continues:

> I get up without washing my face and go outside. . . . The hot sun
> has begun its climb. There's a public water pipe in front of the
> shipping office. I wash my face there, and then drink, gulping
> down the water in an ecstasy of satisfaction. I dab water onto my
> hair and pat it into place.[7]

The aimlessness and disregard of convention that mark the anarcho-
dadaist male poets are here evoked by Fumiko, yet rather than the
anger and/or resentment that generally accompanies the male texts,
Fumiko chooses to relish her situation. The sheer pleasure she derives
from her experiences is unlike anything we find in writings by her
male colleagues. Fumiko's gesture to 1920s Taishō bohemianism is
made in ways that at all times foreground not only her contentment
with herself as subject but also her desire to place this subject on equal
footing with her male counterparts, as we see as the passage continues:

> Walking impatiently through the fresh morning air, I come to the
> front of the university. In a fruit shop a man is polishing apples.
> The phantom apple I haven't had in my mouth for years is in reality
> shiny red and round. Pears, grapes, figs, there's a smell like the
> dripping of fresh water. *Sayankane, dassa, sayankane, ondabutte, butte,
> onda, rattan dariraaaaa.* . . . This is a poem by Tagore. I don't know
> what it means, but occasionally I sing it when I'm bored.[8]

Here, Fumiko's desires are brought into sharp focus, materializing as
the sight and smell of fresh fruit in front of an elite, males-only institution. Both fruit shop and university, however, are closed to her,
the former due to poverty, the latter due to class and gender distinctions. As we might expect, Fumiko's reaction approaches the anarcho-
dadaistic as she turns the situation into a series of nonsense syllables,
yet unlike the dadaists, Fumiko's nonsense words seem to resound
with a kind of sensuous power and in fact are revealed to be actual
words of poetry from another language. Fumiko thus both appropriates and confounds the dadaist insight that words in themselves
are meaningless. "Meaning," in fact, is hers to confer. The smell of
dripping water over fresh fruit acquires an audial dimension as

Fumiko's borrowed language picks up and reiterates the sound and sense of that image . . . *ondabutte, butte, onda, rattan dariraaaaa*. Fumiko's chant, like the falling drops of water, caresses the delicious-looking fruit, imparting an unexpected feeling of well-being to the vagabond's experience. By conferring her own meaning upon Tagore's words, the young writer seeks to define and demarcate her own textual place. At the same time, in associating herself with the illustrious and world-renowned Bengali poet, the unknown Fumiko basks in a reflected glory through which she can proclaim her own abilities as a perceptive and knowledgeable writing individual.

Nonetheless, in spite of this attempt by Fumiko to erase limitations imposed upon her by economic deprivation and gender discrimination through the citation of a foreign male poet, in the end, she seeks to resist the male text. The poet Tagore may be useful for impressing or surprising an audience, but Fumiko is also quick to point out that his meaning is not hers; she doesn't really know what Tagore's words "mean." She has appropriated Tagore and his words for effect. Thus, Fumiko lets us know *she* is the one in control of Tagore's language, not the other way around. Her final assessment of Tagore's song, "I sing it when I'm bored," reveals much of Fumiko's ambivalent response to male writers. On one hand, we read an attempt to ally her own burgeoning literary persona with the words of an internationally acclaimed male poet and writer. On the other hand, however, there also appears an eagerness to relegate this poet to the realm of the trivial and insignificant. Fumiko's witty remark, shifting between the poles of self-deprecation and self-assertion, underlines her difficulty in denying the male-written literary text in order to construct a text of her own.

Fumiko continues to reflect on such matters as she brings her observations on male writers closer to home in the final lines of this section:

> Takahashi Shinkichi is a good poet. Okamoto Jun, too, is a fine poet. Another surprisingly good poet is Tsuboi Shigeji. He wears a black Russian shirt and lives in lodgings so cramped and narrow [that] eels could sleep there. Hagiwara Kyōjirō is a passionate poet in the French style. He wears a jacket striped like a bumblebee. What's more, all these poets are supremely poor, just like me.[9]

Briefly Fumiko provides capsule sketches of two male Japanese poets and mentions two others. In contrast to Tagore, however, Fumiko offers no quotations from these poets' work. Instead, she focuses on appearance and lifestyle, barely recognizing poetic ability, preferring to caricaturize Tsuboi Shigeji and Hagiwara Kyōjirō in terms of bumblebees and eels. The only connection that Fumiko wishes to note between the senior Japanese male poets and herself is that of poverty, a fact that she uses to place male and female on equal ground. In this passage, Fumiko's concern seems twofold: to present herself as an equal and at the same time to create a shift in perspective that will allow and/or include her own (female) subjectivity. Although acknowledging the abilities of the male poets, Fumiko nonetheless prefers to concentrate on their personal idiosyncrasies, a strategy that reveals a desire not only to appraise but also to control. Thus, Fumiko's amusing descriptions, while praising the male poets, also seem to comprise an oblique critique of their work. The comparison of Kyōjirō to a bumblebee, for example, suggests that his poetry is like that of a busily buzzing insect, accompanied by a great deal of noise and display but ultimately of little substance. Likewise, the image of Shigeji as he creeps into his gloomy quarters like an eel more than hints at the negativity and self-denial advocated by this poet. Fumiko, writing from her experiences as a female and a social outcast, seems unwilling to join the male anarchist club. Although Fumiko gestures to the meaningless absurdity of language as frequently employed in dadaist writings by her mock-serious treatment of Tagore and does in general share some traits in common with her literary anarchist fathers —in particular, their impertinence and defiance of the status quo— she is also keenly aware of these poets' inherent privilege as members of the male literary establishment, no matter how tenuous their connection to the accepted canon. As a female, as an impoverished member of the lower classes, as an illegitimate child, as a provincial from a distant part of the country, Fumiko has no claim to such connections, literary or otherwise. Doubly, even quadruply marginalized, Fumiko is nonetheless determined to insinuate herself into literary discourse. Skillfully appropriating the rebellious stance of her anarcho-dadaist male mentors, Fumiko seeks recognition and acceptance even as she undertakes to surpass their irreverence with her own, playfully chiding them for their avoidance of the human, the experiential, the female.

Unlike the modernist male poets, Fumiko is painfully conscious of gender. She writes herself in the previous quotations first of all, as female; second, as poverty-stricken, and above all, *hungry*. Fumiko's hunger is not easily assuaged. In fact, hunger is one of the outstanding features of her text. Batting about from place to place, from man to man, Fumiko seldom lets a moment pass without registering her desire for food. Whether guzzling down cool water, savoring a cheap bowl of hot noodles, or simply imagining the delights of juicy red apples, Fumiko's text is replete with gustatory imagery. Extremely effective as a narrative technique that continually foregrounds Fumiko's dire straits, the hunger motif has further significance, as a marker of Fumiko's desire for success and recognition and also as a signifier of her debt to another, anterior text, that is, *Hunger,* by Knut Hamsun.

Published in 1890, Hamsun's *Hunger* (*Sult* in the original Norwegian) was the text Fumiko most often acknowledged as the inspiration for *Diary of a Vagabond.* First translated into Japanese in 1921, *Hunger* was quickly adopted by the Japanese literary establishment, appearing eventually as part of a Shinchōsha series, *Collection of World Literature (Sekai bungaku zenshū)* in 1928. Certainly the positive reception in Japan was due in part to Hamsun's having received the Nobel Prize for Literature in 1920, albeit for another novel, *Growth of the Soil* (1917), and thus his works were decidedly au courant. Another reason for Hamsun's popularity can be traced to the proletarian literature (*puroretariya bungaku*) movement, a response by Japanese writers and intellectuals to issues and events arising from the Russian Revolution of 1917. Many proletarian writings emphasized poverty, deprivation, and the miseries of the industrial workplace, themes echoed in *Hunger,* which, more than Hamsun's other writings, struck a chord with the Japanese. Akutagawa Ryūnosuke (1892–1927), writing in the literary magazine *Bungei shunjū* in 1927, praised Hamsun thus: "The poetry of sexual desire has been discovered by former writers. However, we have had to wait for Hamsun to give us the poetry of our desire to eat. How stupid we've been!"[10] Although Akutagawa's assessment of Hamsun does not refer specifically to any Hamsun text, "the poetry of our desire to eat" is a clear allusion to *Hunger.* Fumiko in turn seems to have been captivated by this aspect of Hamsun's writing and determined to construct her own text accordingly (see figures 5.1 and 5.2).

Certainly there are a number of correspondences between *Hunger* and *Diary of a Vagabond.* In *Hunger,* for example, an impoverished young writer roams the streets of a Norwegian town, unable to scrape up enough money for a square meal, unable to find a job, reduced to the extremes of starvation. A first-person autobiographical narrative,

Figure 5.1. Hayashi Fumiko

Hunger records the steady downward spiral of a protagonist whose ironic awareness of his miserable situation brings no comfort or solace in the descent to abject depravity and hallucination. *Diary of a Vagabond*, too, takes as its subject a starving writer, buffeted by circumstance from one unprofitable encounter to another. Also like Hamsun, Fumiko lets her protagonist speak in the first person, giving vent to thought and emotion in a fast-paced, quick-changing narrative. At the same time, however, there are major differences between the two texts, two of the most prominent being the constructed personae of each text and the motif of hunger itself.

Figure 5.2. Knut Hamsun

In *Hunger* the starving hero seems truly demented. As his physical situation deteriorates, his mind becomes ever more sharply focused, his mental processes delineated in a manner that, according to one critic, reflects the "general turn towards inwardness in European thought at the end of the nineteenth century."[11] In Hamsun's case, such soul-searching results not in renewal and/or regeneration but in gloom and despair. The pessimistic protagonist, devoid of hope, descends ever deeper into the miserable morass of his own psychological hell. Fumiko, on the other hand, in *Diary of a Vagabond,* cultivates a brash and wildly hopeful persona that remains remarkably unfazed by its constant encounters with hardship and misfortune. Just as both writers present very different personas, so, too, do they differ in their treatment of the hunger motif. Hamsun, for example, treats the desire for and consumption of food very differently from Fumiko, as in the following passage:

> "Would you be so good as to give me a bone for my dog?" I said. "Just a bone—it doesn't have to have any meat on it, just something he can carry around in his mouth." . . .
>
> I got a bone, a gorgeous little bone with some meat still on it, and put it under my coat. . . . I sneaked into a blacksmith's yard, as far as I could go. . . . the darkness was sweet and thick all around me; I started chewing on my bone.
>
> It had no taste at all; a nauseating odor of dried blood rose from the bone, and I started throwing up immediately. I couldn't help it; I tried again—if I could only keep it down, it would do some good. . . . But I vomited again. I grew angry, bit fiercely into the meat, ripped off a small piece, and swallowed it by force. That did no good either—as soon as the small pieces became warm in the stomach, up they came again. I clenched my fists madly, started crying from sheer helplessness, and gnawed like a man possessed. I cried so much that the bone became wet and messy with tears. I vomited, I swore, and chewed again . . . and threw up again. Then I swore aloud and consigned all the powers of the universe to hell.[12]

Although Fumiko finds herself gnawed by similar pangs of starvation, she does not share Hamsun's obsessive ferocity nor his frantic urge to self-destruct. As Fumiko observes:

> Mother went out and bought a big cabbage. When I saw it, I imagined it submerged in bubbling hot water, in which pork cutlets had once cooked. I lay down and looked up at the ceiling of the bare room. It would be wonderful if only I could make myself as small as a mouse and go around gobbling up all kinds of things.[13]

Even though both writers focus on the most basic of desires, that is, the desire to eat, Fumiko's homely mouse is in telling contrast to Hamsun's hopelessly ravenous beast. While Hamsun seems compelled to satisfy his desire by coercion and destruction, Fumiko finds satisfaction in imagination and fabrication, as we see even more clearly in the following:

> Eels and bananas, oranges and pork cutlets, these are the kind of things I really want to eat. When my feelings are at a low ebb,

> strangely enough, I feel like scribbling something. "Bananas and pork cutlets," I wrote that on the wall with my finger.[14]

For Fumiko, eating and writing are conjoined in the production of text. Writing is, in a sense, like eating. Both activities relieve feelings of lack, of emptiness, and bring fulfillment and gratification: a full stomach, a full page.

Unlike Hamsun, Fumiko does not find hunger fearful. Her acceptance of the physiological is in sharp contrast to Hamsun's hatred. Although it may be tempting to make here an essentialist argument for female awareness of the body versus male denial, I prefer to read Fumiko's writing of hunger primarily as literary strategy. That is, Fumiko, in her desire for textuality, seeks first of all to ally herself with those writers who are already accepted and acclaimed, as we have seen in the case of Tagore, or who are of some particular repute, as in the case of the anarcho-dadaist poets. In this respect, Hamsun, having recently won the Nobel Prize for Literature, is an entirely suitable choice. Itagaki Naoko, in one of her several critical studies of Fumiko, remarks that "Fumiko read (Hamsun's *Hunger*) and learned that it was possible to use hunger (as the topic of) a text."[15] Indeed, Fumiko was a quick study. Her attempt to emulate Hamsun's "hunger" is thus born partly from a desire to give her own text a kind of literary-establishment stamp of approval. At the same time, however, a closer look at Hamsun's male protagonist suggests a further reason for Fumiko's attraction to this text. In spite of Hamsun's portrayal of the starving writer as a weak and pathetic loser, the figure comes across as extraordinarily determined, unexpectedly resourceful, wildly uncompromising. The sheer powerfulness of this starving figure in spite of his lowly status is one of the most outstanding features of Hamsun's work. I would argue that Fumiko's construction of a similarly powerful and/ or empowering figure in her early text may owe much to her reading of Hamsun's hero. Mori Eiichi, in his recent analysis of Fumiko's writings, wonders at the number of times Hamsun's *Hunger* is mentioned in *Diary of a Vagabond*. Mori speculates that Fumiko, who had yet to produce her own work, was so smitten with Hamsun's text that she sought to "emphasize the existence of (such) an 'I' (in her own *Diary of a Vagabond*)."[16] If Hamsun's hero was indeed Fumiko's model, then Fumiko undoubtedly faced some difficulty in trying to follow her ideal. At issue here is the construction not of a powerful and convincing textual figure but of a powerful and convincing *female* textual figure, a matter that Mori's critique fails to address and yet is crucial to an understanding of Fumiko's early writing. In short, although Fumiko both admired and desired Hamsun's power, being female of necessity altered and problemized her own textual "hunger."

Thus, in spite of her admiration for Knut Hamsun's tale, Fumiko did not hesitate to challenge his text in the pages of her own. At one point in her text, Fumiko, caught in an altercation between a prostitute and a policeman, comments: "I bet there's nothing like this in Knut Hamsun."[17] Indeed, Hamsun's protagonist would never have faced such sexual harassment. And later, as *Diary of a Vagabond* draws to a close, Fumiko remarks:

> I read Knut Hamsun's *Hunger*. That hunger is somehow more of a paradise. It's a novel by a person from a country where one can think and walk about freely. Words like Evolution and Revolution crop up. At this point I have no patience for such things as these. . . . I'm suffocating, barely alive. When I can't stand it anymore, god don't you know, I want to carve graffiti everywhere, with a knife.[18]

In short, Fumiko finds Hamsun's hunger to be cultural and gender specific. Hamsun's country, for example, where even a starving writer has freedom of thought and action is in stark contrast to Japan, where social and political conditions stifle any attempt at individual self-expression. In Japan, Fumiko finds herself silenced again and again; if she is to write, then her message cannot be written in the usual way. Her text is not likely to occupy a position of privilege or centrality. Compared with Fumiko, Hamsun's protagonist enjoys the rare luxury of choice, a fact amply demonstrated in the conclusion of *Hunger*, when the destitute writer escapes his pitiful situation by finding work on a ship and sailing away. For Fumiko, with her focus on the corporeal female body and its problematical relationship to the Japanese social and literary status quo, Hamsun's text reads as overwhelmingly escapist, male, privileged. Fumiko, in the writing of her own hunger, comes to write against such canonical texts, and thus, any act of writing by her as a poor and underprivileged female may and should be read as a resistance directed not only toward texts like Hamsun's but toward the preferred literary order as well.

Although Fumiko's desire to chronicle her own "hunger" may have been inspired in part by reading Knut Hamsun's autobiographical narrative as well as through her association with the anarcho-dadaist poets, Fumiko also drew inspiration from a number of other male writers, in particular the well-known naturalist writer Tokuda Shūsei (1871–1943), who supplied not only encouragement but also actual sustenance in the form of food and money.

Nurturing the Vagabond: Shūsei Sensei and Fumiko's Hidden Hunger for Fiction

Fumiko's decision to abandon modernist poetry and autobiography in favor of naturalist prose fiction is one of the most surprising about-faces in the history of modern Japanese literature. Having achieved literary and financial success beyond her wildest dreams with *Diary of a Vagabond,* Fumiko might have gone on to become an important, influential poet. Yet she chose not to do so. Instead, she embarked upon one of the most difficult undertakings of her entire career: she determined to master the writing of prose fiction. The reasons for this decision are diverse, yet, by and large, one primary note sounds clear: Fumiko's great admiration for male fiction writers, such as Guy de Maupassant (1850–1893); Charles-Louis Philippe (1874–1909), particularly his novel *Bubu de Montparnasse;* and as already mentioned, Tokuda Shūsei. Moved by these writers' authentic portrayal of lower-class city life as well as by the appearance in their texts of strong female figures, Fumiko began tentatively to explore a new literary realm. Of these writers, I would like to focus on Shūsei, because this writer comes closest perhaps to fulfilling the role of mentor or teacher to Fumiko in her early years as a vagabond and poet. Once Fumiko became well known, she also formed close associations with other Japanese male writers, including Kawabata Yasunari (1899–1972) and Ibuse Masuji (1898–1993). This matter is certainly worth further investigation, given that Fumiko seldom made such alliances with women writers, with the possible exception of Hirabayashi Taiko (1905–1972), a writer with whom Fumiko's name is often linked. The two women, however, did not maintain their close friendship after Fumiko's rise to fame.

Fumiko's personal contact with Tokuda Shūsei began in 1925, while she was still a young poet roaming the Tokyo streets. Turning up at his house one day without an introduction (in the best anarchist fashion), Fumiko planned to interview Shūsei and sell her effort to a current magazine for some hard cash. Fumiko recalls:

> The first time I met [Shūsei sensei], I hadn't eaten anything, and since I was living with a man who had T.B. in an apartment in Kagu-

razaka, I wanted money. . . . I was not particularly fascinated with
Shūsei's writing.[19]

For the young and impudent Fumiko, Shūsei, an established male
writer, is merely a means to an end. If she can, she will figuratively
gobble him up.

Shūsei, however, turns out to be neither snobbish nor affected.
Treating Fumiko honestly and openly, he encourages her in her own
writing, lending her money, reading her manuscripts, offering constructive critique. Fumiko remarks:

> In all the long time that I knew him, he never once lied to me.
> He behaved as if I were a favorite pupil, and whenever I went
> there he treated me to food brought in from somewhere in the
> neighborhood.[20]

Tokuda Shūsei's encouraging manner and generosity toward young
and/or unknown writers has been treated elsewhere[21] and certainly,
as Fumiko attests, was remarkable and refreshing. Rather than having
to cadge an interview and hopefully food and drink, Fumiko found
herself on the receiving end of a relationship that proved both wel-
coming and nurturing.

The hungry poet did not hesitate to respond in a daughterly fashion
to this new literary "father." Fumiko comments in her literary autobiography:

> I showed my poems to sensei. . . . He read them, took off his glasses,
> and wept. At that moment, I thought how I would like to spend
> my life as a maid in his house. I was in despair and felt I could not
> possibly go on living. When he said simply: "This is a good poem,"
> it gave me courage. . . . When I think about it, I can't help but feel
> that Shūsei sensei started me on the road that has brought me to
> today.[22]

Not only does Fumiko find herself treated fairly and favorably by
Shūsei, she seems ready to respond, however uncharacteristically, by
adopting traditional modes of behavior—as loyal servant, diligent
pupil, dutiful daughter. Further, Shūsei is given credit for his role in
fostering Fumiko's writing, in making her what she is.

As a result, when Fumiko began to write prose fiction, she seemed
to be in two minds about the form her productions would take; that
is, she continued to write pieces that were very much in the vein of

her popular *Diary of a Vagabond,* such as "Fūkin to uo no machi " (The accordion and the fish town) and "Seihin no sho" (A record of honest poverty), both published in 1931. At the same time, she began to experiment with the writing of what she called "true" *shōsetsu,* which would seem to be writings of the realist or naturalist type, i.e., the kind of *shōsetsu* written by Tokuda Shūsei. Slowly turning away from auto-biographical pieces such as those mentioned above, which she considered to be "ransacked" from her *Diary of a Vagabond* notebooks, she began seriously to attack the new object of her desire. From 1930 until 1935, Fumiko worked toward her goal of producing well-crafted prose fiction and at last succeeded in winning recognition for several writings, chief among them "Kaki" (The oyster, 1935), which was praised by critics as being particularly reminiscent of the work of Tokuda Shūsei. Later, one critic went even further, offering to bestow upon Fumiko the sobriquet, "the female Shūsei"[23] for her achievement in this particular story. Fumiko, it seems, had succeeded beyond expectations in her appropriation of the Shūsei text. Illegitimate by birth, she had managed throughout her life to avoid the "name of the father," yet as a successful writer, she was labeled a literary daughter by the patriarchy. Even so, being designated a "female Shūsei" was not enough to assure her a place in the modern literary canon, particularly since Tokuda Shūsei himself was to be excluded from such status. Although Shūsei's writing brought him great acclaim and respect while he was alive, he fared less well at the hands of critics in the years immediately following World War II. Deemed unsuitable for inclusion in standard literary series and histories, Shūsei seems to have been so singled out because of his unrelenting focus on the lives of the lower classes, particularly working-class women. In his study of Shūsei, Richard Torrance notes that "the reason why many academics objected to Shūsei was a disinclination to come to terms with real class divisions within Japanese society."[24] Thus, like his literary daughter Fumiko, Shūsei became a kind of outcast, hovering on the periphery of "literature," his genius refused and unrecognized.

The label "the female Shūsei," then, reads as a somewhat dubious compliment, acknowledging Fumiko's talent but also serving to further distance her from acceptance and inclusion in the literary mainstream because of that talent. Having Shūsei for a literary "father" is no guarantee of canonization. In fact, Shūsei as a father figure is a good example of what Patricia Yaeger and Beth Kowaleski-Wallace see as paradoxical and contradictory in their *Refiguring the Father: New Feminist Readings of Patriarchy*. They note that when the "power of an individual father becomes conflated with the power of patriarchy, we miss the ways in which fathers inhabit a shifting series of ideological positions in which men are also misshapen by . . . social values."[25] Although a literary "father," Shūsei is also a male writer whose writings have been misrepresented and misread and are greatly in need of reconstruction. Much of Shūsei's predicament, I would also argue, may be attributed to his concern with and attempt to understand the female position(s). Not only are female writers unwelcome in the modern Japanese literary canon, but so, too, are male writers who would challenge the orthodoxy. Like father, like daughter, Shūsei and Fumiko are perhaps two of the best-known, noncanonical writers of twentieth-century Japanese literature (see figure 5.3).

Pleased as Fumiko was with such praise that likened her to Shūsei and as much as such paternal influence was accepted, recognized, and made the most of by Fumiko, at the same time, I believe, such influence was distrusted, at least initially, and perhaps, on a long-term basis,

Figure 5.3. Hayashi Fumiko (seated on the right in the checked kimono) with *(left to right)* Uno Kōji, Satō Haruo, Tokuda Shūsei, Hirotsu Kazuo, and Hasegawa Shigure. The person on the extreme right is unidentified.

resented. In Fumiko's "Literary Autobiography" *(Bungakuteki jijoden)* quoted above and in numerous other writings, Fumiko reports that although she showed Shūsei her poems, she never *ever* showed him her *shōsetsu.*[26] This is strange, given that Shūsei, one of the most skilled prose writers in Japan, was also recognized as a helpful and magnanimous critic as far as young writers were concerned. Perhaps Fumiko felt more confident of her poetry than of her early fiction? Even so, her professed love and trust of Shūsei seem also to have harbored some measure of doubt. My contention is that, although surprised by and grateful for Shūsei's support, Fumiko was also extremely jealous of her own independence and her own talent. She had made her mark writing from the position of female outsider; she had no intention of altering or relinquishing that position to suit anyone else. Because Fumiko's *shōsetsu,* rather than her poetry, are the basis of her claim to achievement, her continued assertion throughout her life that Shūsei had never helped her with these writings seems to be, in fact, Fumiko's attempt to reclaim her writing as her own and to some extent negate the Shūsei connection.

Another factor in Fumiko's distrust of the father can also be read in her own biography, in which biological father and foster father appear as unsatisfactory, unreliable, and/or ineffectual. Fumiko's mother, on the other hand, stands out as a much loved and powerful figure. Although uneducated and possessing no particular talents, Fumiko's mother, Kiku, lived her life in defiance of patriarchal tradition. Not recognized by Fumiko's biological father as wife, Kiku was quick to take another male partner, the so-called foster father, and embark with him and with Fumiko upon a life of peddling on the open road. The figure of the bold, strong-willed Kiku, more than a match for male partners who would seek to control her, offered Fumiko from a very young age an assertive female role model unfettered by convention and unimpressed with male power.[27] Unrecognized by the paternal and denied admittance to patriarchal society, Fumiko was affiliated with her mother and the maternal family whose surname she bears. Fumiko thus has no "position" in Japanese society save that of *shiseiji* (unrecognized child), and she remains, no matter what her accomplishments, a nonconformist female outsider.

Not content to rest on such laurels as were bestowed by acceptance of her work as a Shūsei "read-alike," Fumiko continued to turn out fictional writings at an astonishing rate, eventually filling twenty-three volumes of collected works by 1951, the year of her death. Although the identification of her writings with Tokuda Shūsei was limited to those pieces produced in the early 1930s, Fumiko was still being praised as a great "naturalist" writer in 1954, in this case, for her often translated short story "Late Chrysanthemum" *(Bangiku)*, called "one of the ten best Naturalist pieces ever written in Japan."[28]

Understandably, Fumiko's desire for recognition and success was never completely fulfilled. The countless hungry, dissatisfied, struggling heroines of her writings all testify to the sense of displacement and dispossession that underlines her texts. Fumiko's female protagonists are eaters and consumers, as we have seen, hungry for more than simply the food they can stuff into their mouths. A case in point is *Meshi* (Meals), one of Fumiko's last, incomplete works. Here, Fumiko deliberately used the prosaic Japanese word *"meshi"* in her title to mark the most ordinary, plain, and quotidian of diets, a choice that upset the publishers who preferred a grander title. In *Meals,* food is written about not only as bland and commonplace but also as particularly unsatisfying, as the female protagonist rebels against the new postwar world where men go out to work and women stay home to cook. The mindless repetitive tasks undertaken by the heroine during the course of her daily life become so unspeakably stultifying that she decides to leave home and husband rather than prepare one more miserable *bentō*.

Meals is not only a close and careful indictment of the narrowing of women's roles after World War II to the immediate household environment, but it also hearkens back to Fumiko's earliest writings, in particular one of her first poems, "Kurushii uta" (Lament, 1926), in which Fumiko deplores her inability to enter the social order as a female who is productive, respected, *and* satisfied:

> Neighbours
> relatives
> lovers
> what are they to me?
>
> If that which I eat in life doesn't satisfy me
> then the pretty flowers I have painted will wither away
> though I want to work cheerfully
> I squat so pathetically small
> amidst all kinds of curses.

I try to raise both arms high
but will they all betray such a pretty woman?
I cannot always hug dolls and keep silent.

Even if I am hungry
or without work
I must not shout "Wo-o!"
lest the fortunate ones knit their brows.

Although I spit blood and die in agony
the earth certainly won't stop in its tracks
they are preparing healthy bullets
one after another
in the show window
there's freshly baked bread
ah, how lightly beautiful like the sound of a piano
is the world I've never known.

Then all at once
I feel like crying out: goddammit![29]

Indeed, in "Lament" as in *Meals,* basic fare may not be impossible to come by, but what cannot be gotten is "freshly baked bread," that is, *delicious* food, "bananas and pork cutlets," as the vagabond poet would have it, in short, a rare and much-sought-after item that would give true satisfaction. Denied by the constraints of poverty, class, and other social and financial barriers that limit women to secondary, inferior roles and categories, such foodstuffs seem almost impossible of attainment. Thus, Fumiko's ever-hungry heroines remain outside the bakery window, looking in. To enter the Western-style bakery would mean to enter the world of the male power-mongers with their "freshly baked bread," and their "healthy bullets," and hence, to lose the impact of one's marginal status and the position from which one speaks and writes. For Hayashi Fumiko, the attempt to intervene in literary and cultural production was fraught with the danger of being naturalized by the very system she sought to appropriate, of acquiring status as a literary "daughter" rather than becoming a literary mother. Although Fumiko did eventually enter the bakery and sample its delights, she was never comfortable in its environs and, troubled by the mediated position in which she found herself, continued, in her writings at least, to send her hungry heroines back outside again and again into the cold.

Notes

All translations in this chapter are mine unless otherwise indicated.

1. In keeping with Japanese literary practice, I have chosen to use the given name rather than the surname when referring to this writer. Early in her career, Fumiko altered the spelling of her given name, replacing the native syllables with Chinese characters, a move that made "Fumiko" her artistic as well as given name.

2. The present version of this text consists of three parts. Parts one and two appeared in the late 1920s and part three in 1948. According to Joan Ericson, parts one and two constitute the "true" *Hōrōki* (pers. comm., Harvard University, 4 May 1996). For details, see Ericson, *Be a Woman*. All three parts are included in the numerous editions appearing after 1948 and in both editions of *Hayashi Fumiko zenshū* (The collected works of Hayashi Fumiko), Fumiko's long-term involvement in the formulation of this text is indicative not only of her struggle to win acceptance but also of her determination to consolidate and control earlier gains, an undertaking that, as time passed, showed an increasing awareness and sensitivity to the male text, not the reverse. Accordingly, a large percentage of Fumiko's commentary on male writers occurs in part three of *Diary of a Vagabond*.

3. Itō, "Aka to kuro," p. 6.

4. Hagiwara, "Shikei senkoku," p. 206.

5. Ibid., p. 208. This final hodgepodge of words, represented by Chinese characters in the original, gives a more graphic/pictorial impression than is possible in English translation.

6. Hayashi, *Hōrōki*, p. 469.

7. Ibid.

8. Ibid., pp. 469–470.

9. Ibid., p. 470.

10. Akutagawa, "Zoku bungeiteki na," p. 177.

11. Bly, "The Art of *Hunger*," p. xiv.

12. Hamsun, *Hunger*, p. 161.

13. Hayashi, *Hōrōki*, p. 281.

14. Ibid., p. 272.

15. Itagaki, *Hayashi Fumiko no shōgai*, p. 107.

16. Mori, *Hayashi Fumiko no keisei*, p. 91.

17. Hayashi, *Hōrōki*, p. 274.

18. Ibid., pp. 543–544.

19. Hayashi, "Shūsei sensei," p. 53.

20. Ibid., pp. 53–54.

21. For an excellent source in English, see Torrance, *The Fiction of Tokuda Shūsei*.

22. Hayashi, "Bungakuteki jijoden," p. 4.

23. Adachi, *Gendai nihon bungaku arubamu 13*, p. 210.

24. Torrance, *Fiction of Tokuda Shūsei*, p. 211.

25. Yaeger and Kowaleski-Wallace, p. xi.

26. Hayashi, "Shūsei sensei," p. 53.

27. For a further discussion of the relationship between Fumiko and Kiku, see my essay, "Re-writing the Maternal."

28. Nakamura, "Hayashi Fumiko ron," p. 438.

29. Hayashi, "Kurushii uta," p. 8. This translation has appeared previously in my recent introduction to Fumiko's early poetry: *Hayashi Fumiko's I Saw a Pale Horse and Selected Poems from Diary of a Vagabond.*

Works Cited

Location of Japanese publishers is Tokyo unless otherwise noted.

Adachi Ken'ichi. *Gendai nihon bungaku arubamu 13: Hayashi Fumiko* (Modern Japanese literature album 13: Hayashi Fumiko). Gakushu kenkyūsha, 1974.

Akutagawa Ryūnosuke. "Zoku bungeiteki na, amari ni bungeiteki na" (Literary, all too literary—a continuation). In *Akutagawa Ryūnosuke zenshū,* vol. 5, pp. 175–184. Chikuma shobō, 1971.

Bly, Robert. "The Art of *Hunger.*" In Knut Hamsun, *Hunger,* trans. Robert Bly, pp. xxiv–xxvii. New York: Farrar, Straus and Giroux, 1967.

Brown, Janice, trans. *Hayashi Fumiko's I Saw a Pale Horse and Selected Poetry from Diary of a Vagabond.* Ithaca, N.Y.: Cornell East Asia Series, 1997.

————. "Re-writing the Maternal: 'Bad' Mothers in the Writings of Hayashi Fumiko." In *Mothers in Japanese Literature,* ed. Kinya Tsuruta, pp. 369–393. Vancouver: Department of Asian Studies, University of British Columbia, 1997.

Ericson, Joan E. *Be a Woman: Hayashi Fumiko and Modern Japanese Women's Literature.* Honolulu: University of Hawai'i Press, 1997.

Hagiwara Kyōjirō. "Shikei senkoku" (Death sentence). In *Gendai nihon bungaku taikei* (An outline of modern Japanese literature), vol. 67, pp. 167–208. Chikuma shobō, 1968.

Hamsun, Knut. *Hunger.* Trans. Robert Bly. New York: Farrar, Straus and Giroux, 1967.

Hayashi Fumiko. "Bungakuteki jijoden" (A literary autobiography). In *Hayashi Fumiko zenshū* (The collected works of Hayashi Fumiko), vol. 10, pp. 1–9. Bunsendō, 1977.

————. *Hōrōki* (Diary of a vagabond). In *Hayashi Fumiko zenshū* (The collected works of Hayashi Fumiko), vol. 1, pp. 263–547. Bunsendō, 1977.

————. "Itaru tokoro Aoyama ari" ("Destination Aoyama"). In *Hayashi Fumiko zenshū* (The collected works of Hayashi Fumiko), vol. 16, pp. 128–133. Bunsendō, 1977.

————. "Kurushii uta" (Lament). In *Hayashi Fumiko zenshū* (The collected works of Hayashi Fumiko), vol. 1, p. 18. Bunsendō, 1977.

————. "Shūsei sensei" (My teacher Shūsei). In *Hayashi Fumiko zenshū* (The collected works of Hayashi Fumiko), vol. 16, pp. 53–56.

Itagaki Naoko. *Hayashi Fumiko no shōgai: uzushio no jinsei* (Whirling tides: the life of Hayashi Fumiko). Daiwa shobō, 1965.

Itō Shinkichi. "Aka to kuro" (The red and the black). In *Nihon kindai bungaku daijiten* (Dictionary of modern Japanese literature), vol. 5, pp. 6–7. Kōdansha, 1977.

Mori Eiichi. *Hayashi Fumiko no keisei—sono sei to hyōgen* (The formation of Hayashi Fumiko: her life and its representation). Daiwa shobō, 1992.

Nakamura Mitsuo. "Hayashi Fumiko ron" (A study of Hayashi Fumiko). In *Gendai nihon bungaku taikei* (An outline of modern Japanese literature), vol. 69, pp. 434–440. Chikuma shobō, 1968.

Torrance, Richard. *The Fiction of Tokuda Shūsei and the Emergence of Japan's New Middle Class.* Seattle: University of Washington Press, 1994.

Yaeger, Patricia, and Beth Kowaleski-Wallace, eds. *Refiguring the Father: New Feminist Readings of Patriarchy.* Carbondale: Southern Illinois University Press, 1989.

Chapter 6

A Room Sweet as Honey
Father-Daughter Love in Mori Mari

Tomoko Aoyama

Miss Mori Mari: the most exceptional grace and sacrament in post-war literature. A splendid hermaphrodite whose writing abounds, within the most masculine and classical physique, with the most feminine sensitivity. She has this exquisite quality: she remembers detail, and while her eyes can see through to the heart of the matter, they refuse reality and never cease to dream. A young girl and a beast. . . . A princess and a pauper. . . . A painter and a composer who uses words like colors and music. The highest sanity in the postwar era with a pretense of insanity. . . . An indescribable, to whom one can only take off one's hat.

Mishima Yukio, "Mudai (Mori Mari san)," *Mishima Yukio zenshū*

Mori Mari (1903–1987) is a contemporary of Uno Chiyo, Enchi Fumiko, and Kōda Aya, each of whom is discussed in this volume. Like Enchi and Kōda, she had a famous father, Mori Ōgai, widely regarded as one of the founding "fathers" of the modernization of Japan, a "fighting patriarch"[1] who made numerous important contributions not only in literature but also in medicine, philosophy, aesthetics, military studies, and many other fields. Mari was the eldest daughter of Ōgai and his second wife, Shige.[2] Like Kōda Aya, Hagiwara Yōko (b. 1920, daughter of Hagiwara Sakutarō), and many other "literary daughters" (i.e., writer-daughters of famous writer-fathers),[3] Mari began her writing career after her father's death. When Ōgai died in 1922, Mari, then aged nineteen, heard the news in Europe, where she remained with her husband, Yamada Tamaki, until the following year. Although she had published some essays *(zuihitsu),*[4] memoirs, translations, and reviews from 1929 onward, it was not until the late 1950s that she gained recognition as a writer. When her first collection of essays, *Chichi no bōshi* (My father's hat, 1957) was published, she was in her mid-fifties. The collection, however, was awarded the Fifth Japan Essayist Club Prize and was followed not only by more essays and memoirs but also by fiction, which brought her two more literary prizes.[5]

Privilege on the Margins: The Daughter Memoirist

It is certainly not rare for daughters to write about their writer-fathers, and there are publishers, editors, and the father's friends and disciples eager to publish such writings. Daughters, as are other family members of celebrated figures, are encouraged to participate in, and contribute to, the maintenance and proliferation of the *bundan* (literary world).[6] In Ōgai's case, just about everyone related to him, including Mari's younger sister Kobori Annu, published at least one book on this great literary figure.[7] Significantly, the inclusion of women in this kind of memorializing seems to be more or less confined to the *bundan;* outside it, when political and other leaders are remembered as fathers, the writers are always sons with their own successful careers.[8] "Literary daughters" are therefore privileged and yet marginalized: they are given opportunities to write, but they are constantly reminded of their peripheral and parasitical positions. Not unnaturally perhaps, some of these literary daughters were closely associated with each other in public and in private. Between Kobori Annu's and Mari's books, Kōda Aya's memoirs of her father, Rohan, were published,[9] and an *entretien* between Annu and Kōda Aya appeared in 1950 in *Mainichi gurafu* (The daily graph). Mari had a very close friendship with Hagiwara Yōko, who, like Mari, received the Essayist Club Prize for her book on her father.[10] Ironically, such associations seem to have reinforced their identity as daughters rather than as authors in their own right. Despite the prizes and despite some exceptionally high praise from a few established writers and critics such as Mishima Yukio, Mari remained a minor writer. To date, none of her works has been translated into English.

The marginality of the literary daughters is, moreover, reflected in the fact that studies of Japanese literature have preferred to focus on the theme of father-son and mother-son relationships—the very relationships that, according to Jungian psychologist Kawai Hayao,[11] determine the development of male consciousness, the dominance of which would, if one was to follow Kawai, offer an interesting explanation for the long neglect of themes addressing mother-daughter or father-daughter relationships (the latter of which in Jungian terms constitutes the development of femininity within paternal restrictions). Furthermore, as Kawai himself admits, the Jungian analysis of the four parent-child "constellations" has invited a view that places the four in developmental hierarchy, with the father-son, which is seen as representing Christian-European, at its pinnacle, followed by the "complementary" constellations of mother-son and father-daughter, with the mother-daughter, regarded as the "unconscious," "natural," and "non-European" at the nadir. Although Kawai's insistence on recognizing the importance of the "complementary constellations" is a step toward amending the gender-determined hierarchy, there is no reason for us to assign a "complementary" status to the father-daughter relationship. It seems perfectly possible to treat it as existing in its own right and to examine it in all its complexity, or, as Patricia Yaeger and Beth Kowaleski-Wallace suggest, "to move outside an oedipal dialectic that insists upon revealing the father as law, as the gaze, as bodiliness, or as the symbolic, and to develop a new dialectic that refuses to describe the father function as if it were univocal and ahistorical."[12]

Mari's writing provides material uniquely suitable for this purpose, for the father that appears in it, be he the historical father or a fictitious one, does not fit into any set mold. It was Jacques Lacan who asserted that we must recognize in the *name of the father* "the support of the symbolic function which, from the dawn of history, has identified his person with the figure of the law."[13] Be that as it may, for Lacan's daughter, Sibylle, the illustrious *name* of her father was nothing but a burden, and his absence a source of anxiety and of jealousy of her half-sister. Many other women have written about the fear of going against the father-as-law and the penalty for such disobedience.[14] However, as we shall see, in Mari's writing the father figure never threatens, neglects, or restricts the daughter. Her textual "father" certainly seems closer to "the imaginary father" proposed by Julia Kristeva[15] as her alternative to the Lacanian "symbolic father." The paternal function, according to Kristeva, not merely includes castration threats and law; "the imaginary father," as a mother-father conglomerate, "provides the loving support that enables the child to abject, or separate from, its mother and enter the social." Our interest here, however, is not so much in the psychoanalysis of Mari's personality as in how she creates the father in her writing—for even when it takes the form of memoirs of her father, it is distinctly her own creation, or reimagination.

Pappa and the Long, Long Happy Days

In Mari's memoirs, the prime focus is the "long, long, happy days"[16] with her father. All the other Ōgai children, with the partial exception of the eldest son, Oto, write about their blissful childhood under paternal love and protection. What distinguishes Mari's texts from the others' is the little girl's intense and sensuous gaze upon her father, as in this example:

> I liked my father in his army uniform, with its loose collar showing a streak of white shirt. His face was sun-tanned, his chin squarish, and his sharp eyes shone bright. Around the immaculate curve of his lips I could almost see the aroma of a Havana. When he sat with his legs crossed, his jacket bulged open between the buttons. Inside it was the object of my love and trust that completely filled my little heart. "Pappa"[17]—that was the whole of my heart. Inside his breast, too, my little loving heart was always warmly welcomed. This was our dear uniformed breast that held my childhood love and my mother's heart within it.[18]

As the last line shows, the mother is not completely forgotten. Indeed, some of Mari's essays present the mother's viewpoint. And the sympathetic presentation of that viewpoint may be in part due to Mari's own experience of having acquired a distinctly negative reputation, just as her mother, Shige, did,[19] after the first of her two divorces.[20] There is no doubt, however, about the centrality or about the sensuality of the father-daughter relationship. As we shall see, unlike her siblings or many other children of famous fathers, Mari is uninterested in answering the question of what it was like to have Ōgai for a father.[21]

The individual voice and maturity of Mari's writing, which, as we have seen, received Mishima's extraordinary praise, is clearly audible even in her earliest essays.[22] She depicts in minute detail the decor surrounding this "love affair": the house, its interior, the garden, trees, plants, the sky, clothes, crockery, food, and so on. Colors in Mari's text are not just the basic palette; they include numerous traditional Japanese hues and European tints. Sounds, smells, texture, and tastes are also described exquisitely. Events and incidents are carefully and skillfully reconstructed, as are conversations, combining her own recollection and imagination with the information she selected from the written and oral accounts of other people. Among her oral informants, her mother was the most important. The written sources include Ōgai's texts and many volumes of memoirs written by other family members. Mari by no means provides a comprehensive review of these texts; she uses only the parts that she finds fitting to her (re)-construction, and either ignores or rejects the parts that would contradict or destroy her "love affair." Whereas Annu's memoirs deal mainly with the final year of her father's life, Mari's favorite episodes belong to her early childhood in late Meiji, when "Pappa" was strong and healthy. The vivid and detailed descriptions in Mari's text suggest a passionate desire to bring the past and her late father back to life through writing.

Mari wrote some of her memoirs in the third person. The earliest examples are two short pieces (included in *My Father's Hat*)[23] published in 1949 as an appendix to *Ōgai zenshū* (Selected works of Ōgai). These can certainly be regarded as forerunners of her arguably autobiographical fiction. They are also Mari's earliest published accounts of the whooping cough, which, in 1908, when Mari was five, nearly proved fatal. Mari's baby brother Furitsu died, and she herself was about to be given a lethal injection to end her suffering. Thanks to the opposition of her maternal grandfather, this plan of last resort was not carried out and, miraculously, she recovered. Ōgai's 1909 text "Konpira" deals with this incident, though without mentioning the proposed euthanasia.[24] The story, told with Ōgai's typical reserve and understatement, is nevertheless a moving account of the death of a baby and of the miraculous recovery of a six-year-old daughter of a philosopher. The only hint, and it is a faint one, at euthanasia in this text is to be found in certain doubts of the doctor and the philosopher-father about continuing treatments such as heart stimulant injections and poultices when they seem to have no effect but to prolong the suffering of the children. It seems unnecessary to speculate as to Ōgai's motivation for suppressing the actual issue of euthanasia in this seemingly autobiographical story; he was happy to deal with the issue in the safer historical setting of "Takasebune" (The boat on the River Takase, 1916).[25] Mari, too, was to write about the episode in many other essays and in fiction. It was indeed not only one of the most sig-

nificant incidents in Mari's life but also it created controversy among
the brothers and sisters as to who it was who proposed the euthanasia.[26] Mari, however, appears most interested in what she sees as
the dramatic contrast between the tragic death of her baby brother
and her own miraculous recovery rather than the pursuit of historical
facts or the continuing conflict within the family; its lasting significance for her was that it made it possible for her to continue the
"long, long happy days" with her father.

There was a stage, however, when Mari felt this perfect world of
father and daughter fading. One of Mari's earliest published essays,
entitled "Toge" (A thorn; first published in 1933, included in *My
Father's Hat*), deals with the distance she sensed between herself and
her father before her departure to Europe. Mari, married but still
only in her late teens, felt deserted by him.

> Some time after our marriage, I said to my husband, "I have put
> my memories of Pappa in a pretty box and *I'm going to keep it
> locked.*" Hidden in these words were my little lament and a certain
> pride. I believed that the love between my father and myself was
> beautiful, and that my father had within him a poetry, *which my
> husband lacked.* (Emphasis added.)[27]

Only after her father's death does she realize, in conversation with
her mother, the true cause of that fading:

> My father purposely created the distance from me [so that Mari
> would be closer to her husband than to her father], enduring his
> own loneliness. He must have thought about his own approaching
> death, and decided not to sadden me with the knowledge, and that
> it would be best for every one to let me go to Europe.[28]

What seemed to be a faded love has now gained new depth and
intensity. She compares her grief over her father's death to the trauma
caused by the suicide of a lover.[29] Despite her declaration that she
would keep her little treasure box locked, she was in fact to open it
again and again and contemplate its precious contents.

The legacies inside this treasure box include what she terms the
"human goodness" *(ningen no yosa)* of her father. She describes how
he never showed hostility even toward disagreeable people, how he
never once interfered in others' business, and how free he was from
obsessions of any kind. She believes that it is this goodness that makes
his face beautiful. And, she feels, this "goodness" needs protection:

To his family he was a picture of good-naturedness, which sometimes made him as vulnerable as a baby. When I was small, I always
felt his goodness, and after I learned the word "god," it became in
my mind identical to my father. We feared that someone might
bully our father. Once a nightmare disturbed me and woke me in
cold sweat; it was about some men approaching my father working
at his desk and attacking him from behind.[30]

She also defends her father against his critics, who have accused him
of being, among other things, a cold-hearted man of reason,[31] while
at the same time recognizing an impassive core, or "lump" *(katamari)*,
in him as well as in herself.

It was not his fault if his love, despite its depth and greatness,
lacked warmth. Like a creature carrying its shell, he had this lump
inside him and yet he loved people. I can see this clearly in my
mind's eye. This thought has made me feel his love more deeply
than in my childhood, when I passionately loved him, jumped at
him, and longed for the aroma of his cigars. Since I reflected upon
my own character and since this thought about my father occurred
to me like a fresh breeze coming into a closed room, I came to
feel my self standing face to face with his person, with the understanding that one human being has of another.[32]

Many of Ōgai's texts deal with this impassive core. In "Konpira," for
example, the protagonist Professor Ono muses on his way home from
Shikoku:

He thought about his wife and children. There were, after all,
things in this world such as love between husband and wife and feli-
city within the home and these were parts of human life. However,
they were insufficient to fill up the void he felt within himself.
Wife and child were merely bound to his own engine by rotten
hawsers of convention. How dreary, how lonely, he thought, as he
fell asleep.[33]

And after the death of his baby son:

Although the professor had contemplated how very sad it would
be if his son were to die, he was shocked at how exceedingly
shallow and insignificant his grief now seemed. It was as if he felt
none of the deep sorrow he had expected. He felt that his sense of
empty loneliness was somewhat sharper than usual. At the same
time, the scene in the room struck him with vivid, objective, dread-
ful clarity.[34]

It is naive, and dangerous, to confuse the narrator, the protagonist, and the writer, even when the story seems to be autobiographical.[35] The mildly comic descriptions of Ono's meticulousness and "stinginess" and the small in-joke of having Professor Takayama (the protagonist of another seemingly "autobiographical" story, "Hannichi") as Ono's neighbor clearly indicate the distance between the author and the protagonist. The narrative also tells us that Ono, despite his view of family ties as "rotten hawsers of convention," shortens his stay in Shikoku precisely because he misses his family. More important, the tragedy of the infant's death is intensified because of Ono's painfully acute observation and reflection. With all this narrative complexity and irony, however, one must admit that what Mari terms the "lump" forms the core of her father's literature: *asobi* (play), resignation, and many other key terms of Ōgai's literature are all closely related to this "lump."[36] Mari refuses to use this "lump" against her father: she identifies the same kind of "lump" in herself and makes it into yet another bond between herself and her father.

In the same way she treats her father's anger as another legacy to be cherished. She remembers that his anger was of two kinds. First "minor" but fierce anger at trifles such as impudence on the part of shop assistants, train conductors, and waiters.[37] The second kind of anger concerned scholarly matters, including the matter of orthography. She confesses that as a child, when she asked him how to write a particular character, she would find his meticulous explanation irksome. Beneath his gentle manner, she sensed an intense fury directed not against her, but against orthographical errors and against indifference to the issue. We are close here to the notion of the "symbolic father" as law. It may also seem to conflict with some of her descriptions of his "human goodness." Mari writes, however, that she loves his second kind of anger as dearly as she loves the first, and she compares it to the roaring of a lion.[38] His explanations may have been irksome to a child, but the roar never intimidated her. Episodes of paternal anger appear repeatedly in many of her later essays.[39] Mari seems totally unconcerned about repeating her favorite anecdotes; to her they are fresh each time she writes or talks about them. Moreover they are her valuable property, which (unlike her jewelry[40]) would never be lost, stolen, or parted with for living; they stay "locked up" in her pretty box. Her own annoyance at matters great and small appears frequently in her text,[41] reminding the reader of her inherited "treasure."

Writing Daughterly Revolt

If Mari's writing is dominated by the father, real or reimagined, it is
—interestingly—also an act of daughterly revolt. The daughter representing the dead father or acting in his place is, as Tanaka Takako
points out, a common (if hitherto neglected) theme in classical Japanese literature.[42] In Mari's case, however, it is neither vengeance
nor an inherited project that connects her with her father. While
defending the goodness, and even the "lump," of her father, she at
the same time criticizes, as a weakness, his writing's lack of *"akuma"*
(or *ma,* demonic elements). Mari's observation is unique in Ōgai criticism. Indeed, although she acknowledges the intellectual and aesthetic
values of some stories, she candidly expresses her dissatisfaction with
his fiction *(shōsetsu),*[43] believing that his greatest literary contributions
were in fact his translations.[44] She finds his historical works frankly
tedious; the only part that amused her in the biography of the nineteenth-century Confucian scholar-doctor, *Shibue Chūsai,* which many
have acclaimed as Ōgai's best, is the description of Chūsai's aversion
to slugs, an aversion she shares.[45] In an interview in 1975 Mari commented thus:

> I think fiction [*shōsetsu*] should be interesting [*omoshiroi*]. So I try
> to make mine interesting. Even great writers produce uninterest-
> ing novels. Take, for instance, Ōgai. His writing is beautiful, of
> course, like exquisite engravings on an ivory plaque. What I don't
> like about it is that it has no *akuma.*[46]

Mari's view that *shōsetsu* should be interesting in fact reminds us of
Ōgai's essaylike story "Tsuina" (Exorcising demons, 1909), in which
the narrator asserts that *shōsetsu* should not be confined to the shackles
of certain styles and subjects but may be written in any fashion and
about any subject.[47] Ironically, his efforts to explore new styles and
subjects were only partly recognized by his daughter: from her viewpoint, his subjects were not as perfect as his style. Mari's revolt was
not only to criticize the weakness of Ōgai's writing but also to create
her own alternatives to "uninteresting" fiction produced by "great
writers." These alternatives fall into three groupings: autobiographical
stories and sketches; romantic novels; and her single full-length novel,
Amai mitsu no heya (Sweet honey room, 1975).

The autobiographical stories and sketches, loosely structured with
no clear plot, are often characterized by a comic self-mockery. Most

of the characters are easily identifiable. Some of the stories describe her reveries in her tiny apartment, and others narrate her encounters with *bundan* figures and with neighbors. In these texts the only clear sign that indicates their generic difference from essays is the parodied or caricatured names. Some texts in this group may be regarded as a parodic expansion of Ōgai's texts. One of the earliest examples is "Yume" (Reverie; first publication date unknown, included in *My Father's Hat*), which reminds the reader of Ōgai's essaylike stories, particularly "Mōsō" (Daydreams, 1911). "Mōsō" is structured with introductory and concluding passages in the third-person narrative, and the middle section, presented as the memoirs and thoughts of "an old man," are told in the first person *(jibun)*. "Yume," on the other hand begins with the first person *(watashi)*, but after the first two lines *watashi* is replaced by the third person "Marii," an obvious variation of Mari, with the long final vowel and different Chinese characters. Both the "old man" and "Marii" view life as shadow, a phantom, a winged vision.

Ōgai's "old man" in "Daydreams:"

> Even after such experiences, my mind remains as before, chasing visions of the future and ignoring present realities. What is this phantom we seek, even while we know our life to be already on the downward path?[48]

Marii:

> Life to Marii seemed like "a shadow"—a shadow that reflects shapes and colors in a person's eye and disappears. This strange shadow flits away moment by moment. Sometimes Marii felt that she heard the sound of the wings of the shadow as it flew away.[49]

Ōgai's text concludes on the following ambiguous note:

> So the old man spends the rest of his days, already numbered, neither in fear of death nor in love with death, but with the sense of a dream unfinished. Sometimes his reminiscences reveal the traces of many years in an instant, like a long, long chain, and at such times his keen eyes stare out over the distant sea and sky.
>
> This is an odd scrap jotted down at just such a moment.[50]

Although the concluding section of Ōgai's text is written in the third person, its final line with the ambiguous "this," which could be interpreted as indicating only the middle section or the whole text, blurs the difference in viewpoint between first and third persons, as if to sum up the illusory nature of life.

It is possible to regard these texts of Ōgai and Mari as a meditative variety of *shishōsetsu*. Mari herself, however, did not believe that any of her writing belonged to the *shishōsetsu* category. In fact she generally detested the genre, accusing it of a lack of imagination.[51] This, too, faintly echoes Ōgai's critical view of naturalism. It is interesting that both father and daughter subverted the genre by producing their own versions of it, adding to it what each believed the existing examples of *shishōsetsu* lacked. In Ōgai's case, it is articulate and erudite reflections, whereas in Mari's writing, everyday items such as empty glass jars and bottles are transformed into magical and aesthetic objects. Poverty, which is an important ingredient in many canonical *shishōsetsu* texts, becomes a comic and at the same time aesthetic setting in Mari's texts such as *Zeitaku binbō* (Luxurious poverty). In these texts all this is accompanied by a strange mixture of passion and comic detachment. The protagonist of "Luxurious Poverty," for example, is called Mure Maria, again a playful disguise of the author's name,[52] with the Chinese character for *ma* adopted from that in *akuma*.

> Maria is poor, almost in destitution. And yet she truly hates all things penurious, and loves the colors of luxury. Hence she devotes herself to eradicating and expelling the reek of poverty from her shabby six-*tatami* apartment and replacing it with a luxurious atmosphere. This is done by methods uniquely her own. One may well wonder what exactly is supposed to be luxurious in the room.[53]

Middle-class materialism and its concern for reputation she attacks fiercely, as an example of *"binbō zeitaku"* (wretched luxury), the opposite of her principle. The texts also depict the comic misadventures of "Maria" as a writer on the periphery of the *bundan*—an indirect criticism, it would seem, of the smug seriousness of the *bundan* and their tediously serious products. One text, entitled "Kuroneko Jurietto no hanashi" (The story of the black cat Juliet; included in *Zeitaku binbō*), has a feline narrator, as has Natsume Sōseki's celebrated *Wagahai wa neko de aru* (I am a cat). The device allows the everyday life of "Maria" in her apartment, and her mumbled thoughts and animadversions, to be reported with humor and irony. "Maria" calls the texts that compose this first grouping "a kind of comic fiction" and compares them to "a bottomless barrel."[54]

From Clumsy Romance to the Sweet Honey Room

The stories in the second group—"clumsy romantic novels" on the theme of love-murder, according to "Maria"—have overtly fictional characters, structure, and plot. This group consists mainly of the male homosexual love stories to be found in the two collections *Koibitotachi no mori* (Lovers' forest, 1961) and *Kareha no nedoko* (The bed of fallen leaves, 1962). Each story involves a wealthy, beautiful, and socially and intellectually powerful man and a young, pretty, but socioeconomically powerless boy. All the stories are set in Japan, but many protagonists have parental and/or cultural connections with Europe.

Idealized images of Europe, especially of France, are everywhere in Mari's writing, regardless of genre and period. Her admiration for Europe is based partly on her 1922–1923 visit, but more important, it is strongly associated with her father.[55] Europe was where her father had stayed between 1884 and 1888, and it was also the birthplace of all the cultural and intellectual products he pioneered in introducing into Japan through his translations and other writing. He is the one who made it possible—despite financial problems, oppositions from relatives, and his own illness—for her to join her husband, who was studying in Europe. Finally, it was in Europe where Mari heard the news of her father's death. Mari's Europe was framed by Ōgai. Thus Europe was another cherished treasure in her little box. Mari's Europe, however, is by no means identical to her father's; she had selected for her treasure box only what appealed to her—the individualistic, sensuous, romantic, and even frivolous aspects of European culture.

Although *Lovers' Forest* was awarded the Tamura Toshiko Prize, these stories left the majority of the *bundan* at a loss; only a few, Mishima Yukio among them, commented on their merits.[56] As I have pointed out elsewhere,[57] Mari's treatment of male homosexuality resembles certain *shōjo manga* (girls' comic book) stories of the 1970s and 1980s that depict boys in love; it is neither like that in her father's *Vita Sexualis* (1909) nor like that in Mishima's texts. The father-daughter love story seems to have given way to a romance between a man and a boy: in these stories the sensuous gaze is not fixed on the father but is exchanged between the lovers. It is, however, not difficult to see a pseudo-father-daughter relationship in the male couples; the older man with his power and infatuation loves and protects the boy, who is described as having feminine, even infantilistic features. In this sense these homosexual love stories helped pave the way for Mari's next phase of her father-daughter love affair: her full-length novel, *Amai mitsu no heya* (The sweet honey room, 1975).

This novel is her clearest challenge to her father. Additionally, it offers a full catalog of the treasures in her little box. It took her ten years to complete this three-part novel—more than 500 pages in its paperback form—about an innocent "demon" of a girl Moira and her "sweet honey room" with her father. When its second part was published in 1967, Mishima wrote an extremely warm review, praising Mari's stylistic and technical virtuosity and the "sensuality" of her novel, to which, he believed, no other modern Japanese fiction, with the exception of Kawabata Yasunari's *Nemureru bijo* (The house of sleeping beauties, 1961), was comparable.[58]

As shown in table 6.1, many of the characters in *Sweet Honey Room* are identifiable. Changing parts of names is of course not new to Japanese writing: it is commonly used in the traditional theater.[59] The same device of parodic names is also found in some of Ōgai's texts and, as we have seen, in Mari's texts of the first group. However, the comic tone of the latter is absent from this novel.[60] In addition to the easily identifiable names, some episodes familiar from her other texts and from Ōgai's texts also appear in the novel. The most obvious example is the whooping cough. The issue of euthanasia, however, is suppressed, for a completely different reason from Ōgai's in "Konpira": it is simply unthinkable that Moira's father should give his assent to ending her life.[61]

Despite its apparent adherence to the biographical facts, the novel contains many other deliberate changes. Moira, for example, is born in early Taishō, that is, about ten years later than Mari. Her father Rinsaku is neither a writer nor a doctor, but owns a trading company in Yokohama.[62] Moira's mother dies soon after giving birth to her, and there is no brother or sister in the story. Thus Mari creates an ideal situation for her infant heroine to monopolize her father in an environment surrounded by European luxury.

> For Rinsaku, Moira was like a little lover, and he sees her more often than anyone else. He would, of course, have to give this lover away in ten and a few years' time. . . . Underneath the father's love that he felt for her, he had a sweet "honey-like" premonition that she would maintain this close love with him and would never be able to slip out of its deep tenderness.[63]

Table 6.1
Parodic Names of Characters in *Amai mitsu no heya* and Other Works by Mori Mari

	Amai mitsu no heya	*Other texts by Mari	Ōgai's texts
Family:			
Mori Ōgai 鷗外	Mure (Ōgai) mentioned as one of Marius's favorite writers	Mure (Z) Ōgai 欧外 (Ba, Z)	Mōri *(Seinen)* Ōson *(Seinen)*
Rintarō	Rinsaku (trading businessman. b. ca. 1875)	Rinnosuke (Ba)	
Mari 茉莉	Moira 藻羅 (b. ca. 1913)	Marii 未里 (F, Y), Maria 魔利 (Ba, Z), Yuria 由里 (Bo)	Tama 玉 (Hannichi), Yuri 百合 (Konpira)
Mineko (Ōgai's mother)	Tomone (mentioned only once)		
Shige (Ōgai's wife, Mari's mother)	Shigeyo (dies after giving birth to Moira)	Setsu (Ba) Take (Z)	
Atsujirō (Ōgai's brother)	Tatsuji (mentioned only once)		
Oto (Mari's elder brother)	—	Otokichi (Ba)	
Furitsu (Mari's younger brother)	—	Furittsu (different characters) (F)	Hansu (Konpira)
Annu (Mari's younger sister)	—	Emma (Ba)	

*Other text by Mari:
Ba: "Barakuihime"   Bo: "Botchicheri no tobira"   F: "Futari no tenshi"   Y: "Yume"
Z: *Zeitaku binbō*

Family:

Rui (Mari's younger brother)	—	Rin (Ba)
Yamada Tamaki (Mari's first husband)	Amagami Marius	Kamada Tamaki (Z)
Araki Hiroomi (Mari's maternal grandfather)	Gōda Shigeomi	
Jakku (Mari's son)	—	Jan (Ba)

Friends, other writers:

Natsume Sōseki		Ōseki (Z)	Hirata Fuseki *(Seinen)*
Hagiwara Yōko	Nobara Noemi (Moira's classmate)	Nobara Noemi (Z)
Hagiwara Sakutarō	Nobara Sakuya	Sakujirō (Ba) Nobara Yōnosuke (Z)
Murō Saisei	Moro Saisen	Moro Tensei (Ba) Iraka Heishirō (Z)
Shiraishi Kazuko		Aoishi Namiko (Ba)
Yagawa Sumiko		Yano Fumiko (Ba)
Mishima Yukio		Majima Yoshiyuki (Ba, Z)

As Moira grows up, she attracts many admirers, all fictitious characters, and, just as in the homosexual love stories, almost all with some
European connection. A young groom, Jōkichi, later to be called
Dumitori, has a Russian father and a Japanese mother. Moira's piano
teacher is a Frenchman, and the young medical student "Pītā" is Russian. Amagami Marius, whom Moira marries at the age of sixteen—
just as Mari married Yamada Tamaki at sixteen—is Japanese but has
the face of a "handsome Englishman." Rinsaku, who is depicted as
sexually attractive, has a German mistress[64] after Moira's mother's
death. The story very nearly conforms to a *shōjo manga* story.[65] And as
in *shōjo manga,* there are enemies who out of jealousy try to interfere
with the heroine's happiness.

The pretty little treasure box of the *My Father's Hat* phase is now
the "sweet honey room" of the father and daughter. All the men
charmed by Moira understand instinctively its perfection; none succeeds in stepping into the room, let alone in replacing Rinsaku. Neither can her enemies tarnish or lessen the perfection. It is notable that
all the men attracted to Moira except her father have something religious or pious about them. Their peace of mind, however, is savagely
destroyed by the innocent demon in Moira. Rinsaku explains Christianity to Moira as a teaching intended, just like those of Confucius
and of Lao-tse, to allow people to live harmoniously in this world with
others.[66] But Moira is not interested in harmony with others: she is a
voracious "carnivore of love," as her father observes,[67] and she thrives
on his love and that of others. She is by no means a victim. This father-
daughter love is quite unlike the gentle simulacrum of a love affair suggested in Annu's memoirs; neither is it the object of a study of sexuality after the manner of Ōgai's *Vita Sexualis.* In the novel it is Pītā and
Marius who become Moira's lovers. These sexual encounters, however, only deepen the love between father and daughter. Neither the
daughter nor the father is punished, for no violation takes place, which
contrasts markedly with the treatment of daughter-father incest in
stories written by other women writers about the same time as this
novel.[68]

Yagawa Sumiko remarks—perceptively—that Rinsaku's smile is the
basso continuo of the novel and that each of the three parts ends with
his smile.[69] Although Mari insists in her *entretien* with Yagawa that Rinsaku was modeled after the business entrepreneur Fujiyama Raita and
that to have chosen the name so similar to her father's [Rintarō] was
simply an oversight, she concedes that this smile was taken from her

father.[70] Scattered all over Mari's memoirs are the bright, gentle, comforting smiles of her father.[71] Rinsaku's smile, however, contains the "demon" that Mari believed was absent in Ōgai. It is a smile of complicity in his daughter's nascent "carnivorous" sexuality.

> Rinsaku, even when he is not smiling, has a faint shadow of a smile on his dark cheeks, which, like a gentle breeze, makes Moira's heart rustle. In this shadow of a smile she sees the depth of his cherishing of her, his admiration set deeper than anybody else's.[72]

And at the end of the novel, after Moira's husband commits suicide:

> Rinsaku felt a sharp pain about his heart. Inside him, however, there is another Rinsaku, with a smiling face. . . . Was it the joy of bringing Moira back to his house? A beautiful smile, which might have been mistaken for an expression of embarrassment, appeared on his face. The smile lingered around the dimple on one of his cheeks that looked as if it had been pressed by a fingertip. This was a smile of victory: Moira was at last his own. It was the smile of a fearless beautiful demon, an impudent smile which seemed to have spread from his cells to Moira's, a pleasure in rebellion against all the world.[73]

Mourning Work: The Reluctant Electra

If this novel can be read as a daughter's challenge to her father's Apollonian texts, it can also be read as Mari's bold response to the charges leveled (or which she believed to be leveled) at her personality: the diagnosis of an "Oedipus (or Electra) complex,"[74] the label "spoilt child," the accusations of infantilism and narcissism. In 1961 Mari took a Rorschach test with the psychologist Kataguchi Yasufumi, who tested twenty other writers. Kataguchi found her responses "just like [those of] a child reporting the nightmare she had last night" and concludes thus:

> The tendency to lock herself up in her inner world is remarkable. External stimuli do not bring immediate responses. It is not easy for her to observe reality objectively; subjective judgment is always predominant. Moreover, when one idea becomes dominant, there is no room for other ideas. She is easily frightened, just like, one might say, an infant.
>   This childishness is so prominent that one wonders whether it is a pose. It might be more appropriate, however, to conclude that a childhood mentality is still abundantly preserved in her mind.[75]

As Kataguchi himself acknowledges, many of his informants, and other critics, have questioned the validity of his method and of his conclusions. If one is unwilling to accept his comments on Mari's personality as scientifically proven truth, it is true that her "childishness" seems to be a fact, and an ambiguous one: in many of her essays and letters she expresses her annoyance at being treated like a child, and yet she likens her anger to that of a child being ignored by adults.[76] In *Sweet Honey Room,* however, infantilism is unambiguously victorious, for all the maturity of the prose style. Moira should perhaps be seen as Mari's alternative to the persona of an old man that appears frequently in Ōgai's texts. Just as Ōgai created this persona in his late forties, Mari, in her sixties and early seventies, invented her infant heroine.

The same paradox applies to a supposed Oedipus/Electra complex: although Mari insists Rinsaku is not Ōgai Rintarō in essays and interviews, in *Sweet Honey Room* she depicts, almost obsessively, the exclusive love between father and daughter. Mari is certainly aware, if somewhat vaguely, of Freudian theory; but that does not inhibit or modify her creation of her father-daughter romance in any way. When Moira, aged fifteen, shows signs of mild "hysteria," Rinsaku muses on a case reported by a psychoanalyst:

> It was about a little girl, whose condition was not unlike that of Moira now. When I [i.e., Rinsaku] heard about this case, I felt so sorry for the girl. It was well before Moira was born. The girl, ill in bed, told her father who visited her to sit when he was standing, and when sitting, to stand. Irritated by her own tantrum, the girl started to cry and could not stop crying for a long time. . . . It was a fit caused by her desire to see her father's love with her own eyes. There must be something else—a kind of anxiety, for example, at the time of sudden physical change.[77]

Such apparently objective considerations, however, turn out to have no practical effect on Rinsaku's relations with his daughter; the love affair continues.

As to narcissism, Mari makes no excuse but simply pursues it in her writing. This itself seems to provide evidence against Mishima's unambiguously sexist view of narcissism.[78] Mishima believes that it is impossible for women to be narcissist because they lack objective self-criticism, which, in his opinion, is just as essential to Narcissus as his beauty. Five years after the publication of his essay on narcissism,

Mishima expressed his amazement at the discovery of an exception to his theory in Mari's homosexual story.[79] The only way for him to come to terms with the fact that a woman can understand and write about narcissism was to see her, as we saw in his passage quoted at the beginning of this chapter, as a hermaphrodite. To some extent Mari herself was complicitous with gender bias. As I mentioned in a previous essay,[80] Mari's texts, including *Sweet Honey Room,* often show stereotypical images of women—as ignorant, jealous, hypocritical, or simply banal. The story of Moira, however, goes beyond stereotypes in that it presents a girl's narcissism to the fullest extent and in a manner perhaps no other writer has attempted. It would seem that Mari sensed the ultimate *desire* of *shōjo* and set an example with her texts, as is enthusiastically acknowledged by many ex-*shōjo* writers, including Yagawa Sumiko, Kanai Mieko, and Shiraishi Kazuko.[81]

It will have already become obvious that none of Mari's texts, despite the fact that her illustrious father plays a central role in their genesis, can be regarded as memoirs, that is, if one takes "memoir" to mean, among other things, a text that could safely be used as a primary source for any Ōgai biographer.[82] Whether any of them are really about Ōgai at all is debatable; what they are certainly about is Mari's own psyche, a crucial element of which was her need to cope with the spell of the dead father. Through writing, she transforms her position from the protected to the protector. In her literary exploration of the father-daughter love affair, she actually invented male homosexual romance and pioneered in representations of *shōjo*. The "father" in her texts is not the Lacanian disembodied entity but is "re-membered" by the daughter's "mourning-work" and "through the echolalias of the daughter's desire."[83] As for the father's writing, it is not simply resurrected and embedded in the daughter's but is judged, modified, and parodied.[84]

Notes

This chapter is part of my ongoing project on father-daughter relationships in Japanese literature, funded by the Australian Research Council. An earlier version of this essay was given as a paper at the Association for Asian Studies Fifty-first Annual Meeting, 11–14 March 1999, under the title "Mari and Annu." My special thanks to Drs. Copeland and Ramirez-Christensen for their encouragement and valuable suggestions. Translations from Japanese texts are mine, unless otherwise stated. The short (eight lines in total) untitled passage used as the epigraph here was written by Mishima in November 1970, just before his suicide.

1. This is Yamazaki Masakazu's term in his *Ōgai: tatakau kachō*.

2. All of Ōgai's children have European names: Otto, Marie, Fritz, Anne, and Louis. In this paper, however, the *kana* readings of the characters adopted for these names are used instead of their European spellings. Although it is customary to cite the writer's surname (e.g., Enchi, Mishima) unless there is an elegant sobriquet (e.g., Ōgai, Sōseki, Ichiyō), I shall use the given name Mari in this chapter, mainly to distinguish her from other members of the Mori clan, but also because she uses it and its parodic variations within her stories.

3. Other "literary daughters" include Kobori Annu (b. 1909, Mari's younger sister), Mitsui Futabako (b. 1918, daughter of Saijō Yaso), Satō Aiko (b. 1923, daughter of Satō Kōroku), Murō Asako (b. 1923, daughter of Murō Saisei), Yoshiyuki Rie (b. 1939, daughter of Yoshiyuki Eisuke), Tsushima Yūko (b. 1947, daughter of Dazai Osamu), Kaikō Michiko (1952–1994, daughter of Kaikō Takeshi and Maki Yōko), Yoshimoto Banana (b. 1964, daughter of Yoshimoto Takaaki). Others who have written essays include Iizuka Kuni (1899–1994, adopted daughter of Tsubouchi Shōyō), Kaji Ruriko (daughter of Ueda Bin), Togawa Ema (b. 1911, daughter of Togawa Shūkotsu), Murai Yoneko (daughter of Murai Gensai), Mori Fujiko (daughter of Yosano Hiroshi and Akiko), Agawa Sawako (daughter of Agawa Hiroshi), Dan Fumi (daughter of Dan Kazuo), and Takeda Hana (daughter of Takeda Taijun and Yuriko). Daughters of famous writer-mothers include Aoki Tama (daughter of Kōda Aya), Aoki Nao (Tama's daughter), and Ariyoshi Tamao (daughter of Ariyoshi Sawako).

4. Although for convenience' sake I use the term "essay" for short prose pieces usually called in Japanese *zuihitsu,* or more recently *essē,* they are somewhat different from the genre in European literature, just as *shōsetsu,* which is usually translated as "fiction," does not share the same definition as European fiction. *Zuihitsu,* unlike traditional European essays, do not necessarily express a particular viewpoint or persuade the reader to accept some general proposition. They can consist of miscellaneous thoughts or accounts of everyday life, usually addressed to a general readership. Mari, being aware of the Montaigne tradition, hesitates to call her writings essays; she instead uses "belles lettres," though adding modestly that using this term for her own writing might sound overconfident.

There is a similar problem regarding the term "memoirs," which in this paper is used rather loosely for written reminiscences *(omoide).* Memoirs are generically distinguishable from autobiography in that they do not place emphasis on the author's developing self but on the people he or she has known and on the events he or she has witnessed (Abrams, *Glossary,* p. 15). As we shall see, Mari's writing clearly has herself as its central interest, even when it is generally regarded as memoirs of her father.

5. These were the Tamura Toshiko Prize for *Koibitotachi no mori* (1961) and the Izumi Kyōka Prize for *Amai mitsu no heya* (1975).

6. Hagiwara Yōko's *Tenjō no hana* and *Rinne no koyomi* (the third part of her trilogy *Irakusa no ie*) recount how she was encouraged to write and how often she was judged in comparison with her father and with other literary daughters.

7. Mori Oto (Ōgai's eldest son from his first marriage, to Akamatsu Toshiko) and Mori Junzaburō (Ōgai's younger brother) edited *Ōgai iju to omoide* (1933). Junzaburō also published *Ōgai Mori Rintarō den* (1934) and *Ōgai Rintarō* (1942). Oto's other publications include *Kaibōdai ni motarite* (1934), *Mori Ōgai* (1946), and *Chichioya to shite no Mori Ōgai* (1955). Kobori Annu wrote *Bannen no chichi* (1936) and a few other books. Ōgai's younger sister, Koganei Kimiko, published *Ōgai no omoide* in 1956, and in the same year Ōgai's youngest son, Mori Rui, published *Ōgai no kodomo-tachi.*

8. The 1936 publication *Chichi no eizō* (Inukai et al., rev. ed., 1988) is a collection of essays written by twelve "brilliant sons" of twelve "great founders of modern Japan." The 1943 publication *Chichi no shosai* (Arishima et al., rev. ed., 1989), on the other hand, includes thirty-three essays on writer/scholar fathers, out of which six are written by daughters. The former includes Mori Oto's essay, and the latter has Kobori Annu's. The "Kaisetsu" (commentary) included in each volume also marks the gender division: Shiroyama Saburō is the commentator for the former, and Hagiwara Yōko for the latter.

9. Kōda Aya, *Chichi—sono shi* (1949). See chapter 9 in this volume.

10. Hagiwara, *Chichi, Hagiwara Sakutarō.*

11. Kawai, *Mukashibanashi to,* pp. 251–252.

12. Yaeger and Kowaleski-Wallace, *Refiguring the Father,* p. xi.

13. Lacan, *Écrits,* p. 67.

14. See, for example, Owen, ed., *Fathers.*

15. Oliver, ed., *Portable Kristeva,* pp. 133–134, 157–159.

16. Mori Mari, *Chichi no bōshi,* p. 56.

17. This, with the accent on the first syllable, is the special term Mari used to address her father from early childhood. In late Meiji, "papa" was not a common household term. All the three children of Ōgai and Shige (and in fact the parents themselves) used this word, while they seem to have called their mother by the usual "Okāsan" or "Okāchan."

18. Ibid., p. 42.

19. *Bundan* journalism has represented Shige as an impossible wife, daughter-in-law, and stepmother. The reputation has as its main sources Ōgai's short stories published around 1909 and the memoirs of Mori Oto.

20. Many other "literary daughters," including Kōda Aya, Hagiwara Yōko, Satō Aiko, and Tsushima Yūko, experienced divorce. Rather than jumping to hasty conclusions and seeing an Oedipus complex as the major cause, they should be treated individually. The negative reputation of Mari as a terrible wife and uncaring mother seems to have been orchestrated by her first husband, Yamada Tamaki, and his friends and colleagues. Mari's younger brother, Rui, recalls a nightmare he had after her divorce, in which he was chased by Yamada Tamaki (*Ōgai no kodomo-tachi,* pp. 128–129).

21. Katherine Tait, Bertrand Russell's daughter, opens her book on her father with the question she has "been asked all her life and [has] struggled vainly to provide concise and honest answers": "What was it like, having Bertrand Russell for a father?" Tait, *My Father,* p. xvii.

22. Yagawa Sumiko, too, emphasizes the maturity of Mari's writing from the earliest stage of her literary career. Yagawa, *"Chichi no musume"-tachi,* p. 11.

23. Mori Mari, *Chichi no bōshi*, pp. 57–64.

24. Mori Ōgai, *Ōgai zenshū*, vol. 5, pp. 519–567. The story is translated as "Kompira" by James M. Vardaman Jr. and is included in the collection of Ōgai's stories edited by J. Thomas Rimer, *Youth and Other Stories*. A brief discussion of this story is to be found in Bowring, *Mori Ōgai and the Modernization of Japanese Culture*, p. 131.

25. Set in the late eighteenth century, the story depicts a man sentenced to banishment for his mercy killing of his brother. As noted in the brief introduction to Edmund R. Skrzypczak's translation of this story in Mori Ōgai, *The Historical Fiction of Mori Ōgai*, p. 223, the story is one of the most widely admired of Ōgai's stories and has been translated into English several times.

26. Tanaka Miyoko (in Hirakawa et al., eds., *Ōgai no hito to shūhen*, pp. 254–284) carefully examines the discrepancies among the accounts of this incident given by Ōgai, Mari, Annu, and Oto. Oto writes that it was Shige who requested euthanasia, which was never carried out. Annu categorically denies this and insists that the idea came from one of the doctors. In the 1949 text, Mari writes sympathetically that after Furitsu's death her mother could not bear to see Mari's suffering any longer and requested her husband to administer an injection. In a later essay, however, she suggests that it was Mine, not Shige, who first consulted the family doctor about euthanasia. From all these accounts, Tanaka concludes that Furitsu's death was not a natural death but by morphine injection, proposed by Ōgai's mother (ibid., p. 271).

27. Mori Mari, *Chichi no bōshi*, p. 93.

28. Ibid., p. 99.

29. She uses the metaphor of a young rose thorn, "tender and supple" and "all the more painful because of its tenderness" (*Chichi no bōshi*, p. 100). Like the "box" and many other metaphors she uses, it makes the reader wonder whether Mari has deliberately chosen such words that invite Freudian analysis.

30. Ibid., p. 192.

31. See, for example, Etō, *Ketteiban Natsume Sōseki*, p. 351.

32. Mori Mari, *Chichi no bōshi*, pp. 182–183.

33. Mori Ōgai, *Youth and Other Stories*, pp. 111–112 (Mori Ōgai, *Ōgai zenshū*, vol. 5, p. 533).

34. Ibid., p. 127 (Mori Ōgai, *Ōgai zenshū*, vol. 5, p. 555).

35. Komori Yōichi presents a convincing argument on this point in his reading of Ōgai's "Hannichi," in "Kaku kazoku shōsetsu."

36. *"Asobi"* comes from the title of Ōgai's short story (*Ōgai zenshū*, vol. 7; Vardaman's translation is included in *Youth and Other Stories*). "Resignation," on the other hand, is the term that appears in his essay "Yo ga tachiba" (*Ōgai zenshū*, vol. 16).

37. *Chichi no bōshi* (pp. 7–8) begins with an episode of her father at a hat shop. As his head was unusually large, none of the hats in the shop fitted him. This, combined with his unusual appearance and demeanor, gave rise to sneers among shop attendants.

38. Ibid., p. 10.

39. *Chichi no bōshi*, pp. 7–10; *Zeitaku binbō*, pp. 174–177; *Kioku no e*, in *Mori Mari zenshū*, vol. 3, pp. 360–363; "Barakuihime," in *Mori Mari zenshū*, vol. 5, pp. 112–113.

40. All her treasured necklaces, pearls, and rubies were either mislaid or stolen. After World War II, with no income and few savings, she was forced to sell her diamond ring. See *Mori Mari zenshū*, vol. 3, pp. 49–50, 356–359.

41. For example, *Zeitaku binbō*, pp. 155–177; *Watashi no bi no sekai*, in *Mori Mari zenshū*, vol. 3, pp. 148–210; *Kioku no e*, in *Mori Mari zenshū*, vol. 3, pp. 370–373; "Barakuihime," in *Mori Mari zenshū*, vol. 5, pp. 92–126.

42. Tanaka, *Nihon fazakon bungakushi*.

43. As mentioned in note 4, above, *shōsetsu* is different from fiction in that it encompasses a wider range of prose writing, including not only novels and short stories but also what seems like biography, essay, journal, and criticism. The term originally came from Chinese and was used during the Edo period to denote trivial discourse. During Meiji it was used by Tsubouchi Shōyō as a translation of the term "novel." See Noguchi Takehiko's comprehensive explanation in *Ichigo no jiten: Shōsetsu*. The difference between fiction and *shōsetsu*, particularly its sub-genre *shishōsetsu*, has been discussed in many recent studies, including Fowler's *Rhetoric of Confession*.

44. *Chichi no bōshi*, pp. 184–185; *Zeitaku binbō*, pp. 66, 155; *Mori Mari zenshū*, vol. 3, pp. 392, 654. Notably many of the works Ōgai translated, including those by Goethe, Strindberg, Wilde, and d'Annunzio, do contain *akuma*.

45. *Mori Mari zenshū*, vol. 3, p. 394.

46. Yagawa, *"Chichi no musume,"* p. 90.

47. Mori Ōgai, *Ōgai zenshū*, vol. 4, p. 588. John W. Dower's translation of the text is included in *Youth and Other Stories*, pp. 65–70.

48. Trans. Bowring, in Mori Ōgai, *Youth and Other Stories*, p. 176.

49. Mori Mari, *Chichi no bōshi*, p. 140.

50. Trans. Bowring, in Mori Ōgai, *Youth and Other Stories*, p. 181.

51. *Mori Mari zenshū*, vol. 3, p. 348.

52. See the table of parodic names in her texts and Ōgai's. While her father used Mori Ōgai, Kanchōrō Shujin, Yume Miru Hito, Koshi Bentō, and various other pen names, Mari always used her own name for her writing; parodic names appear only within her texts.

53. Mori Mari, *Zeitaku binbō*, pp. 7–8.

54. Ibid., p. 137.

55. One of Mari's parodic names for Ōgai has the character for Europe instead of seagull for "Ō."

56. See Mishima's review "'Hanakage' to 'Koibitotachi no mori,'" in *Mishima Yukio zenshū*, vol. 30, pp. 149–151.

57. Aoyama, "Male Homosexuality," pp. 191–196.

58. Mishima, "Anata no rakuen."

59. Mari also writes (*Zeitaku binbō*, p. 119) about how she enjoyed the parodic or punning names in the adaptations of French novels by Kuroiwa Ruikō (Akazawa Ruikoku in her text).

60. The first few pages of the novel, however, do show the same features as in the first group. Comic names such as Iboyama Azako (Wart-hill Birthmark) and Hirutani Namako (Leech-valley Sea Cucumber) are cited as those of Moira's enemies. Mari seems to have completely abandoned pursuing the comic caricature after these few pages.

61. There are many other subtle differences between "Konpira" and *Amai mitsu no heya.* For example, while in Ōgai's text (*Ōgai zenshū,* vol. 5, p. 565; *Youth and Other Stories,* p. 133) the father cannot understand his daughter's mumbled words until the nurse interprets them for him, in Mari's text (p. 56) the father immediately understands Moira's request.

62. Yamada Tamaki's father, Yōsaku, was also in the trading business.

63. Mori Mari, *Amai mitsu no heya,* p. 21.

64. This reminds the reader of "Maihime" and other stories by Ōgai depicting a relationship between a Japanese man and a German woman.

65. Although the genre of *shōjo manga* itself does not seem to have interested Mari, in the mid-1970s she wrote that she found stories in the comic magazine *Big Comic* much more interesting than contemporary fiction (*Boyaki to ikari no Maria,* p. 404). She was also fascinated by the theater and films and often gained inspiration from magazine photographs. As she writes in many essays, a photograph of the French film actors Jean-Claude Brialy and Alain Delon inspired her to write the male homosexual love stories. Mari also told her editor and friends that she had the image of Peter O'Toole in mind in her creation and depiction of Moira. From the late 1970s, television was another source of imagination. In her stories she mixes techniques and visual images from such sources with her childhood memories and transforms them into what Mishima Yukio called "words that are never found in department stores but are sold only in the Mori Mari store" (Mishima, "Anata no rakuen, p. 13).

66. Mori Mari, *Amai mitsu no heya,* p. 404. Rinsaku's words faintly remind us of the *"als ob"* (*ka no yō ni,* as if) theory of Vaihinger, the subject of Ōgai's 1912 story "Ka no yō ni" (As if).

67. Ibid., p. 58.

68. Among such stories are Kanai Mieko's, including "Usagi" (1972), and Kurahashi Yumiko's novel *Seishōjo* (1965). See Atsuko Sakaki's chapter in this volume on Kurahashi and Sharalyn Orbaugh's chapter in *The Woman's Hand,* ed. Schalow and Walker, for discussion of Kanai's stories.

69. Yagawa, *"Chichi no musume"-tachi,* pp. 47–48.

70. Ibid., pp. 41, 78, 85, 91.

71. In Annu's and Rui's memoirs, too, Ōgai's smile is remembered with deep affection. In Oto's writing, however, Ōgai's smile is not always cheerful but often expresses embarrassment and bitterness (*Chichioya to shite no Mori Ōgai,* p. 119).

72. Mori Mari, *Amai mitsu no heya,* p. 353.

73. Ibid., p. 508.

74. Jung, taking up Freud's ideas on the Oedipus complex, renamed the girl's oedipal conflict the Electra complex, which Freud rejected (ibid., pp. 12–13).

75. Kataguchi, *Sakka no shindan,* pp. 52, 54. Mari caricatures this experience in "Kuroneko Jurietto no hanashi" (included in *Zeitaku binbō*), pp. 106–110, in which "Maria" expresses dissatisfaction with "Katagai"'s comment that her childishness might be a pose.

76. *Mori Mari zenshū,* vol. 5, pp. 109–124.

77. Mori Mari, *Amai mitsu no heya,* pp. 155–156.

78. "Narushishizumuron," in *Mishima Yukio zenshū,* vol. 32, pp. 375–390. This essay first appeared in the July 1966 issue of *Fujin kōron,* one of the major women's

magazines. Its lingering influence upon male writers and critics can be seen, for example, in Hasegawa Izumi's 1976 article "Gendai joryū sakka no yōsō," in which he accepts Mishima's gender-biased view of narcissism and asserts that literature requires this male property.

79. In his review of *Koibitotachi no mori* (*Mishima Yukio zenshū*, vol. 30, p. 150), Mishima writes: ". . . women are never expected to achieve such cruel and clean narcissism; it is the secret of all secrets men possess. It is astonishing that a woman writer has uncovered it."

80. Aoyama, "Male Homosexuality," p. 194.

81. Yagawa wrote in a letter to Mari that the novel depicted the complete picture of *shōjo* (*"Chichi no musume"-tachi*, p. 78). Shiraishi writes in her "Kaisetsu" of the novel that no other writer in Japan has ever portrayed a creature/*shōjo* like this (Mori Mari, *Amai mitsu no heya*, p. 516). See also Kanai, *Kaku koto*, pp. 255–256.

82. That Mari's writing would make unsafe source material might seem a cause for regret, in that the biographer would naturally seek to build up a portrait of the private Ōgai. Yagawa (p. 28) has pointed to the lack of the viewpoint of *onna kodomo* (women and children) in Ōgai studies. However, recent studies, such as those by Kaneko Sachiyo and Hirakawa et al., do go some way toward incorporating this viewpoint, using Oto's and Annu's memoirs generally in preference to Mari's writing.

83. Yaeger and Kowaleski-Wallace, pp. xiv, xvii.

84. Besides those mentioned above, there are many other examples of parody and allusion. Mari's use of the word *"giyō"* (*Amai mitsu no heya*, pp. 18, 97) is somewhat different from Ōgai's in *Vita Sexualis*. The deliberate misuse of honorifics for comic effect is seen in both Mari and Ōgai, but Mari uses it far more frequently and emphatically. It would also be interesting to compare the physicality of the father-daughter relationship in "Hannichi," as observed by Komori Yōichi, with that in Mari's texts.

Works Cited

Location of Japanese publishers is Tokyo unless otherwise noted.

Abrams, M. H. *A Glossary of Literary Terms*. 3d ed. New York: Holt, Rinehart and Winston, 1971.

Aoyama, Tomoko. "Male Homosexuality as Treated by Japanese Women Writers." In *Modernization and Beyond: The Japanese Trajectory*, ed. Gavan McCormack and Yoshio Sugimoto, pp. 186–204. Cambridge: Cambridge University Press, 1988.

Arishima Yukimitsu et al. *Chichi no shosai*. Chikuma shobō, 1989.

Bowring, Richard. *Mori Ōgai and the Modernization of Japanese Culture*. Cambridge: Cambridge University Press.

Etō Jun. *Ketteiban Natsume Sōseki*. Shinchō bunko. Shinchōsa, 1979.

Fowler, Edward. *The Rhetoric of Confession: Shishōsetsu in Early Twentieth-Century Japanese Fiction*. Berkeley and Los Angeles: University of California Press, 1988.

Hagiwara Yōko. *Chichi, Hagiwara Sakutarō*. Chūkō bunko. Chūō kōronsha, 1979.

———. *Irakusa no ie: sanbusaku*. Shinchōsha, 1998.

———. *Tenjō no hana: Miyoshi Tatsuji shō*. Shinchōsha, 1966.

Hasegawa Izumi. "Gendai joryū bungaku no yōsō." *Kokubungaku kaishaku to kanshō* 530 (September 1976): 6–14.

———. *Mori Ōgai ronkō*. Meiji shoin, 1962.

Hirakawa Sukehiro, Hiraoka Toshio, and Takemori Ten'yū, eds. *Ōgai no hito to shūhen*. Vol. 1 of *Kōza Mori Ōgai*. Shin'yōsha, 1997.

Inukai Takeru et al. *Chichi no eizō*. Chikuma shobō, 1988.

Kanai Mieko. *Kaku koto no hajimari ni mukatte*. Chūkō bunko. Chūō kōronsha, 1981.

Kaneko Sachiyo. *Ōgai to "josei"—Mori Ōgai ronkyū*. Daitō shuppansha, 1992.

Kataguchi Yasufumi. *Sakka no shindan: rōrushahha tesuto kara sōsaku shinri no himitsu o saguru*. Shin'yōsha, 1982.

Kawai Hayao. *Mukashibanashi to Nihonjin no kokoro*. Iwanami shoten, 1982.

Kobori Annu. *Bannen no chichi*. Iwanami bunko. Iwanami shoten, 1981.

Kobori Keiichirō. *Mori Ōgai bungyō kaidai: hon'yaku-hen*. Iwanami shoten, 1982.

Koganei Kimiko. *Ōgai no omoide*. Iwanami bunko. Iwanami shoten, 1999.

Komori Yōichi. "Kaku kazoku shōsetsu to shite no 'Hannichi': sei to shōhi no gensetsu kūkan." *Mori Ōgai kenkyū* 5 (January 1993): 21–43.

Kurahashi Yumiko. *Seishōjo*. Shinchō bunko. Shinchōsa, 1981.

Lacan, Jacques. *Écrits: A Selection*. Trans. Alan Sheridan. London: Travistock Publications, 1980.

Lacan, Sibylle. *Aru chichioya: Puzzle*. Trans. Nagata China. Shōbunsha, 1998.

Marcus, Marvin. *Paragons of the Ordinary: The Biographical Literature of Mori Ōgai*. Honolulu: University of Hawai'i Press, 1993.

Mishima Yukio. Mishima, "Anata no rakuen, anata no gin no saji—Mori Mari sama." In *Mori Mari zenshū*, vol. 4, "Geppō 2," pp. 9–16. Chikuma shobō, 1993. Reprinted from *Fujin kōron* (March 1967). Also in *Mishima Yukio zenshū*, vol. 32, pp. 561–567 (Shinchōsha, 1975).

———. *Mishima Yukio zenshū*. 36 vols. Shinchōsha, 1973–1976.

———. "Mudai (Mori Mari san.)." In *Mishima Yukio zenshū*, vol. 35, p. 231. Shinchōsa, 1976.

Mitchell, Juliet, and Jacqueline Rose, eds. *Feminine Sexuality: Jacques Lacan and the École Freudienne*. London: Macmillan, 1982.

Mori Mari. *Amai mitsu no heya*. Shinchō bunko. Shinchōsha, 1981.

———. *Barakuihime, Kareha no nedoko*. Kōdansha bungei bunko. Kōdansha, 1996.

———. "Barakuihime." In *Mori Mari zenshū*, vol. 5, pp. 91–126. Chikuma shobō, 1993.

———. "Botchicheri no tobira." In *Koibitotachi no mori*, pp. 7–76. Shinchōsha, 1975.

———. *Boyaki to ikari no Maria*. Ed. Kojima Chikako. Chikuma shobō, 1998.

———. *Chichi no bōshi*. Kōdansha bungei bunko. Kōdansha, 1991.

———. "Chichi no bōshi." In *Chichi no bōshi*, pp. 7–10. Kōdansha bungei bunko. Kōdansha, 1991.

———. "Futari no tenshi." In *Chichi no bōshi*, pp. 57–60. Kōdansha, 1991.

———. *Kioku no e*. In *Mori Mari zenshū*, vol. 3, pp. 307–531. Chikuma shobō, 1993.

————. *Koibitotachi no mori.* Shinchō bunko. Pp. 7–76. Shinchōsha, 1975.

————. *Mori Mari zenshū.* 8 vols. Chikuma shobō, 1993.

————. *Watashi no bi no sekai.* In *Mori Mari zenshū,* vol. 3, pp. 6–210. Chikuma shobō, 1993.

————. "Yume." In *Chichi no bōshi,* pp. 135–166. Kōdansha, 1991.

————. *Zeitaku binbō.* Kōdansha bungei bunko. Kōdansha, 1991.

Mori Mayumi. *Ōgai no saka.* Shinchōsha, 1997.

Mori Ōgai. *The Historical Fiction of Mori Ōgai.* Ed. David Dilworth and J. Thomas Rimer. Honolulu: University of Hawai'i Press, 1991.

————. *Ōgai zenshū.* 38 vols. Iwanami shoten, 1971–1975.

————. *Youth and Other Stories.* Ed. J. Thomas Rimer. Honolulu: University of Hawai'i Press, 1994.

Mori Oto. *Chichioya to shite no Mori Ōgai.* Chikuma bunko. Chikuma shoten, 1993.

Mori Rui. *Ōgai no kodomo-tachi.* Chikuma bunko. Chikuma shoten, 1995.

Mure Yōko. *Zeitaku binbō no Maria.* Kadokawa shoten, 1996.

Nakano Shigeharu. *Ōgai sono sokumen.* Chikuma gakugei bunko. Chikuma shoten, 1994.

Noguchi Takehiko. *Ichigo no jiten: Shōsetsu.* Sanseidō, 1996.

Oliver, Kelly, ed. *The Portable Kristeva.* New York: Columbia University Press, 1997.

Owen, Ursula, ed. *Fathers: Reflections by Daughters.* London: Virago, 1983.

Schalow, Paul Gordon, and Janet A. Walker, eds. *The Woman's Hand: Gender and Theory in Japanese Women's Writings.* Stanford, Calif.: Stanford University Press, 1996.

Senuma Kayō et al. *Meiji joryū bungakushū.* Vol. 2. *Meiji bungaku zenshū,* vol. 82. Chikuma shobō, 1965.

Tait, Katharine. *My Father Bertrand Russell.* Bristol: Thoemmes Press, 1996.

Takahashi Yoshitaka. *Mori Ōgai.* Vol. 1 of *Gendai sakkaron zenshū.* Satsuki shobō, 1957.

Takemori Ten'yū. *Ōgai sono monyō.* Ozawa shoten, 1984.

Tanaka Takako. *Nihon fazakon bungakushi.* Kinokuniya shoten, 1998.

Tanizaki Jun'ichirō. *Tanizaki Jun'ichirō zenshū.* Vol. 17. Chūō kōronsha, 1973.

Tsukakoshi Kazuo. "Mori Mari." *Kokubungaku kaishaku to kanshō,* no. 651 (50.10) (September 1985): 146–147.

Yaeger, Patricia, and Beth Kowaleski-Wallace, eds. *Refiguring the Father: New Feminist Readings of Patriarchy.* Carbondale: Southern Illinois University Press, 1989.

Yagawa Sumiko. *"Chichi no musume"-tachi—Mori Mari to Anaisu Nin.* Shinchōsha, 1997.

Yamazaki Masakazu. *Ōgai: tatakau kachō.* Shinchō bunko. Shinchōsha, 1980.

Chapter 7
Enchi Fumiko
Female Sexuality and the Absent Father

Eileen B. Mikals-Adachi

Hidden in the depths of Tokyo's Yanaka Cemetery is one literary daughter who, while enjoying an impressive reputation in her own right, was eternally haunted by her father's image. Enchi Fumiko (1905–1986), one of postwar Japan's most acclaimed women writers in life, is positioned in death alongside her father, Ueda Kazutoshi (1867–1937)[1]—and significantly so. The cemetery's "Directory of Celebrities" lists this 1985 recipient of Japan's highest of honors, the Imperial Cultural Medal *(Bunka kunshō)*, as simply "novelist; oldest daughter of Kazutoshi."[2] Indeed, Enchi is better known to many Japanese as the daughter of this renowned philologist and classicist than for her long list of literary accomplishments and awards. This choice of burial sites was, moreover, the writer's own. Rejecting a tradition that would have meant placement in her husband's plot, Enchi insisted on this arrangement, in short demanding eternal entombment as "Daddy's girl."[3] Through this bold gesture, she reiterated the fascinating dichotomy present in the patriarchal structure that she had explored in her literature.

Patriarchy, Jane Gallop explains in *The Daughter's Seduction,* is rooted in the uprightness of the father.[4] In the Ueda burial plot, the father's tombstone, larger and overshadowing his daughter's, stands as testimony to what Gallop would term the "phallic uprightness" of patriarchy. Yet, in Enchi's world the ideology and the man himself are frequently presented as two distinct entities, related but not synonymous. Father figures, as discrete characters, are conspicuously absent in Enchi's works. Thus, even though the author is critical of the patriarchal system that oppresses women, she retains the purity of the father by keeping him outside the text and apart from the order that he would normally represent. Leaving the father undefined within

194

the pages of her fiction allows the author to protect him from charges that he could be less than perfect. Separation of the father and patriarchy is, however, not always clear-cut for Enchi. Inevitably there is overlap, just as the roles of daughter and writer occasionally become indistinguishable.

Emotionally seduced by the power of the father image, as a young woman Enchi was unable to sever ties with the man whose name would mark her as his permanent property in life and in death. Not even her own successful career as a literary figure, a career spanning over half a century, could erase Enchi's attachment to a father long gone. Enchi's last complete work, *Between Dreams and Reality* (*Yume utsutsu no ki,* 1987), a journal of random recollections about her father, remains behind as a sad farewell to the world in which the writer was enwrapped until her dying days, a world "between dreams and reality," a world defined by a daughter's desire for an unattainable father.

Reality: Dutiful Daughter

A student of B. H. Chamberlain at Tokyo University, Ueda Kazutoshi introduced Western research methods into the study of Japanese language and linguistics after four years of research in Germany and France. Then, as a professor at his alma mater, Ueda trained researchers in his capacity as a member of the National Language Research Committee (Kokugo chōsa iinkai) and published a number of books on Japanese linguistics: *For the Japanese Language,* volumes 1 and 2 (*Kokugo no tame,* 1895–1903); *Ten Lectures on the Japanese Language* (*Kokugaku no jukkō,* 1916); and a Chinese character dictionary entitled *Daijiten* (1917). Best known among his publications is the Japanese-language dictionary *Dai Nihon kokugo jiten* (1915–1919), which he wrote in collaboration with Matsui Kanji (1893–1945). Ueda was clearly respected in his field and quite well known in the literary circles where his daughter hoped to make her name.

Enchi was Ueda's third and youngest child, and apparently his favorite. Information about this daughter-father relationship is limited, however, and what is available concerns only Enchi's early years. Most important among these few accessible details is Ueda's role in introducing his daughter to literature and, in a sense, sending her on the road to a career as a writer. At the age of four, Enchi began accompanying her father to the kabuki theater. She was constantly in the presence of the numerous professors, scholars, and students of Japanese linguistics who frequented the Ueda home, and she was conveniently blessed with access to her father's extensive library. Enchi's early interest in literature was soon elevated to a passionate desire to become a part of her father's world of letters. When the home economics–oriented curriculum at her high school could not satisfy her thirst for that world, Enchi left school in 1922 to pursue English, French, Chinese, and Bible studies on her own—a move Ueda encouraged and abetted by supplying tutors. In 1928, moreover, with the publication of her first major literary work, a full-length play entitled *Noisy Night in Late Spring (Banshun sōya)*, Enchi modified the way her name was inscribed by changing Fumi, written with the Chinese characters for "abundant beauty," to Fumiko, or "child of letters." Although by birth she was Ueda's daughter—his "abundant beauty," by her own choice she identified the literary world itself as being responsible for her paternity.[5]

Distinguishing herself from her renowned father was clearly not as easy as a simple name change. Even so, being the daughter of a famed scholar was certainly not a disadvantage for a young writer. Through his fame and connections, Ueda provided the introductions that would allow his daughter entrance to influential literary circles. For example, it was through his network of acquaintances that Enchi was able to join a drama seminar conducted by Osanai Kaoru (1881–1928), then leader of the modern theater movement. It was this association that enabled Enchi to publish a number of minor plays—thus inaugurating her debut in 1926. Why she chose to change her name in 1928 is not clear, nor does the writer herself ever discuss this matter in her writing. Facts about Enchi's life at this early stage in her career are vague. Her association with members of the proletarian movement is known, as is her attraction to one of these political activists, Kataoka Teppei (1894–1944), a married man and a target of police surveillance. But why Enchi chose only a few years later to distance herself from those connected with the movement is left unexplained. Most likely, as she implies in her subsequent fiction, she removed herself from this politically dangerous association in an effort to protect her father's name from potential scandal.

Perhaps for similar reasons, Ueda's daughter entered into a respectable relationship with Enchi Yoshimatsu, a newspaper columnist ten years her senior. Her acquaintance with Yoshimatsu and their subsequent marriage in 1930 was masterminded, significantly, by one of her father's colleagues. It was not a happy union, and Enchi, who until the marriage had consistently written for the stage, turned to the prose-fiction for which she is so well known today. Enchi's first important piece of fiction, the short story "Original Sin" *(Genzai)* was written in 1938, the year following her father's death. But then the war intervened, and Enchi began to suffer from a variety of ailments. Further literary production was delayed until 1953 when she published "Miserable Times" *(Himojii tsukihi)*, for which she received the 1954 Women's Literature Prize. This date thus marks the true beginning of Enchi's career as a writer. During the three decades that followed, she produced a wide array of literary masterpieces, including more than twenty plays, more than fifty short stories, thirty full-length novels, ten collections of essays, and a number of modern translations of classical works such as *The Tale of Genji.* In recognition of these feats, she also received six major awards of distinction.

Ueda never witnessed his daughter's success. Instead, he died with, in a sense, the satisfaction of knowing that she had become a respectable woman through marriage and motherhood. Enchi does not discuss the effect, if any, that Ueda's actual death had on her writing. Yet, his departure from her life seemed to allow her to open up in ways that had not been possible when he was alive. Moreover, the void that he left in her life is replicated in her fiction—in story after story of family plots with conspicuously absent or certainly nondescript fathers. As stated earlier, Enchi's seemingly intentional reluctance to paint fatherly portraits leaves the father figure in an illusionary state of perfection. Enchi the writer might have matured with her father's death, but Enchi the daughter was apparently unable to free herself of the fatherly hold on her emotions. Rather than facing the phantom, she used language as a clever screen—shielding her father from exposure and protecting herself from confrontation with him. Confronting the father might have meant rejection by or, even worse, disintegration of her idol, and Enchi wanted, most of all, to retain her position as Daddy's favorite. Now, as the "child of letters," she had the creative ability to preserve memories of what were—when compared with her present situation—surely the happiest days of her life. And she did so by leaving them untold.

Between Dreams and Reality—The Fictionalized Father

Rather than introducing a dominant father into her narratives, Enchi leaves him undefined, his influence only implied—a technique that,

in effect, strengthens the father's position and reinforces the power
he has over his daughter. As Paul Rosefeldt explains in his study *The
Absent Father in Modern Drama*, "the corporeal presence of a father
can be attacked," but "the invisible father, only a step away from presence, is what ensnares his daughters and holds them bound to him."[6]
In Enchi's world, the absent father too maintains a subtle grip on the
daughterly writer who in turn creates women, like herself, who are in
search of the self suppressed by the system he represents. Together
with her protagonists, Enchi struggles to be free of the man behind
the scenes.[7]

Although many of her novels involve families, few describe familial
relationships. Rarely does the author focus on parent-child ties or
the husband-wife bond. Rather, Enchi pursues the story from the
wife's point of view, discussing the illicit affairs these women have
with married men, younger men, or some other "inappropriate"
male partners. Moreover, she characterizes these affairs as attempts
on the part of her female protagonists to escape unhappy marriages
or relationships and to liberate themselves, or at least feel liberated,
from the misery of the situations they are forced to endure. Although
Enchi did not proclaim herself a feminist, her texts abound in subtle
protests against the patriarchal system that is at the root of her protagonists' woes. At the same time, she insists, however, on maintain-
ing the purity of the father throughout her literature and intentionally avoiding any confrontation with his flaws.

Even in novels that revolve around families and include prominent male characters, the absent father prevails. In *The Female Slope*
(*Onnazaka*, 1957; translated by John Bester as *The Waiting Years*, 1971),
for example, the protagonist Tomo turns only to her mother for advice
and guidance. Her father is never described. Moreover, Tomo's husband, Yukitomo, who is father to a number of children, is depicted in
his roles as spouse, provider, and lover of numerous mistresses, and
although his relationships with women young enough to be his children are quite suggestive, hinting at an incestuous pact, that with his
own daughter never becomes the writer's concern. By refusing to describe the father-daughter relationship in detail—positive or otherwise
—Enchi absolves the father (though not the man) of tyranny and
creates a sacred space for the father-daughter dyad.

In another well-known work by Enchi, *Female Masks* (*Onnamen*,
1958; translated by Juliet Winters Carpenter as *Masks*, 1983), no por-
tion of the story is set aside for a description of the father-child rela-

tionships, even though children are central to the vengeful scheme of the protagonist Mieko. Mieko's husband is portrayed as the spouse who deprived her of happiness, and the other men in the story are seen as but pawns in the cynical game she chooses to play. In a subtle reversal of the concept of "borrowing the womb"[8] to continue family lines, Enchi skillfully presents men as mere objects from which to extract the seed of life. Mieko's lover from the past is acknowledged only for his assistance in creating her children, and the young man Ibuki is recognized simply for his role in impregnating Mieko's mentally impaired daughter to ensure the continuance of her family line.

In both of these novels, and indeed in the majority of Enchi's works, the writer refuses to elevate any man to the position of "father." Imprisoned in the illusion of his perfection, Enchi is unable to portray another in the father's place and through this absent father, she too is seen as a victim of the system he represents. For patriarchy, as Rosefeldt explains, "like all ideologies, oppresses less by force than by conditioning" and "this ideology leaves the daughter always hoping for the lost father, looking always for Daddy's approval."[9] Not wanting to tarnish the father's name, Enchi circumvents the issue with elaborate descriptions of women like Tomo or Mieko that overshadow any would-be contender for the paternal throne, and thus she preserves the image of an almighty father in the everlasting world of illusions.

The subject of father is similarly avoided in the numerous essays credited to Enchi's name. The most detailed picture of this father-daughter team is presented in *Between Dreams and Reality*. Although this too is a meager sketch, it reconfirms Enchi's desperate desire to please the man who meant the most to her. First, she offers readers a cheerful picture of a little girl enjoying her position as the youngest child and the privileges afforded the Ueda's "family pet."[10] The mood of the account soon changes, however, when the daughter labeled as Kazutoshi's favorite confesses that her father never spoke of his love for her and that instead he made it quite clear that she was not as ladylike as he would have desired. Scarred by her father's words, words that she suggests echo those spoken to Murasaki Shikibu—"It's too bad you're not a boy"[11]—Enchi frantically attempts to become the woman Ueda wanted his daughter to be.[12] She agrees to marry an undesirable man only because she knows that her father will be "relieved" by the arrangement and then finds to her dismay that "her husband was not at all like the father whose place he was supposed to take."[13]

Still craving the love of her father long after his death, Enchi stays
with Yoshimatsu for more than forty years and lives in misery merely
out of fear of "losing her father" if they divorced.[14] The husband
essentially chosen by the father comes to represent the patriarchal
system Enchi had been conditioned to accept. A divorce from Yoshimatsu would have meant rejection of her father's ideals and, in a
sense, of the man himself—a move that Enchi was not willing or prepared to make.

Although one would expect Enchi to be more critical of a man who
failed to recognize his daughter's worth and who was clearly insensitive to her misery, nothing could displace the perfect father in the
eyes of his adoring child. Even if, at some point, Enchi sensed that as
a little girl she had been deceived into believing in the extent of her
father's affection, over the years theirs became, in her mind, a mutual
and perpetual love. Fortunately, the enchantment of this father-
daughter relationship did not extend to that of Ueda Kazutoshi the
scholar and Enchi Fumiko the writer. Here, Enchi was able to be a
bit more realistic. Revealing that she "knew almost nothing about her
father's work,"[15] she asserts that on a professional level she wanted to
succeed on her own. She also confides that as a writer, being "labeled
as Kazutoshi's daughter"[16] was something that she despised. The father
might have interfered with her life, but Enchi was not about to let
him dominate her career.

The only other reference to living under the pressure of a famed
father's name is seen in the collection of random jottings titled
Dressed to Travel (*Tabi yosoi*, 1966). Here, in the short essay "Dad: Ueda
Bannen" *(Oyaji: Ueda Bannen)*, Enchi explains:

> For the past ten years or so, I have been able to accept people re-
> ferring to my father when they speak to me, and now, in a way, I
> even enjoy those moments. But before I reached this point, I was
> embarrassed by references to my father—both before and after he
> died—and I would deal with the matter by changing the subject.
>
> This was, by no means, because I despised my father. Instead, I
> wanted to avoid having such words tickle my inner being—the
> depths in which I kept my father's image. On the other hand, there
> was a time when I had a very twisted view of the whole situation
> and the fact that my own name was always crowned with my father's
> hurt my pride. In my youth, I was distressed by the fact that any-
> thing other than my own self—even a parent—should be my crown-
> ing glory.[17]

The peak of Enchi's agony comes when a middle-aged woman she has just met cannot remember which famous scholar, Ueda Bin[18] or Ueda Bannen, is Enchi's father. Not only are the repeated references to a father long deceased annoying, but comments like "your father is the only reason people remember you" prove to be devastating, crushing "the tiny bit of pride" the young writer had for herself.[19] Although Ueda had introduced Enchi to the world of literature, he had also instilled in his daughter the horror of living in the shadow of his fame:

> Sons of extraordinary fathers are often plagued with an inferiority complex and develop a type of second generation personality. Supposedly in the case of daughters, having a father with a respectable social position frequently fosters their growth instead of burdening them with complexes. Perhaps it was because I was not a very feminine type, but apparently I did have a complex towards my father. For, did I not, on the professional level, unconsciously view my father as a potential rival?[20]

In not being a typical daughter, perhaps Enchi, like Murasaki Shikibu, surpassed the "boy" her father had wished she could have been.[21]

Determined not to be defeated professionally by her "rival" or to let her own "complex" penetrate her writing, Enchi's initial intention was to keep her roles as daughter and writer completely separate. She soon discovered, however, that this was not an easy task, and her two worlds inevitably began to overlap as she wrote about women like herself, constantly searching for the self that can define itself rather than be defined by and within the confines of a patriarchal society. The protagonists' problems develop out of the writer's own, and just as Enchi's identity revolves around the image of her father, the self-identity of her women becomes closely tied to the patriarchal system he represents. Drawn by the father's palpable absence into a quest for a substitute to fill his place, Enchi's women go from lover to lover looking for, but never finding, the perfect man.

Beginning with her 1938 short story "Original Sin," about a widow involved with a married man, forbidden relationships abound in Enchi's fiction, as her protagonists try to satisfy what Enchi defines as "natural instincts." In "Village of Falling Flowers" (*Hana chiru sato*, 1961), for example, a middle-aged, childless woman falls in love with her stepson, and in the novel *A Ray of Komachi* (*Komachi hensō*, 1965), a beautiful but aging actress has an affair with a man young enough to be her own child, the son of her lover from years past. When inappropriate relationships such as these—particularly relationships of infidelity—occur in Western literature, as Jane Gallop notes, they often suggest a feminist ploy to undermine the "Name of the Father," destroying from within the marriage system that buttresses the Father's Law. In Enchi's works, however, while each of these women tries to affirm her identity through a sexual relationship, none of them experiences a happy ending. As Enchi explains, in Japan "women in particular are taught to suppress their sexuality,"[22] and having broken the rules, these daughters have to pay the consequences. Father, after all, is always watching.

The space set aside for the father in real life might translate into an empty void in Enchi's narratives, but his image is constantly hanging over the men her protagonists encounter. Before continuing with these women in the pursuit of the self, the writer felt the need to define the father she had kept within. In "Dad: Ueda Kazutoshi," Enchi explains:

> Once I was over fifty years old and able to fully exhibit my ability through my work, the feeling that I was burdened with my father's name was gone. I no longer had the chip that had weighed on my shoulders. I sincerely felt happy about being my father's child— not because of anything that was outwardly obvious, like the fact that my father was socially renowned or that I had spent my youth in a pile of books. It was because the first man I had met in my life was the most masculine of men—my father.[23]

Daddy's girl had matured and was ready to confront her father on the written page. She was also prepared to examine that part of her own identity so closely connected to him and his "masculinity": her own sexuality. Ironically, however, it was only after she had passed her sexual peak that Enchi was able to confront this problem. Recovering from a mastectomy (1938) and a hysterectomy (1946), the writer herself was, at this time, suffering the psychological pain of having lost those parts of her body normally described as defining the "feminine." Questioning how she could still be a woman without the physical proof of her sexuality, Enchi apparently felt, to borrow Sidonie Smith's words, "homeless inside her own body."[24]

As a result, during the 1950s and 1960s, Enchi's attention is noticeably turned to the physical attributes of her characters. Female body parts are openly discussed, and many of her women suffer, like their creator, from some feminine ailment. Throughout her life, Enchi had suppressed her sexual desires and individual identity to play the roles assigned a proper lady and thereby please her father. Having denied her body the gratification it deserved for so long, she was now eager to finally reveal the passionate feelings of her innermost self. Enchi felt betrayed, however, by the physical being that housed that self and by the society that had forced her to keep it within, and she clearly knew that what she now needed was some vehicle of expression other than her body.

Dreams: Paternal Phantoms

The only concrete appearance of a father figure in Enchi's fictional world is in the award-winning trilogy *Stripped of Crimson* (*Ake o ubau mono*, 1956–1968), a semiautobiographical work that includes the novels *Stripped of Crimson* (*Ake o ubau mono*, 1956), *Wounded Wings* (*Kizu aru tsubasa*, 1962), and *Rainbow and Carnage* (*Niji to shura*, 1968). In this trilogy, Enchi attempts to "go public," so to speak, by presenting her own interpretation of the father-daughter experience in the fashion of an "autobiographical manifesto," as defined by Sidonie Smith in *Subjectivity, Identity, and the Body*.[25] This is, it should be noted, Enchi's sole autobiographical piece of fiction and the only time she is able to enter the emotional territory set aside for a paternal parent. The sacred seat of father is clearly reserved for but one man, Ueda Kazutoshi, and never before, or after, this trilogy does she attempt to confront her own father or the role he played in her identity.

When accepting the Tanizaki Literary Prize for this trilogy, Enchi states that "being in her fifties at the time she wrote this series, she was fully aware of her role as a novelist" and she "realized that when trying to put down in words what she wanted to say, it was easiest, and yet most trying, to look back on the road she herself had followed."[26] In *Unsolicited Commentary on Edo Literature* (*Edo bungaku towazugatari*, 1960), she also explains that "art is born from events in real life,"[27] and in *Stripped of Crimson* she clearly tells her personal story as she "looks back" on her own life. For purposes of continuity, Enchi uses the same protagonist in the entire trilogy and, through the character Shigeko, tries to "leave her mark in literature by writing about every possible aspect of one woman's sexuality."[28]

In this journey through time in the trilogy *Stripped of Crimson*, a web of self-identity is woven, and the writer's own self is reconstructed.

Such autobiographical accounts demonstrate, as Morwenna Griffiths explains in *Feminisms and the Self,* "how social circumstance, material circumstance (including embodiment), change and growth all come together to make the self."[29] Right from the onset of *Stripped of Crimson,* the similarities between writer and protagonist are evident. In the opening scene, set in a dimly lit dentist's office, Shigeko reflects on the aging state of her own body as her teeth are extracted in preparation for a set of dentures. Though she feels "strong remorse over having an important part of her self taken from her," Shigeko knows that this is not the first, but the third time she "is watching a part of herself die." The first two "deaths" she is forced to witness occur during operations identical to Enchi's own, a mastectomy and a hysterectomy. Shigeko recalls the anxiety she felt over "losing her feminine characteristics" and her grief at having "more than half of her female sexuality taken from her body."[30] The "dry cavity"[31] that fills her toothless mouth is as empty as the body Shigeko now has, and her pain and fear represent the writer's own.

By using Shigeko's body as her vehicle of expression in a manner similar to that described by Elizabeth Grosz in *Volatile Bodies,* Enchi is able to take what is essentially private and make it available to her reading public.[32] Enchi goes past the physical void to unveil that which is concealed within. She believes that, like the dentures for an empty mouth, there must also be a way to fill the sexual cavity caused by her physical loss and describes her protagonist as being pleasantly surprised when her attraction to a surgeon ignites a "passionate kind of love" inside the "self that had supposedly lost its womanhood."[33] The writer, concerned about her own physical condition, thus shows that not even a decaying body can erase the "sexuality alive in her emotions."[34]

As Shigeko ponders questions of self-identity, the most prominent image in the novel becomes blood, to borrow Smith's term, the "metonymic marker of 'woman.' "[35] Paralleling the divisions in the story, this sanguineous element marks the three important stages in the development of the protagonist.[36] The first menstrual period, the loss of her virginity to a married man, and an affair with a considerably younger man after her hysterectomy announce, affirm, and then, in a sense, negate Shigeko's femininity. Not only are the physical changes significant, but the lack of understanding shown by the men in her life is also essential in developing Shigeko's awareness of her own self. Social circumstances inevitably affect the development of the self, and for Enchi and the women she portrays, all of whom have been conditioned to believe that self-worth is based on relationships with men, such circumstances involve members of the opposite sex. Moreover, the writer inevitably brings the discussion of self back to the man who has played the most influential role in her life, the father.

Shigeko's introduction to the reality of life is described through her discovery of the onset of her first menstrual period, a momentous occasion at which her father is present. In her depiction, Enchi presents a protagonist shocked by the physical changes and distraught at her own inability to tell her father what is happening to her body. Hoping that the person for whom she has the utmost respect and love will notice the changes in his daughter's body, Shigeko is left dumbfounded by her father's silent indifference. The father, whose absence had earlier permeated Enchi's fiction, is now being colored in by the anger of one made to feel inferior about a very feminine experience merely because her father refused to celebrate, or even notice, his daughter's womanhood.

In a "logical" sequence of events, the next blood to appear in the trilogy signifies the loss of Shigeko's virginity to her married lover, Hitoyanagi. After their rendezvous, Shigeko looks in the mirror and begins laughing until her face becomes "distorted into an ugly smile"[37] and her sadness fills the blank page of yet another man's indifference to the sexuality one woman is trying to affirm. To avoid being ostracized by a society that expects women to conform to successive roles of daughter, wife, and mother, Enchi has her protagonist marry an "ordinary" man in a "safe" marriage—notably a carbon copy of the writer's own. Her individuality is thus sacrificed for her identity as first a daughter, then a wife, and finally a mother. This does not mean, however, that Enchi has lost faith in discovering the self. Shigeko's awakening comes from reflections on a life that has been played by the rules, a life lived by the writer and now projected into her literature.

After the first meeting with her husband-to-be, Shigeko sees "a dream where she is walking on the beach with Hitoyanagi who has become blind." Enchi then has her protagonist suddenly awaken with the realization that the man in the dream was "her father in the form of Hitoyanagi"[38] and that both of these men are equally "blind" concerning her own self. Another dream after her mastectomy, in which the man she thought to be her lover turns out to be her husband, further demonstrates that the men in her life are interchangeable—each blurring in the void she had reserved for the perfect man. And in a third dream that occurs during Shigeko's hysterectomy, Enchi zooms in on the problem, bringing everything into sharp perspective. This time the man in question is undoubtedly her father, and his little girl deliriously calls out to him in a final, though vain, attempt to acquire his approval.

In this climactic ending to Shigeko's dreams, Enchi has her protagonist walking along the beach with her father when the blood of the first menstrual period begins to flows from between her legs. Not at all embarrassed by this incident, Shigeko is instead disappointed in her father's failure to notice the "red drops about the size of a dog's footprints" that she has left marking their trail. The father is again described as being "blind" and together with her protagonist, the writer wonders if "this is because he is a man." The daughter runs frantically after her father yelling: "a very important thing is happening to Shigeko's body," and "this is what it is to be a woman."[39] Her words fall upon deaf ears, however, and she wakes up feeling frail and empty. How could the father she so adored be completely oblivious to the feelings of the daughter that had put him up on his pedestal?

Enchi does not let her protagonist despair for long, though. Not only does Shigeko survive the operation, but her vision is enhanced by her father's "blindness." The role of father and daughter are, in a sense, reversed, thereby empowering the woman whose view had been blocked by the shadow of her father. Now it is the woman who becomes the observer, the sightless father bereft of power. With her vision, she is able to fix upon the father—and to name him. The man she had so blindly admired, she can clearly see, is no different from any other man. The image of her father as the "perfect" man is crushed instantly by the woman who comes boldly forward from deep inside of Shigeko. Liberated from an "Electra complex,"[40] Shigeko is now ready to start a healthy relationship with a man. Ironically, however, just when the shadow of her father is removed from the picture, Shigeko finds that her body is "full of deformities."[41] "Incapable of ever joining a man sexually," she is haunted by dreams of her first period and continually reminded that physically "she is no longer the same person" she used to be.[42] Yet, through these whispers of the night, Enchi also tells her protagonist that even without the physical proof, she still is, and always will be, a woman:

Not even Shigeko realized that the dream of her first menstrual period, the dream that she was strangely reliving over and over again, came to her as the final breath of the woman inside herself—the woman that had fallen into a deep and bottomless well the moment Shigeko had lost her sexual organ.[43]

The narrator who needed to define the father in her search for the self now knows that it is time to unveil the woman who has matured within, the woman breathing the dreams of her own heart.

The posthysterectomy Shigeko is described at first as being deeply depressed because of the "the burial hole" that has replaced her reproductive organs in the graveyard of her body.[44] She dreads being touched by anyone and fears, most of all, the possible damage that might be inflicted on her body "by the reckless force of a man."[45] For a woman whose identity had been defined through her relationships with men, lack of a physical vehicle for expression accentuates the author's feeling of "not being home" in her own body. As Smith explains, "this experience of homelessness in the body derives from the relationship of specific bodies to the cultural meanings assigned bodies in the politic."[46] To save herself from the cultural innuendoes "assigned" her "deformed" body, Shigeko had to look at her body as the other and to look at the inner, not the outer, self as the essence of her being. Interestingly, this is accomplished through yet another graphic description of female blood.

In a final attempt to assert the physicality of her womanhood, Shigeko has an affair with a younger man. And although the blood that consequently flows from her body would normally indicate the end of her life, to this writer it suggests a new beginning. Reassured by her doctors that she is physically sound and encouraged by the young lover who cannot see her as anything but a woman,[47] Shigeko realizes how special this blood is. By way of contrast, the menstrual and virgin blood had left anything but pleasant memories for this protagonist:

The memory of some thirty years ago when I experienced my first period was irritating. I had felt so ashamed and dirty with that blood wrapped like glue around my insides that I couldn't tell my father about it . . .

When I met Hitoyanagi in that hotel room in Yokohama with a view of boats all decorated with lights, a small amount of virgin blood stained the toilet paper.[48]

Although Shigeko is now "a woman full of deformities—without a breast and without a uterus,"[49] her body no longer emits the menstrual blood of an inferior color. The oppressive menstrual cycle that tied her to a miserable marriage and to negative memories of her father is over, and Enchi's protagonist progresses toward the last and liberating stage of a life fully lived. All the men involved in defining Shigeko's sexuality—her father, her married lover, and now the younger man with whom she falls in love—have been associated with blood, the ink that moistens the seal of womanhood. Yet, through this new blood, Shigeko witnesses "the woman inside herself once again coming to life."[50] and she regains the self-respect she had been deprived of by the shadow of her father and that she had later been denied by the silent robber of her virginity, her first lover. In such earlier works as "Earrings" (*Mimi yōraku*, 1952) and "A Bond for Two Lifetimes—Gleanings" (*Nisei no en shūi*, 1952; trans. 1982), Enchi had described the pain of protagonists who, like Shigeko, had suffered from a hysterectomy as the "cry of the womb," but now she lets her writing echo with the call of the woman within, a call that fills the "vacant cavity" in Shigeko's body with renewed energy.

Together with this "call from within" comes, moreover, a significant change in the terminology used for the female gender in Enchi's literature. Although *josei,* the combination of characters meaning woman and sex/sexuality, designates her early protagonists, Enchi later uses only the first of these characters, the single word *onna,* or woman, to represent those who, like herself, have lost the physical symbols of femininity but who are, and always will be, women. Since children are labeled as *onna no ko,* or the combination of characters meaning woman (female) and child, the cycle of life presented in Enchi's literature is evident: female child—sexually functional female—female person. This definition of womanhood, it should be noted, was established only because the writer had come to terms with her own sexual identity.

In Enchi's world of elderly and "deformed" women, sexual identity is almost synonymous with self-concept, and the only way for the writer to define these terms was to put her relationship with her father into perspective. Although known more for her references to the Japanese classics than to foreign sources, the most telling passage found in her oeuvre that concerns self-identity is in one of the few non-Japanese quotes inscribed, and in its original language:

> No bird soars too high
> If he soars with his own wings[51]

These two lines from "Proverbs of Hell" in William Blake's *A Mar-riage of Heaven and Hell* are first introduced in the play through which Enchi entered literary circles, "A Noisy Night in Late Spring," and they are then reiterated here in *Stripped of Crimson,* her one and only autobiographical work. Brief as these words might be, they clearly reinforce the thread Enchi has woven into her literature—the coexis-tence of dreams and reality and, moreover, the need for Enchi's women to separate themselves from the father. With the trilogy *Stripped of Crimson,* Enchi shows us how in the end her protagonist finds the strength to use her "own wings" and fly out of the paternal nest. Shi-geko knows that her self-expression has been hampered by "wounded wings," as is suggested by the title of the second novel and expressed in the protagonist's thoughts:

> I want the courage to be able to act on my own . . . I want to say
> that I did something with my own power. But, I have always been
> controlled by someone else and never seem to have my own will.[52]

She consequently decides that "to live as her real self, she should create a world through writing."[53] Shigeko begins to feel, moreover, as if "she will deteriorate" if she does not write, that "she cannot live if she does not write," and that "she herself does not exist if she does not write."[54] All of the emotions burning inside Shigeko obviously re-flect the writer's own—a writer who, while lying bedridden after a stroke the year before her death, constantly kept her right hand in motion while saying, "As long as I have this hand I will be fine."[55]

Through Shigeko, Enchi shows how literature becomes the "deeply merciful god that will save" her,[56] and how writing can actually reju-venate both her characters and indeed herself. Filled with what Enchi calls an almost "religious type of passion,"[57] Shigeko feels as if the young girl she has buried deep within has come back to life. Hav-ing learned about sex in her youth by reading books from, signifi-cantly enough, her father's library, Shigeko became strongly attracted to "the artificial light of a second world"[58] she found in literature. The young Shigeko had been interested not in "physical things" but in more abstract and spiritual feelings, and the same is true when she reaches old age. Once able to detach herself from the image of the father inseparable from the formation of her self-concept and to deemphasize the physical aspects that symbolize her sexuality, Shigeko, and Enchi, are free to fly to those dangerous heights of ecstasy they had both dreamed of as young girls.

At the end of *Stripped of Crimson,* Shigeko is seen writing a story that focuses on the problems of sexuality and aging, and in 1965 Enchi published a novel dealing with that very topic, *A Ray of Komachi.* The trilogy that began with a protagonist "stripped of crimson" because of a hysterectomy and tinted with the "artificial light" of illusions thus ends with a woman who will create her own "second world" through literature, coloring it with the numerous hues of the rainbow with which she ends the trilogy. This "second world" will not, however, include any trace of a father image. Instead, it will show that the woman introduced to literature by her father became a writer who found the space to spread her wings to the fullest.

After this semiautobiographical trilogy, Enchi is clearly more comfortable portraying female writers. She continues to focus on women close to her own age, with many of the subsequent characters appearing as older women, well established in their careers but still struggling with issues of self-identity. Viewing Japan as a "paradise for children and men, but an extremely cruel nation for elderly women,"[59] Enchi's objective becomes portraying the victims of this harsh world. In such works as *Wandering Spirits* (*Yūkon,* 1971), her protagonists are seen roaming in "illusions" where they are able to become young girls in the "thoughts separate from reality" that Shigeko had described.[60] As Rosefeldt explains, daughters like Enchi, "in their personal quests to vindicate, escape and/or replace the father who has died or who is in the process of dying . . . become victims of the invisible structure of patriarchy which consumes them in illusions or leaves them in despair."[61] While in her maturity, the writer was seemingly able to remove the father from the picture she painted, the "illusions" of elderly women searching for happiness in youthful days kept his spirit alive. These final pages plainly show that absent as the real father might have been from Enchi's last novels, the father and the patriarchal system he represents were still potent and present.

Conclusion: Eternal Embrace of the Father

Enchi ends her literary career with reminiscences about her father and with side excursions into her own land of "illusions." While clearly recognizing some of the imperfections of the corporeal man in *Between Dreams and Reality,* she maintains that any faults her father might have had stemmed from his position in the patriarchal society of which he too was a victim. Until her dying days, Enchi chose, in both her real and fictitious worlds, to separate her father from the system she so detested, and she refused to let anything destroy the image she held or the bonds that tied them together. As her father, Ueda would always be perfect and as his daughter, she would always be Daddy's little girl. When reality became too vivid, she erased that which she did not want to see; when dreams were too blurred, she filled the lines in with the pen of creativity. For Enchi, this father and daughter were to stay together for eternity in a world she created between dreams and reality, be it in the depths of Yanaka Cemetery or on the written page.

Notes

1. He is also known as Ueda Bannen, and his daughter referred to him as simply Bannen. "Kazutoshi" is used here because that is how he is known more commonly.

2. "Yanaka Cemetery—Tombstones of Famous People" *(Yanaka reien chomeijin bohi),* n.d. Distributed by the office of Yanaka Cemetery and received in June 1995 by the author of this essay during a visit to Yanaka to pay respects to Enchi Fumiko at her grave. The actual status of Fumiko in the Ueda family is youngest child, second daughter.

3. Enchi's tombstone is one of three in the Ueda plot, the other two being for members of the Ueda and Fuke (Enchi's daughter) families. The Ueda grave contains the remains of Enchi's father and mother, and the Fuke grave those of her granddaughter. Positioned between the two, Enchi's tombstone is engraved with both her name and her husband's, Enchi Yoshimatsu. Only Enchi's remains are buried here, however, because Yoshimatsu's own tombstone is located in another cemetery. For family reasons, her name and some of her remains have been included in Yoshimatsu's grave, but her real place of final rest is beside her father in the Ueda plot.

4. Gallop, *The Daughter's Seduction,* p. 75.

5. Although "Fumiko" is in a sense the name this author elected for her self, she is referred to as Enchi in most scholarship today, and this chapter follows suit.

6. Rosefeldt, *Absent Father,* p. 132.

7. Interestingly, the process that Enchi's characters undergo is not unlike that observed in Colette's creations of daughterly characters. See Flieger, *Colette.*

8. See Lebra, "Motherhood."

9. Rosefeldt, *Absent Father*, p. 128.

10. Enchi, *Yume utsutsu no ki*, p. 6.

11. Ibid., p. 87.

12. See chapter 4 in this volume, "Mother Tongue and Father Script," by Joshua S. Mostow.

13. Enchi, *Yume utsutsu no ki*, pp. 144, 148.

14. Ibid., p. 156.

15. Ibid., p. 166.

16. Ibid., p. 123.

17. Enchi, "Oyaji: Ueda Bannen," in *Enchi Fumiko zenshū*, vol. 15, p. 364.

18. Ueda Bin (1874–1916) was a poet, critic, and scholar of English literature active in the literary scene during the same time as Enchi's father, who was known to many by his similar-sounding name, Ueda Bannen.

19. Enchi, "Oyaji: Ueda Bannen," p. 365.

20. Ibid.

21. Note that both Enchi and Murasaki had brothers, but their fathers felt—and rightfully so—that, had they been boys, their exceptional literary skills might have been better recognized.

22. Enchi, "Hana chiru sato," in *Enchi Fumiko zenshū*, vol. 6, p. 256.

23. Enchi, "Oyaji: Ueda Bannen," p. 365.

24. Smith, *Subjectivity, Identity, and the Body*, p. 128.

25. Smith suggests that, through an "autobiographical manifesto," the autobiographer resists the sovereignty of the "universal subject"—that small segment of society that offers to "speak for all"—and endeavors to "bring to light" her own diverse and marginalized experiences. She will reject "the object status to which cultural identities have confined her." Ibid., pp. 157–163.

26. Enchi, "Tanizaki Junichirō shō o ukete," in *Enchi Fumiko zenshū*, vol. 12 p. 442.

27. Enchi, *Edo bungaku towazugatari*, p. 28.

28. Enchi, "Araremonai kotoba," p. 151.

29. Griffiths, *Feminisms and the Self*, p. 93.

30. Enchi, *Ake o ubau mono*, in *Enchi Fumiko zenshū*, vol. 12, pp. 7–8.

31. Ibid., p. 44.

32. Grosz, *Volatile Bodies*, p. 9.

33. Enchi, *Ake o ubau mono*, p. 321.

34. Ibid., p. 9.

35. Smith, *Subjectivity, Identity, and the Body*, p. 3.

36. In her article "Bound by Blood," Nina Cornyetz similarly analyzes Enchi's use of the blood image in the novel *Masks*. Interestingly enough, this novel too is divided into three chapters that represent the different stages of the development of the protagonist Mieko, whose name conveniently means "child of three layers." Menstrual blood and the ability to bear children are, however, what empower the women who appear in *Masks*, as opposed to the experience of Shigeko, who finds that entire cycle to be oppressive and whose name "bountiful child" implies that she is full of a different kind of knowledge.

37. Enchi, *Ake o ubau mono*, p. 75.

38. Ibid., pp. 91–92.

39. Ibid., pp. 317–318.

40. Ibid., pp. 26, 317. Enchi uses the term "Electra complex" in a rather nonchalant fashion and writes it in *katakana*, or the syllabary for foreign words, without any explanation for the term or its usage. Her intention in doing so is unclear, especially since her audience's comprehension of this term is questionable. Perhaps, for Enchi, her own understanding of the term was sufficient because she was, after all, dealing with a subject very close to her own personal experience.

41. Ibid., pp. 257, 404.

42. Ibid., p. 257.

43. Ibid., p. 318.

44. Ibid., p. 402.

45. Ibid.

46. Smith, *Subjectivity, Identity, and the Body*, p. 128.

47. Enchi, *Ake o ubau mono*, p. 403.

48. Ibid.

49. Ibid., p. 404.

50. Ibid., p. 403.

51. "A Noisy Night in Late Spring" (Banshun sōya, 1930) can be found in volume 1 of *Enchi Fumiko zenshū*.

52. Enchi, *Ake o ubau mono*, p. 166.

53. Ibid., p. 228.

54. Ibid., pp. 145–146.

55. These words were spoken directly to the author of this essay during a visit with Enchi Fumiko in Juntendo Hospital, Tokyo, in June 1985.

56. Enchi, *Ake o ubau mono*, p. 311.

57. Ibid., p. 44.

58. Ibid., p. 228.

59. Enchi, *Watakushimo moeteru*, in *Enchi Fumiko zenshū*, vol. 8, p. 328.

60. Enchi, *Ake o ubau mono*, pp. 399.

61. Rosefeldt, *Absent Father*, p. 135.

Works Cited

Location of Japanese publishers is Tokyo unless otherwise noted.

Cornyetz, Nina. "Bound by Blood: Female Pollution, Divinity, and Community in Enchi Fumiko's *Masks*." *U.S.-Japan Women's Journal, English Supplement* 9 (December 1995): 29–58.

Enchi Fumiko. "Araremonai kotoba—Sei o dō kangaeru ka." *Gunzō* (April 1965): 147–151.

———. *Edo bungaku towazugatari*. Kōdansha, 1978.

———. *Enchi Fumiko zenshū*. 16 vols. Shinchōsha, 1977–1980.

———. *Yume utsutsu no ki*. Bungei shunjū, 1987.

Flieger, Jerry Aline. *Colette and the Fantom Subject of Autobiography*. Ithaca, N.Y.: Cornell University Press, 1992.

Gallop, Jane. *The Daughter's Seduction: Feminism and Psychoanalysis.* Ithaca, N.Y.: Cornell University Press, 1987.

Griffiths, Morwenna. *Feminisms and the Self.* London: Routledge, 1995.

Grosz, Elizabeth. *Volatile Bodies: Toward a Corporeal Feminism.* Bloomington: Indiana University Press, 1994.

Lebra, Takie Sugiyama. "Motherhood." In *Japanese Women: Constraint and Fulfillment,* pp. 158–216. Honolulu: University of Hawai'i Press, 1984.

Rosefeldt, Paul. *The Absent Father in Modern Drama.* New York: Peter Lang, 1996.

Smith, Sidonie. *Subjectivity, Identity, and the Body.* Bloomington: Indiana University Press, 1993.

Chapter 8

Needles, Knives, and Pens
Uno Chiyo and the Remembered Father

REBECCA L. COPELAND

Some women may become mothers, wives, sisters, or aunts. But all women—from birth to death—are daughters. They are daughters biologically to parents who may or may not figure in their lives, and if they live in patriarchal societies, they are daughters politically, ideologically, and symbolically to a culture that venerates phallic law. How women respond to and experience "daughterhood" differs across cultures, across generations, and across the span of individual lives. In her narratives, the writer Uno Chiyo (1897–1996) reveals a woman whose struggle with her "daughterhood" began as an act of defiance, a refusal of the silence and submission that her father—and, by extension, the society he represented—would have imposed on her. Yet Uno would gradually discover that by defying the father, she would become in her defiance "like" him—the one who had authority. She thus entitled herself to his name,[1] his signature, and his room.

Born the first child of the ne'er-do-well scion of a sake-brewing family, Uno Chiyo and her five step-siblings were raised in perpetual fear of their father's explosive temper. He died when Uno was sixteen, thus freeing her from his tyranny, although not from her almost obsessive need for his recognition and affection, a need that surely reasserted itself in her unsuccessful and frequently scandalous relationships with men. By the time she was seventeen, Uno had been ostracized in her hometown of Iwakuni, a small castle town on the Inland Sea, for her involvement in a love affair. She fled to the anonymity and freedom of Tokyo, determined to make her way as a "significant woman." Instead, she established herself as a femme fatale. Beautiful, passionate and ever eager to shock, Uno Chiyo easily aroused both admiration and censure in pre–World War II Japan, capitalizing on her promiscuous love life by mining her experiences for the subjects of her stories.

The Birth of the Uno Heroine

As a young writer, Uno entertained her readers with brash and brazen heroines who sauntered through life in search of a moment's happiness. Once Uno "outgrew" romance, her heroines, too, were transformed into feisty old women ready to beguile their listeners with spice-laced memories. Because many of her writings fall into the category of *shishōsetsu,* or "I"-fiction—a curious blend of fiction and lived experience—readers are tempted to conflate Uno's creations with the author herself. For example, in her 1971 novella *Aru hitori no onna no hanashi* (The story of a single woman; trans. 1992), generally described as a *shishōsetsu,* the protagonist, Kazue, is strikingly similar to the implied author. They are the same age and gender. They hail from similar native homes and experience similar romances. And yet, instead of the intimacy of an autobiographical, first-person account, we find an omnipotent narrator who mediates between her subject, Kazue, and the seventy-year-old implied author. This unnamed narrator gently prods Kazue (but not *herself*) through her paces, commenting with amused, often ironic detachment on her many missteps. In the *shishōsetsu* tradition the author thus reinvents himself or herself as an accommodation of "truth"—a rearrangement, or distillation, of historical experience within the framework of a conscious fiction. The following excerpt from Uno's 1970 short story "Kōfuku" (Happiness; trans. 1982), metaphorically illustrates the *shishōsetsu* creative process. In this scene the Uno narrator describes her alter ego, again named Kazue, as she "re-creates" herself before her mirror, thus suggesting the author's own approach to her self-referential writing:

> Every time Kazue gets out of the bath, she stands in front of the mirror and examines her naked body for a moment. She uses the towel in front for modesty and turns her hips slightly, standing at an angle. Her skin has turned slightly pink.
> "I look like her," she thinks.
> She thus notes her resemblance to Botticelli's Venus. There is the similarity in the way she is standing, although no seashell supports her. She also has the same feet and the slightly rounded stomach. This description might imply that Kazue enjoys staring at

herself at length, but in fact this is not the case. She just notes the resemblance and soon gets dressed.

In fact, Kazue does not very deeply believe that her naked body resembles Venus. A body with more than seventy years behind it is hardly likely to come close to Venus's. Perhaps Kazue's skin bears blemishes in places and occasionally sags. But her eyesight is failing and the steam from the bath makes the objects before her even more obscure. Kazue includes these shortcomings when she enumerates the happy aspects of her life. In this manner, Kazue collects fragments of happiness one after another, and so lives, spreading them throughout her environment. Even what seems odd to other people, she considers happiness.[2]

Then in her seventies, Uno wrote "Happiness" and other "I"-fiction from within a fog of memory, allowing her eyes to see shapes as she would have them seen, permitting her pen to tell stories as she would have them told. What is seen and what is told may not exist, but it gives the author pleasure to describe it so, to make it so. Uno recreates her personal history by picking fragments of memory and arranging them in a narrative mist that reveals, through swirls, images of a mythic life. Her life becomes just that—an autofiction, or what American autobiographer Audre Lorde has termed a biomythography.[3] Like Kazue standing before her steamy mirror, she sees what she knows is not there and likes what she sees. She invents a myth story and lets it stand in place of the "truth" that is her life.

The challenge for readers of Uno's works is not to mine the myths for historical truths, to expect the image in the mirror to reflect backward on the figure before it, but to accept the image for the inner life it represents—that is, to see metaphorically. This is the kind of reading William Sibley recommends for Shiga Naoya (1883–1971), discovering in Shiga's works a single character who, though identified by different names, social roles, and ages, shares the same viewpoint and suggests the same inner life throughout the Shiga oeuvre. Sibley terms this character the "Shiga hero" and thus "distinguish[es] this persona, alter ego, surrogate, etc., from Shiga's 'real self,' who is unknowable."[4]

In this essay, I am similarly concerned with an "Uno hero," or "heroine," whose viewpoint consistently informed the production of the Uno story—be it "I"-fiction, interview, literary memoir, essay, or autobiography. As with Shiga, this viewpoint so dominates Uno's narratives that all other characters are ancillary and function more or less as parameters for the mediating inner life, suggesting its boundaries and thereby contributing to the definition of the Uno heroine —and by "heroine," I refer not only to the self-described characters in Uno's texts but also to the persona of the author herself, as projected over time. One way to approach this heroine is through an analysis of her relationships with the secondary characters who inhabit her narratives, both self-referential and fictional.

Using these narratives, I will focus on Uno's reconstruction of a father figure, on how she reflected her vision of her father in the mirror of her texts. This exploration will not (cannot) uncover a definitive relationship between an actual woman and her biological father. Rather, it will reconstruct, or reorder, the myth narratives that the author spun out for herself in response to her position as both historical and fictional daughter. What is of interest—and what *is* accessible—is Uno's articulation of the role of father, the identity she assigned to father-described characters in her varied narratives, and the way these roles and identities changed over the course of her career. In her texts, Uno transforms the father figure of her youth, the monolithic tyrant who bars the young heroine from all she desires, into a gentle spirit who becomes the very object of the daughter's desire.

An analysis of this transformation of the father figure from foil into goal not only illuminates Uno Chiyo's narratives—and, to a certain extent, the struggle of Japanese women writers in seeking to define themselves in a literary patriarchy—but also offers suggestions as to how modern Japanese women in general have to renegotiate their positions as daughters to both biological and metaphorical fathers when entering traditionally male spheres. This phenomenon is not limited to Japanese society by any means but is equally relevant to other modernizing patriarchal cultures, whether in Egypt, China, or America. Western feminist critics, in particular, have paid specific attention to the relationship between daughters and fathers and the implication this relationship has on the developing identities of women who move outside socially inscribed enclaves of femininity. As diverse as these studies are, in fields ranging from psychology to literature, they seem to concur that "successful" women are, by and large, "father-identified." Although there are differences between Western and Japanese patriarchies, the similarities in this "father-identification" are compelling enough to suggest traces of common

ground. It is on this common ground that I build my argument, referring occasionally to Western literary studies that are applicable to
the Japanese context, even though these studies do not discuss Japanese society in particular.

The Daughter Writer

While young, Uno Chiyo earned fame as a "love-sick writer," a "writer
of illicit love," with narratives that consistently involved love entan-
glements—love gone awry ("Shifun no kao" [Painted face], 1921); love
lost ("Tanjōbi" [Birthday], 1929, "Miren" [Regrets], 1936); and occasionally even love won ("Koi no tegami" [Love letters], 1939)—but
always love on the margins of respectability (*Irozange* [Confessions of
love], 1935; trans. 1989).[5] Her stories were drawn in sharp perspective; emotions were ragged, and though she rarely gave vent to the
anger or remorse often associated with women's writing in Japan,
Uno did allow glimpses of bitterness and hurt. With age, however, her
narratives grew more temperate. No longer involved in love affairs
herself, she become dependent on memories. In works such as *Kono
oshiroi-ire* (This powder box, 1967; trans. 1992), she goes back over
the familiar territory described earlier in *Confessions of Love* (1935)
and "Regrets" (1936). Far from being frustrated by the unreliability
of memory, Uno used its mistiness to permit greater aberration and
fantasy. The faces of the men in her memories overlapped and
blurred, her sharp vision replaced by nostalgia. Curiously, in these
later, more consciously self-referential narratives, such as *The Story of
a Single Woman* (1971), the man who begins to emerge most distinctly
from the collage of faces is Uno's father—or the father figure she con-
cocts of him. In this story, which I shall discuss below, memories of
the father provide the frame for the narrative.

Although I will argue that her father has been a presence in Uno's
narratives all along, it wasn't until she reached her seventies that she
began to insert father figures into her stories consistently and consciously. Moreover, the father portraits in these memoir-fictions illu-
minate her earlier narratives, rewarding the seeker of the Uno myth
for reading back and forth across the course of her career. That is to
say, scenes that seem innocuous or mysterious in earlier stories become
rich with implication when reread against the backdrop of her later
works. More significantly, the absence of a father in the earlier pieces
is so striking that this very absence becomes a form of presence. *The*

Story of a Single Woman (1971), the best-selling autobiography *Ikite yuku Watashi* (I will go on living, 1983), and others of Uno's more recent biomythographies thus open up her earlier stories to new readings and interpretations, adding depth and direction to the early Uno heroine.

The Father Remembered

The Story of a Single Woman begins and ends with memories of the father. Overtly the account is a rumination on a love odyssey, as the narrator traces Kazue's path from one man to another, but covertly it reads as the quest for a long-absent father. Early in the story we learn of the horrific events that led to the death of Kazue's father. It had snowed heavily, an unusual occurrence in her town on the Inland Sea. With no one attending him, Kazue's bedridden father disappeared from his sickroom, only to be discovered staggering through the snow:

> He was waving something that flashed in the sun. A knife. . . . In his condition, how had he managed to take the knife from the kitchen? The snow had stopped falling and the sun glittered down brightly, so strong it was hard to believe it was a winter day. Kazue's father coughed and blood spattered the snow.[6]

As household members carried him inside, others hurriedly brushed the snow clean, erasing the blood-writ signature he had left behind, though not before its lettering was imprinted on his daughter's mind. Seventy years later, Kazue still struggles to decode her father's message:

> The scene that snowy day was brutal. But, unbelievable as it may seem, the brutality of the moment has faded over the expanse of those seventy years or so, leaving Kazue with only a beautiful picture. Perhaps this is because of the snow. Now that Kazue has reached the age she has, she thinks she can understand what must have gone through her father's mind when he crawled out into the snow and coughed blood. Did he mean to end his own life in that crazed moment? Did he mean to kill someone he hated? No. That wasn't it. Kazue believes without a doubt that he wanted in that briefest of seconds to right, if he could, his life of dissipation and waste. If he had been able, he would have started a new life—one that was right and good in the eyes of the world. Was his not the final act of a madman spurred on by impatience?[7]

The end of Kazue's historical father marks the beginning of her quest to reconstruct him, to read his signature in the snow. But though the circumstance of his death was horrific, time has ameliorated the visual impact of the scene, much as the bathroom mist in "Happiness" turns the seventy-year-old protagonist into Venus. Kazue is able to interpret her father's last moments with a benign nostalgia. In looking back, she finds him vulnerable—a crumbled figure in the snow—whose last act is to be interpreted not as a threat but as a generous directive intended to protect his daughter: "Do not go where I have gone."

The Desire-Bound Daughter

Kazue's assessment of her father is in stark contrast, however, to that of Michiyo—an earlier incarnation of the Uno alter ego. In "Michiyo no yomeiri" (Michiyo goes to wed, 1925), one of Uno's earlier "I"-fictions, there is nothing fuzzy around the edges of Michiyo's memory, no ameliorating snow. Her father stands out in sharp relief as a jailer and a tormentor.

> It happened long ago, when she was still a child. Her father was in the Clock Room . . . drinking sake from a bottle he warmed over the hearth. For some reason, no one else was in the room with him but Michiyo. She sat obediently at his side and poured his sake. He twisted his face into a hideous smile—the like of which she had never seen before—and peered directly into her eyes.
>
> "Today I'm going to buy you whatever you want," he said. "Whatever Michiyo wants she can have. Well, what'll it be?"
>
> Michiyo shrank back slowly. She said nothing. She could not trust her father's face. When he saw this, he repeated over and over, "I'll buy you anything."
>
> Suddenly Michiyo realized that her father was playing a game with her. . . . She thought it would be fun to play along, maybe even tease her father a bit, too. She laughed happily. There was something she wanted. "A red ribbon. I want a red ribbon."
>
> Her father put on a different mask. He spread his arms out wide and seemed ready to pounce on her.
>
> "You want what? A ribbon? You shameless little fool, you wasted no time spitting that out."
>
> He looked around the room for the sash her mother used to carry the baby on her back and found it tied to the pillar behind him. He trussed Michiyo hand and foot and hung her from the ceiling like a rabbit. Her tiny head, caught between her shoulders, fell backward. Tears ran in a line down her cheek. She thought she would die.

Her father sat beneath her drinking his sake. Had he meant to
teach her a lesson? Was she supposed to respond, "No! There is
nothing I want!" whenever asked about her needs? Or was her
father simply amusing himself with her because he was drunk?
Michiyo thought about it for a long time. There was that sort of
meanness in the man.[8]

The father in this scene obligingly (almost too obligingly) offers
himself as a metaphor for patriarchy. When we come upon him, he is
sitting in "the Clock Room," his room, the room of measured time
and order. Full of desire himself, he tricks his daughter into articu-
lating her own. But once she does so, she is punished. "The father
desires and forbids desiring," Lynda E. Boose notes of the biblical
narrative. "He simultaneously wants but does not want the transgression he has provoked but will deny and punish."[9] In Uno's narrative,
however, the daughter is punished not only for desiring but also for
naming. Naming is the father's prerogative.[10] He names the daughter
with words (a "shameless little fool"), but he also defines her with the
ropes he uses to bind her—the mother's sash, the one she uses to
bind her children to her back. Michiyo longs for a red ribbon, a sign
of her own budding narcissism. Perhaps in her desire to make herself attractive, the ribbon signifies her attempt to "seduce" the father,
to play his game, to tie him to her.[11] But instead of a ribbon, her father
gives her a sign of female bondage. In binding Michiyo with the
mother's ropes, the father ties her physically to her figurative role of
daughter. She becomes the father's possession, named by him, kept
in his house until he transfers her to another man—the bonds of marriage replicating the sash with which she has been trussed.

In the narrative, the association between the daughter's confinement and marriage is made tangentially. This scene of the daughter's
punishment is embedded as flashback into a larger narrative describing Michiyo's betrothal. Her father tricks her into marriage by sending her with no warning to her maternal cousin's house. When she
returns after dark, accompanied by her male cousin (her future bridegroom), her father beats her, berates her, and later indicates that
marriage shall be the punishment for her "wantonness." Like the sash
used to bind her, marriage reminds Michiyo that she has no will of
her own. She is bereft of agency—a daughter soon to be a wife. As
Boose and other Western feminist critics have noted of the daughter's
position within the family, "the daughter, unlike the son, is the temporary sojourner."[12] She is legitimized and named by being transferred beyond its boundaries.

While the daughter is in her state of flux, her only recourse, it would seem, is to please the father and, by extension, the husband to whom she will be bequeathed. And yet the rebellious daughter longs to remain independent and unassigned. In the scene in which Michiyo returns after dark, she cowers in the dirt while her father kicks her, wishing he would cripple her rather than send her away in marriage. She longs to protest to her father that she is a "good girl," but she has no voice. She cannot name herself or her desire. Instead, she scrambles to the well to fetch water so that she might wash her father's feet.

The Father's Law

The Uno father figure consistently denies his daughter access to language—which becomes, consequently, the sign of his authority. In Uno narratives, father-daughter verbal communication is always one-sided. The daughter is never allowed to address the father of her own volition but must wait silently for him to summon her—to permit her speech. In *The Story of a Single Woman,* the Uno narrator relates how no one, especially Kazue, ever questioned her father. To do so, she explains, would be tantamount to a farmer questioning the weather: one simply accepts whatever comes one's way.

The written word, and writing itself, also become taboo for the daughter—both as a form of self-expression and as a source of outside knowledge. Out of pettiness, Kazue's father refuses to let her purchase new pencils but insists that she use her old ones until they are stubs too small to grasp. Kazue cleverly ties empty brush caps to her tiny pencils and thus extends their usefulness. In other biomythographies, such as the delightfully humorous essay-memoir "Watashi no seishun uchiake banashi" (Confessions of my youth, 1955) and her two-volume autobiography, *I Will Go On Living* (1983), the Uno narrator suggests that the practice of writing with such tiny instruments cramped her calligraphic style and is responsible for her now-famous crabbed characters.[13] The father, in his obsessive desire to deny his daughter access to language, is ironically present in every word she writes, as every word becomes a transgression of his law. He is visibly present as well in the very shape her letters take.

In "Mohō no tensai" (A genius of imitation, trans. 1987), an essay-memoir Uno wrote in 1934, she states that her father beat her if he caught her reading the serialized novels she found stashed in his storehouse. The novels, she asserted, introduced her to an unknown

adult world. This was territory her father transgressed freely, it would
seem, for the novels were his. This world of the father, the child protagonist discovers, is defined by heterosexual love, for in the storehouse she also find her father's old love letters—documents of his
second life, a life beyond the child's imagination. It is for this life,
this world beyond, that the Uno child hungers. But it is just this life
that her father is determined she will not explore, and so he keeps
her trussed and tied.

Thus it is that with her father's death, the Uno heroine not only
feels profound relief but also gains access to her own sexuality and
verbal self-expression. As the protagonist says in "Genius of Imitation":

> After offering their condolences, the neighbors said to my mother
> and me, "But I'm sure your life will be a lot easier now," and they
> even congratulated themselves on his death. . . . I cried bitterly, but
> somehow I was happy at the same time, thinking that I could now
> do whatever I wanted.[14]

The protagonist, who is representative of all Uno heroines, goes on
to engage in one love affair after another, indulging herself with a
near vengeance in the very knowledge her father had forbidden her.
She also goes on to write. But to her dismay, she discovers that transgressing her father's prohibitions does not free her from his law. As
the narrator observes in *The Story of a Single Woman:*

> All the old taboos were forgotten. And yet the house was not the
> same as one that had never known taboos. Whenever Kazue did
> something, she could not help reminding herself: "This used to
> be forbidden." . . . The taboos had been torn aside, but did that
> make her happy? Whenever she thought about them, she felt her
> father's shadow looming darkly in front of her. She would watch
> herself squeeze past the shadow and run far, far away.[15]

Fleeing the Father's House

> Father-daughter stories are full of literal houses, castles, or gardens
> in which fathers . . . lock up their daughters in a futile attempt to
> prevent some rival male from stealing them.[16]

The daughter-father relationship in Uno's narratives is often
fraught with erotic tension. While in her father's house, the Uno
heroine is made to be his handmaiden—serving his sake, rubbing his
legs, avoiding his displeasure and angry blows. After his removal from

the story, she writes herself into the roles of women he adored—geisha and illicit lovers. Thus she places her partners in the role of his surrogate. In so doing, Uno reverses the direction of the standard patriarchal system, which would have the daughter confined by the father's law until he is ready to transfer her by marriage to another man. In Uno's narratives, it is the father who is exchangeable—substituted as it were, for one lover after another. Not only is the father himself exchangeable, but so is his house—the spatial enclosure with which he would define his daughter.

The Uno heroine is ejected as a child from the paternal space and made to find her place as a "signified woman," a wife, in the house of another man. But she continually rejects this paternal injunction, seeking to situate herself in her own room and make of herself not a woman "signified" but a "significant woman." In her quest to do so, she finds herself transgressing former boundaries and entering threatening territory. Nestlike rooms that promised protection soon metamorphose into prisons. The hold in the ferry that offers the heroine an escape from her claustrophobically small town in "Okon no shukkyō" (Okon goes to the capital, 1923) is transformed into a microcosm of that town when she is caught alone with strange men who seem intent on molesting her. The upstairs-room hideaway her lover provides becomes an airless room inducing dreams of suffocation in "Yoru" (Night, 1924). In "Shiroi ie to tsumi" (A white house and crime, 1924), the Uno heroine's illicit encounter with a lover leads to a jail cell where she is questioned by a seedy policeman on charges of prostitution, her lover nowhere to be found. In another narrative, "Shiroi mokusaku no aru ie" (House with the white fence, 1926), she is troubled by her husband's infidelities and constantly dreams of a house with an imposing white fence, only to discover that the house of her dreams is the sanatorium to which she must deliver her syphilitic husband.[17] Houses and rooms, though offering comfort and promising joy at first, thus become metaphors for confinement, assuming a near "character" quality in their own right, as the Uno heroine maps her narrative progress via the houses she has built and fled.[18] Each enclosure is defined by the man or the marriage that inhabited it, although it is clear that the mediating principle behind each structure is always the father. As each story reaches its conclusion, the narrator discovers that she is still a daughter confined in her father's room.

At the end of *The Story of a Single Woman,* for example, Kazue meets

the charmingly dangerous Tanabe, a thinly veiled portrait of Tōgō
Seiji, Uno's lover from 1930–1935. Tanabe has recently recovered from
a suicide attempt, his neck still bearing the scar of his knife thrust. In
Tanabe, Kazue finds both her father's provocative power and his
wounds. Left alone in Tanabe's room, Kazue imagines that she is
back in her family home:

> Suddenly Kazue was seized with the illusion that she was alone in
> her house back in the country, a house she had not seen for so
> many years. She imagined that the sound she heard was the wind
> blowing through the thicket beneath her house. That was the
> sound. . . . It was the sound of the wind that had swept over the
> figure of her father as he crawled on to the road that snowy morn-
> ing, coughing blood.[19]

Kazue squeezes out of Tanabe's room, just as earlier she had
squeezed past her father's dark shadow, and sets off down the road.
The reader is left to wonder whether she is running away from her
father or now running toward him.

The Feminized Father and the Daughter's Pen

In early Uno narratives, the direction of the heroine's flight was
never in doubt. The author depicts the father figure as such a tyrant
that her heroine's survival hinges on her ability to escape him. In
"Michiyo Goes to Wed," for example, Uno presents the father as a
monolithic power. He exists as an "enormous abstraction," hardly
manifest in human form: faceless save for a seductive smile; bodiless
but for arms that spread out in a winglike span, not to shelter but to
pounce. (Ironically, the bodilessness of the father is amplified by the
physicality of the daughter. She has arms and legs that can be trussed,
eyes that cry.) Beth Kowaleski-Wallace suggests that women writers
turn fathers into gargantuan oppressors in order to avoid their own
limitations and frustrations: "We seek to protect ourselves by perpet-
uating the myth of paternal omnipotence, since our own 'castration'
is made most apparent when we are forced to recognize the limitations
of the father and his language."[20] With "Michiyo Goes to Wed" and
similar narratives, Uno portrays her own "daughtering," her awareness
of her "castration" at the hands of an abstract and despotic power. By
positioning herself as victim, as the innocent recipient of a father's
whims, she absolves herself of responsibility—suggesting that it was

never hers to take—and so colludes in the myth of patriarchal power and female victimhood.

Ironically, however, in the process of erecting a monolithic father, Uno reveals him as flawed by showing him to be a desiring creature. In the extract cited already from "Michiyo Goes to Wed," for example, it is the father's desire to abuse his daughter, his desire *for* the daughter, that renders the scene so volatile and threatening. And yet, by showing the father's desire—his *want*—the author exposes his "lack," thus removing him from his pinnacle and rendering him human, vulnerable, fallen. As Jane Gallop has observed in *The Daughter's Seduction: Feminism and Psychoanalysis,* daughters "feminize" fathers when they expose male desire:

> Since the phallic order demands that the law rather than desire issue from the paternal position, an exposure of the father as desiring, a view of the father as prick . . . feminizes him. . . . The phallic role demands impassivity; the prick obviously gets pleasure from his cruelty. The evidence of the pleasure undermines the rigid authority of the paternal position.[21]

The "feminized' father must be protected. As Uno's narratives progress, and as the author gradually finds greater assurance in her own voice, the Uno heroine comes to feel affection for the afflicted father, seeing in him her own wounding. Second son that the father was, and therefore superfluous, he too had been cast out of the family home and made dependent on an older brother's largesse. Thus the tyrannical father is something of a daughter himself. Identifying with her father's neediness, the prodigal daughter returns to his house, where, in sympathetic complicity with him, she makes efforts to hide his inadequacies. Lynda Zwinger, writing on the literary implications of father-daughter representations in the Western novel, suggests that the "daughter" writer "props the patriarch up, straightens his collar, reties his cravat, and makes him look like what the heterosexual fiction says he is. She ventriloquizes the father's part, temporarily assuming the patriarchal authority left unclaimed because of a paternal power vacuum."[22] Uno Chiyo also asserts her own daughterly authority in her effort to re-create the father in her texts. As a writer she has "authored" the father, after all, by naming him in her narratives, confining him to her texts, and defining him with her pen, just as assuredly as she imagined him earlier defining her with his knife and ropes. Indeed, her reconstruction of the father figure becomes her substitute knife, her figurative phallus. Stepping into the "paternal power vacuum," Uno positions herself as a replacement *for* the father. Here we see that Uno's is not an Electra story. She does not long for the father so much as she longs to *be* him, to take his place, to wield his knife, and to make his room her own.

Her Father's Heir

Having recognized the father's flaw, his *need,* the Uno daughter is ready to offer herself as the heir to his room, his name, his knife. Again, as Boose observes of the structures of the daughter-father relationship in Western culture: "By asserting her desire for the sign that confers exclusive rights to the male, she symbolically challenges every privilege of the sex/gender system that the father's phallus signifies."[23] The Uno author likewise challenges the father's privilege by presenting her heroine in these later narratives as more a son than a daughter.[24] In *The Story of a Single Woman,* for example, the narrator takes pains to show just how closely identified Kazue is with her father. Although the father has other children—and some of them sons—they are never depicted as having a relationship with him, or even as *relating* to him. The father does not speak to the other children but reserves his words for Kazue, as though she alone has been designated his heir. Alignment with the father offers Kazue autonomy and authority—it releases her from the mother-bonds of submissiveness that the father figure had imposed on her earlier.

The Uno author is also able to wrest herself free from the father's suffocating authority by writing. With her pen she humbles the cruel tyrant, transforming him into a gentle invalid. In this way the Uno author symbolically emasculates the father figure. She literally castrates him and takes his authorizing pen, his knife, as her own.

Daughter's Word, Father's Knife

In *The Story of a Single Woman,* drawing on the last vision she had of her father, Kazue "fetishizes" the knife into a symbol for the absent patriarch and also for the phallus. The knife becomes the sign of her own "missing phallus" as well as the agency of her destiny. Banished from her home because of her wanton behavior following her father's death, Kazue refuses to be chastened, reviving her father's earlier cycle of debauchery. She returns to her hometown, eager to reclaim her place in her present lover's heart, and along the way stops to buy a knife, though she hardly knows why. In other variants of this myth narrative—such as *I Will Go On Living*—the Uno heroine "reasons" that her mother must now be lacking her kitchen knife, since she is missing her husband. She means to return the knife to her mother, to replace the knife/father in her mother's house.[25] In a way Kazue does become the surrogate husband for her (step)mother. Throughout the narrative, the stepmother, who is only fourteen years older than Kazue, is never positioned as a "mother" to this child. Rather, she is treated as "the father's wife." She has children of her own, and Kazue often views her surrounded by her brood but, significantly, never counts herself among their numbers. Kazue's identification is with the father and with the fatherly way of relating to the mother/wife.[26] As a child, it was Kazue who had to entice (seduce) the mother back into her father's house after she ran away in horror at the man's cruelty. And as an adult, it is Kazue who turns her paycheck triumphantly over to the mother, offering the financial solace and protection the father's death has denied her.

Whereas the mother welcomes Kazue's performance as putative patriarch, the lover misinterprets the gesture as threatening. When Kazue appears on his doorstep ready to "seduce" him, her knife tucked into her sash, he throws her out. She returns, knife intact, to her father's room.

The knife remains a constant symbol in Uno's oeuvre, though frequently it is replaced by the pen or the needle. The knife was her father's instrument of power, the signifier of his "law." But at his death it became his writing implement, cutting over the blank sheet of snow, cutting into his daughter's imagined memory. She inherited the text he left in the snow, his blood signature—his memory. And with her pen she re-creates his signature on her own snowy pages—dark squiggles on a white ground. That signature is re-created not only in the physical appearance of the words themselves but also in the images she reconstructs. Uno constantly writes of scattered leaves, scattered petals, scattered drops of blood on a white ground. Nowhere is this more pronounced than in her accounts of Tōgō Seiji and his blood-spattered futon.[27] In a text of another kind, we find the author's metaphorical vision given tactile shape in the pattern she creates as a kimono designer. With her fabrics she draws over and over again her

Figure 8.1. Uno Chiyo, wearing a kimono of her design with her trademark "cherry petal" motif. The photograph was taken at her eighty-eighth birthday celebration, held at the Imperial Hotel in Tokyo, 30 November 1985.

father's blood on the snow—his final words to her. The "signature" motif she adopts features white cherry petals scattered over dark cloth —a color reversal of the blood writing on the snow, the blood on the futon (figure 8.1). In a gender reversal as well, the feminine image has replaced the masculine: needles as implements of creative self-expression replace the pen, which had in turn replaced the knife.

The Re-membered Father

Perhaps it is the assuaging power of the feminine which relieves the knife of its deadly authority in Uno's narratives as well, although this is a passage that would take Uno some sixty years to complete. Uno's earlier narratives are defined by the father's betrayal of his daughter, his denial of her desire. In revenge, the Uno author must continue to kill off the father. "Michiyo Goes to Wed," for example, begins and ends with the father on his deathbed. *The Story of a Single Woman,* written some fifty years later, is similarly framed. To gain her own voice, the Uno author must remove the father from her narrative space; she must literarily castrate him, emasculate him in memory, usurp the knife. And yet, just as his taboos remain in the house he left behind, so his memory remains to restrict and confine the daughter who inherits them—until, that is, she learns to accept her inheritance.

In Uno's essay-memoir "Kokyō no ie" (The house where I was born, 1974), the father's death takes place outside the narrative frame. Within the frame of the story, the Uno narrator describes a nostalgic trip back to her hometown. But the motivation for her return is more than nostalgia. Uno is returning to "re-member" the father, to suture the division between them with her needles and pens. Because she cannot reclaim the historical father, the Uno heroine seeks to restore those attributes that belonged to him, those attributes that she associated most closely with him: the knife, the enclosing house/room, and the signature in the snow. No longer fraught with threatening potential, these attributes are still an essential part of the father quest. For example, in "The House Where I Was Born," the Uno heroine comes upon a hardware store where, unlike in earlier narratives, the knives are not set out in a glittering display. The Uno narrator is enthralled, rather, by the haphazardness of the display and the nonchalance of the old metalsmith:

"I'd like this knife, please," I called to him.

"Help yourself," he answered without turning to look at me.

"This kitchen knife here. How much is it?"

"The price is written right there on the tag. Just leave your money on the table."

I finally realized that the old man was much too busy with his work to stop. Even so . . . no, precisely because of this, I wanted that kitchen knife all the more.[28]

The keeper of the knife has grown old and is no longer interested in its potential as symbol. Divested of its threat, the knife has been restored to its utilitarian (feminine?) roles as a kitchen implement: it has, in a sense, been "domesticated," tamed. The houses, too, which formerly loomed threateningly before the Uno heroine, have grown familiar and inviting. Her family house is desolate and in need of repair. She fusses over it—loving daughter that she is—dusting off the years, straightening the roof tiles, much as the Uno author earlier "prop[ped] the patriarch up, straighten[ed] his collar, retie[d] his cravat."

The Uno heroine returns to the geisha house where her father once disported himself. She describes the curious blend of admiration and awe she had felt as a girl standing outside the house waiting for her father: "He could do no wrong. Even if what he did hurt my mother, my siblings, me—it didn't matter. If he did it . . . it was good. For me, as a child, the more immoral my father was, the more I admired him for his immorality."[29] But now the geisha house—reduced to a shabby structure, devoid of its magical past, save in the memory of the girl-woman who stands before it—seems to welcome the Uno heroine, to want her there, so that it might relive but briefly its lively past. She steps inside and spends the night in the room where her father—or so she imagines—once led his enchanted life. She takes the stairs he took, sits where he sat, and an old geisha, too young to have known her father, waits on her.

In "The House Where I Was Born," the Uno heroine reconstructs her father's memory by first restoring him to his manhood. He is bigger than life, a legend, a lady's man. Next she rehabilitates the structures that once enclosed her father—both literally, by rebuilding the family house, and literarily, by charting the course of her father's life through the rooms he once inhabited (the second floor of the geisha house, the Clock Room). Earlier, the Uno author used houses and rooms to map out her own life and relationships; now such enclosures do not threaten. Instead, she pulls the rooms around her shoulders like a familiar mantle, slipping into her father's identity as she does so. She sits in her father's room—the Clock Room—and looks out over the garden, where she has placed a Buddhist statue. In earlier narratives the Uno heroine found images of a former husband in Buddhist statuary.[30] Now it seems she finds her father replicated there:

> Sitting there, on its mound of yellow earth, how much more naked the stone made my naked garden look! It left me feeling the presence of some kind of invisible weight. Had I really been standing there the whole time? An hour must have passed. As I grew accustomed to the Buddha's expression, I found that the suggestion of seductiveness around his eyes and lips gave way to the strange kind of peace that death brings.[31]

Figure 8.2. On the veranda of her Iwakuni house, 1987. Uno had the house restored in 1973.

In Her Father's Place

Returned to her father's place, inhabiting his room, the daughter cannot escape the weight of her father's presence. But his presence is no longer intimidating. The seductive, enigmatic smile of the tyrant has given way to peaceful resignation, the father's shadow become a comforting caress. Just as the divisive threat of the knife is "domesticated" by the therapeutic nature of the pen, so the fearsomeness of the father has been tamed. In the swirling fog of memory, the outlines that once so clearly marked the boundaries of characters have blurred, as father and daughter overlap and merge (figure 8.2).

Notes

A version of this essay first appeared in the *U.S.-Japan Women's Journal* 11 (1996): 3–22. I am grateful to Sally Hastings, coeditor of the journal, for her help with this essay. I would also like to thank the journal's copy editor, Victoria Scott, for her helpful suggestions and corrections.

1. Uno Chiyo's first stories were published under what was then her "married" name, "Fujimura Chiyo." Although she married two more times after this and legally assumed the names of her husbands each time, she consistently used her father's name "Uno" as her publishing, public name from 1924 on.

2. Uno, "Happiness," p. 134.

3. See Leigh Gilmore's description of Audre Lorde's autobiographical experimentation in *Autobiographics,* pp. 26–34.

4. Sibley, *The Shiga Hero,* p. 8.

5. None of Uno's earliest works are translated. For more on her early reputation as a writer, see Copeland, "Uno Chiyo." For a translation of *Irozange,* with a substantial introduction, see Uno, *Confessions of Love,* trans. Phyllis Birnbaum.

6. Uno, *Story of a Single Woman,* p. 34.

7. Ibid.

8. Uno, "Michiyo no yomeiri," pp. 325–326.

9. Boose, "The Father's House," p. 56.

10. From the beginning of Japanese mythological time, ever since the female deity Izanami spoke out of turn, man has been in charge of the discourse and particularly of the naming of desire. In the "Meeting at the Pillar of Heaven" section of the Izanami-Izanagi myth sequence, it was deemed inappropriate for Izanami to assume prominence in expressing her desire. The male deity, Izanagi, usurps her position and co-opts her language in the process, thus suggesting the triumph of a patriarchal system over an earlier matriarchal society. See "Legends Concerning Shinto Deities," pp. 24–26.

11. In other narratives the future mother-in-law dresses the Uno heroine's

hair with a ribbon, so as to make her more attractive to her bridegroom. But the child rips the ribbon from her hair before she returns to her father, as if to suggest her allegiance to him. She will remain unattractive, unmarried, and by his side.

12. Boose, "The Father's House," p. 21.

13. Perhaps in response to her father's tyranny, Uno was known to keep a mountain of needle-sharp pencils on her writing desk.

14. Uno, "A Genius of Imitation," p. 190.

15. Uno, *Story of a Single Woman*, p. 36.

16. Boose, "The Father's House," p. 33.

17. Ironically, it is in similar white-walled buildings—be they prison stockades or hospitals—that the Uno heroine will later locate her errant father, confining him as once he had her. Although written in the form of a *kikigaki*, or "hear-write tale," and not "I"-fiction, *Kaze no oto* (The sound of the wind, 1969; trans. 1992) features a white-walled stockade. The male protagonist, Seikichi, whom Uno claims to have modeled on her father, is confined in this stockade on the charge of murder. A similar prison is described in *The Story of a Single Woman*, though this time the father is held there on gambling charges.

18. In "Happiness," for example, the Uno narrator traces her life back through the thirteen houses she had inhabited.

19. Uno, *Story of a Single Woman*, p. 132.

20. Kowaleski-Wallace, "Reading the Father Metaphorically," p. 309.

21. Gallop, *The Daughter's Seduction*, p. 38.

22. Zwinger, *Daughters, Fathers, and the Novel*, p. 127.

23. Boose, "The Father's House," p. 55.

24. The author, Uno Chiyo, was equally proud of her father-identification and accompanying "son-hood." She was fond of recalling how the writer Hirotsu Kazuo asserted, after observing Uno interact with her family, that she behaved like the oldest son. In *The Sound of the Wind*, which she claimed to have modeled on her father's life, the child who corresponds to Uno is a son. Many Western feminists —psychologists and literary critics alike—cite the frequency with which writers and successful women in other professions admit to father-identification and often view themselves as honorary sons. See for example, Hill-Miller, "The Skies and Trees of the Past," pp. 361–383.

25. See, for example, *Ikite yuku Watashi*, p. 72.

26. As a corollary, it is interesting to note that Uno's identification with her father may have contributed to her tendency to write from the male perspective, as she did in *Confessions of Love*, (*Ohan*, 1957; trans. 1961), and other fictional works.

27. In Uno's many accounts of her affair with Tōgō Seiji, she recalls how she went to meet him at a café—planning to interview him for a love-suicide scene she was preparing to include in a novel she was serializing. Tōgō still wore a bandage on his neck—a remnant of his abortive love-suicide attempt. When he invited Uno back to his atelier to spend the night, Uno accepted. Upon awaking the next morning, she found that the futon they had slept on was caked with the blood from the suicide attempt. "Had I been a normal woman," she was to write in a later memoir-essay, "I would have fled in terror at the sight. But to the contrary, I felt all the more inclined to remain right where I was!" Uno, "Watashi no

bungakuteki kaisōki," p. 159. It should be noted that Uno's accounts of the affair enjoy the same mist of memory encountered in "Happiness."

28. Uno, "Kokyō no ie," p. 218.

29. Ibid., p. 206.

30. In *Ame no oto* (The sound of rain), for example, the Uno narrator describes buying a statue of Jizō because it reminds her of a former husband (p. 154).

31. Uno, "Kokyō no ie," p. 215.

Works Cited

Location of Japanese publishers is Tokyo unless otherwise noted.

Boose, Lynda E. "The Father's House and the Daughter in It: The Structures of Western Culture's Daughter-Father Relationship." In *Daughters and Fathers,* ed. Lynda E. Boose and Betty S. Flowers, pp. 19–74. Baltimore: Johns Hopkins University Press, 1989.

Copeland, Rebecca. *The Sound of the Wind: The Life and Works of Uno Chiyo.* Honolulu: University of Hawai'i Press, 1992.

———. "Uno Chiyo: Not Just a Writer of 'Illicit Love.'" *Japan Quarterly* 35.2 (April–June 1988): 176–182.

Gallop, Jane. *The Daughter's Seduction: Feminism and Psychoanalysis.* Ithaca, N.Y.: Cornell University Press, 1982.

Gilmore, Leigh. *Autobiographics.* Ithaca, N.Y.: Cornell University Press, 1994.

Hill-Miller, Katherine C. "'The Skies and Trees of the Past': Anne Thackeray Ritchie and William Makepeace Thackeray." In *Daughters and Fathers,* ed. Lynda E. Boose and Betty S. Flowers, pp. 361–383. Baltimore: Johns Hopkins University Press, 1989.

Kowaleski-Wallace, Beth. "Reading the Father Metaphorically." In *Refiguring the Father: New Feminist Readings of Patriarchy,* ed. Patricia Yaeger and Beth Kowaleski-Wallace, pp. 296–311. Carbondale: Southern Illinois University Press, 1982.

"Legends Concerning Shinto Deities." In *Sources of Japanese Traditions,* ed. Ryusaku Tsunoda, Wm. Theodore de Bary, and Donald Keene, vol. 1, pp. 24–26. New York: Columbia University Press, 1958.

Sibley, William. *The Shiga Hero.* Chicago: University of Chicago Press, 1979.

Uno Chiyo. *Ame no oto.* In *Uno Chiyo zenshū,* vol. 8. Chūō kōronsha, 1978.

———. *Confessions of Love.* Trans. Phyllis Birnbaum. Honolulu: University of Hawai'i Press, 1989.

———. "A Genius of Imitation." Trans. Yukiko Tanaka. In *To Live and to Write: Selections by Japanese Women Writers, 1913–1938,* ed. Yukiko Tanaka, pp. 189–196. Seattle: Seal Press, 1987.

———. "Happiness." In *Rabbits, Crabs, Etc.: Stories by Japanese Woman Writers,* trans. and ed. Phyllis Birnbaum, pp. 133–147. Honolulu: University of Hawai'i Press, 1982.

————. *Ikite yuku Watashi*. Mainichi shinbunsha, 1983.

————. "Kokyō no ie." In *Uno Chiyo zenshū*, vol. 7, pp. 205–221. Chūō kōronsha, 1978.

————. "Michiyo no yomeiri." In *Shinsen Uno Chiyo shū*, pp. 323–345. Kaizōsha, 1929.

————. *The Story of a Single Woman*. Trans. Rebecca Copeland. London: Peter Owen, 1992.

————. "Watashi no bungakuteki kaisōki." In *Uno Chiyo zenshū*, vol. 12, pp. 122–238. Chūō kōronsha, 1978.

Zwinger, Lynda. *Daughters, Fathers, and the Novel: The Sentimental Romance of Heterosexuality*. Madison: University of Wisconsin Press, 1991.

Chapter 9

A Confucian Utopia

Kōda Aya and Kōda Rohan

Ann Sherif

The Father is all too often villainized as oppressive originator of the Law, as capitalist, and as dictator; he is rapist, molester, pervert, and abuser, and readers tend to collapse all these different manifestations into a single figure. That is, we often conflate the individual father, the socioeconomic and political systems of patriarchy, the phallus, the Law in the symbolic order, men! Clearly, such oversimplification cannot lead to a sophisticated theory of gender and gender relations nor enhance feminism. I believe one of our tasks in this volume is to distinguish among the several aspects of the figure we call the Father and paternalism and so arrive at a more nuanced understanding of women writers' relationship to this figure in both its monolithic and plural manifestations. Only in this way can we get away from the pitfalls of a gendered binarism.

This chapter will focus on the particular daughter-father relationship between Kōda Aya and Kōda Rohan, a relationship that has invited precisely this sort of conflation and confusion. I will argue that the narrative realm created by Kōda Aya in her autobiographical essays presents in fact a utopian vision of the family, a unified moral and aesthetic realm that is an alternative to the despair at the failed patriarchy and matriarchy expressed in the texts of many of Kōda's contemporaries. Kōda's world view finds inspiration in Confucian ideals of moral and bodily discipline within the domestic setting. And the father-daughter relationship evoked in her writings is never an exclusive one, for mothers, grandmothers, aunts, and other women also function as essential players in her accounts of the family.

Writing the Lettered Father

Kōda Rohan (1867–1947) was arguably one of modern Japan's preeminent men of letters. He launched his career as a critically acclaimed writer with novels such as *The Five-Story Pagoda* (*Gojū no tō*, 1891) and later established himself as a critic and public intellectual as well. Unlike many of his peers, Rohan trained his gaze not primarily on the Anglo-European world, emphasizing instead Japan's Asian literary and philosophical heritage. Exhibiting tremendous versatility in style and topic, he produced everything from dense and stylistically challenging historical novels about ancient China to books written in a highly colloquial style about urban planning or premodern literature, and essays on fishing and cinema.

In contrast, Rohan's daughter Kōda Aya (1906–1990) began her writing career as her father's biographer, with numerous essays about her home life with the eccentric, famous Rohan. At the start of her career, Kōda Aya had the advantages of a famous name and a tolerant age. The postwar era encouraged an outpouring of literary creativity and fostered a diversity of voices and interests. In this exhilarating atmosphere, Kōda grappled with the assignment given her of presenting her late father's home life to an admiring readership. She also faced the tasks of supporting herself and finding a place in the world when she no longer had the responsibility of caring for her father. During the 1940s and 1950s, Kōda's numerous autobiographical essays drew the attention of many Japanese readers because they succeeded brilliantly in providing an intimate view of the personal life of the idiosyncratic Rohan, a celebrated writer who did not run with members of the literary establishment *(bundan)* and whose revered works held an ambiguous position in the modern canon and the debate on tradition and modernity. Kōda herself acknowledged her father's ambivalent status as cultural figure, and also as a family man:

> Some people praise my father as a formidable scholar; others call him an eccentric *(fūgawari no henjin)*, but Father had a different interpretation: "It's not that I'm a great scholar; anyone who thinks so must be greatly ignorant," he'd say, or "People who think I'm strange just don't realize how many people don't fit into the same mold as they do." At times, I agreed with him. In any case, I learned about housekeeping from my father not because he was a scholar who felt compelled to teach me. Nor were my lessons the warped

inheritance of an eccentric. Rather, it just happened that way naturally; my father acceded to act both as father and mother to me
because the circumstances at home demanded it. After my mother
died when I was eight, I had to depend on the kindness of my stepmother, a woman who was superior to my first mother, I understand,
in matters of learning, but who fell short when it came to managing
a home.[1]

The emblematic invocation of Rohan the father here might suggest
an individual and an author so bound to her paternal origins that a
sense of individuality outside of identification with the father seems
an impossibility. According to Kowaleski-Wallace, for some Anglo-
European "father-identified daughters" for whom "paternal existence
gives shape and meaning to . . . life, to speak directly of [the father's]
failings would be to undermine the terms of her own self-image," a
situation that leads to an extreme idealization of the father and the
resulting suppression of the mother.[2] However, Kōda's case is somewhat different from this. A paradoxical and ambiguous aspect of her
memoirs is that they exalt the father while also exposing his human
failings. They use the father as a reference point, but in an abstract,
distant manner, while exploring in a much more nuanced fashion the
two mothers Kōda knew, as well as the other women who played important roles in her life. The same subtle treatment may be seen with
the many female characters who are central in her fiction.

Thus, despite the father figure's supposed prominence in Kōda's
narratives, she actually writes extensively in the memoirs about the
women in her family as well. The figure of Rohan takes on an exag-
gerated presence out of sheer repetition, and partly out of the conceit
(and readerly expectation) that the famous man is the central preoccupation of her oeuvre. More than once, indeed, Kōda recalls a
point in her career when she could write of nothing except memories
of her father: "After I had completed *Good for Nothing*, I was stuck; my
pencil would not work for me. Of course, I had reached an impasse,
because I had neither will nor self-cultivation, and wrote only about
my memories of my late father."[3] For many readers and critics whose
horizons of expectation are aligned with the canon, this apparent
focus on the death of the father evokes its significance as a theme sig-
naling the son's entrance into manhood and is extremely compelling
because this topos has occupied such a central position in many canonical modern prose works.

For Kōda, however, although Rohan did represent an entire erudite tradition, by no means was this a tradition inaccessible to her mothers. If anything, she had available a variety of models, including women in her own family who excelled in Western classical music, such as her aunts Nobuko and Ando Kōko, as well as in writing. Her stepmother, Yayoko, was a poet and devout Christian whose library included the works of Kant and the dialogues of Socrates, along with the Bible.[4] Significantly, these women artists' links were with orthodox and respectable traditions of verse and music, whereas Rohan started his career as a dabbler in fiction.

Unlike novelist Enchi Fumiko, who registers surprise when readers inquire about the influence of her famous father, writer and scholar Ueda Kazutoshi (Bannen), Kōda Aya reveled in creating a body of narrative works describing the relationship of a father and a daughter. In her life, Kōda spent many years serving her father, cooking for him, cleaning house, and nursing him. Some readers will view Rohan as a lucky man because he had a daughter willing to serve him like a wife throughout his long life; others will regard his strength and her attitude of self-devaluation as representative of patriarchy's relationship to women, and even as legitimizing it. However, such a quick conflation of the individual father with the patriarchal system and a facile equation of Kōda's life with servility renders her works utterly tainted and unpalatable.

The Daughter Apprentice:
Lessons in the Nobility of Normalcy

As a matter of fact, Kōda claims considerable authority and talent for herself as a writer and a woman. In a 1977 public lecture in Kyoto, she related her initial realization of her capacity for, and the transformative power of, *kandō* (heightened emotion or aesthetic response). Also remarkable in this speech is its status as performance. As her narration approaches the moment of epiphany, the pitch of her voice becomes significantly higher, the pace of her speech more rapid, and she modulates the volume of her voice subtly to fashion the precision of her description:

> The pencil that started my writing career came rolling over to me. It was not something I sought out. In my family, my father always taught me that I must try whatever is served to us. As children, we were not allowed to refuse something for the reason that we didn't like it or because it was new to us. My parents were especially strict

with girls about this. Father instructed me that if I were served food unfamiliar to me, I must not hold back. He would not tolerate such behavior from me. "Try everything," he said. "If you absolutely can't swallow it, then just spit it out. But that alone would be rude, so, in order to avoid insulting the other person, you must then say, 'Regretfully, I am unable to accept this. I beg your kind forgiveness,' and then leave." That's what he told me. For, you see, the inferior child must be told exactly what to do, down to the last detail, down to the last word.

Do you know that if you scribble down a few sentences and get them published, people will address you as "Sensei?" I'd been a homemaker all of my life, and then one morning, all of the sudden, I was "Sensei." . . . Psychologically, I couldn't stand all the pressure, and friends told me that I needed a rest, so I decided to go to Hakone. It was May, and the mountains there were lovely. . . . The people at the inn where I was staying recommended a walk in the mountains because there were fine bush warblers to be seen there. The whole thing seemed a bit dubious to me, but I went up anyway, and, what do you know, I found one. I couldn't see the warbler because it was high up in the trees, but I knew that it was there when I heard its beautiful song. I listened and guessed that he or she likely had a nicely rounded throat—the song sounded round to me. I heard it singing *"hokkekyo,"* for indeed that is the way the bush warbler sings. It's so very pretty, the song, but I wondered how the bird could sing so marvelously with a small little throat like that. They can't possibly have very big bodies. So there I stood listening to the warbler's song, when all of a sudden it stopped. Just like that, and the mountain was absolutely quiet. I could hear the quiet. I looked out and the May breeze came blowing from afar, and the green was all waving about like this, and that wind swept lower into the grasses in the fields and about my feet. The May breeze felt wonderful, and I realized what I had just heard. And I felt it. Suddenly, my heart cleared up. I knew that it didn't matter if people called me Sensei or whatever. This is where I exist. . . . I am simply an old woman, a person who knows nothing of art and learning. But I can do things like this and I can feel. . . . Hadn't I heard something fine and felt deep emotion? Had I not been moved? If I go out into the world, I will be moved. I only needed to search for it, and then everything would be all right. With that, the stress vanished from me and I was ready to come home right away. Once home, I enjoyed my life. . . .

I realized something else because of that bush warbler. I was amazed that the warbler, with its tiny throat and lungs, could produce such a voice from such a small place. I realized that if I too sang from my small, lonely corner, with my meager breath, but with my five senses, I would exist. . . . By that time, I was already an old woman, but all the things that I had been interested in as a small child came back to me—pebbles of all colors and shapes, dogs, bright yellow rape flowers, the clouds floating by in the blue sky, gourds, moss, tadpoles, the Sumida River, fields of tall grasses. They said to me, here we are. Of all these, I chose to concentrate on trees. At that point, even my feelings of jealousy for my brilliant sister disappeared.[5]

Kōda's many essays about life with Rohan include the early pieces that she penned around the time of his death, such as "Random Notes" (*Zakki*, 1947) and "Death of my Father" (*Chichi: sono shi*, 1947). There are also numerous later individual works and collections of essays, such as *This Sort of Thing* (*Konna koto*, 1956), *Good for Nothing* (*Miso-kkasu*, 1951), and *Scattered Clouds* (*Chigiregumo*, 1956).

Critics often cite the publication of Kōda's first full-length work of prose fiction, *Nagareru* (Flowing, 1956), as the true beginning of her career because it marked her accession to the position of novelist. However, the reader can detect a significant shift in her writings much earlier, one that determined the form and substance of her essays and established her as an important narrative presence. In her first essays, Kōda obediently responds to the assigned task of writing about Rohan, and her inclusion of minute physical detail, nuances of emotion, and compelling style makes these initial works extremely evocative. In the space of a few short years, however, Kōda developed an approach to narrative form, perspective, and subjectivity that would become her hallmark. This is evident from the essay "Notes from Sugano" (1948), which, like the first writings, describes her daily life with Rohan during his later years. Instead of using the chronology of her father's illness as the primary structuring device, however, she organizes the later essays around different tropes, such as wandering *(sasurai)*, war, evanescence *(karisome)*, confusion *(mayoi)*, sudden awareness of absence *(totsuzen no natsukashisa)*, potential for failure *(masaka)*, waiting, and especially heightened emotion *(kandō)*.[6]

This new method has the effect of altering the nature of the narrative voice. The shift from a linear temporal strategy to a highly conceptual, thematic structure highlights the narrator's subjectivity and also signals a seizing of narrative authority. It is possible that Kōda's pose of humility and insistence on foregrounding her links with her father have distracted readers from her considerable literary accomplishment: the evocation, through narrative, of a symbolic realm of stability, unity, and moral certitude rare in postwar Japanese literature.

Over the course of her career, Kōda did pass through long periods of ambivalence about her roles as a writer and as a woman in society. Readers similarly have approached Kōda's texts and biography with suspicion. Because of her adherence to the role of homemaker for much of her life, and the reverence accorded to the father, Kōda's figuring of gender may initially seem regressive and based on conservative constructs of men's and women's social roles. In addition, Kōda's narratives do not overtly share much with texts ordinarily categorized as early feminist fiction, described succinctly by Maryellen Toman Mori as stories that "usually revolve around alienated female protagonists who oppose patriarchal society's values and its prescriptions for women's lives." She continues, "These protagonists resent or reject marriage, reproduction, and child rearing, because they entail women's subordination to men and their confinement within the domestic sphere." Although published in the same decades as authors like Takahashi Takako and Kōno Taeko, Kōda in her writing further exhibits an indifference to the "search for sexual transport and spiritual rejuvenation" and "women's quest for jouissance" evident in their feminist fiction.[7] Instead, while denying involvement in the learning and artistic aspirations of the illustrious forebears in her family, Kōda presents a vision of personhood grounded in sensual and emotional response to and close observation of the phenomenal world; in belief in the possibility of recovery from trauma and of personal maturity; and in the rejection of loss as a central trope signifying the reality of Japan's postwar culture. The moral certainty and the belief in continuity expressed in her narratives stem from a dedication to the notion of the family, in whatever form, as a primary and constructive social unit.

Transcending Inadequacy: The Depth of Life Lived Narrowly

One of the qualities that attract readers to Kōda's memoirs lies paradoxically in the fact that the essays form a remarkable portrait of a life that, in outline, seems to lack interest because of its utter conventionality, apart from her connection with Rohan. From her adolescent days, Kōda performed much of the domestic work in the Kōda household, even while she was a student. Then she married and had a child and finally became her father's companion and, during his later years, his nurse. Only near the very end of his life did Kōda begin writing, and even that was not an act of rebellion but one of homage. Again, her biography is surprisingly unpunctuated by the expected varieties of social resistance and rebellion:

> My father was a professional writer, but I never for a moment imagined that the day would come when I made money writing. I had no interest whatsoever in my father's work. In those days, women could get by without thinking about earning money. When I was young, I depended on my father; when I got married, I looked to my husband. After my divorce, I again went back to my father. Such a life was comfortable, I suppose, but I grew tired of its narrowness. I occasionally thought of striking out on my own, perhaps starting a small business. It never occurred to me that I might do Father's work.[8]

The memoirs are fascinating because they suggest a life thoughtfully considered and already unconventional in nuance, detail, and perspective even before Kōda was forced by circumstances to find an identity apart from her relationship with her father and husband.

Her father became both "mother and father" to her, not so much by virtue of the literal absence of a mother—for two women occupied the role of mother in the Kōda household—but because Rohan had grown up in a family whose poverty and traditional ethos dictated that male children too learned to do housework, which meant that Rohan knew what to teach his daughter about running a home. His own parents had not tolerated idleness, nor had they regarded Rohan's own youthful declaration that he wanted to become a novelist as an excuse from making himself useful around the house. In 1887, after Rohan quit his job as telegrapher in rural Hokkaido and returned to Tokyo to respond to Tsubouchi Shōyō's imperative concerning the future of Japanese literature, his mother, Yū, set him to work washing rice at the neighborhood well and other housework, tasks with which he was familiar from the time he was a small boy.[9] This also serves to remind us that, for many Japanese in prewar days, productive work ("producing essential goods and income") and reproductive work ("childrearing, cooking, and housekeeping") took place in physical proximity.[10] The separation, both in spatial and gender terms, of the public sphere and productive work from the domestic sphere and reproductive labor, respectively, did not become the predominant model in many households until after World War II.

In his childhood home, Rohan performed housework both as service to his family and as a form of discipline. Part of his attachment to his first wife, Kimi, stemmed from his admiration for her capable handling of the household budget and labor; her talents also allowed him to devote himself principally to his writing.[11] In turn, Rohan deemed it essential that his youngest daughter, Kōda, learn these skills as well. As Kōda described in an essay:

> It was my father who taught me how to sweep the floor and wipe up. My lessons with him went beyond the realm of cleaning, and he taught me the sort of things one normally learns from a mother. We never did make it to the proper placement of hairpins when you're doing a permanent for curly hair, but Father did show me how to powder my face, how to cut up tofu into nice neat cubes, how to re-cover paper sliding doors, the best things to say when I need to borrow money, and even the ins and outs of love.[12]

The long memoir "Incantations" (Atomiyosowaka, 1948) contains dazzling passages describing in detail Kōda's apprenticeship to Rohan in household work, which she calls her "private lessons in cleaning" (sōji no keiko), as one might refer to lessons in a traditional art, such as Noh chanting or tea ceremony. Kōda credits this strict upbringing not just to her father but also to her grandmother Yū, whom she felt was "always watching her from afar, certainly not willing to allow her granddaughter to be spoiled or raised as an undisciplined country girl." Rohan's study was her classroom.[13] Rohan's exacting approach to teaching his daughter the proper ways to handle water or a broom, described in "Incantations," demonstrates that, far from disdaining reproductive labor in the home, Rohan regarded such work with utter seriousness and, furthermore, as the perfect opportunity to instill in his daughter his own Confucian-inspired values and philosophy. He taught his daughter that the Confucian dictum kakubutsu chichi (the investigation of all things) extends to the most quotidian activities. He emphasized that individual behavior and thought should be understood within the framework of a moral worldview and, specifically, his brand of Confucianism:

> The next morning, the scoldings started early. The glue that I had cooked up the day before seemed too stiff to me and I certainly didn't want him complaining again, so I decided to add some water.

But then as I was mixing up the glue, it turned lumpy, and Father's reaction was of course devastating. "Trying to come up with something clever on your own is tantamount to ignoring Confucius's teaching. He wrote that it is best to learn from observation."

When I do something without consulting with Father and it turns out poorly, usually the venerable Confucius comes and rests his weight upon me, a four ton boulder, just to make sure I have understood the error of my ways. Even worse than not having consulted with Father, it seems, was my failure to have shown proper respect to Confucius, and no amount of discussion or apology could absolve me. To a girl raised in the village of Terajima, Minami Katsu-shika-gun, the revered words of Confucius from many millenniums before seemed distant and murky at best. And how in the world could my making lumpy glue be construed as disrespect for Confucius? And then Father told me that girls like me, who have no sense of humility, are evil and won't do anyone any good. My life was useless, he said.

Father regarded Confucius as worthy of great respect and used polite language when he referred to him, but, in my eyes, it was Father who was absolute, not Confucius. I was in trouble because that Absolute came raining down on me, bringing the Honorable Confucius with him. My heart torn apart, I wished that I could disappear, but even that I was not allowed. One must, he told me, try again, come to life again. Feeling momentarily relieved, I then learned that I still was in error: this time, his approach took the form of "Are you going to live your whole life in fear of Confucius? That's a coward's way." It seems that I must discard that desire to disappear and assume a new attitude of fortitude.[14]

The Confucian slant of Rohan's teaching reinforced the emphasis on this world: "Confucius' effort to take things at hand—ordinary daily affairs—as the basis for his ethical teaching makes Confucian learning an intrinsically moral activity at whose core is the task of developing a refined knowledge of oneself."[15] Rohan's emphasis on the importance of good physical form also derived from a Confucian approach to self-cultivation: the "ritualizing [of] bodily behavior . . . represents a concerted effort to transform the body into a fitting expression of the mental and spiritual resources within."[16] The initial steps toward the goal of "becoming an exemplar of personal knowledge" involve ritual acts of "elementary learning," such as cleaning the floor and calligraphy. The eight steps of "Great Learning" that facilitate this aim during adulthood include the "investigation of

things" *(kakubutsu;* Chinese *ke-wu)*, a "form of knowing in which the
knower is not only informed but also transformed by the known."
That is, investigation is not simply a "disinterested study of external
facts by an outside observer."[17] Much of Kōda's autobiographical writings explore her training by Rohan in ritualized "body behavior" and
emphasize the explicit link made between cleaning and self-cultivation. Her claim, moreover, of possessing a well-defined aesthetic and
moral sensibility stems from the notion of the transformative power
of observation and from her conviction that knowledge is linked to
moral improvement.[18] During Edo and Meiji, furthermore, women
were not completely exempt from the encouragement of their fathers:
"[It] behooved the conscientious head [of the household] to make
sure that the heir was carefully groomed to shoulder the household's
social obligations and ply its trade. This concern applied especially
to eldest sons, but fathers have devoted attention to other children
as understudies to the heir."[19]

Most contemporary readers of Kōda's early essays would have
been attracted to the opportunity to learn more about Rohan's home
life and his personality. Within a relatively short period, however,
Kōda proved—though all the while professing her status as amateur
—that her writerly presence and the perceptions manifest in her narrative provided a great deal of interest, whether or not she wrote
about her father, with the result that readers would want to know
Kōda's authoritative view on morality, on the family, and on old age
and to come into contact with her words and style. Some critics have
asserted that Kōda's works exhibit no literary influence from Rohan.[20]
The question of influence between the father and the daughter, it is
generally agreed, lies primarily in Rohan's transmission of the practice of the Neo-Confucian *kakubutsu chichi* ("investigation of all things
through observation" with the aim of self-cultivation), and Kōda's gra-
cious mastery of this practice.[21] The glaring omission from this equation is an examination of the meaning of this act of transmission from
father to daughter and also of the link between powers of observation
and the act of narrating itself. Thus, critics have dubbed Kōda a *seika-
tsusha* (one who lives), rather than a *sakusha* (one who creates, or a
writer), as if her capacity for observation and investigation could be
known in the world outside the medium of her writing, or as if the
intellectual practice of writing itself did not give expression, or more
accurately, lend shape to the cognitive processes and the signs of cultivated knowing.[22]

Kōda herself rationalizes her father's focus on teaching housework by first comparing herself with her siblings. For Utako, the eldest daughter and, by Kōda's account, the child most beautiful and beloved, Rohan bought special plants and trees for the garden at Kagyūan in order to cultivate Utako's native intelligence and fascination with nature.[23] Rohan, Kōda tells us, meant to make a botanist out of Utako. Kōda, by Rohan's standards, lacked natural curiosity and aptitude for art or learning—or so she tells us—so by default he chose to train her strictly in cooking, cleaning, and budgeting. Curiously, he did not include in her home education lessons in tea ceremony or flower arranging required of a young woman being readied for marriage.[24] Kōda remarks that her father did not demand of his long-awaited—but ultimately dissolute—son Ichirō the same competence in anything that he expected of his daughters and in fact spoiled the boy terribly. In the end, both Utako and Ichirō died young, and only Kōda Aya survived, almost too well prepared for the several lives and careers ahead of her. In retrospect, Kōda describes such family dynamics as affecting her thus:

> The hard outer shell may contain only one chestnut, or some may shelter two, making it a double chestnut, or three—a triple chestnut. If you peel a single chestnut, the nut inside has a nice rounded belly and back. Everyone loves this kind. The meat of double chestnuts have flat bellies, but their backsides are still nice and round. This is the second most well loved type. But a triple chestnut has three nuts inside, and the one in the center is, well, I suppose you'd call it pathetic. It gets pressed in from both sides and smashed flat. That was the way I was—stuck between my sister and brother and crushed flat. . . . And so—and I'm not complaining, but—I don't think that I was given much love . . . My father was the fourth child in his family and got smashed quite a bit too . . . But even so Father would say things to me such as "You are rather slow, aren't you?" Not stupid, mind you, slow.[25]

The complexity of her relationship with her father and siblings, and her maturation as an individual come through clearly in this passage. Kōda at once posits an inferior status for herself within the family and asserts a strong emotional bond between herself and Rohan, thus elevating her textual self. The reader can only interpret as ironic Kōda's citing of Rohan's belittling comments at the end of the passage, because of her tremendous stature as a writer and her talent.

Kōda's repeated mention of Rohan in many of the essays that she

wrote over four decades would seem to refute the claim of a newly
found confidence in her relationship both with her own creative abilities and her audience, as would her constant unfavorable compari-
sons of her own abilities with her father's. As Alan Tansman notes,
however, this "rhetoric of inadequacy" became a means of fashioning
a narrative presence in the world.[26] On careful examination, that narrative presence bears an authoritative vision of the meaning of maturity, of aesthetics and morality, and challenges the reader to reconsider
the common notion of a break *(danzetsu)* between tradition and modernity, between pre- and postwar Japan.

The habit of self-deprecation goes hand in hand with the powerful
emotions with which Kōda regarded her father, whom she portrays
as, in several senses, her partner for life. Rohan becomes variously
her teacher, her home, her authority figure, her charge, her muse, her
tormentor, her means of support, her companion, and the primary
object of her affection. The parent-child relationship evoked in the
narrative is, however, conspicuously devoid of sexual overtones. Eroticized parent-child bonds have been given bold treatment most notably by Okamoto Kanoko (1889–1939) in "A Mother's Love" (*Boshi jojō*,
1937) and Tanizaki Jun'ichirō in "The Bridge of Dreams" (*Yume no ukihashi*, 1959) and other works. In contrast, only once does the daughter
in Kōda's essays wonder about the nature of her feelings for her father.
The context for this is the days of the incendiary bombing of Tokyo
by the Allied Forces in spring, 1945. Worried to distraction over
the safety of her bedridden father, Kōda devises a makeshift bomb
shelter for him in a closet filled with bedding. She realizes the futility
of her attempt but feels compelled to go to any length to avoid losing him. In a sober moment, she wonders, "Could my feelings for
him be likened to those of a mistress *(mekake)*?"[27] But she purposely
phrases this extremely rare flirtation with taboo in the abstract terms
of social relations (i.e., married man and mistress), which utterly lack
the evocative and frankly erotic force of, for example, Okamoto
Kanoko's mother character, who regards her son as a "man," or the
heady indulgence of Tanizaki Jun'ichirō's male protagonists who
long for the milky scent of mother.[28] A writer such as Kanai Mieko,
who was conscious of Freudian and Lacanian "models of Oedipal relations," utilized explicit imagery of the body and addressed eroticized
parent-child relations in stories such as "Boshizō" (Portrait of mother
and child, 1972) and "Usagi" (Rabbits, 1972).[29] In contrast, Kōda

constantly looked to Confucian-inspired notions of familial relations, which were based on moral and ethical concepts of propriety and self-cultivation and prohibited eroticized relations within the family.

But this Father also has a negative aspect: he drinks, he scolds, he is unreasonably demanding. He expects others to attend to his needs. It would seem, however, that the rewards of association with this father more than compensate for the drawbacks. Through narrative, Kōda can rehearse the death of the Father again and again, either in great detail, as in her first works, or merely by referring to him as "my late father" *(bofu)*, rather than as "my father" *(chichi)*, as she comes to do in the later essays.[30] The measure of control afforded by the act of writing ultimately has various benefits: it quells the father's anger, abates the child's fear, and puts an end to his drinking. It also allows the persona to conclude that she has, after all, "pleased him" and earned his love. Although the essays display a mixture of both fear and adoration of Rohan, the negative emotion is transitory because the father's anger passes quickly, while the sense of debt, love, and longing for their life together remains constant. This expression of affection in the earlier works sometimes is cloaked in the language of extreme emotion, as in the short piece "A Fragment" (*Kakera,* 1948), describing Kōda's visit to the bombed-out ruins of the Koishi-kawa family home:

> The burnt ruins are a treasure chest, and the earth yields so much. Buried in it are things that, above the ground, had purpose, but now, broken, are useless, like fragments of china and dishes, and warped pans and spoons. While the soil seems willing to settle back into its old routine, now dancing up in the wind, now sinking down under the falling rain, the things in the earth are content only if they can push their way up out of the soil so as to see the sun once again. Every object that appears has some memory attached to it, especially the things directly linked to Father. When I come across one of those, I feel like raising my face to the sky in celebration of the opportunity to remember, and at the same time like lying down on the earth to cry over my loneliness. Just this morning, I could scarcely believe my eyes when I saw a glint of dark blue in the ice that covered the ground. It was a fragment of a tray Father had adored—a nice Kyoto Shonzui piece with a low rim. . . . I imagine that [my first] Mother used it to carry a bottle of sake, a cup, and some tasty morsel out to Father each evening.[31]

Over the course of her career, the mention of Rohan and Kōda's own inadequacy continues, but becomes markedly more formulaic and occupies less space in her narrative.

Of Kōda's marriage and divorce, Inoue Kazuko asserts that Rohan's extraordinarily rigorous training ruined Kōda's "potential for happiness" in a married relationship. Kōda's many strengths and skills "were useless in a marriage which was predicated on the construction of the identity of a wife as one who relied on her husband's strengths," Inoue writes. "Kōda's sharp perceptions, furthermore, allowed her to see through the fallacy of marriage under patriarchy."[32] Indeed, Kōda has seldom written critically of the system of marriage, but most relationships predicated on the establishment of social and economic bonds would pale against the intensity of emotional and moral unity that she describes as having had in the domestic arrangement with her father, which elevated the mundane to the moral, spiritual, and intellectual level and which was predicated on a complementary model rather than an oppositional one.

Despite Kōda's assertions of inadequacy in the face of her father's high standards, her writings highlight not only their mutual affection but, more important, her ability to spar with this most demanding of partners, whether it be over the correct way to polish the floor, poetry, or the best way to recover from a traumatic experience. Repeatedly, Kōda describes the pain of "defeat" after a lesson or an argument with her father, but then she reveals that she would acquiesce only after fighting back. Such images stand in stark contrast to other father-daughter relationships depicted in prose narrative, such as Uno Chiyo's evocation of the strict father who would lock up or tie up the daughter.[33]

Conclusion: The Authority of Daughterhood

For Kōda Aya, the notion of Father became equated with the language of transcendence. Rather than as a famous writer, the Rohan of her narrative realm has authority that evokes the teachings of Confucius and, as seen above, transcends even the authority of that philosophical past:

> I have, since my childhood, had the strong urge to resist the absolute power of this father. For some reason still unclear to me, in my forty-four years of struggle, I have not once succeeded in escap-

ing from this "Absolute." Only that would give me relief. After Father died and was no longer a person in my life, the "Absolute" became even more absolute. I came to crave the "Absolute" once I could no longer see it with my eyes or hear it with my ears, and for the first time I cried. When Father picked a fight with someone, he never took into account his partner's height, and instead spoke exclusively from his own intellectual level. He would go on and on about matters beyond my comprehension. One minute it would be Socrates, and the next Ninomiya Sontoku. Without warning, he'd switch the topic of conversation from the *Kojiki* to race car engines.[34]

Constant in Kōda's evocations of Rohan the father is the dizzying mixture of the cultural icon: the sage teacher, the beleaguered family man, the manic constantly in search of new texts and new cultural phenomena, and the spiritual partner of Kōda, for whom only a man of Rohan's breadth and depth will suffice.

Overemphasis on Kōda's seemingly masochistic tendency for self-denigration and her extreme identification with her father will distract the reader from appreciation of her narrative accomplishments. Many of her later essays, such as "Private Tutor" (*Kojin kyōju*, 1971), start out with a rhetorical positioning of Kōda Aya as someone lacking potential in the arts and scholarship, though a member of a family of talented musicians, writers, and scholars. But they end with a celebration of the gifts she received from her father: the ability to observe nature and the training in the rhetorical means, both poetic and prosaic, to express beauty and perceive connections between the natural world and human society.

The persona's sense of inadequacy is attributed to multiple sources: her parents' disappointment that she was not a boy; her feelings that she is neither a good daughter nor a good mother; the constant comparison of herself with the extraordinary father; her own sense of being different and unloved. At points in the essays, the declaration of inadequacy takes formulaic forms of modesty: as a child, when she mistakes the church where Rohan and Yayoko's wedding is held for a movie theater (never having been to a church before and uninformed about the event in progress), she concludes, "I am so stupid."[35] At other points, she declares herself ugly, lazy, and unable to be a worthy recipient of the teachings of her father.[36] One driving force behind this rhetoric of self-denigration is the potential for forgiveness and reevaluation. In fact, Kōda's narrative leads ultimately not to self-hatred or the desire for self-destruction but rather to resolution and

recovery. In the essay "At the Writing Desk," self-forgiveness is expressed in a passage in which Rohan declares to her, "Even people
who aren't brilliant have their place in the world."[37]

Another reason that I regard textual humility as a discursive strategy
for self-presentation relates to the idiosyncrasies of the Kōda household, which in turn resonate with certain social mores in society at
large. In that admittedly unusual family, Rohan unceasingly demanded
discipline and perfection, linking these qualities with the Confucian
dictums that equate laziness with evil *(aku)* and place even the most
mundane of household chores in the realm of spiritual and moral
training. Thus, Kōda's repeated insistence that her links to Rohan
are "through the kitchen" rather than being discursive in nature implies much more than that she knew Rohan only as a servant or ser-
vile wife who cooked and served his meals. As suggested above, ordinary daily activities such as cooking took on an "intrinsically moral"
sense, as the site of self-cultivation. Thus, the seemingly simple assertion suggests, without spelling it out, the degree to which Kōda succeeded in rising to Rohan's challenge—not only in preparing meals
that taste good but also in making correctly an entire cluster of moral
and aesthetic choices in the context of the unified realm that she
evoked, in narrative, as their home. Rather than buckling under the
unreasonable demands of her father about the proper way to hold a
feather duster or to handle water in a bucket, she rose to the occasion
and succeeded where she could, in the realms of action and observation: "Father taught me to look at nature, since I wasn't suited to art
or learning."[38]

Similarly, Kōda's constant refrain that her life was one "lived narrowly" stands in ironic relation to the body of her essays. The majority
of these essays aim precisely at illustrating the depth of a life narrowly
lived, if one has the aesthetic and moral wherewithal to perceive and
be moved by the sounds of a knife chopping vegetables, by the sight
of sparrows in a tiny garden, by the pale face of an aged man as he
lies dying. The body of Kōda's essays exists precisely to evoke this vast
and profound perceptual realm and this aesthetic sensibility.

Admittedly, an integral part of Kōda's method lies in the compulsion to create harshly lit and often unflattering portraits of a man
who was lionized in the public domain, a man whose erudition and
ability to wield archaic and difficult styles rendered him an object of
awe, even as his novels and essays became increasingly inaccessible
even to educated readers. Kōda knocked Rohan down to an utterly

human level by presenting him both as an overdemanding parent who had unreasonable expectations of the child who tried the hardest to please him (and only him) and as a very mortal man of flesh, vulnerable to the ravages of time, illness, and aging. Her characteristic fondness for precision and detail, received as part of Rohan's education in *kakubutsu chichi*, extends to sketches of Rohan himself, whether it be the cold, biting sting of his words, or the blood that he coughed onto the sheets of his sickbed during the last days of his life.[39] For example, "Notes from Sugano" contains a passage in which Kōda examines, by the glaring light of a bare light bulb, Rohan's bleeding gums and the bloody strings of mucus that came out of his mouth and nose. After the bleeding stops and Rohan manages to spit out the blood, Kōda asks her daughter Tama to bring the lamp closer, so she can examine the contents:

> The bulb illuminated for me not only the red blood in the pail, but every detail of Father's face as well. I detected no trace of fear or despair or laxness there, or, of course, any expression of pleasure. All I saw were his eyes looking, just as he does when he is reading, with the muscles beneath his brows slightly tensed, those eyes looking at the blood. The stink of the blood rose from the pail.[40]

But the practice of repetition, of reducing Rohan to the status of an ordinary man, sometimes cruel, sometimes loving, suggests the profundity of his influence, and the extent of their attachment. Only by trying to tame this man, who was larger than life not only in the public eye, but at home as well, could Kōda grapple with her own literary and philosophical inheritance.

A means of evoking a mythological realm, or biomyth, in her memoirs can be seen in Kōda's evocation of Rohan as a man of letters *(bunjin;* Chinese, *wenren).* This image of Rohan as the last of the literati also existed in the popular discourse about him. In fact, he successfully cultivated the aura of a writer and thinker living apart from society, fond of poetry, philosophical matters, and liquor. Rohan's other biographers also mention his fondness for drinking, but Kōda's depiction of this habit of his is distinctive in its ambiguity. There is much nostalgia for the cups, trays, and other objects associated with serving him his evening sake, the flowers, poetry composition, and wine. On the other hand, there are gut-wrenching descriptions of the father and husband under the influence, ranting at his wife, making his children cower in the corners, attacking his companions. Yet the more positive and sentimental depictions are striking for their allusiveness, both to the *bunjin* tradition in general and to Rohan's own texts.

Because of Kōda's complex portrayal of Rohan, the bond between them cannot be reduced simply to the level of a masochistic daughter and cruel father but remains on the biomythic level of the Chinese lion that pushes its cubs off a cliff in order to make them prove themselves. Through this mythologizing strategy, Kōda achieved a place for herself in the narrative pantheon and also paid tribute to a father whose lessons had given her the enviable ability to view with wonder a world most of us miss and to write of the strength and love that she has come to possess.

The extent to which Kōda succeeded in sustaining and enhancing this biomyth becomes clear when one reads her daughter Tama Aoki's books, *The House in Koishikawa* (*Koishikawa no uchi*, 1994) and *The Home That I Longed For* (*Kaeritakatta uchi*, 1997). Although many incidents and the atmosphere of the Kōda home are already familiar to readers from Kōda's writing, Tama allows us a glimpse of an unknown Aya: a woman who was as strict and demanding as her perfectionist father, Rohan. Tama also portrays in a more thorough and balanced manner her own father, Ikunosuke. A similar conceit of self-deprecation runs through both mother's and daughter's narratives. Tama chooses only to shoulder the mantle of unworthy daughter (and granddaughter), while Aya assumed inadequacy in a much grander manner: not only did she paint herself an unworthy member of the accomplished Kōda family—by virtue of her ordinariness—but she also bemoaned her shortcomings as a writer and an artist.

Over the course of her career, Kōda produced a huge volume of essays for inclusion in journals targeted both at specialized audiences (literary journals, women's magazines, ones focusing on *shōgi*, poetry, kimono, and language education) and at a more general readership (*Shinchō, Nami, Gakutō,* and others), and she wrote for the major newspapers as well. The essays have subsequently been collected in single-volume editions.

In these pieces, Kōda stated her views on an astonishing array of topics—and these short pieces inevitably bear topical titles related to nature or culture, literature or politics, objects or people, encounters or incidents. A random list of their subject matter will give an idea of her range: on crows, a natural disaster, a famous site, snow, Christmas, gourds, Bashō's poetry, Rohan's complaints, poverty, the month of August, the month of May, weeds, men, rulers, scissors, kimono, light and dark, ice, furniture, publishers, the emperor, rags, sounds, green soybeans, chopsticks, old age, nicknames, fish, Kyoto women, the *Apollo* mission to the moon, temple architecture (pagodas), her father's career, her childhood, aging, and the changes in Japanese society since the war. Many of the earlier pieces, such as "Dolls for a Special Day," "The Medal," and "The Black Hem," can easily be read as short stories, because they were longer and she structured them around plot and character. Many of them were, in fact, promoted by publishers as—and called by critics and reviewers—either *"shōsetsu"* or autobiographical fiction *(jidenteki shōsetsu)*.[41]

Other of Kōda's numerous *zuihitsu*/essays, published subsequently in bound editions such as *Scattered Clouds, Smoke over the Moon* (*Tsuki no chiri*, 1994), and *Reminders of the Season* (*Kisetsu no katami*, 1993), never tempt the reader to regard them as fiction, but they are nonetheless highly entertaining and edifying. Somewhat formulaic in their repetition of the elements of careful observation, interpretation, and statement of emotional appeal, the essays are yet always stunningly beautiful, balanced, and pleasing to read and savor, and they form the core of Kōda's oeuvre and her public persona.[42] It is through these works that Kōda created and asserted her textual authority.

The notion of literary authority, or the question of "what allows the text and its creators to maintain the ability to speak within . . . society at a specific time," is obviously crucial in the case of a writer like Kōda.[43] Throughout her long career, Kōda unabashedly employed the name of her father and his celebrity. Given the high praise that critics and her reading audience accorded her novels, she could doubtless have remained successful without the explicit reminders of Rohan. However, apparently feeling apologetic primarily for the rhetorical and conceptual distance between his idea of art and narrative and her own, she created and tended her reputation as Rohan's daughter through her own writings and repeatedly reaffirmed her position vis-à-vis this man.

One prominent feature of Kōda's essays is the emphasis on affect. The earlier works convey the complexity of emotion during mourning: anger, grief, joy, depression. In the essays Kōda wrote later in her life, she also places great value on expressions of affect, but in these texts, emotion, rather than flowing from within, becomes something poetic and transcendent, liberating and curative. Rather than social

intercourse, it is contemplation that gives rise to emotions and aesthetic response. Experiencing heightened emotion, however, does not
constitute an end in itself. The ability to observe, to be transformed,
and to narrate the experience becomes the basis of her moral realm.

In her later essays on the topics of trees and landslides, Kōda reiterates her narrative aim: she scrambles up steep slopes and gets strong
men to carry her up unblazed mountain paths in her search for heightened emotion, or excitement *(kandō o motomete)*. Here, the heightened
emotion previously available within the "narrowness" of her own
home life can now be found only by means of a quest. At the same
time, Kōda represents herself as someone well qualified to search for
and to articulate such transcendent values:

> Even if I have no ability as a scholar, I am still able to go out and
> see things with my own eyes. If I am then able to seize the height-
> ened emotion of landslides, weave that emotion into words and
> convey it to my readers, I will be satisfied. Even a natural disaster
> of a small scale involves a tremendous amount of energy, and it is
> inconceivable that one cannot find heightened emotion in a place
> where the earth has moved with such force. As for the nature of
> that emotion, sometimes one may feel horrified, and at others sad
> and desolate. I hope to convey to my readers the emotion that I
> have seen and heard, the emotion that speaks of the fate of this
> country Japan. I would like to be the messenger of that emotion.
> If one has few prospects as a scholar, then she must use her physical
> faculties instead, and go out and see with her eyes and listen with
> her ears.[44]

In this way, Kōda situates herself in yet a new relationship with her
narrative Father. In this passage, the implicit comparison of herself
with her father ("I have no ability as a scholar") serves as a preface to
what she views now as her true and legitimate role, that of "messenger
of emotion."[45]

Among the numerous father-daughter pairs of writers in Japan,
Kōda remains among the notable minority of women writers for whom
the authority to write does not derive from the Romantic figure of
the original, creative individual. If anything, Kōda positions herself in
a time-honored tradition of learning in Japan, one that is based on a
master-disciple relationship that itself echoes the parent-child relationship. Such a structure lays emphasis on transmission of the master's
spirit, and doing as the master does is the method of learning. In
Rohan and Kōda Aya's case, the gender imbalance between master

and disciple may be said to be compensated for by Rohan's marginalized position in the world of canonized letters. As Esperanza Ramirez-Christensen has noted, "it is fitting that Kōda became the disciple he never had, the one who permanently inscribes his name and work in cultural history, who rejects 'a woman's happiness,' and appropriates for herself the more authoritative role of transmitter of privileged knowledge."[46]

Although it might seem presumptuous to claim moral authority for an author who writes about kimono, birds in the garden, and sounds in the kitchen, that is precisely the stance that Kōda Aya assumes, a wise person with the authority to speak about the moral and symbolic order in daily life with the voice of experience and moral certitude. Her stance, as well as her father's, is especially evident when contrasted with those of their literary contemporaries who, in the face of modernity, lack the wherewithal and certainty to assert their sense of personhood, much less the harmony or disharmony of heaven and earth.

Recalling Kōda's speech about her epiphany at Hakone, Kōda makes no direct reference to artistic or literary precedents for such profound connections between viewer, nature, and the subsequent discursive activity that reproduces the epiphanic moment in the narrative. In the lecture, she claims it as her moment, her way, her emotion. Written all over this revelation and her account of it, however, are traces of multiple cultural and personal moments: Rohan and Kōda's shared acute powers of observation, and Rohan's admiration for premodern poet Bashō and contemporary poet Masaoka Shiki and especially for their aestheticism.[47]

Although it is true that the *zuihitsu* essay genre, in its various forms as memoir, reminiscence about people, and meditation on objects, has found great favor with the modern Japanese reading public, generic popularity alone cannot explain the constant demand for and praise of Kōda's essays. Her works tend to concentrate on certain topoi, such as a childhood home (in her case, the semipastoral Mukōjima on the banks of the Sumida River); wandering; loss; her assumption of the role of homemaker at a very young age; emotional reactions to natural phenomena or specific sights or sounds; the strictness of her upbringing and her father's teachings at home; expressions of inadequacy (personal or professional); and interpretations of a father's regard (initially perceived as negative, subsequently as an expression of love).

During the postwar decades, Kōda's figuring of the Father was potentially highly anomalous but attractive to readers and citizens of a defeated nation who literally had to cross out the lessons of the past, as presented in school textbooks, with opaque black ink. Kōda's essays about Rohan will always be a moving account of one woman's love for her parent and the process of mourning him and learning to live on her own. However, consciously or not, Kōda also invests great symbolic weight in the Father by repetition and constant reexamination of it as a positive figure whose stability is associated with his grounding in a past, and whose teachings and moral outlook, while challenging, were something to be embraced rather than categorically rejected. Even if the parent-child bond and the family have primacy, as in Confucian terms, Kōda puts her own postwar spin on the relationship. She depicts the dynamics of her relationship with Rohan, which, on an initial glance, would seem to put her in a subordinate, disadvantaged position. But what the subtext silently inscribes is her strength and pride as a survivor, her enjoyment in drawing in her writing on the rich material of her father's life, personality and narrative, her family, and her own success.

Apart from interest in Rohan and the quality of his prose and voice, Kōda's writings are attractive to readers on a symbolic level because they narrate the loss of the Father and suggest the possibility of maturity and psychological integrity in the aftermath of such trauma. In prewar canonical fiction, the reader frequently encounters the topos of the death of the Father, for example in Sōseki's *Kokoro* and Shimazaki Tōson's *The Broken Commandment (Hakai)*. Alan Tansman has brilliantly analyzed the critics' appropriation of Kōda's works as signs of cultural conservatism and the nativist discourse concerning "Return to Japan" *(Nihon kaiki):* "critics agreed with Mishima about the feminine quality of Aya's writing, most valorized her style as essentially Japanese and thus an antidote to male overintellectualization and overreliance on foreign modes of thought. To these critics 'feminine' language was somehow more authentically native and could restore a true, untainted, and life-sustaining quality to Japanese cultural and literary life."[48]

Kōda's writings must also be read in light of postwar debates that employ what are essentially psychoanalytic categories to consider texts, gender relations, and national identity. The criticism of Etō Jun, Katō Norihiro, and Ueno Chizuko, for example, exhibits an interest in an oedipal framework as a tool for understanding the family. In addition, much prose fiction by male authors in the prewar period intimated such a quest for a second father, a spiritual father.[49] On the basis of her writing alone, it would be prudent to ask whether it is not against just such cultural criticism that Kōda wrote.

Notes

Portions of this chapter have appeared in a slightly modified form in my book *Mirror: The Fiction and Essays of Kōda Aya.*

1. Kōda, "Atomiyosowaka," p. 93.

2. Kowaleski-Wallace, *Their Father's Daughters*, p. 23.

3. See the newspaper article "Watakushi wa fude o tatsu," in *Kōda Aya zenshū*, vol. 2, pp. 11–13; also the afterword of 1983 paperback edition of her collection of essays *Good for Nothing (Misokkasu)*, p. 218.

4. Kowaleski-Wallace, *Their Father's Daughters*, p. 11; Kōda, *Misokkasu*, pp. 89–90.

5. Kōda, "Kōen 'Deai to kandō,'" in *Kōda Aya zenshū*, cassette tape attached to vol. 23.

6. Kōda, "Sugano no ki."

7. Mori, "The Quest for Jouissance," pp. 207–208. On the variety of feminist strategies in literature, see also Orbaugh, "The Body in Contemporary Japanese Woman's Fiction," pp. 121–124.

8. Kōda, "Eiyaku 'Kuroi suso' ni soete," in *Kōda Aya zenshū*, vol. 6, p. 185.

9. Kōda, "Atomiyosowaka," p. 94; *Misokkasu*, pp. 37\tsff.

10. Uno, "Women and Changes," p. 27.

11. Kōda, *Misokkasu*, pp. 17\tsff.

12. Kōda, "Atomiyosowaka," p. 145.

13. Ibid., pp. 146–147.

14. Ibid., pp. 170–171.

15. Tu, *Way, Learning, and Politics*, p. 31.

16. Ibid., p. 33.

17. Ibid., pp. 39–40.

18. At the same time, Rohan, by providing a good education for his daughter, drew on familial practices in evidence both in the Edo period and earlier in Meiji. The Edo poet-painter Ema Saikō (1787–1861), for example, learned calligraphy, painting, and literature from her father, Confucian and Rangaku (Dutch Learning) scholar Ema Ransai (1747–1838). Other precedents include the venerable sage Ninomiya Sontoku, who gave his daughter Fumiko what a writer in 1909 termed "the best education of the time: she learned to read and write and to sew and cook, as well as the fine arts of tea, poetry, and calligraphy"—best because the Meiji writer sought to extol "hard work, endurance, and education" as feminine virtues, in accordance with the state's policies concerning the roles of women. Tomeoka Kosuke, "Joshi ni taisuru Ninomiya Oo no risō," *Shimin* 4.4 (28 May 1909), pp. 61–62, quoted in Nolte and Hastings, "The Meiji State's Policy," p. 168; Fister, "Female *Bunjin*," pp. 110, 113.

19. Higuchi Ichiyō's father, for example, recognizing her intelligence and talent, afforded her more attention and better educational opportunities than her less apt brother. Uno, "Women and Changes," pp. 31–32; and Danly, *In the Shade of Spring Leaves,* pp. 11–13.

20. Interview with Noborio Yutaka, April 1986.

21. In addition, Kōda herself, Aoki, Tansman, and many Japanese critics concur on this aspect of "influence" and of their relationship.

22. Alan Tansman, in his fine study, discusses Kōda's use of objects in her work. See especially his chapter "A World of Objects," in *The Writings of Kōda Aya,* pp. 70–101.

23. *Misokkasu,* pp. 14–15, 73.

24. Again, Rohan may have been following a model such as that of Ema Saikō and her father, for whom painting and calligraphy were not *hanayome shugyō* (training for marriage) but part of the education of a literate, or *bunjin.* Fister notes: "the earliest female *bunjin* . . . were primarily the wives, sisters, or daughters of well-known *bunjin* artists . . . many scholars, inspired by the actions of contemporary masters in China, now encouraged women to join their ranks." "Female *Bunjin,*" p. 108.

25. Kōda, "Kōen," in *Kōda Aya zenshū,* p. 23, cassette tape.

26. Tansman, *Writings of Kōda Aya,* p. 4.

27. Kōda, "Sugano no ki," pp. 27–29.

28. Yaeger, Kowaleski-Wallace, and Ursula Owens note that only a few frameworks exist for feminists viewing father-daughter relationships. One is the Freudian view that "focuses on the sexual bonds between father and daughter, emphasizing the daughter's sexual feelings and her elaborate mechanisms for denying those feelings," and the other approach lies in institutionalized forms of patriarchy that determines "what part women shall or shall not play and in which the female is everywhere subsumed under the male." In *Fathers: Reflections by Daughters* (New York: Pantheon, 1983), p. 3, quoted in Yaeger and Kowaleski-Wallace, *Refiguring the Father,* p. xiii.

29. See Orbaugh's illuminating essay "The Body in Contemporary Japanese Fiction," esp. pp. 128–129, 149–153; and Cornyetz, *Dangerous Women, Deadly Words.*

30. I am grateful to Ken Ito for this point.

31. Sherif, "A Dealer in Memories," pp. 221–222.

32. In contrast, Uno Chiyo describes her relationship with her sadistic father in blunt terms and makes it clear that she became a writer despite his attempts literally to bind her. See chapter 8, by Rebecca Copeland, in this volume and also her *Sound of the Wind.*

33. Inoue, "Onna no isshō," p. 111.

34. Kōda, "Atomiyosowaka," pp. 140–141.

35. Kōda, *Misokkasu,* p. 84.

36. Ibid., p. 153; *Kuzure,* pp. 11\tsff.; "Gozaimasen," in *Kōda Aya zenshū,* vol. 20, p. 58; "Renzu," in *Kōda Aya zenshū,* vol. 1, pp. 62\tsff.; "Zen," in *Kōda Aya zenshū,* vol. 2, pp. 72–73; "Sugano no ki," p. 59.

37. Kōda, "Kihen," in *Kōda Aya zenshū,* vol. 15, p. 63.

38. Kōda, "Kusabue," in *Kōda Aya zenshū,* vol. 21, p. 3.

39. Examples of such evocations of Rohan can be found in Kōda's "Chichi— sono shi," "Sugano no ki," and other works.

40. Kōda, "Sugano no ki," p. 24.

41. The shift in generic classification occurs in the United States too: what had earlier been promoted as "fiction" because of sensitive material is later packaged as autobiography.

42. Tansman uses the term "persona" in his book.

43. Larson, *Literary Authority*, p. 161, n. 1.

44. Kōda, *Kuzure*, p. 26.

45. Kōda, *Tsuki no chiri*, p. 23.

46. Personal correspondence with the author, 14 September 1996.

47. Rohan and Shiki admired each other's work, but Rohan discouraged Shiki from becoming a novelist.

48. Tansman, *The Writings of Kōda Aya*, pp. 132\tsff., 151.

49. I thank Paul Anderer for pointing out the predominance of the search for a second father. The most obvious examples of this are in Sōseki's *Kokoro* and Tōson's *Hakai*.

Works Cited

Location of Japanese publishers is Tokyo unless otherwise noted.

Bernstein, Gail, ed. *Recreating Japanese Women: 1600–1945*. Berkeley and Los Angeles: University of California Press, 1991.

Copeland, Rebecca. *The Sound of the Wind: The Life and Works of Uno Chiyo*. Honolulu: University of Hawai'i Press, 1992.

Cornyetz, Nina. *Dangerous Women, Deadly Words: Phallic Fantasy and Modernity in Three Japanese Writers*. Stanford, Calif.: Stanford University Press, 1999.

Danly, Robert Lyons. *In the Shade of Spring Leaves: The Life and Writings of Higuchi Ichiyō, A Woman of Letters in Meiji Japan*. New Haven, Conn.: Yale University Press, 1981.

Fister, Patricia. "Female *Bunjin*: The Life of Poet-Painter Ema Saikō." In *Recreating Japanese Women: 1600–1945*, ed. Gail Bernstein, pp. 108–130. Berkeley and Los Angeles: University of California Press, 1991.

Harari, Josue V., ed. *Textual Strategies*. Ithaca, N.Y.: Cornell University Press, 1979.

Inoue Kazuko. "Onna no isshō—Kōda Aya to kimono." In *Gengo bunkabu kiyō*. Hokkaidō Daigaku, 1994.

Kōda Aya. "Atomiyosowaka." In *Chichi—Konna koto*. Shinchōsha, 1956.

———. *Chichi—Konna koto*. Shinchōsha, 1956.

———. *Kōda Aya zenshū*. 23 vols. Iwanami shoten, 1995–1997.

———. *Kuzure*. Kōdansha, 1991.

———. *Misokkasu*. Iwanami shoten, 1983.

———. "Sugano no ki." In *Chichi—Konna koto*, pp. 9–90. Shinchōsha, 1956.

————. *Tsuki no chiri.* Kōdansha, 1994.

Kowaleski-Wallace, Elizabeth. *Their Father's Daughters: Hannah More, Maria Edge-worth, and Patriarchal Complicity.* New York: Oxford University Press, 1991.

Larson, Wendy. *Literary Authority and the Modern Chinese Writer.* Durham, N.C.: Duke University Press, 1991.

Mori, Maryellen Toman. "The Quest for Jouissance in Takahashi Takako's Texts." In *The Woman's Hand: Gender and Theory in Japanese Women's Writing,* ed. Paul Schalow and Janet Walker, pp. 205–235. Stanford, Calif.: Stanford University Press, 1996.

Nolte, Sharon, and Sally Hastings. "The Meiji State's Policy toward Women, 1890–1910." In *Recreating Japanese Women: 1600–1945,* ed. Gail Bernstein, p. 151–174. Berkeley and Los Angeles: University of California Press, 1991.

Orbaugh, Sharalyn. "The Body in Contemporary Japanese Woman's Fiction." In *The Woman's Hand: Gender and Theory in Japanese Women's Writing,* ed. Paul Schalow and Janet Walker, pp. 119–164. Stanford, Calif.: Stanford University Press, 1996.

Sherif, Ann. "A Dealer in Memories: The Fiction and Essays of Kōda Aya." Ph.D. dissertation, University of Michigan, 1991.

————. *Mirror: The Fiction and Essays of Kōda Aya.* Honolulu: University of Hawai'i Press, 1999.

Tansman, Alan. *The Writings of Kōda Aya: A Japanese Literary Daughter.* New Haven, Conn.: Yale University Press, 1993.

Tu, Wei-Ming. *Way, Learning, and Politics: Essays on the Confucian Intellectual.* Albany: SUNY Press, 1993.

Uno, Kathleen. "Women and Changes in the Household Division of Labor." In *Recreating Japanese Women: 1600–1945,* ed. Gail Bernstein, p. 17–41. Berkeley and Los Angeles: University of California Press, 1991.

Yaeger, Patricia, and Beth Kowaleski-Wallace, eds. *Refiguring the Father: New Feminist Readings of Patriarchy.* Carbondale: Southern Illinois University Press, 1989.

Chapter 10
Ōba Minako and the Paternity of Maternalism

SHARALYN ORBAUGH

Remind me how we loved our mother's body / our mouths drawing the first / thin sweetness from her nipples // our faces dream-
ing hour on hour / in the salt smell of her lap Remind me / how
her touch melted childgrief // how she floated great and tender
in our dark/ or stood guard over us/ against our willing // and how
we thought she loved / the strange male body first / that took, that
took, whose taking seemed a law // and how she sent us weeping /
into that law / how we remet her in our childbirth visions // erect,
enthroned, above / a spiral stair / and crawled and panted toward
her // I know, I remember, but / hold me, remind me / of how her
woman's flesh was made taboo to us

Adrienne Rich, *Sibling Mysteries*, Part 2

The Family Romance

The idea of the family romance—that is, "the story we tell ourselves
about the social and psychological reality of the family in which we
find ourselves and about the patterns of desire that motivate the interaction among its members"[1]—has been related frequently in recent
years to the study of narrative fiction. Ever since Harold Bloom's
Anxiety of Influence (1973) appeared, the filial nature of the relationship between a male writer and his male predecessors has been explored. More recently, feminist literary scholars have inflected
the question of filiality to investigate the different relationship that a
literary daughter may be presumed to have to her literary forebears, both fathers and mothers. This chapter will address the relationship between models of the family and the fiction of a particular
contemporary writer, Ōba Minako (b. 1930). Precisely because I am
interested here in the stories that people tell themselves in the construction of filial relationships, I feel I must begin this study with a

personal anecdote, explaining how I came to be interested in Ōba in this context.

I first encountered Ōba Minako's work in 1981,[2] and although I have continued to read and to teach her work in both English and Japanese ever since, I had never until quite recently been tempted to make Ōba's work an object of study. Something had always kept me from being engaged by her work with the same enthusiasm that I have for several other women writers who appear to touch on similar themes, such as Tsushima Yūko, Kōno Taeko, Kanai Mieko, and Hirabayashi Taiko.

During a year spent in Tokyo in 1994–1995, I met with Ōba Minako twice and finally was able to identify the source of my resistance to her work. At the first meeting, she was accompanied by her daughter, Ōba Yū, who had just translated Ōba's novel *Urashimasō* into English. Yū was exactly my age, and it was in my immediate identification with her that I realized for the first time that Ōba Minako is not writing simply from the position of woman-as-subject (which could be argued for the other women writers I mentioned), but rather Ōba Minako is often writing specifically from the position of *mother*-as-subject—and, significantly, a bourgeois, nuclear-family mother-as-subject—something that is not true of those other writers.[3] In addition, I realized for the first time that, vis-à-vis that maternal subjectivity at the center of Ōba's works, I was reading from the position of daughter.

It is relatively rare even in feminist scholarship that the story or voice of the mother is considered. When we think of a woman speaking her life experience, we think of her doing so as an autonomous already-constituted subject, whatever narrative we use to conceptualize that process of subject formation (such as the oedipal narrative, for example). Moreover those various narratives of subject formation always focus on the younger generation in the scenario: the son or daughter. In these narratives the mother is merely what Marianne Hirsch calls "the *object* of the child's process of subject-formation and the *ground* on which the conflict between father and son is played out" (my emphasis). And although Hirsch goes on in her 1989 study, *The Mother/Daughter Plot,* to address explicitly the story and/or voice of the mother, she acknowledges that narratives written in such a voice or focalized exclusively through the maternal experience are few. In attempts to privilege a female-centered discourse, to *parler femme,* the speakers or centers of consciousness are generally adult daughters (whether or not they also have children of their own). As Hirsch sums it up: ". . . while psychoanalytic feminism can add the female child to the male, allowing women to speak as daughters, it has difficulty accounting for the experience and the voice of the adult woman who is a mother."[4]

There are, of course, a large number of narratives by daughters speaking *about* mothers or maternity. This is the case, for example, in the Adrienne Rich poem from which the epigraph is excerpted. Even though the speaker is herself a mother, she appeals to her sister(s) in their shared position as daughter to their mother; it is through the meaning of that original motherhood that the speaker wishes to understand and define herself, with the help of her sister(s). But in contrast to this, Ōba Minako's protagonists and narrators often are mothers, and they speak as such. Ōba somehow has managed to construct a seemingly complete and effortless maternal discourse, what we might call a discourse of *parler mère,* or, more appropriately in this case, *haha-gataru.* It is this mother-centered discourse that I refer to in the title of this essay by the word "maternalism."

When I began this project on Ōba Minako in 1996, I was thirty-eight years old. It is worth noting that when my mother was thirty-eight, I was nineteen. When my mother's mother was thirty-eight, she was a grandmother. When Ōba Minako was thirty-eight, she published "Sanbiki no kani" (The three crabs, 1968; English translations, 1978, 1982),[5] her first story, and the one I'll be concentrating on here. I list these facts to emphasize that there is nothing about my physical age that prevents me from understanding the discourse that I am here calling by the shorthand term "maternalism." But the fact remains that I have never been a mother, and the only process of subject formation I have ever experienced is as a daughter. Having thus finally recognized my position as eternal daughter vis-à-vis the maternal subjectivity at the center of Ōba's work,[6] I also became aware of another major source of my discomfort with her fiction: that is, my heretofore unexamined preference for identification with my father or, more accurately, with "the role of fatherliness"—my aspiration to emulate a paternal model, characterized by psychic integrity, social power, and autonomy, as opposed to the more ambiguous, amorphous, socially constrained maternal model.

Some of the general questions I was working on just as I began thinking about Ōba Minako were the following: Can one make the distinction between a "men's literature" and a "women's literature" in modern Japan? (As is well known, that distinction is commonly made—the question therefore concerns its validity.) Which women writers try to demonstrate their female identity in their writing, and which try to erase the gender distinction? How have women writers been reviewed by the literary establishment that their cultural fathers have constructed?[7]

In my preliminary consideration of Ōba's work, it seemed that Ōba's maternalist discourse would certainly constitute a "women's literature," which, being so fundamentally tied to the reproductive body, emphasized rather than erased gender distinctions. And, as we shall see, the "cultural fathers" of the male critical establishment gave Ōba's mother-focused work an overwhelmingly positive welcome, despite some significant undercurrents of discomfort. Ōba Minako would therefore appear to have constructed an apparently effortless, seamless discourse of maternalism. Even such a mother-centered construction, however, must be considered in the context of its own familial relationships. If a literary text, writer's oeuvre, or constructed discourse can be conceptualized (metaphorically) as the product of familial structures, then the "paternity" both of and in Ōba's writing is worthy of consideration. What sort of "fatherhood" is it that could help to produce such a mother-centered body of texts? For the remainder of this study, I will investigate the paternity of Ōba's maternalist discourse.

Literary Paternity

I will explore here two kinds of paternity vis-à-vis Ōba's work. The first refers to the traditional kind of cultural fathers mentioned above: the men who inspired Ōba to write, those whose models influenced her work, as well as the men who introduced her into Japan's literary world. A list of such "fathers" in Ōba's case would have to include the following figures:

1. The men who developed and dropped the atomic bomb on Hiroshima, because Ōba frequently refers to her experience of that event at the age of fourteen as the impetus for her eventual literary career.[8]

2. Franz Kafka (1883–1924). Ōba has said that her reading of Kafka, specifically his story "The Metamorphosis" (Die Verwandlung, 1915), while she was in the United States in 1967 taught her what literature really was, and the immediate result was her writing of "The Three

Crabs," which in 1968 won her both the Gunzō New Writers Award and the Akutagawa Prize.[9] This stunning debut effectively launched her long and prestigious career in Japanese literary circles.

3. The distinguished members of the eleventh Gunzō New Writers Award committee that first heralded her work: Etō Jun, Noma Hiroshi, Ōe Kenzaburō, and Yasuoka Shōtarō. (The average age of the committee members in 1968 was forty-two.)

4. The members of the even more prestigious 59th Akutagawa Prize committee: Mishima Yukio, Ishikawa Tatsuzō, Ishikawa Jun, Inoue Yasushi, Kawabata Yasunari, Niwa Fumio, Funabashi Seiichi, Takii Kōsaku, Ōoka Shōhei, Nagai Tatsuo, and Nakamura Mitsuo. (Average age sixty-two.) The fifteen members of this and the eleventh Gunzō New Writers Award committees, comprising two exclusively male generations of the *bundan,* represent the absolute center and apex of literature and criticism in 1968.

5. The literary figures (all male) to whom these prize committees referred in their evaluations of Ōba's work: American dramatist Edward Albee (b. 1928), author of "Who's Afraid of Virginia Woolf?" (1962), to which "The Three Crabs" is repeatedly compared (see, for example, the comments of Etō and Yasuoka); Arishima Takeo (1878–1923), author of *Aru onna* (A certain woman, 1919), because Yasuoka identifies Yōko, the protagonist of *Aru onna,* with Yuri, the protagonist of "The Three Crabs"; and, finally, Norwegian playwright Henrik Ibsen (1828–1906), because Funabashi Seiichi compares Yuri to Nora of "A Doll's House" (1879), in the scene in which Nora dances the tarantella with tambourine in hand. Certainly these male writers and their feisty female protagonists have a rightful place in a list of Ōba's cultural influences, but let me point out in passing that none of the female characters in these works—Martha (of "Virginia Woolf"), Yōko, or Nora—is, in fact, a mother in a bourgeois nuclear family, as Yuri is. In all three cases the motherhood of the protagonist is either spurious or rejected. These protagonists do not speak or act from the subject position of "mother."[10] Nor is it their maternal aspects that interest the critics who cite them in connection with Ōba's work.

This then is a rough list of candidates for the first kind of paternity I am addressing here: the traditional cultural fathers, who exist prior to and outside of Ōba's texts and who, through either inspiration or endorsement, helped to bring her discourse of maternalism to the literary world.

The second kind of paternity I plan to address is *internal* to those texts. This type of paternity refers not to the father or "role of father-liness" that produces Ōba's maternalism as an offspring, but rather it refers to the father or "role of fatherliness" produced *within* Ōba's constructed literary universe. This includes depictions of a female protagonist's father, one generation up, as well as depictions of a pro-tagonist's husband/male partner, in the position of father to the protagonist's child(ren). In the remainder of this study, I will focus on these two types of paternity—external and internal to Ōba's texts —as they work separately and together in the construction of Ōba's maternalist discourse.

External Paternity

In the June 1968 issue of *Gunzō,* the eleventh New Writers awards were announced, the winning pieces were published, and each of the four members of the awards committee contributed an essay explaining the selections. In that year, rather than awarding one prize for fiction and one for criticism, the committee awarded a special Overall Winner prize *(tōsensaku)* to Ōba's "The Three Crabs" and then made the two normal Awards for Excellence *(yūshūsaku),* to Fukai Tomiko for fiction and Komatsu Masako for criticism.[11] That "The Three Crabs" so far outdistanced the competition that it necessitated a special award category, and that the three winners were all women, are points remarked on repeatedly by the four judges.

The essay by the extremely influential critic Etō Jun, titled "Michisū no sugomi" (Immeasurable ghastliness) is the first. He begins by draw-ing attention to the large and increasing numbers of women students in university literature departments but insists that this phenomenon is unconnected to the fact that the three 1968 winners are all female. The three winners are all his age, he emphasizes—Etō, born in 1933, was thirty-five in 1968; Ōba, born in 1930, was thirty-eight—and there-fore these new women writers are too old to belong to the university generation of women, who were then so politically vocal.

Rather, Etō characterizes the work of the female writers of his generation as the "personal statements of women who were seri-ously made to bear responsibility for the heavy burden of the *'bōkoku'* [the 'national defeat' of World War II]." They share this responsibility with the men of their generation but, in Etō's view, respond to it differently:

> [I]n order to gloss over the humiliation of "national defeat," men have built up elaborate bluffing self-deceptions, but women on the contrary have tried to throw themselves bodily into the fissures between reality and the fabrications created by these ruined men [*dame ni natte shimatta otokotachi*]. This of course warps and tears these women.[12]

Therefore, he asserts, the three women prizewinners have been forced to produce something new, something different from any earlier generation of Japanese women writers, through the enormous and painful pressure of this national destruction. He adds:

> Perhaps because of this [their work exhibits] a palpable touch of life. That this life is desolate is because our contemporary life is desolate. If the women who have thrown themselves into the fissures have eyes that can see, naturally life will appear in that form.[13]

Among the writers of these new, desolate works, Etō singles out Ōba both for her exceptional talent and for what he terms the "immeasurable ghastliness" of her work—the title of his essay.

The essays of Ōe and Noma generally concur in Etō's high praise of Ōba's talent. More interesting, however, is the essay of the final committee member, Yasuoka Shōtarō, titled "Osorubeki joryū" (Terrifying women writers/women's writing). Yasuoka also attributes the emergence of this wave of terrifying, talented women writers to the effects of the war and the defeat. He relates a conversation in which Etō had solemnly said to him:

> "Ōba Minako is roughly the same generation as we are, and this has a close connection with the theme of her story. That is: for her, the weakening of the males has reached a point of such desolation. . . . I apologize, but "men" for Ōba does not mean all of us of this generation; it means men the age of her husband. Yasuoka-san, it is the weakness of men of exactly *your age* that is the problem." [Yasuoka, born in 1920, was forty-eight at this time.]

Yasuoka continues:

> Of course I was taken aback, but this opinion is probably valid and should be examined seriously. The fact that no exciting new male writers have appeared since Ōe Kenzaburō should not be attrib-

uted to chance, but rather we men should turn around and take a
good look at ourselves.[14]

Before I turn to the Akutagawa Prize committee reactions, let me
underscore two points about Etō's and Yasuoka's evaluations. First,
both make note of a sense of ghastliness, something they find profoundly disturbing, even terrifying, in Ōba's work, while they also
praise its genius; and second, both attribute the freshness *and* the
ghastliness of her work to historical contingency: her relationship to
the war and its discursive aftermath, a relationship specific to her
gender, they argue.

The eleven-member Akutagawa Prize committee each produced a
much shorter essay explaining the decision process. In fact, the Fifty-
ninth Akutagawa Prize was split between two stories: besides "The
Three Crabs," Maruya Saiichi's "Toshi no nokori" (The remains of
the year) was honored.[15] The committee was sharply divided: some
preferred Maruya and some preferred Ōba. Several thought that a
brand-new writer such as Ōba should not be awarded the extremely
prestigious Akutagawa Prize.[16] This prize is meant to highlight the
accomplishments of writers relatively new to the literary world but
nonetheless is often not awarded until several years into a writer's
career. Maruya Saiichi, for example, Ōba's co-winner, had been publishing actively for eight years before he won the Akutagawa Prize.
Most winners in the postwar years have been nominated unsuccess-
fully at least once before being awarded the prize.

In general the Akutagawa Prize committee essays address questions
of style and "literary merit" more than those of the Gunzō Award
committee did. Several mention "problems" with Ōba's work, particularly of dialogue or language and structure, although none analyzes
those problems at length.[17]

It is significant, however, that none of the Akutagawa Prize essays
refers to the war as a probable influence on Ōba's writing. Nor does
any refer to gender per se. But two or three essays do provide an
obliquely gendered sociological explanation for the theme of "The
Three Crabs." Niwa Fumio, for example, writes:

Ōba Minako's "The Three Crabs" was an effectively shocking story.
This married woman [i.e., the protagonist] has already slept with
a foreigner, and is the sort of woman to advise her friend that if

she plans to have an affair she should look for a man with whom there will be no lingering ties. . . .

It seems that things that are difficult to do in one's own country become easy when one is in a foreign country surrounded by foreigners. That is, for the purpose of [achieving freedom in] both action and thought, some people remove themselves from their fellow Japanese. But there are also cases like the wife of a businessman stationed abroad who committed suicide by throwing herself out of a window somewhere around New York.[18]

In contrast to Etō's figure of the war-generation women writers who leap bravely into discursive fissures to bridge reality and male-generated fabrication, Niwa cites a "real case" of a displaced woman for whom too much freedom has resulted in her leaping to her death. (Despite the positive tone of Etō's image of self-sacrificing women, it is significant that he concludes his model by saying, "This of course tears and warps these women." In both critics' illustrative accounts, therefore, the women end up dead and/or mangled. A suspicious reader might infer a concealed hostility even on Etō's part.)

Akutagawa Prize committee member Takii Kōsaku admires Ōba's depiction of such displaced characters but describes the characters in "The Three Crabs" and "Niji to ukihashi" (Rainbow and floating bridge, 1968) themselves in negative terms:

The Americans and other nationalities depicted in these stories are like rootless grasses [*nenashigusa*], and are horrible. Probably not all the people are like this, but these stories are written focusing on a society where there are many such rootless people.[19]

Again the points to be noted from these evaluations are, first, the general discomfort engendered by Ōba's story; and second, the search for the source of that discomfort—in this case explicitly related to the Japanese characters' presence in the rootless, too-free society of the United States. It is interesting to observe an apparent generational split into the younger Gunzō Award critics who see the war, and men, as the problem, versus the older Akutagawa Prize critics who see too much freedom, particularly for women, as the problem. But in both cases the critics recognize the cruel results for the women depicted in Ōba's narratives. None, however, mentions Yuri's identity as a mother. It is the protagonist's behavior vis-à-vis the men in her life that all the critics, regardless of generation, find significant.

These then are the paternal critical responses that launched Ōba
and her work onto the Japanese literary scene. Now I would like to
turn to the paternity constructed within her work, beginning as early
as her first story, "The Three Crabs."

Internal Paternity

In 1920 Franz Kafka (as we have seen, one of Ōba's paternal influences) wrote: "He does not live for the sake of his personal life; he
does not think for the sake of his personal thoughts. It seems to him
that he lives and thinks under the compulsion of a family . . . for which
he constitutes, in obedience to some law unknown to him, a formal
necessity."[20] This perfectly describes the situation of Gregor Samsa,
the unfortunate protagonist of Kafka's "The Metamorphosis," the story
that taught Ōba (in her words) "what literature could be" and inspired her to begin writing fiction. Just as "The Metamorphosis" is a
narrative completely enclosed by the walls of the family, and just as
Gregor's sudden transformation into a giant insect inevitably transforms in turn the nature of each family member's role, so Ōba's work
should also be examined in terms of the "compulsion of a family"
and the ways the protagonist—a mother in this case—"constitutes . . .
a formal necessity" of that family. I would contend that the ghastliness,
fearfulness, and rootlessness attributed by the Japanese male critics
to Ōba's story may have as much to do with her exploration of the
constitution of the family and the subject construction of the mother
as with the external historical or geocultural explanations adduced
by those critics.[21]

When looking at the relationship between narratives of subject
construction within the frame of family and the family as constructed
within the frame of narrative, literary critics refer back to a limited set
of plots: the Freudian and Lacanian plots based on the oedipal narrative; feminist and other recent rewritings of Freud and Lacan, which
still take Oedipus as the point of departure and contention (Chodo-
row, Kristeva, Deleuze and Guattari, and so on); and the Ajase plot,
which has begun to appear recently in Japanese criticism.[22] I do not
intend to focus on or endorse any one of these plots here. But an
understanding of the structural points that all of these subject-con-
struction narratives share is essential to a discussion of Ōba Minako's
alternate strategy for plotting the family.

Both the oedipal and Ajase plots are based on two-generation triangles: father, mother, and child/son. In every case it is the subject formation of the child that is at issue: the subject identities of the parents are taken as fixed within this frame, while the child's identity is in the process of being constituted vis-à-vis the parents' fixed identities.[23] In addition, despite the necessarily triangular nature of these models, in every case the process of subject formation is focused through the interaction of a dyad within the triangle, and the passive "third term" tends to disappear from view. Again, because the focus is on the child/son here, that dyad is never composed of the same-generation figures: the mother and father. Rather, in the oedipal triangle it is the father-son dyadic rivalry that is central, while the mother functions merely as the "object" and "ground" of that rivalry (in Hirsch's words). In the Ajase model it is the mother-son dyad that is central, while the father is merely the original instigator of the mother-son conflict to be resolved.

Ōba Minako's experiments in writing the constitution of mother-as-subject within the frame of narrative replicate some of these structural patterns but necessarily change others. The family narrated in many of Ōba's works, including "The Three Crabs," is a simple two-generational triangle: father, mother, and child. But Ōba does not attempt what would seem a straightforward strategy of "flipping" the oedipal narrative: she recognizes that simply to recast the story from Jocasta's point of view would not change the focus of the plot, which would remain the child's, Oedipus's, subjectivity. Similarly, to cast her protagonist as Queen Idaike would retain the focus on Prince Ajase. In order to construct a maternal discourse, Ōba must write a new plot, taking as her focus the subjectivity of the *mother* as it is constituted through the dynamic of the family.[24]

In addition, the child in Ōba's scenario is a daughter. Therefore the focus is on the issues of identity and separation in the mother-daughter dyad, rather than the father-son rivalry of Oedipus. In Ōba's model it is the father who is the third term against which this dyad plays out the main plotline; it is the father whose subjectivity constantly slips out of sight. As we shall see, Ōba in fact changes her focus back and forth between a mother-daughter dyad mediated by the father, and a wife-husband (or mother-father) dyad mediated through the daughter.[25] I would tentatively argue, however, that looking at Ōba's work as a whole, it is the mother-daughter relationship that receives the most attention.[26] If this is true, then it is significant to look at the nature of paternity as it is constituted as "object" or "ground" in Ōba's work. Although the examples I discuss in this essay are primarily from "The Three Crabs," interesting depictions of paternity as third term can be found in much of her fiction.

In semiotic terms it might well be argued that the sign for adult woman is "enclosure" (vaginal image) and that the sign for mother is enclosure squared or enclosure times ten—some greater order of magnitude, based on a uterine image.

Psychoanalytic literature around the world discusses the fear of women, and perhaps particularly mothers, expressed through tropes of engulfment and enclosure. The "role of motherliness" is figured as amorphous, sticky, s-mothering; Julia Kristeva writes of the "swamp" of the maternal. This is in direct contrast to the "role of fatherliness," which is figured as distant, adamantine, inflexible, powerful. Lest it seem that I am imposing these western cultural models arbitrarily, let me mention briefly two of the many examples of modern Japanese texts that inscribe these same semiotic terms.

Many readers of modern Japanese literature would think immediately of Kōno Taeko's 1961 story "Yōjigari" (Toddler-hunting, trans. 1996) in this context.[27] The protagonist, Akiko, thinks of women in the double terms of the image of a silkworm squirming in a dissected cocoon, and the cocoon itself: the adjectives accompanying this image include "sticky," "liquid," "binding," "dark," "smothering," and "smothered."

Tsushima Yūko delineates the typical view of motherhood in a story called "Mugura no haha" (Bindweed mother, 1975). The first-person narrator speaks and acts in the story as a daughter, but she is pregnant, about to become a mother herself. The story concerns her extremely ambivalent attitudes toward her pregnancy, and her attitudes toward her own mother, who is figured as the *mugura* of the title: a thick, choking, wild vine, which in Japanese classical poetry typically smothers a ramshackle house inhabited by a lone and lonely woman. The young woman protagonist of Tsushima's story thinks of her mother as both a frightening enclosure, threatening to steal away the daughter's autonomy, and simultaneously as the pitiful being enclosed in an impenetrable and undesirable shell: the mother is both the *mugura* and the desolate emptiness it encases. Because the young woman is soon to assume that role herself, and because she is currently in the extraordinary body state of enclosing another living being, the young woman agonizes over her now undeniable identification with this unattractive role model, but eventually comes to terms

—reluctantly—with her new subjectivity. Still, Tsushima's story of maternal subject formation is narrated from the point of view of the daughter, whereas Ōba, as I have already pointed out, places the mother—the figure always already both enclosing and enclosed, entrapping and entrapped—at the center of her narrative.

"The Three Crabs"

In "The Three Crabs," the daughter, Rie, an intelligent ten-year-old, is far too young to have reached the level of consciousness of the relationship between her mother's role and her own that Tsushima's narrator eventually achieves. Although the mother, Yuri, tries to engage Rie's consciousness of their shared identity, Rie adamantly resists. I will sketch briefly the plot of "The Three Crabs" before returning to specific examples of Rie's resistance to the maternal model.

The story opens with the protagonist, Yuri, walking through "a milky morning fog" by an unidentified seashore, where she sees two crabs, whose shells remind her of human faces, crawling together as if their legs are entangled. She boards a bus, only to discover that the money she had had in her wallet "the night before when she left home" is missing. As the bus moves toward her destination, Yuri looks out the window to see a neon sign for "The Three Crabs" hotel.

At this point, with only a line break to mark the transition, the story moves back in time to the afternoon before, as Yuri is baking in preparation to host a bridge party that night. She dreads the party and persuades her husband, Takeshi, to allow her to leave on a pretext after greeting the guests. The bulk of the text then consists of unpleasant conversations among Yuri, Takeshi, and Rie and, later, conversations among the various party guests—Russian, Japanese, and American—most of whom are connected with a local university in some capacity. Through these conversations we learn that both Yuri and her husband have had affairs with some of the people who will be coming to the party.

The next section of the story follows Yuri as she leaves the party and goes aimlessly to an amusement park, where she is drawn to an exhibition of Alaskan native crafts. (It is significant that all of the crafts mentioned synthesize the animal and the human in some way.) There she meets a man in a pink shirt, thereafter known only as *momo iro shatsu,* or Pink Shirt. He tells her he is "one quarter Eskimo . . . one quarter Tlingit, one quarter Swedish, and one quarter Polish."[28]

As they talk idly, Pink Shirt mentions his wife; Yuri also makes it clear that she has a husband. Nonetheless they go together on a roller coaster ride, with Pink Shirt's arm tightly wrapped around Yuri's shoulders. From there they go dancing and end up driving down the coast to spend the night together at the Three Crabs hotel. The story ends with Yuri looking at the sea and imagining the metallic voices of her husband and daughter. Recalling the opening of the story, we realize that it was set on the morning after this, as Yuri wends her way home alone after parting from Pink Shirt.

Let me return now to a consideration of Rie's relationship with her parents and the two social roles they represent. In the scene that opens the narrative chronologically, Yuri is baking a cake for that evening's bridge party, which she is dreading so much that she feels nauseated.

> Rie was whipping the cream. She was looking forward to licking the bowl later.
>
> "Who all will be coming?" asked Rie dipping into the whipped cream with her finger.
>
> "It doesn't matter who's coming. I don't want you to go telling Susan every time your parents have friends over," said Yuri holding back the pain in her stomach.
>
> "Oh all right," said Rie rolling up the whites of her eyes. "Look Rie," continued Yuri, "there is no one else mama can be completely honest with, so every now and then I like to talk to you. To admit things like . . . I hate Sasha, or how I feel that I have to go ahead and bake this cake even though just the thought makes me vomit. But don't go telling everyone what I just said, okay? When mama says strange things like this, just listen to her and think of her as a poor fool. Mama may be a fool but she needs your sympathy. Be kind to her once in a while."[29]

Rie does not respond. Instead Takeshi intervenes, chastising her for saying such things to her daughter. Yuri's offer of a bond of exclusive identity with her daughter ("there is no one else mama can be completely honest with") is disrupted by the father, who intervenes to "protect" the daughter from too much maternal connection. That Rie is in sympathy with her father, rather than her mother, is evident in the story's only sustained conversation between Yuri and Rie:

> Yuri, having made up her mind not to play bridge, was much more relaxed, and she felt like putting on some make-up. As she was putting on eye-liner in the bathroom mirror, Rie came in with her

hands clasped behind her back and *with the voice of a schoolmaster* said, "Oh mama, you want to make yourself look young."

"That's right. Every woman wants to look young."

"But mama, everyone knows I'm your daughter so they're not going to believe that you're less than thirty."

"Some women have children when they're sixteen years old."

"But nice girls don't do that."

"How about it? Do you think your mama looks like she is twenty-six?"

"Well, I know how old you are. I can't pretend that I don't."

"What are you standing there for? It's not good to always go around criticizing people. It's especially odious in young ladies."

"I have to go to the bathroom. That's what I'm waiting for."

"Mama isn't a boy; I'll just look the other way."

"Never mind. I'll wait." Rie flounced out with a toss of her head.[30] (Emphasis added.)

Rie positions herself in this conversation as both identified with patriarchal authority and as a competitor with her mother for male, patriarchal, attention and favor. She chastises her mother "with the voice of a schoolmaster"[31] for attempting to look young and refuses to acknowledge that her mother might, indeed, be attractive. She lays down the law of social (patriarchal) authority a second time as she says: "nice girls don't do that." Despite Yuri's attempt to regain maternal authority, criticizing Rie's "odious" behavior, unsuited to a young lady, and her subsequent attempt to assert at least a gender identification with her daughter, "Mama isn't a boy; I'll just look the other way," Rie is having none of it. The narrator underscores this situation in another passage: "Rie hated her mother when she was like this, and immediately sympathized with her father."[32]

The law that Kafka posited as the rule for subject constitution within the family may be unknowable, as he suggested, but its implacable manifestations are not invisible. Immediately after the above exchange, Yuri is forced to acknowledge the impossibility of overcoming the fixed nature of the interdependent roles of mother and daughter:

The look in Rie's eyes when she looked at Yuri always reminded Yuri of her own mother's eyes. Yuri herself remembered looking at her mother with the same look that Rie turned on her now.[33]

The cycle of the daughter's rejection of identification with the role of motherliness, her preference for the role of fatherliness as both a model of subjectivity and a source of affection and attention, is inescapable. Yuri has been a daughter, behaving toward her parents just as Rie now behaves; Yuri's current identity as mother is just the next loop in an unending cycle, which will inevitably pass through Rie as well, if she should become mother to a daughter. It is only when a woman has reached the position of mother that the cyclic nature of this pattern becomes apparent; this rejection of identification with the mother in favor of paternal identification is invisible to the daughter until she has a daughter of her own and sees the rejection in the daughter's eyes. At the same time, the woman in the position of mother realizes that this rejecting daughter may well eventually become a mother of a girl herself and will someday experience this moment of undeniable identification with her formerly rejected mother.[34]

The circular nature of women's maternal experience is replicated by the chronological structure of "The Three Crabs."[35] The enfolding chronology of beginning and end has Yuri on a bus far from home the morning after her sexual encounter with Pink Shirt, gazing through the "milky," enveloping mist at the neon sign of the Three Crabs hotel.[36] The external narrative circle is therefore the story of Yuri's sexual encounter outside the home. This external circle is characterized by ambiguous roles, fragmentation, and blurred boundaries: the crabs with human faces, oddly locked together; the man identified synecdochically by his shirt, whose ethnicity is so complex; the lack of proper names; the animal-human native artwork; the pervasive fog.

Enclosed within that external narrative circle is the woman's interactions with her husband and daughter and later with the party guests at her house, characterized by fixed, seemingly immutable family and social roles, identification through proper names, and simple, contrasting ethnicities. In his Gunzō Award comments, Yasuoka Shōtarō remarked about this story: *"shikashi iyana shōsetsu da naa, shin ga nai ja nai ka"* ("It really is an unpleasant story, isn't it?—it has no wick/core"). This statement made such an impression on Etō Jun that he quoted it in his own comments.[37]

If Yasuoka sees this story as having no core, only enclosure, then that which is slipping from his view is the thing that occupies the structural center of the story and "ought," in normal discursive terms, to occupy its thematic center: that is, the dyad of father and child, and the patriarchal world organized into clear social roles and proper names. In this case, however, although the father and daughter are two points of the triangle necessary for the constitution of the mother-as-subject within the frame of the nuclear family, they are in the end not the focus. Whereas in the oedipal narrative the mother slips quickly from view, here, in the Ōba narrative, the father and daughter fade into the empty center of the maternalist plot.

A similar structure may be found in other works by Ōba that address paternity. Perhaps the best-known of these is the short work "Aoi kitsune" (The Pale Fox, 1973, trans. 1985), which opens and closes with the female protagonist and her lover, the eponymous Pale Fox, together in a hotel. In the interstices of the narrative of her relationship with this man is another story—that of the protagonist's relationships with her elderly widowed father and with the memory of her mother. Once again the "enclosing structure" of the narrative concerns a woman's activities outside conventional marriage or family relationships, her occasional meetings with a lover, while the paternity in the text is relegated to the background, "in-between" spaces.

This structural pattern directly contrasts with the gender-linked imagery in "The Pale Fox," in which the father is dominant and powerful (as is Takeshi in "The Three Crabs"). The father in the story works with metalcraft: he shapes what is hard to suit his own ends. The mother is pierced, at the father's insistence, in order to wear the earrings he has made; her ears never recover from this "violence." The mother is associated with abalone shells lying under moss at the bottom of the sea: tender, enclosed, dark, secret, hidden. The father rips those shells violently from their hiding place to devour them. Like the character identified only as the Pale Fox, the father is associated with predatory animals, the mother with passive prey. And yet, despite the forcefulness and dynamism that characterize paternity here, the father does not in any sense occupy the center of the narrative; his story slips behind the protagonist's relationship with her lover. It is again *her* identity that is at issue, and the "compulsion of the family" is important only as it relates to the adult woman she has become. Nonetheless, in this story too the family is inescapable because of its fundamental role in constituting even her adult identity.

The imagery associated with food and eating in "The Pale Fox" is clearly linked to gendered family roles, even though the configurations are not fixed by gender: the father "eats" and the mother "is eaten"; but in the protagonist's relationship with her partner (the man she lives with, in contrast to the Pale Fox, whom she meets occasionally), she is the devourer and he the devoured—hence his "name," Praying Mantis. The pattern is thus not that all men are predators and all women are prey. Rather, it is the father or paternity that is associated in this work with the aggressive, creative, forceful, predatory activities, and the mother or maternity that is associated with passivity, death, immobility, and enclosure. In this story it is not that the adult woman is figured as, by definition, food; only the mother is so defined. As we have seen, in "The Three Crabs" too the role of mother is defined partly in the context of the discourse of food and eating.

In the modern world, carnivalesque gluttony is associated with premodernity, with the primitive and/or the abject. In the eighteenth century, for example, as Europe moved rapidly toward the modern, there was quite a vogue for the display of monstrous gluttons who ate both huge quantities and inappropriate (nonfood) objects—live animals, iron, wood, stones.[38] Even in twentieth-century sideshows, "geeks" display their inordinate and inappropriate appetites for live chickens, frogs, or other revolting creatures. In all such cases the glutton is identified as coming from the hills, the forests, the mountains—somewhere remote both spatially and socially. In contrast with such displays, modernity and social acceptability are associated strongly with the ability to control one's appetite, to eat what is "normal" and in "suitable" amounts. The glutton's transgressive performance underscores the controlled, suitable, and modern nature of the viewers' means of gratification. In short, monstrous gluttony may arise from a natural and presumably universal human desire for food, but, representing excess, it lies outside the bounds of the modern social order.

Food functions, of course, as a powerful metaphor for sex, and in the case of displays of monstrous gluttony the excessive quality of the inappropriate gratification of desire is directly related to inappropriate gratification of other base, carnal appetites. Conversely, the control of the appetite for sex, like the control of the appetite for food, is a founding block of social order. To indulge in inappropriate, excessive, carnivalesque gratifications of either appetite is to threaten that order in fundamental ways.

The society within "The Three Crabs" is utterly controlled, despite what might at first appear to be dangerous ruptures: the known infidelities of both Yuri and Takeshi. (Note that the Akutagawa Prize critics comment only on her infidelity; that is where they locate the threat to the social order.) These affairs seem to have left the marriage and the friendships intact, if strained; they are normal topics of conversation. Adulterous affairs would not seem, therefore, to represent an excessive gratification of sexual appetites but rather are akin to eating a piece of cake: an occasional special indulgence, but well within the bounds of sanctioned behavior in that particular society.

We recall that in the scene that opens "The Three Crabs" chronologically, Yuri is simultaneously baking a cake for her guests and suppressing her own nausea. She is sick at the thought of the party, of the social intercourse among herself, her husband, her daughter, and their friends.

> Yuri felt a vague discomfort in her stomach as she stirred the cake batter. Mechanically she broke an egg into the bowl and mixed in the butter. As she blended in the baking powder and salt, she felt the nausea rising in her throat like morning sickness.[39]

Yuri's problem is not a desire for excessive gratification, but rather a wish to *refuse* to partake in the social intercourse represented immediately by the food she prepares and the friends, some of them former lovers, who will eat it. Yuri cannot, on this day, flirt and dally because, literally, she has no stomach for it. It is, of course, significant that Yuri associates her nausea with morning sickness (even though that evidently is not its cause), signifying impending motherhood. This suggests that it is her reinscription into the "role of motherliness" that Yuri wishes to refuse. That role requires Yuri to provide the food that will allow gratification within social norms. In addition, it requires her to occupy the position of "nice girl" assigned earlier by her patriarchally identified daughter: remaining entirely outside the competition for male attention (because she's too old, her daughter implies), or remaining at least within the bounds of sexual and other gratification sanctioned by her husband and their society.

Takeshi's strong resistance to her request to be allowed to skip the party signals the degree of unnaturalness her behavior suggests: to refuse to participate in the sanctioned gratification of desires is as potentially disruptive to the social order as grotesque excess. (It is significant here that Rie is waiting anxiously to lick the icing from the beaters: like her father, she takes pleasure in the gratification—within accepted limits—of her carnal desires.)

Another of Kafka's short works presents a paradigm of subjectivity similar to that of "The Three Crabs." In "The Hunger Artist" (1924), the narrative revolves around the larger meanings of food, the socially acceptable gratification of desire, and voluntary abstinence, in the context of modern social norms. Kafka's story features a man who starves himself in public for a living, fasting for a specified number of days inside a cage on public view. At the end of the story, the dying Hunger Artist admits that he is so good at fasting because he never found any food that he enjoyed; if he had, he would no doubt have been as obsessed with food and eating as the public who had watched his fasting in horrified disbelief, he says. But instead he has made his nature, his abhorrence of food, into his art.

Voluntary starvation is in many ways more disturbing than excessive eating, because it involves the denial or suppression of appetites taken to be natural and universal.[40] In Kafka's story, those who watched the Hunger Artist in his cage came away profoundly disturbed, reminded of the carnal nature of their own lives—that carnality highlighted by contrast with his abstinence. Compared with the monstrous gluttons discussed above, the Hunger Artist's public fasting was an unpopular display because it induced in the audience feelings of inferiority rather than superiority of control. But he had recognized that a lack of desire for the sanctioned gratification of food was fundamental to his identity, his subjectivity, and he forced the audience to acknowledge that.

Yuri's refusal to play her role in the economy of socially sanctioned gratification infuriates Takeshi, but it is this refusal that leads her away from the core narrative—the implacable fixity of her identity as constituted through husband and child—and toward the ambiguous, shifting identity that characterizes the enfolding narrative of her encounter with Pink Shirt. It need hardly be pointed out that this is not a utopic, liberating, permanent escape: Yuri must immediately return to the compulsion of the family. Nor does the description of her time with Pink Shirt contain any suggestion of enjoyment or release. Yuri's abstinence, her refusal to take part in the social rituals represented by the bridge party, is not rewarded with approval at home or pleasure abroad. Instead, like the Hunger Artist, she insists on her abstinence, her true identity, despite the lack of explicit reward.

Conclusion: The External and Internal Paternity of Maternalism

The critics who first shaped Ōba Minako's entrance into the Japanese literary world likened her earliest female protagonists to Ibsen's

Nora, Arishima's Yōko, and Albee's Martha: literary characters representing female sexual excess (especially Yōko and Martha), and a (selfish) desire for personal gratification. Even the admirable or pitiable examples cited by Etō and Niwa of real women who end up torn and mangled, can be considered selfish and/or excessive: they have themselves to blame for the choices they have made, leaping into discursive fissures or out of skyscraper windows. That these critics recognize the agency of Yuri as the protagonist of a peculiarly woman-centered narrative discourse, and attempt therefore to link her with existing examples of female agents, is understandable. I would argue, however, that they have misunderstood the nature of her agency. Unlike Nora or Yōko, Yuri does not escape from "the compulsion of the family" into a life of autonomous choice. Nor does her narrative trajectory inscribe a brave, if damaging, one-way leap out of social constraints altogether. Instead, her narrative is circular; she returns quietly to the compulsion of the family.

Far from excessive, rebellious gratification, Yuri's actions represent a Kafkaesque playing out of (self-)loathing and the austere acceptance of an unsought (and unsatisfactory) personal subjectivity. The Japanese critics in search of literary precursors might therefore have done better to look to Gregor Samsa or the Hunger Artist to find a model for Yuri, despite the gender difference. However, even Kafka's characters are on a one-way, self-chosen trajectory *out* of the compulsion of familial and social structures: both are dying, or dead, by suicide at the end of their narratives. But unlike Gregor Samsa or the Hunger Artist, Yuri goes on living, playing out a particularly female-identified (circular, ambiguous) and maternal (bleak, entrapped) subjectivity. Given the extreme rarity, and the inescapable ghastliness, of such a depiction, it is not surprising that Ōba's external literary fathers were perplexed, disturbed, and yet still profoundly impressed by her writing.

Notes

1. Hirsch, *Mother/Daughter Plot*, p. 9. My thanks to Andra Alvis, who first drew my attention to this book.

2. That year I read "Sanbiki no kani" (The three crabs, 1968) in a graduate seminar taught by Chiyuki Kumakura at the University of Michigan. The following year, Ōba's "Yamauba no bishō" (The smile of a mountain witch, 1976) appeared in English translation by Lippit and Ochi. Both stories deal with the rela-

tionship between mother and daughter, and it may be significant that my first exposure to Ōba's work was through them.

3. In fact, all of those writers, and many other women whose work interests me, write stories featuring protagonists who are mothers. And yet they do not seem to produce a discourse as intensely "maternal" as that of Ōba. In Tsushima's case, her mother-centered stories usually concern the trials of a single mother; in Hirabayashi's, the special concerns of an adoptive mother; and so on. These are cases of "special" mothers, and to the extent that their stories take motherhood as a main theme, it is the social and personal consequences of living within a non-normative family structure that are stressed.

4. Hirsch, p. 4. Mizuta Noriko makes the same point in "Bosei o tou," p. 185.

5. First published in *Gunzō* 23.6 (June 1968); references here are to the version in *Ōba Minako zenshū,* vol. 1. Unless otherwise noted, passages quoted in the text are from the translation by Kohl and Toyama. "The Three Crabs" has also been well translated by Tanaka and Hanson.

6. As suggested in the arguments of Hirsch and others, above, a change in my status to the position of mother to my own child would not necessarily change my relationship to, or understanding of, Ōba's work. It is in this sense that I will remain in the position of "eternal" daughter as I read Ōba.

7. These questions are a paraphrase of a set of guidelines written by Atsuko Sakaki for the workshop at Harvard University in March 1996 at which I originally delivered this paper. I am grateful to Professor Sakaki for bringing up these thought-provoking issues as I was working on this project.

8. For more on this point, see Brown, "Ōba Minako."

9. Ōba writes about this delightful rediscovery of Kafka (whom she had first read in her late teens or early twenties "with no understanding at all") in two short essays: "Henshin—Kafuka" (The metamorphosis—Kafka) and "Yūjin—Kafuka *Shinban*" (My friend Kafka—*The Trial*). These essays make it clear that her familiarity with his work extends far beyond "The Metamorphosis." I am grateful to Professors Sumie Jones and Janice Brown, who originally pointed out to me Ōba's Kafka connection.

10. In "Virginia Woolf," Martha and her husband, George, have a fantasy son, whom George "kills" in the course of the play because Martha breaks the rules of their fantasy world by mentioning the son to the guests. She is not a "real" mother. Nora of "A Doll's House" has three children, whom she must abandon when she makes the decision to leave her husband. Although she is definitely a mother, it is not that aspect of her character that interests Funabashi. In *A Certain Woman,* Yōko has given birth to a child but has abandoned it long since. None of the critics who mention these works makes the connection explicit, but I cannot help wondering whether the motif of the spurious or abandoning mother brought these stories to their minds in the context of "The Three Crabs." This might in some measure explain the tremendous threat to the social order that several critics feel is posed by this story.

11. To give a sense of the cohort in that year: among the Honorable Mentions are Nakagami Kenji for the fictional "Nihongo ni tsuite" (About Japanese) and Karatani Kōjin for the critical essay "<Hihyō> no shi" (The death of <criticism>).

12. Etō, "Michisū no sugomi," p. 114. Translations are mine.

13. Ibid.

14. Yasuoka, "Osorubeki joryū," pp. 120–121.

15. The biannual Akutagawa Prize is awarded by a standing committee of ten to twelve members. In the ten years preceding 1968, the prize was split between two authors only once, in 1963. (Kōno Taeko was one of the two winners.) No prize at all was awarded in five occasions over those years. However, in the four years following Ōba's award, the prize was split between two authors five times; no winner was found on two occasions. (My thanks to Marilyn Bolles for research assistance on literary prizes awarded in the 1960s.)

16. In addition, several committee members commented on their negative reaction to the wave of enthusiastic critical response generated by the previously awarded Gunzō New Writers Award, which had caused them to approach Ōba's work with a somewhat skeptical, jaundiced eye. Of the committee members, Mishima Yukio, Ishikawa Tatsuzō, and Funabashi Seiichi were quite negative in their reactions to "The Three Crabs"; Inoue Yasushi, Ishikawa Jun, Niwa Fumio, Ōoka Shōhei, and Nagai Tatsuo were moderately positive in their evaluations; and Kawabata Yasunari, Takii Kōsaku, and Nakamura Mitsuo were strongly positive in their praise for Ōba's story.

17. For example, several of these critics mention the quality of the cocktail party dialogue, some finding it to be superbly refreshing, and others finding it artificial and stilted (such as Niwa Fumio, who likens it to a bad translation). None, however, presents specific arguments about the language of the dialogue passages to support his argument, whether pro or con.

18. Niwa, "Senhyō" (Evaluation [a generic title used for all the Akutagawa Prize committee's comments]), p. 495.

19. Takii, "Senhyō," p. 498. At seventy-four, Takii is the oldest of the 1968 Akutagawa committee judges.

20. Kafka, *The Great Wall of China;* quoted in Corngold, *Franz Kafka,* p. 4. Walter Benjamin also quotes this passage in an essay, identifying it as central to Kafka's life and his writing ("Franz Kafka," p. 130).

21. I do not intend to pursue this exploration as an "influence study"; that is, I do not intend to trace the merit in Ōba's work back to the earlier genius, Kafka. But Ōba has several times remarked that it was specifically Kafka's work that provided the catalyst for her own fiction, and it is significant that this catalyst is so tightly connected to themes of family and imprisonment. In the 1960s (and on into the 1970s) many Japanese women writers were exploring the Japanese family system in their fiction, using narrative to critique and deconstruct its oppressive elements. As I have pointed out above, however, none does so through a discourse as intensely bourgeois and maternal as Ōba Minako. I am interested, therefore, in analyzing the paternal relationships of her fiction, including its connections to Kafka, at least partly in order to elaborate the source of Ōba's divergence from the "mainstream" of Japanese women writers of the period.

22. The Ajase plot is derived from a story in the *Nirvana Sutra*. Troubled by her childlessness, Queen Idaike met a soothsayer who prophesied that a certain hermit would die three years hence, and his soul would enter her womb to be reborn as her son. Unwilling to wait for the hermit's death, Idaike killed him,

only to be told that the resulting child would grow up to kill his father. Fright-
ened, Idaike dropped the baby, Ajase, from the top of a tall tower as she gave
birth to him. However, he survived.

Upon reaching adolescence, Ajase learned the truth of his birth. Furious at
his mother, Ajase wanted to kill her, but was so devastated by guilt at the idea of
matricide that he developed an unsightly and foul-smelling skin disease. Only
Idaike was willing to get close enough to care for him. Eventually mother and
son were reconciled, and Ajase became a wise and respected King. (Once again,
my thanks to Andra Alvis, who brought Japanese psychoanalytic criticism using
the Ajase complex to my attention.)

23. Again this is visible in the Rich poem. Even in coming to a new identity as
"mother," the speaker positions her changing, not-yet-realized, in-motion identity against the fixed, monolithic identity of her own mother: "we remet her in
our childbirth visions // erect, enthroned, above / a spiral stair / and crawled
and panted toward her. . . ."

24. Although the Freudian/Lacanian and Ajase models feature different
stages of a child's coming to subjectivity, the cognitive "change" occurring at
each stage is figured as occurring once and with results that last for the rest of
the person's life. It has been suggested, however, that in fact even adults reexpe-
rience or re-perform those moments of subject construction throughout their
lives. Because no one is born a mother, to come to a new understanding of oneself in that role would require a post-oedipal set of subject-constituting experiences. It is this set of experiences that Ōba focuses on in much of her maternalist writing.

25. Many of Ōba's stories, including "The Three Crabs," feature a third dyad,
outside the family, of the protagonist and a female friend, often with lesbian
overtones. Many of Ōba's maternalist protagonists perform a subjectivity
that has multiple dimensions, including at times a dimension of "adult subject"
who is (temporarily) no one's mother, no one's wife, no one's daughter, even
though the protagonist is actually married with a child. Although I am focusing
in this essay on the maternal subjectivity in Ōba's works, this is in no way meant
to obscure the complexity and multiplicity of the adult female subjects Ōba
depicts.

26. This essay is not the place to pursue this point at length, but it should be
noted that even though Ōba's protagonists engage in a great deal of heterosexual sex, both inside and outside marriage, the sexual act is rarely (if ever)
described in erotic ways. The pleasure of sex does not seem to be her point.
Rather the focus is on the ways in which these relationships constitute the web in
which the woman's subjectivity is cathected. As I shall argue below, in "Aoi
kitsune" (The Pale Fox), for example, although the narrative begins and ends
with a discussion of the protagonist's lover, the Pale Fox, it is her relationship
with her father and her identification with her dead mother that are the central
points of the story. And in other works, such as "The Three Crabs" or *Garakuta
hakubutsukan* (The junk museum, 1975), the daughter's presence or absence,
her knowledge or ignorance of these relationships, her acceptance or rejection
of them, are as important as the relationships themselves.

27. I am grateful to Professor Kazue Campbell, who reminded me of Kōno's

story at the workshop at Harvard University for which this essay was originally written.

28. Ōba, "Three Crabs," trans. Kohl and Toyama, p. 335.

29. Ibid., p. 324.

30. Ibid., p. 326.

31. In the Japanese the gender of the schoolmaster is made more explicit: the word literally means a female school principal.

32. Ōba, *"Sanbiki no kani"* (my translation).

33. Ōba, "Three Crabs," trans. Kohl and Toyama, p. 326.

34. This is not to suggest that readers who have not been mothers of daughters are unable to understand or appreciate this situation, at least intellectually. Indeed, it is through Ōba's work that I have become aware of my own position in the mother-daughter cycle. Ōba engages the circularity of the relationship between mother and daughter in her nonfiction works as well. See, for example, "Musume to watashi no jikan" (Time for my daughter and me) or "Chichi to haha to toshikoshi no soba" (Father, mother, and year-end noodles).

35. Hatta Kazuko, in *Joryū sakka no shinzui* (The essence of women writers, p. 224), points out the circularity of the conversations in "The Three Crabs." Hatta argues that Ōba is critiquing the lot of the bourgeois housewife, using this circularity to show the tedium and loneliness of that life. This is certainly true. But Ōba is also reinscribing in structural terms a particularly maternally structured discourse, and in so doing bringing a maternally defined subjectivity into centrality. This kind of circularity, too, is a structural analogic repetition of the spatiality of maternal subjectivity: spatiotemporal enclosure, discursive circularity, generational repetition/looping.

36. The image of three crabs, suggested by the hotel name, may be representative of the three-person family through which Yuri is constituted. At the beginning of the story, Yuri sees two crabs crawling along the sand, their legs interlocked. These would seem to be the father-daughter dyad, walking in lockstep. Or, because some species of crabs are so linked when they are mating, it is also possible to interpret them as representing Yuri and Pink Shirt. The ambiguity of the image provides an interesting structural analog, this time to Ōba's deconstruction and rewriting of the triangles and dyads of the family structure through which maternal subjectivity is constituted.

37. Etō, p. 115. This lack of a (phallic?) wick/core is a feature of many of Ōba's stories. On the other hand, in all of her work, signs of mother, milk, the breast, and mist/fog are frequent at every level of language. (We have seen the example of the "milky fog" in the first line of "The Three Crabs.") See Mizuta, *Monogatari*, chapter 5, for examples and discussion of such images.

38. For discussions of gluttonous displays and modernity, see Camporesi, *Bread of Dreams;* Falk, *The Consuming Body;* and Cheesman, "Modernity/Monstrosity."

39. Ōba, "Three Crabs," trans. Kohl and Toyama, p. 324.

40. The bingeing and purging of bulimia, while potentially equally damaging, is less threatening to the social order than anorexia because bulimia appears to be based on a "natural" if excessive indulgence of appetite. This may partly explain why bulimia has heretofore been discussed—but, thus far, less thoroughly theorized—in feminist scholarship than anorexia.

Works Cited

Location of Japanese publishers is Tokyo unless otherwise noted.

Akutagawashō zenshū. Bungei shunjū, 1982.

Benjamin, Walter. "Franz Kafka: On the Tenth Anniversary of His Death." In *Illuminations,* ed. Hannah Arendt, trans. Harry Zohn. New York: Schocken Books, 1968.

Brown, Janice. "Ōba Minako—Telling the Untellable." In *Japan Quarterly* 45.3 (July-September 1998): 50–59.

Camporesi, Piero. *Bread of Dreams: Food and Fantasy in Early Modern Europe.* Cambridge, UK: Polity Press, 1989.

Cheesman, Tom. "Modernity/Monstrosity: Eating Freaks." In *Body and Society* 2.3 (September 1996): 1–31.

Corngold, Stanley. *Franz Kafka: The Necessity of Form.* Ithaca, N.Y.: Cornell University Press, 1988.

Etō Jun. "Michisū no sugomi." *Gunzō* 23.6 (June 1968): 114–116.

Falk, Pasi. *The Consuming Body.* London: Sage, 1994.

Hatta Kazuko. *Joryū sakka no shinzui.* Funi shuppan, 1987.

Hirsch, Marianne. *The Mother/Daughter Plot: Narrative, Psychoanalysis, Feminism.* Bloomington: Indiana University Press, 1989.

Kōno Taeko. "Yōjigari." First published in *Shinchō,* December 1961. Trans. Lucy North. In Kōno, *Toddler-Hunting and Other Stories,* pp. 45–68. New York: Directions Book, 1996.

Mizuta Noriko. "Bosei o tou—<Haha to musume> to iu shudai." Roundtable discussion, in *Haha to musume no feminizumu: kindai kazoku o koete,* ed. Mizuta Noriko, Kitada Sachie, and Hasegawa Kei. Tabatake shoten, 1996.

———. *Monogatari to han-monogatari no fūkei: bungaku to josei no sōzōryoku.* Tabatake shoten, 1993.

Niwa Fumio. "Senhyō." In *Akutagawashō zenshū,* vol. 8, pp. 495–496. Bungei shunjū, 1982.

Ōba Minako. "Aoi kitsune." 1973. First published in *Bungei,* October 1973. Trans. Stephen W. Kohl. In *The Shōwa Anthology: Modern Japanese Short Stories,* vol. 2, ed. Van C. Gessel and Tomone Matsumoto, pp. 337–347. Kōdansha, 1985.

———. "Chichi to haha to toshikoshi no soba." In *Watashi no erabu watashi no basho,* pp. 138–141. Kairyūsha, 1982.

———. *Garakuta hakubutsukan.* Bungei shunjū, 1975.

———. "Henshin—Kafuka." In *Ōba Minako zenshū,* vol. 10, pp. 241–242. Kōdansha, 1991.

———. "Musume to watashi no jikan." In *Watashi no erabu watashi no basho,* pp. 100–103. Kairyūsha, 1982.

———. *Ōba Minako zenshū.* 10 vols. Kōdansha, 1991.

———. "Sanbiki no kani" (1968). In *Ōba Minako zenshū,* vol. 1, pp. 9–50. Kōdansha, 1991.

———. "The Smile of a Mountain Witch." Trans. Noriko Mizuta Lippit, assisted by Mariko Ochi. In *Japanese Women Writers,* ed. Lippit and Kyoko Selden, pp. 194–206. New York: M. E. Sharpe, 1991.

————. "The Three Crabs." Trans. Stephen Kohl and Toyama Ryōko. In *Japan Quarterly* 25.3 (1978): 323–340.

————. "The Three Crabs." Trans. Yukiko Tanaka and Elizabeth Hanson. In *This Kind of Woman: Ten Stories by Japanese Women Writers, 1960–76*, ed. Tanaka and Hanson, pp. 88–113. Stanford, Calif.: Stanford University Press, 1982.

————. *Watashi no erabu watashi no basho*. Kairyūsha, 1982.

————. "Yamauba no bisho." In *Ōba Minako zenshū*, vol. 3, 335–352. Kōdansha, 1991.

————. "Yūjin—Kafuka *Shinban*." In *Ōba Minako zenshū*, vol. 10, pp. 245–247. Kōdansha, 1991.

Takii Kōsaku. "Senhyō." In *Akutagawashō zenshū*, vol. 8, pp. 497–498. Bungei shunjū, 1982.

Tsushima Yūko. "Mugura no haha." First published in *Bungei*, 1974.

Yasuoka Shōtarō. "Osorubeki joryū." *Gunzō* 23.6 (June 1968): 120–122.

Chapter 11
Kurahashi Yumiko's Negotiations with the Fathers

ATSUKO SAKAKI

"I experienced the same sensation with this work that I felt when I read Mr. Ōe Kenzaburō's first work," Hirano Ken wrote in his *Mainichi shinbun* review of Kurahashi Yumiko's debut piece, "Parutai" (Partei, 1960).[1] Having favorably reviewed the works on women and politics by the two established women writers of the time—Sata Ineko (1904–1998) and Ōhara Tomie (b. 1912) earlier that year (1960), Hirano (1907–1978) here takes up "Partei," which deals with a female university student's disillusionment with a Stalinist-styled "party," as "another work on politics and sexuality"[2] and praises the talent of Kurahashi (b. 1935) as follows:

> "Partei" impressed me by the way it provides a concrete representation, through the offices of a [female] student, of the patterns in revolutionary movements that are radically pure and ideological in nature. It will be easy for anyone to criticize this work as idea-oriented, but it is not easy to mold an idea into a consistent literary image—and that is just what this unknown writer has managed to do.[3]

Hirano was at the time an influential critic in the Japanese literary establishment; since 1946 he had been writing monthly reviews for the *Mainichi shinbun,* one of the three nationally circulated newspapers. He was also a professor at Meiji University, where Kurahashi had studied French literature since 1956, as both an undergraduate and a graduate student. Moreover, he was a member of the selection committee for the Meiji University President Prize for literary works. Kurahashi's "Partei" won the prize in the 1960 competition and was accordingly first published in the university newspaper, *Meiji Daigaku shinbun.*

Just as Hirano's praise for Ōe Kenzaburō's first published work, "Kimyōna shigoto" (A strange job, 1956) in the *Tōkyō Daigaku shinbun*, had drawn the attention of a wider audience to Ōe,[4] his positive review of Kurahashi immediately put her work in the spotlight. "Partei" was reprinted in the prestigious literary magazine *Bungakukai* in March 1960. Hirano issued further words of support in the same month's issue of another established journal, *Shinchō*, suggesting that he should be right in his high esteem of Kurahashi, given that Ōe (b. 1935), an earlier "discovery" of his, had proved to be a unique talent.[5] In light of such unequivocal patronage, we might attribute the creation of the author Kurahashi Yumiko to Hirano Ken.

With this mighty "father" supporting her, Kurahashi seemed guaranteed a successful literary career. Indeed, she immediately earned successive nominations for the prestigious Akutagawa Prize, first for "Partei" and then for "Natsu no owari" (The end of summer, 1960; trans. 1988).[6] The latter presents a love triangle involving two sisters and a young man, K, which is resolved when the sisters collaborate in murdering K. In both of these stories it was, above all, the detached tone of the narration, as well as the female narrator-protagonist's rare cynicism, that attracted critical attention. In neither of the stories does the narrator-protagonist become emotional when she recounts what might seem to be critical moments in her life: joining a political party and becoming pregnant by a party member in "Partei," and being betrayed by her lover and subsequently murdering him and accidentally killing her sister and accomplice in "The End of Summer." She does not seem to have any illusion about the party or her lover in the first place and observes calmly what might conventionally be described as the object of devotion or love.

Although Kurahashi failed to be awarded the Akutagawa Prize both times that she was nominated,[7] she was not forgotten by the literary establishment. Her short stories were published in major literary journals almost every month in the year following "Partei"'s reprinting —sometimes two stories a month. In a single year, three anthologies of her short stories were published, and in February 1961 she received the *Joryū bungaku shō* (Women's Literature Prize).

Kurahashi's remarkable productivity at this time, and the accompanying media attention, however, solicited a mixture of favorable and antagonistic responses from male critics, who entered into disputes regarding the canonical status of Kurahashi's fiction and its value to (Japanese) literature. In this essay, I will first examine these disputes and then explore the way Kurahashi resisted and later exploited the criticisms her works received.

The "Partei" and "Hebi" Debates

The first of these debates, termed the " 'Parutai' ronsō" (Debates on "Partei"), involved Hirano, Niwa Fumio (b. 1904), Etō Jun (1933–1999), and Okuno Takeo (1926–1998). Critics such as Itō Sei (1905–1969) and Etō responded variously to "Hebi" (Snake, 1960)[8]—a Kafkaesque absurdist story about a university student named K who wakes up to find that he is swallowing a snake, which eventually swallows him up instead. This debate was followed by the so-called "Riarizumu hihan" (Realism critique) between Nakamura Mitsuo (1911–1988) and Okuno. But the most serious debates concerned the author's first novel—or antinovel—*Kurai tabi* (Blue journey, 1961) and were triggered by Etō, followed up by Okuno, and eventually encompassed responses by Kurahashi herself, among others.

What was so controversial about Kurahashi's fiction? The debates listed above suggest three points of dispute: (1) the visible planning of the plot, attributed to the author's methodological awareness of herself as a literary critic; (2) the unrealistic plot development, unaccountable to the logic of causality; and (3) a lack of correspondence to "reality" or "contemporaneity." Niwa Fumio, a fertile *shishōsetsu* novelist, says of "Partei" that though he was not moved by the story, he was nevertheless impressed with the author's skills. He defines the work as a *hihyōka no kandōsuru shōsetsu* (story that critics think highly of) as opposed to a *shōsetsuka no kandōsuru shōsetsu* (story that novelists admire).[9] Evidently, Niwa is here drawing a contrast between the mind (reason, or structure) and the heart (emotions, or force), ascribing the former to the critic and the latter to the writer. Etō Jun is more explicitly negative in his view of "Partei," for similar reasons: the story relies solely on *meiseki-sa* (lucidity), he says.[10] Here we should recall Hirano's review of the work. It is not coincidental that his praise is directed to the author's skill in creating the form, rather than the content, of the story.

The next quality that divided critics into two opposing groups—the metaphorical, nonrepresentational nature of the prose style—is perhaps best illustrated by "Snake," which, as Kurahashi defines it, is a parody of Franz Kafka's "Metamorphosis."[11] Just as there is no apparent reason why Gregor finds himself transformed into an insect in the older work, the snake, which Kurahashi's protagonist K encounters, appears out of nowhere. The rest of the story, right up to the end, when K is himself swallowed by the snake, is equally unrealistic or, rather, does not seem to seek any contact with what we perceive as the real. Hence, Etō's critique:

> This work is not an allegory, but a mere game of concepts. There is most likely no impulse within Ms. Kurahashi to seek expression in allegory. She is simply playing with those concepts that fill her brain, assigning them to characters, and changing and crisscrossing the assignments. Furthermore, these concepts are mere jargon, the currency of which is limited to a group of student activists. . . . Writing of a male student being assaulted and impregnated by a woman is nothing more than a confession of sexual deviation. Value for Ms. Kurahashi is subverted only inside her pink brain. There is nothing easier for a smart writer to do. "Snake" does not convey any message because nothing exists outside the author's brain.[12]

As is evident in the above excerpt, Etō's critical criteria rely on whether the author has a particular message to convey, whether the message is supported by the author's experience in the actual world, and whether this message is acceptable to the "normal" citizen. Indeed, Kurahashi is not interested in sending the sort of message that can be translated into conventional language; she is rather challenging the authenticity of the "natural," "real," and "true" by accounting for the unaccountable. As long as we apply conventional norms in judging the value of her fiction, she will inevitably be judged "deviant." Thus, her project can never be understood.

However, if the reader admits the autonomy of the world of fiction from that of the "real" world, then the question shifts from how realistic the fiction is to how consistent the logic within the fiction is. Itō Sei, a novelist and a scholar of English literature who, in journalistic terms, might perhaps be best known as the translator of D. H. Lawrence's *Lady Chatterley's Lover* and as one of the defendants in the obscenity lawsuit filed against its translation and publication, takes a positive view of Kurahashi's attempt to integrate the text, not by causal or temporal relationships but by *gūwa* (allegory) and *metafā* (metaphor). His stance, however, includes a caveat: although such a compositional method is common in poetry, he challenges its feasibility in the field of prose fiction.[13] Itō first raises a fundamental question, which is particularly relevant to Kurahashi's agenda and to the way her work was received by critics like Etō. "The Japanese literary establishment tends to view writers' lives as the site for practicing ethics, and to evaluate their works according to reports of their lives. Isn't it necessary to question the ethics themselves?"[14] In contrast to Etō, who seems convinced of the authenticity of his ethical values, Itō questions such ethical and judgmental criticism of literature. Then he proceeds to the specific case of "Snake":

> This work of Ms. Kurahashi . . . manages to carry out the difficult task of the continuation of metaphors [in prose], which shows more capacity than a steadily maintained mimetic prose. . . . You do not have to relate the snake to something [in the actual world]; the work will be fine if only you can finish reading without giving up in the middle.
>
> If we view pragmatically the way this work is written, it will serve as a methodology for writing novels, and thus will be of great benefit in enabling writers to write something that cannot be written in *shishōsetsu*, or in the so-called authentic novel [*honkaku-ha shōsetsu*]. It would also become possible to subtly avoid, or entirely dismiss, ethical criticism or the impositions of critics on the plot and view of life in the work. No doubt such a work can and must emerge from modern life, where value no longer rests in the concrete and semi-natural, but has shifted to the abstract and structural.[15]

Itō thus dethrones the authenticized mode of criticism, which evaluates works by seeking correspondences to the author's life or social conditions. Simultaneously, Itō signals his understanding of the social conditions that validate abstract or absurdist writing. If I may expand Itō's argument a little further, any text necessarily emerges out of a particular historical context, but this does not mean that the text has to represent the values of the time. Kurahashi's fiction shows contingency of value by presenting a context completely alien to the contemporary Japanese one, suggesting that what appears to be natural, real, or true appears so only if we accept a certain paradigm.

The "Realism" Debates

The reviews of "Snake" by Etō and Itō appeared in the July issues of two literary journals—*Bungakukai* and *Shinchō*, respectively. It must have been by coincidence that they discussed the same issues from opposite positions. However, another pair of critics—Nakamura Mitsuo and Okuno Takeo—entered into a debate about the proper

function of literature as an indirect result of a discussion of Kurahashi's fiction. This has come to be known as the "Realism Critique,"
mentioned above, which lasted from July to December 1960. Nakamura criticizes Kurahashi's "Mikkoku" (Betrayal, 1960)—a short story
about violence, crime, and the practice of homosexuality among adolescent boys—for its alleged lack of correspondence to human beings.
Having reviewed "Nawa" (Rope, 1960), by Abe Kōbō (1924–1993), as
"psychologically artificial" and having labeled it "a 'poem' made by a
philosopher, rather than a 'prose work' composed by a poet," Nakamura refers to Kurahashi's story as another example of an idea-
oriented work.[16] Indeed, none of the settings of her stories from this
period is specified as being Japanese, no proper place-names are
mentioned, and no manners or customs specific to Japanese culture
or society are described. The names of characters, such as K, L, M, S,
P, and Q, allow any citizenship—if, that is, these characters are even
earthbound human beings. Indeed, the stories develop not according to our everyday logic of causality but rather according to the metaphorical exfoliation of images and absurdist concatenations of events.
Nakamura maintained that Kurahashi had confused the genres of
prose and poetry and ignored the "principal purpose of prose," that
is, to "explain" things.[17]

It was Okuno Takeo, an engineer-turned-literary-critic probably
best known for his work on Dazai Osamu (1909–1948), who came to
Kurahashi's rescue. Okuno had expressed a high opinion of Kurahashi's talent and had written in her defense several times since
"Partei," to the extent that he was chided by some for appearing to
be Kurahashi's "champion."[18] Okuno plunged into disputes with Nakamura, supporting the autonomy of Kurahashi's imaginative world
from the actual world, and her idea-orientedness as opposed to fact-
orientedness.

Indeed, in her essay "Shōsetsu no meiro to hiteisei" (The labyrinth
and negativity of fiction, 1966; partial trans., 1977), Kurahashi herself calls the world of her fiction *"han sekai"* (antiworld), defining it
as the world that operates according to "the logic of dreams" rather
than that of everyday life:

> I, as the author, do not manipulate the characters as would "God."
> Rather, I assign a primary "hypothesis," throw the characters into
> the labyrinth of "imaginary space," and let them walk about in the
> labyrinth and strike the walls with their heads. What I mean by a
> "hypothesis" is something like: "One day K woke up from a nap to

find he had begun to swallow an incredibly long snake." The
"hypothesis" is comparable to an axiom in mathematics, which
remains unaccountable as the novel closes. Plausibility of such a
world has to be supported by the minute construction of details
that appears to make sense. But as a whole the world is like a "nightmare." As mathematics as a system is constructed by formal logic,
the world of my fiction is governed by the logic of dreams. Leaps
and twists inherent to dreams transform this world into a grotesque
form. As the "deformation" reaches an apogee, I disappear suddenly, leaving behind a novel that resembles a mysterious castle,
or a grotesque snake.[19]

Because the Japanese audience was accustomed to reading fiction
as the author's confessions, readers found such an active erasure of
traces of reality around the author disturbing. Some tried to reconstruct the basic story of Kurahashi's life from her fiction. As Kurahashi
mentions cynically in one essay, Etō read "Partei" as the confessions
of the author's guilty conscience after quitting the Japan Communist
Party. Yet this attempt at reading fiction as autobiography ended in
creating a complete fiction, because Kurahashi had never joined the
Japanese Communist Party,[20] nor had she conspired with her sister
to murder their common lover, as the protagonist of "The End of
Summer" does. Though Kurahashi may occasionally draw upon personal experience in her stories, she does so without the intention,
pretense, or illusion of making confessions of her "darker side" so as
to indulge in narcissistic and sadomasochistic ecstasy. Rather, she is
intentionally, unpretentiously, and self-consciously engaged in parodying her personal life, as well as any text that she has read. In her
own words:

> As [André] Malraux says, one transforms oneself into an artist . . .
> by "imitating" the style of a predecessor whom he [*kare*] is obsessed
> with. This truth is, however, not taken seriously as far as literature
> is concerned in Japan—particularly so for the novel. This is because
> Japanese criticism tends to trace [the content of] a novel in the
> author's "life," and to consider fiction as the author's "self-expres-
> sion"—the author's personal "crisis" and the overcoming of it—a
> fashionable pattern, indeed. To explain my own writing, I didn't
> begin to write fiction because I had something to tell about myself,
> but because I wanted to write fiction in someone else's style, or
> like someone else. My own "experience" was merely utilized in the
> process.[21]

This was taken as a deliberate affront to the canonicity of "*shishō-setsu*" and to Japanese "naturalism," both of which are based on the myth of the identity of the author's life and the content of the work, with which the writers, critics, and readers commonly played.[22]

This belief system held by the literary establishment, however, began to erode gradually in the 1960s, and thus, despite the many negative responses to her fiction, Kurahashi had no lack of championing figures. In fact, several writers and critics followed in Hirano's footsteps and, for a variety of reasons, volunteered to be her "cultural father." Many Japanese intellectuals, after all, preferred reading Kafka to Tayama Katai (1871–1930), the paragon of Japanese naturalism. One such intellectual was Haniya Yutaka (1910–1997), a formidable Marxist writer of the postwar period, known for his affinities with Fyodor Mikhailovich Dostoyevsky (1821–1881). He loved Kurahashi for the abstractness of her work. She recalls in the "Author's Note" attached to the *zensakuhin* (collected works) version of her dystopian "Dokonimo nai basho" (A place that exists nowhere, 1961) how Haniya mentored her, inviting her to his house and presenting her with signed copies of his works, and how, in return, she used to peruse his books, scribbling her comments in the margins.[23] Her story is, as the author herself notes, modeled after Haniya's *Shiryō* (The ghosts, 1946–1961), which is itself a pastiche of *The Brothers Karamazov* (1879–1880) and *The Devils* (1871–1872). The female protagonist in Kurahashi's "A Place That Exists Nowhere," L, leaves her husband and visits her long-lost mother in a mental institution, then meets various people for a discussion of the proper function of literature. The whole narrative is written in the present tense, thus violating the unwritten "rule" that stipulates that narratives ought to be about what has already happened and should thus be written in the past tense.

Haniya, the literary father of this work by Kurahashi, reacted with a tone of obvious delight to being parodied by this young protégé:

> I had heard Kurahashi say that she would cannibalize *The Ghosts* . . . . No member of the literary establishment would even have conceived of such! But she is not even aware of this fact, which makes her all the more new and outsider-like. . . . Although Kurahashi and I are from different ages, we belong to the same generation. . . . Her portrayals of sex scenes are interesting exactly because she does not know much about sex and so could write just as her imagination led her.[24]

It is evident in the short excerpt above that Haniya's view of what literature should be is markedly different from that espoused by Etō. Literature for Haniya is a product of the imagination and may be produced out of literature itself, rather than out of the author's experiences in the outside world. Indeed, Etō borrows from Haniya's statement in deriding not only Haniya's works but also the work of the woman who would parody him. Etō dismisses Kurahashi's story as "superficial" and as "a funny caricature" that "enlarges Haniya's shortcomings" and "reveals how ill-bred" Kurahashi's literature is.[25] Etō is thus critical not only of the abstract nature of the type of literature produced by Haniya and Kurahashi but also of the nature of the literary genealogy between the two, which, in Etō's view, consists of "mimicry" and not "memory."[26] Kurahashi is thus doubly denied authenticity; she is not only ill-bred but also fatherless.

This literary "incest"—reading and rewriting (either by reviewing or parodying each other's work)—between Haniya and Kurahashi did not last long, however. Their affiliation dissolved once Kurahashi discovered herself to be a neoclassicist rather than an experimentalist, and a high-brow dilettante rather than a determined member of the avant-garde. As early as December 1961 Haniya noted that he could not expect Kurahashi to be as radically concerned with political issues as he, because she was more interested in fiddling with politics as a possible object of experimentation. Hinuma Rintarō (1925–1968) similarly observed that Kurahashi was not committed to "engagement"—she was inclined to "think before she leaps," and she was, moreover, convinced that thinking is a more courageous act than leaping.[27] She could not remain Haniya's legitimate literary daughter, for unlike him she was not a committed supporter of the New Left movement in postwar Japan. Perhaps in this regard Etō's observation that she was not heir to Haniya's literary heritage may have been right.

An "Illegitimate Daughter": The Price of Challenging the Modern Japanese Novel

Okuno's high esteem for Kurahashi's literary talent was directed not exclusively toward her intellectual qualities but also—and perhaps primarily—toward her unique expressions of female sexuality. He found these to be particularly significant in *Blue Journey*, published in 1961. Kurahashi's first book-length piece, the work features a female graduate student in French literature, identified as *"anata"* (you), who travels from Tokyo to Kyoto when her longtime fiancé disappears without a trace. She also "travels" in an achronological stream of consciousness from one stage to another in her life up until the narrative's present.[28] While this work reveals many of Kurahashi's familiar characteristics, such as the associatively woven rather than logically structured, text, it also shows a radical departure from her earlier work, in that Japanese proper nouns are used for characters. Names of places and businesses—cities, hotels, restaurants, and pubs—are the same as existing ones. Names of manufactured goods (e.g., "Cutex" for a nail polish) and of works of art (e.g., *Fuego,* by Charlie Parker [1920–1955]) are mentioned. Only a few names are represented by letters (Q University, L Women's College, and Mr. G, a passenger on the train for Kyoto). Not entirely irrelevant to this sudden shift to descriptive writing is that some parallels may be found between the story of *"anata"* and Kurahashi's own experience. I will return to this point, which was to become an issue in the "*Kurai tabi* ronsō" (*Blue Journey* debate), but let us first examine Okuno's review of the work in the *Nihon keizai shinbun* (Japanese economic news).

While aware of the differences between this work and Kurahashi's earlier works, Okuno was as positive as ever. In the course of his praise, he makes an important and complex observation regarding "femininity":

> No other novel has made me feel more "the female" than this, which observes "the female" from the interior, and in its essentials. . . . I do not know any other novel which portrays as relentlessly and unrestrainedly a woman as beautiful and erotic. . . . This is a novel which few women could write, and yet which only a woman could write.[29]

A brief description of the sexual content of *Blue Journey* is in order here. The female protagonist and her fiancé, after a period of intimacy, have agreed not to sleep with each other, and to pursue sexual affairs with others on two conditions: each affair should be a one-night stand, and the two are to describe the encounters to each other afterward. As one might expect, the story is replete with sexual acts, experienced by characters either in reality or in imagination, including acts of masturbation. The language nonetheless remains lucid and pedantic, rather than oblique or arousing. The sexual content conveys not a sense of rapture but rather self-detachment and loss, both because the sexual acts are nothing more nor less than performance, to be narrated for another who is absent from the scene, and because all except one scene are reminiscences of the protagonist.

Okuno's observations on female sexuality and on the way it is presented in *Blue Journey* stands on the borderline between performative gender theory, as suggested by Judith Butler among others, and essentialism.[30] If there is any "female sexuality," is it because the text *tells* us of the female, or because the author, the narrator, the protagonist, or a combination of any or all of the three, is female and thus *shows* the female? On one level, Okuno appears to think that women writers might not be able, or willing, to depict female sexuality as "beautiful and erotic." By stating that "few women could write" this novel, Okuno seems to suggest that only male writers, who are granted aesthetic distance, can aestheticize and eroticize female sexuality. To set aside the question of just how many women writers could indeed write of, let alone aestheticize, female sexuality, Okuno here implies that being female and thus familiar with one's own female body does not automatically enable one to textualize that body. On another level, however, he thinks that "only a woman could write" such a novel, for no man could understand female sexuality "from the interior." Here, in contrast to his earlier stance, he takes an essentialist position and suggests that what one is is inherent in, and in control of, what one writes. Writing in this sense is confined to the act of "showing" what one is, rather than that of "telling" what one sees.

Perhaps we may be able to reconcile these two seemingly contradictory views as follows: Okuno suggests that Kurahashi writes like a man what she experiences as a woman. She knows what men cannot know for anatomical reasons, and yet she can write in a way that other women cannot, for she does not allow herself to be carried away with an untested identification with characters of the same gender. The combination of Kurahashi's anatomically given identity as female and her culturally constructed identity as masculine allows her to write *like* a man about female sexuality. Essentially female, Kurahashi becomes performatively masculine. As she says herself:

> I had to write fiction as a hermaphrodite, somewhere between the "girl" and "young man" in my twenties, and perform the role of a "young witch." My fiction is therefore a cooperative work of this "girl" and this "young man." However, one cannot be an authentic "girl" after one turns twenty. Furthermore, the "young man" is also the Other in myself, as I am not male. I have been growing the Other inside myself while writing fiction. The secret of my

literature is, psychoanalytically speaking, the desire to become
masculine.[31]

If we accept Okuno's dualistic comments, then we might conclude
that Kurahashi's fiction is neither a product of male fantasy about
women as the Other, nor a product of a narcissistic female gaze on
women as intrinsically different from that of men. This, perhaps, is
what underlies Kurahashi's unique and isolated position in the literary establishment. As long as she writes under the female name
Kurahashi Yumiko, without "cross-dressing" her name as Victorian
English women authors did, she cannot be accepted as "one of us"
by male writers. On the other hand, she cannot be viewed entirely as
a comrade by female writers either, because of her choice not to represent female subjectivity in the way she writes.

As a matter of fact, this reading of Okuno's review has more to do
with Kurahashi's fiction in general than with *Blue Journey* in particular. Since "masculinity" as a performative gender identity in Kurahashi's writing becomes more evident in her later works, I will postpone further discussion of the notion now and will simply point out
an act of obliteration of the female subjectivity in the making of the
narrative. The choice of "you" rather than "I" for the referent to the
female protagonist allows the narrator to maintain a distance from
the protagonist, enabling the narrator to be the observer of an object,
rather than the subject of the action. Whereas the story never loses
sight of the protagonist, suggesting the narrator's persistent interest
in her, the narrator does not claim to represent the protagonist's
views. In this gesture away from autobiography, the narrator remains
ambiguous as to gender and avoids identification with the protagonist, who happens to be female. The narrator thus does not "show"
the female but instead "tells" of the female, as a genderless subject.

There is another layer of gender performance in *Blue Journey*. Not
only does the text avoid defining the narrator as feminine, but it also
performs discursive femininity in its consciousness of the audience
and in its structure. Okuno wrote later, in a response to Etō's article
on *Blue Journey* (to be discussed shortly), that he felt its "femaleness"
"not because portrayals of women in the novel seem real, but because the novel itself has become female."[32] As I rephrased Okuno
above, he senses that Kurahashi writes as a man what she experiences
as a woman. He also knows, however, that she writes as a man who
knows how to present femaleness. Although Okuno may not be artic-

ulate in defining what he means by the statement "the novel itself
has become female," we could locate the femaleness of *Blue Journey*
in several structural characteristics. First, although I have argued that
the second-person narrative is a sign of the narrator's detachment
from the female protagonist and thus of genderlessness, another
reader might find this same narrative approach intensely "feminine." That is to say, it could be possible to conclude that because
the narrative is not dependent on an authoritative narrator but is
instead left to the reader to construct, the overall structure represents passivity and flexibility. This kind of passivity might easily strike
a reader like Okuno as "feminine," insofar as femininity is conventionally defined. Second, the text consists of numerous fragments,
none of which shows any necessarily chronological or logical connection to those immediately before or after it. This elliptical, achronological, and "illogical" formation of the text might also appear to
Okuno as feminine.

Thus, Kurahashi not only de-genders her text but also reengen-
ders it. Her anatomical identity as the female is bracketed by distanc-
ing the narrator from the protagonist, and then is reconstructed in a
feminine discourse. This doubly deceptive gender performance is
appropriate for the theme of *Blue Journey*. The female protagonist
has been struggling to accept herself as a sexual being since her first
menstruation at the age of twelve, which she takes as "an execution
of feminization" in a body that up to then had been "neither male or
female, just a child."[33] She tried to look at her own vaginal opening
reflected in a mirror and contemplated how to deal with having been
"forcibly made into a woman." She concluded: "I will have to perform being a woman—that is the only way to retaliate on the world
and liberate myself."[34] In the words of her boyfriend, she "happen[s]
to assume the role of a woman."[35] Just as the protagonist of the novel
decides to act as a woman only to escape her anatomical gender identity by replacing it with the performative one, Kurahashi as the author
chooses a feminine discourse to construct femininity artificially, rather
than straightforwardly representing her womanhood. Okuno's review
reflects such an artificially constructed femininity in and about *Blue
Journey*, whose author only happens to be female.

Despite Okuno's positive review, the publication of *Blue Journey*
nearly provoked Kurahashi's journalistic ostracism. Etō returned to
the attack, writing reviews that triggered what was called the *Blue Journey* Debate, mentioned above. Etō first accused Kurahashi of a lack

of authenticity in her description of real places and things. For example, of Kamakura, where the novel opens, he suggests: "I have lived in Kamakura for several years, and thus, I know that this is not the true Kamakura."[36] He further maintains that the range of goods, works of art, and places mentioned in the novel merely show how shallow and materialistic the author's life is and that these objects have not been internalized into the author's sensitivity. Given his earlier criticisms of Kurahashi for not describing things in the real world, Etō's critique suggests that Kurahashi is unable to write descriptively—even when she tries. And for Etō, descriptive writing is the only authentic way to write fiction.

Etō's untested assertions about what is and is not real are relevant to a gender distinction in the act of reading. What appears to males, including Etō, as authentic, natural, and real may well not appear to females, including Kurahashi, as such. Neither will the things that seem to males literary or artificial necessarily be taken as such by females. What males call reality is in fact a male construction of what is real and is thus gender specific. A female version of reality may well be radically different. As Kurahashi writes in her response to Etō's critique,

> he deplores that the Kamakura I presented in my writing does not look like the "true Kamakura"—and I wonder what "true Kamakura" could be. . . . There is nothing but your Kamakura, Mr. Etō's Kamakura, or my Kamakura. Moreover, my Kamakura exists in my writing, but Mr. Etō's does not, unless it is written about.[37]

This is not to confirm, however, an essential contrast between male and female versions of reality. For one thing, the two versions are not symmetrical. The female version, when it is written for publication, and thus with an awareness of reviews that will be written predominantly by male critics, becomes either a repetition of the male version, or a reaction to it, or both. Feminine vision has been thus more significantly affected by masculine sensibility than has male vision by feminine sensibility in modern Japan. Similarly, a feminine discourse in modern Japanese language has been sought and established through a process of either simulating or challenging masculine discourse, while the converse has not been the case.

For most of the history of modern Japanese literature, female writers have needed to define their styles in comparison with those of male writers and thus, whether they liked it or not, have had to become aware of the degree to which they wrote as men, whereas male writers could afford not to think about how much distance they should maintain from female writers' style, or whether they would claim autonomy from, or acknowledge indebtedness to, earlier writers. For male writers, the question of whether they should write as "essentially male" or "disguised as women" was largely irrelevant.

A more serious accusation than the "failure" to represent the truth that Etō made against Kurahashi concerns her alleged plagiarism of *La Modification* (The change of heart, 1957; trans. 1958), by Michel Butor (1926–). The book had been translated into Japanese as *Kokoro gawari* in 1959—only a few years before the publication of *Blue Journey*,[38] and Etō found a number of parallels between the two novels, such as the setting of the story in a train, and the use of the second person to refer to the protagonist, without any "I" inside the text.

Apparently, in writing *Blue Journey*, Kurahashi overestimated the degree of reading knowledge on which her readers would draw in determining whether the work was to be considered a parody, a forgery, or an original. She mistakenly expected her readers to be able to discern the sources immediately and to enjoy comparing a source with its rewritten version. Instead, readers such as Etō thought that she had tried to conceal the modeling of her work on Butor's.[39]

Etō's criticism—focusing on the foreign origin of Kurahashi's work —raised the issue of the status of Japanese literature in the world, as well as that of foreign literature in Japan. Okuno writes in response to Etō:

> What mystifies me is the censorship of literary works influenced by foreign literature as being unforgivable forgeries and fakes, while those indebted to Japanese precursors are praised for their traditional methods or for growing out of the tradition.
> Despite his seeming criticism of foreign literary influences, Mr. Etō's writing reveals that he privileges foreign literature.[40]

Etō's accusation of Kurahashi for her affiliation with a non-Japanese precursor sounds as if he, as an "indigenous Japanese man," or a legal, nonbiological father, were bashing a racially hybrid daughter, as a devil's child or an illegitimate daughter of the alien. Etō is a rejecting father who tries to defend Japan from being "soiled" by foreign blood. Kurahashi is "contaminated," a dishonor to the nation, and thus to be expelled as illegitimate. As Okuno suggests above, the "daughters" of Japanese or indigenous fathers are spared such bashing. One might consider, for example, the rewriting of *The Tale of Genji* by Enchi Fumiko (1905–1986), which drew little criticism of her integrity as a professional writer. Neither have I heard of any accusations of plagiarism made against Natsume Sōseki (1867–1916) or Mori Ōgai (1862–1922), who published novels with very similar settings and themes almost contemporaneously, such as *Sanshirō* (1908; trans. 1977) and *Seinen* (The youth, 1910; trans. 1994), respectively. As long as an author works in harmony with indigenous Japanese literature, it seems, he or she is excused when showing, at times openly and intentionally, the influence of others. This was not, however, the case for Kurahashi. Her crime stemmed from the foreignness of her sources.

Gender distinctions are relevant as well in examining the extent of foreignness in literary production. Although other "inauthentic" writers of modern Japan, such as Abe Kōbō and Ōe Kenzaburō, also came under attack from nativist critics, they were not exposed to the kind of radical denunciations that were directed at Kurahashi. For male writers to reveal foreign origins is to convert to the beliefs of the enemies of their cultural fathers. For female writers, however, it means something more than a child's betrayal of her parents, for such female transvestites highlight their literary fathers' "femininity" by contrast and thus destabilize gender distinctions as well as cultural distinctions.

Modern Japanese critics tend to define Japanese literature vis-à-vis Western literature in terms similar to those they might use in defining the female vis-à-vis the male. Consider the pairs of opposing concepts —natural versus artistic/artificial, static versus dynamic, archaic versus modern, flora versus fauna, silent versus vocal, enigmatic versus articulate, emotional versus intellectual, physical versus intellectual, immediate versus detached, and so on. These pairs of oppositions can be applied both to the Japan-West and to the female-male contrasts. Furthermore, the fact that Japan tends to be conscious of how it appears to the West, and tries to define itself in terms of the hegemonic Other, i.e., the West, suggests Japan's "femininity," given that it is women who show the more pervasive tendency to define themselves—and let themselves be defined—either as similar to, or different from, members of the opposite sex. Thus, Japan or the female feels an urge either to demonstrate or to renounce its femininity against the Other's masculinity, whereas the West, or the male, can afford not to think of the Other.

In this formula, Japanese writers, both male and female, assign to themselves the feminine role, vis-à-vis Western writers, to whom they assign the masculine role. Thus Japanese male writers are "emasculated" in their relation to Western writers. If, therefore, some Japanese male writers happen to look more "Western" than "Japanese" or to achieve worldwide recognition, it simply means that they have recovered their masculinity. Others may envy them, but there is no subversion of the gender hierarchy. However, when Japanese female writers become Westernized, it is quite another story. The Westernized, and thus "masculinized" women are subversive and threatening to "castrated" men. Consequently, male writers, with the exception of those able to transcend the binary opposition between feminine Japan and masculine West, seem intent on decapitating such women, depriving them of their intellectual activities.

It is significant in this context that the "victim" of the alleged plagiarism, Michel Butor, remained silent throughout these disputes. Apparently, Japanese literary journalists did not bother to ask him for his impressions of Kurahashi. Neither did he, apparently, know of the existence of his literary daughter who (unfortunately) happened to be born in Japan.[41] Kurahashi remained obscure and illegitimate in this sense too. Like the daughter in Anaïs Nin's (1903–1977) *Winter of Artifice* (1939)—and unlike the author of that novel, who is publicly acknowledged as a literary daughter of Henry Miller (1891–1980)— Kurahashi was a deserted and forgotten daughter of a Father, who was significantly present only in his absence. Her construction of identity inevitably involves a search for the lost Father, who does not even know he is being sought.

This is not the fault of Kurahashi alone. For Western writers, Japanese reception might not have meant much—Japan was little more than an exotic land, with virtually no legible literature for them. Translations of their works into Japanese would not guarantee them anything other than perhaps financial success. Linguistic and literary currency exchanges operate as unfairly as their monetary counterparts. Until recently, Euro-American writers have not been particularly intimate with their Japanese offspring. Japan, the deserted daughter of the Euro-American literature and literary criticism that holds the patriarchal authority in the world literary market, is marginalized and forgotten.

This is all the more reason for the Japanese literary fathers to bash the illegitimate daughter Kurahashi. She aspired to the center— the Euro-American literary canon—from which they were forbidden.

In order to claim their own territory, male critics were thus engaged in immuring themselves within the myth of a Japanese native literature pure of foreign, contaminating influences. Kurahashi had eaten forbidden fruit and was accordingly to be expelled from paradise.

Construction of Fathers: The Daughter Takes Charge

Given the seriousness of the charges against Kurahashi as surveyed above, it is a little surprising that she managed to stay active in the Japanese publication industry. How was she able to do this? Perhaps she learned her strategy from Shimizu Tōru (1931–), Michal Butor's translator. The *Tōkyō shinbun,* in which the *Blue Journey* Debate had taken place, solicited Shimizu, in the place of the French literary father, to make a definitive announcement, appropriate to the authority of a Father, about the standing of Kurahashi's literary work. Shimizu's judgment was nuanced. He suggested, rightly, that Kurahashi should either have drawn upon Butor more openly or reduced traces of his work to a minimum, to escape the accusation of plagiarizing him. In the former strategy, Kurahashi's indebtedness to Butor would have been shared by the reader, her work would have been acknowledged as an intentional parody, and thus no accusation would have been made. In the latter, Kurahashi could have successfully concealed her indebtedness.[42]

Although it is not clear whether Kurahashi was following Shimizu's advice, she did begin to name some of the sources of inspiration within her subsequent texts. She has her fictional characters associate what they see, hear, and experience with what they have read. Instead of herself revealing or concealing traces of her Fathers' texts, she has her characters refer to them, paraphrase them, and cite them. At such moments, her characters become readers, and her text, a form of reader-response criticism. Rather than anticipating or parrying readers' suspicions about the originality of her texts, Kurahashi actively highlights their intertextuality.

An example of such tendency, her novel, *Shunposhion* (Symposium, 1985)[43] is almost a reading list, in which characters name the novel's literary fathers one after another, citing their texts and comparing and contrasting them with their own experiences. Characters who spend a summer at the seashore residence of a former prime minister compare their way of spending time—discussing literature, art, music, cuisine, and so on—to sympotic literature such as Plato's *Symposium,* to which the title of the novel is indebted. Subtle and drastic changes of weather are experienced in association with the weather presented in poems by Su Shi (1036–1101), Matsuo Bashō (1644–1694), Fujiwara Teika (1162–1241), and others. Inquiries into culinary art and wine selections draw on various ancient sources from China, India, Europe, and Japan. Paintings are copied from masters such as Paul Klee (1879–1940), Raoul Dufy (1877–1953), and Henri Matisse (1869–1954). Jazzlike improvisational variations are performed on the tunes of classical pieces by established composers such as J. S. Bach (1685–1750).

One quality is shared by the wide range of artists mentioned here. They are all renowned for consciously parodying others and/or for being parodied by others. Kurahashi seems to imply here the view she once expressed in response to Etō: "pastiche is the royal road of art."[44] Another side attack on the literary establishment might be intended in the following conversation between the heroine and hero of the novel—Satoko, an extremely well-read young woman, and Akira, an associate professor of Greek and Latin—whose love forms the novel's central plot. Akira confesses that he has not read much of modern Japanese literature—despite his wide knowledge of European and Asian classics—and asks Satoko,

> "Incidentally, if you were to recommend a handful or so of the twentieth-century Japanese novels which we in the subsequent century might inherit, what would you say?"
>
> "Could I answer your question by selecting authors all of whose works I would be tempted to read?"
>
> "Certainly. That would be more irresistibly interesting, and useful for me, too."
>
> "Sōseki—the earlier works only, though—Ōgai, Tanizaki, Mishima. That makes four. It's difficult to make up a handful."
>
> "Less than five? That does make me feel relieved. I have read hardly any post–Meiji-era Japanese novels, you know."
>
> "That must be the case with all but scholars or excessively addicted readers. Most Japanese novels are simply materials for literary history, only to be stored in data bases or libraries now."[45]

Satoko declares that most post-Meiji Japanese writers are not worth reading, except by professional or dilettante literary historians. Her choice of exceptions to the rule and the exclusion of Sōseki's later works, known for pro-naturalist tendencies, suggest that Satoko thinks highly of those who developed omnivorous styles, relying on their for-

midable reading knowledge, rather than those who seem to strive for
a unique, less literary style. Alternatively, the dichotomy may be viewed
as a preference for intellectual writers over impressionistic writers.
Consider the canonized authors who did not make the list: Shiga
Naoya (1883–1971) and Kawabata Yasunari (1899–1972), for example.

Another reason for Kurahashi's survival as a professional writer is
that she increasingly turned to the dead, canonized, and/or Japanese
sources for her literary fathers. The oppressive existence of national
fathers (or the persistent claims for their existence) and the irrecover-
able absence of literary fathers launched Kurahashi, the disowned/
deserted daughter, on a new project. This time she was determined
not to search for but to construct her Fathers. In so doing, Kurahashi
ventured into antiquity and/or canonicity, whether native or not.

This change is usually viewed by critics as a return to her native culture that she naturally experienced as she was nearing middle age
and that coincided with her geographical return to Japan from the
United States, where she had stayed from June 1966 to September
1967 as a Fulbright artist.[46] Such an interpretation will be acceptable
only if we ignore the references and allusions to European sources
that continue to be made as frequently as ever in Kurahashi's fiction.
We can make better sense of this change by viewing it not as a move
from Eurocentrism to nativism, but as the result of a shift in allegiances
from the avant-garde to what we might call neoclassicism. The notion
of literary citizenship was necessary to many critics in Japan who
needed to construct the illusion of the contrast between the West and
Japan. The illusory nature of such a formula, however, is evident in
that it is absent from Western thought as a self-explanatory concept.

The non-Japanese origin of Kurahashi's fiction in later years is obvious even in the works that are considered to mark the turning point:
Han higeki (Anti-tragedies), an omnibus of five stories, which was published from November 1968 through 1971, breaking two years of
silence in publication of fictional works, and "Nagai yumeji" (The long
passage of dreams, trans. 1998), a story published in December 1968.[47]
While drawing upon noh plays such as *Adachigahara* and *Ōhara gokō*
(The imperial visit to Ōhara gokō), the first work is also indebted to
Greek tragedies for more than its title—to *Electra, Orestes, Medea,* and
Oedipus at Colonus, among others, as the author explains in the note
added to the book version published in 1971.[48]

"The Long Passage of Dreams" centers around a man dying in
Japan and his daughter who has come back from the United States

to see him for the last time. The text is generously studded with references to noh plays, such as *Kayoi Komachi, Sotoba Komachi, Kagekiyo, Adachigahara,* and *Tamakazura,* whose last line (*"nagaki yumeji wa same-nikeri"* [The long passage of dreams has come to its end]) is echoed in the story. Additionally, the story is indebted to Greek tragedies, such as *Medea, Oedipus at Colonus,* and *Antigone,* and other classical works of both Japan and the West, as the two major characters cannot help but associate themselves with literary figures as they recollect their own experiences in the past. (The man, for example, courted his wife for ninety-nine nights, just as Fukakusa no shōshō came to visit Ono no Komachi for ninety-nine nights in the Komachi-based noh plays; he eventually eloped with her, as Jason did with Medea.) In their hallucinations and dreams, moreover, they transform themselves into these figures. Again, the literary sources are explicitly mentioned, as it is characters who make the associations.

Two reviews of the work deserve special attention in the context of our discussion of literary father-daughter relationships. Hirano Ken, Kurahashi's "original" father, who had earlier reviewed "Partei" in the pages of the *Mainichi shinbun,* decided to resign from his position as critic for the newspaper. In his last assignment, he reviewed "The Long Passage of Dreams." The tone is not forthrightly positive. "I am not sure if this is a success," he says. But the way he phrases his negative impressions shows how concerned he was with Kurahashi's reputation and, by extension, how fatherly he still felt toward her: "Although one may be impressed with [the complexity] typical of Kurahashi . . . , it is possible that readers might be repelled by the fact that the author cannot help being pedantic even when dealing with a topic as serious as a father's death."[49] With this caution, Hirano retired from fatherhood, though he continued to write retrospectively about Kurahashi's birth as a writer and his involvement in the event.

The other review to be examined here was written by Yoshida Ken'ichi (1912–1977). Son of a former prime minister of Japan (Yoshida Shigeru), Yoshida was also a Cambridge dropout with hardly any institutional education in Japan (he had spent most of his younger years abroad with his diplomat-father), a Meiji University professor, and, most important, a critic of European literature and Japanese culture. He is one of the three people for whom Kurahashi has written elegies, the other two, incidentally, being Mishima Yukio (1925–1970), as I will discuss shortly, and Nakamura Mitsuo, her former thesis adviser at Meiji University and, as we saw earlier, a one-time disowning "father." Kurahashi, along with other Japanese Europhiles such as Shimizu Tōru, whom I mentioned above, loved Yoshida's style and imitated it.

Yoshida's review reveals that the appreciation was mutual, thus constituting a rare reciprocally acknowledged literary father-daughter relationship:

> Greek myths and noh plays are verbal expressions, as are contemporary Japanese novels. Then we must consider it a normal usage of language to incorporate words of Japanese and foreign myths and classics into one's own writing, and establish the world of fiction on the basis of the mixture. . . . Modern Japanese novelists did not invent language. A neologism is not part of language. That is the very reason why writers have to read more than they write. Quotations in "The Long Passage of Dreams" mature into part of the reality constituting this work, to the extent that the reader realizes literature itself is a dream of language. I have no reservation in awarding the praise previously given to [T. S.] Eliot (1888–1965).[50]

"Great poets steal" must be the phrase Yoshida had in mind as the compliment Kurahashi deserved. The praise is meaningful for two reasons. One is that it demonstrates Yoshida's support of Kurahashi in her war with the critics who put a premium on originality, and it legitimates her art of pastiche. The other is that Kurahashi is compared with a non-Japanese writer, T. S. Eliot, with no consideration of the national boundaries between the two. Whereas critics like Etō attacked the tie between Butor and Kurahashi because of their difference in nationalities, Yoshida here looks at compositional methodologies and acknowledges a "lineage" that crosses such boundaries to bind Eliot and Kurahashi. A Japanese citizen whose first language was English, Yoshida is in effect questioning whether European and Japanese literatures must appear in any essential contrast, beyond the simple fact that they employ different languages.

Kurahashi's experimentation with pastiche continued. Thus, *Sumiyakisuto Kyū no bōken* (The adventures of Sumiyakist Q, 1969; trans. 1979) features the self-absorbed and dogmatic protagonist Q, an echo of the title character of *Don Quixote* (1605, 1615), while the generous sprinkling of existentialist conversations is reminiscent of those in *The Brothers Karamazov,* and the framework of the story—the protagonist visiting an isolated place filled with quintessential people and discussing philosophical matters—resembles that of *The Magic Mountain* (1924), by Thomas Mann (1875–1955).[51]

Yume no ukihashi (The floating bridge of dreams, 1971)[52] draws its title from a poem by Fujiwara Teika—*Haru no yo no / yume no ukihashi / todae shite / mine ni wakaruru / yokogumo no sora*[53]—while inevitably echoing the last volume of *The Tale of Genji* and the story of the same title by Tanizaki Jun'ichirō (The bridge of dreams, 1959; trans. 1963), as Saeki Shōichi and Fumiko Yamamoto[54] have noted. The style—third-person narrative with an omniscient narrator, whose viewpoint nonetheless remains closely tied to the protagonist for most of the story—is, according to the Author's Note, learned from Kawabata Yasunari.[55] The plot—a love hexagon—seems to owe much to *The Severed Head* (1961), by Iris Murdoch (1919–1999), who is often mentioned by the protagonist of *The Floating Bridge of Dreams* as her favorite novelist.

One may note that such "flirtatious" claiming of many fathers removes the stifling bond between literary father and daughter that we observed in the first stage of Kurahashi's career—a bond based on genealogy, monopoly, obligations, and loyalty. The literary daughter now chooses her own fathers. Authenticity is no longer an issue, nor is the Father in control of his daughter. Rather, the daughter constructs fathers for herself and is entitled to replace one father with another as she chooses. The origin and its uniqueness are denied. Instead, a trace constructs its origin—performatively, and playfully. Indeed, as Jorge Luis Borges says in reference to Kafka:

> In the critics' vocabulary, the word "precursor" is indispensable, but it should be cleansed of all connotation of polemics or rivalry. The fact is that every writer *creates* his own precursors. His work modifies our conception of the past, as it will modify the future. In this correlation, the identity or plurality of the men involved is unimportant.[56]

Interestingly, as Kurahashi persists with her construction of Fathers, the literary critics of a younger generation—Miura Masashi (1946–), Kawamura Minato (1951–), Kanai Mieko (1947–),[57]and others—have become engaged in guessing the sources of her texts. They discuss Kurahashi's borrowings in their reviews and *kaisetsu* (readers' guides) of her works, not to criticize her but simply to enjoy examining literary relationships. It is not only Kurahashi the author who has changed. The Japanese literary establishment itself has come a long way—it now takes the lead in appreciating the literariness of literary works, rather than censoring "plagiarism" or forbidden foreign elements.

The Hero Who Fell from Grace:
Kurahashi Rewrites Mishima

Within the sort of ontological subversion outlined above, the literary daughter can even name her fathers only to dethrone them. Indeed, she can afford to ridicule them by writing parodies in the narrow sense. Although Kurahashi has mocked many male writers of established status from antiquity up to the present day, dead or active, perhaps the most conspicuous example of a literary father whom she has admired, claimed, and then disowned is Mishima Yukio.

In her essay, "Eiyū no shi" (The death of the hero, 1971), which she contributed to the special commemorative volume for Mishima Yukio, Kurahashi recollects how her praise of Mishima misled the police into suspecting her of political collaboration with him at the time of his theatrical suicide. According to Kurahashi, an officer came to stay at her house that day, without explaining the reason. Several hours had passed when another officer arrived. After an inconsequential conversation with Kurahashi, the newly arrived officer finally said to her, "Don't you watch TV in the daytime? He died, you know? It's now being broadcast on TV."[58] Kurahashi took the person who died to be her husband and was bewildered at the thought of what her husband might have done to warrant a TV broadcast. When she turned on the TV, her first bewilderment was replaced by another. At this point the police officer was convinced that Kurahashi had had no previous knowledge of the plans for Mishima's ritual suicide.

This reaction of the police to the Mishima incident offers a caricature of some Japanese literary critics who tend to read fiction as the author's confession. In fact, there is no trace of Kurahashi's ever having been an advocate for imperial sovereignty. It is also hard to believe that Kurahashi, the determined meritocrat, could have lightly accepted any claim to worth derived simply from a bloodline. Moreover, she is anything but a fanatic. When she reportedly said that she wished she were a man so that she could join Mishima's private army, "Tate no kai," it must have been the ritualistic nature of the organization that she had in mind, and not necessarily its explicitly political activities.

It would be absurd to claim that Kurahashi is somehow uniquely ideology-free. But it would be equally absurd to assume a complete identification between the ideologies of Kurahashi and Mishima. She admired Mishima, not as an activist but primarily for his relentlessly masculine and Westernized literature, for his sharp, logical, and intellectual style, for his elaborate structures, and for his sophisticated art of pastiche. In other words, Kurahashi was fascinated with Mishima's performance of masculinity. Indeed, Mishima is the perfect father for Kurahashi in that he could be said to read as a woman and to write as a man.

As I suggested earlier, Kurahashi wrote as a man in a feminine discourse in the beginning of her career. But she subsequently began to write in a distinctively masculine discourse. Masculine speech is naturally accepted when a male character assumes the responsibilities of the narrator, as with the case of *Sei shōjo* (Divine maiden, 1965; partial trans. 1989).[59] Its primary narrator, *"boku,"* narrates like a man, whereas the secondary narrator of the novel, a young woman, writes like a woman, referring to herself as *"atashi."* With an increasing number of Kurahashi's novels, however, the narrator is omnipresent and thus not identified either as male or female, and the tone of speech assumes detachment and objectivity. Kurahashi's choice is almost always the established written discourse—that is to say, "masculine" discourse, whose gender marker is neutralized, or naturalized —as gender-free, thus obscuring its masculine origin. There are few works by Kurahashi after 1968 that display the discursive femininity that I hypothetically defined earlier on behalf of Okuno Takeo. Thus, Kurahashi becomes discursively, as well as intellectually, masculine.

Nakamura Shin'ichirō (1918–1998), a Europhilic novelist and critic who had been sympathetic with Kurahashi,[60] reviewed "Himawari no ie" (The house of sunflowers), the first story in her omnibus, *Anti-Tragedies.*[61] Therein he appropriately compares Mishima and Kurahashi:

> Ms. Kurahashi has to face a new difficulty, which did not occur to Mr. Mishima, who distanced his narrative from everyday life . . . employing a reserved classical style. Ms. Kurahashi's fictional world is originally phlegmatic, which gives a sensual realism to her abstract and fictitious stories. However, when she superimposes Greek myths and contemporary Japanese life, the phlegm results in a schism in the narrative.
>
> For example, when Orestes, hiding himself behind his father's tombstone, eavesdrops on conversations among women in the town, their tone of speech is a grotesque mixture of classical and colloquial, and thus is an artificial and clumsy conversation without any sensuality. This disappoints the reader.

> . . . It is evident that the author will be troubled by the question of how to compromise her own phlegmatic nature with the transparency of Greek tragedies in a given work.[62]

Nakamura seems to note the gender distinction between Mishima and Kurahashi. Whereas it is easy for Mishima to erase the marks of his existence as a person, because he does not have to erase the marks of masculinity in writing in a masculine discourse, Kurahashi has to somehow reconcile the femininity as the anatomical gender with the masculinity as the culturally constructed gender. Although Mishima did not encounter the same dilemma, some would assert that his masculinity is not a reflection of his anatomical gender but rather a willful construction of cultural identity—a twofold gender performance, similar to that in *Blue Journey*. Moreover, granted that he is a "converted son" of the Japanese literary fathers, his "foreignness" did not cost him the label of sexual misfit. Probably to resolve the dilemma, Kurahashi longs to become asexual:

> If it is still impossible for me to masculinize my body with the aid of modern medical technology, then I would wish to diminish the body to a minimum, just sufficient to keep the spirit [in this world], in order to get out of the "femaleness." That is, I would wish to become an elderly person. . . . What is the pleasure of the elderly? I imagine that it must be to control others not by the body but by the mind.[63]

Once she is liberated from the body, which carries the marks of femaleness, Kurahashi seems to think, she could write only as the mind, without any intervention of her female sensuality.

It is more than interesting to note in this context that Kurahashi's gesture of "disowning" this father of hers is made in *Popoi* (1987),[64] narrated, as in many of her earliest works, in an unmistakably feminine discourse. This futuristic novel, set in the twenty-first century, is narrated in the first person by the protagonist, Mai, a granddaughter of the lover of Satoko's grandmother in *Symposium*. Kurahashi chooses for the narrator's statements (*ji no bun*) a combination of the written discourse with *"da"* and *"de aru"* sentence endings, which tend to neutralize the gender identity of the addresser, and a conversational tone of speech that immediately identifies the speaker as a sophisticated schoolgirl, in which sentences end with informal, introspective, and also feminine *"deshō?" "kashira,"* and *"keredo . . ."*—the last being uncharacteristic of Kurahashi's writing, especially after 1968, as I stated earlier. Kurahashi, who has read Mishima as masculine, here assumes a female readership and expresses how unappealing Mishima could be to women.

What is consistent in the alternate modes of speech in this novel, as well as with other works of Kurahashi, is its pedantry. The examination of sources of references and allusions reveals an impressive breadth of the author's knowledge of literature and art, Euro-American in particular.[65] The text echoes lines from T. S. Eliot's "Burial of the Dead," which functions both to signal seasonal changes (e.g., "April is the cruellest month") and to suggest similarities between the hyacinth bulb in the poem and the severed head of a terrorist around which the Kurahashi story evolves.

The terrorist—named Popoi, after a Greek word of exclamation—committed ritualistic suicide in a manner that reminded the twenty-first–century populace of Mishima. As she takes care of the head, which has remained alive, Mai becomes interested in Mishima. That Mai, an extremely intelligent and knowledgeable young woman, did not know much about Mishima until this time is an oblique suggestion of the mortality of Mishima's fame:

> I do know the similarities between the recent incident and Mishima's disembowelment as far as they have been reported by some of the mass media. But I don't know the details of the incident, nor do I know much of Mishima Yukio himself. From what little I happened to hear somewhere from somebody, he seemed so oppressive that I did not feel like approaching him. So I was reluctant to think about the possible influence Mishima might have on Popoi. . . . I am not sure if I can like Mishima yet.[66]

Upon her inquiry into Mishima's death, her grandfather's private librarian suggests that she read his novels such as *Kamen no kokuhaku* (Confessions of a mask, 1949; trans. 1958), *Kyōko no ie* (The house of Kyoko, 1959) and *Hōjō no umi* (The sea of fertility, 1965–1970; trans. 1972–1974). Mai, however, reads John Nathan's biography *Mishima,* prior to reading Mishima's fiction, which seems to suggest that Mishima's fiction has not retained any value independent of his eccentric life and death. The reading experience does not seem to have changed Mai's views of Mishima, either. She does agree with Satoko, who loves to read Mishima, that he is "a virtuoso of style,"[67] but she does not at all seem to become enthusiastic about either his work or his death. Rather, she thinks of him as a lunatic, the cause of his death incomprehensible, and she feels a detached sense of incomprehension. "I do not understand how the lucid brain of Mishima could have gone mad while not losing lucidity."[68] Thus, Mai fails to gain a sympathetic understanding not only of Mishima's work but also of his life and death. The Mishima incident is no longer relevant to Mai, the reader of the next century.

A more radical dismissal of Mishima is seen in *Kōkan* (Pleasure exchange, 1989),[69] presenting some of *Popoi*'s major characters—namely, Mai's grandfather Irie and his mistress Keiko—in their younger days. Keiko, a widow in her forties, is the heroine of the story. She is the president of a publishing house specializing in literature. The way she manages the various activities of her company shows how critical Keiko is of the conservatism in the Japanese literary establishment. The publisher sponsors an annual literary prize, and the selection of the winner is made by reviewing anonymous manuscripts —they may be written by new writers or by established authors. This practice is intended to remove any possibility of the kind of favoritism common in a society bound by mentor-disciple relationships, as the literary establishment has traditionally been. Also unique to this prize is the presence of two non-Japanese reviewers on the selection committee—an English woman who is a graduate student at Oxford and an American man who has written a book radically questioning the authority of Motoori Norinaga. Their presence serves to denaturalize values that have gone untested and unequivocally accepted in the Japanese literary establishment.

Another reviewer, a young poststructuralist named Mishima Hideo, has the following discussion about his name with Keiko:

> Mishima Hideo said that he had been contemplating renaming himself.
> "My name sounds like nothing but a compound of a great author and a critic, doesn't it? I don't like that. Still this is not my pen name, but the name that my parents gave me."
> "I know that well."
> "By whatever coincidence, I happen to detest both of them."
> "I am not surprised to hear that."
> "You agree with me, don't you, Keiko?"
> "I could not possibly make any comment in my place."[70]

Of course, the "great author" is Mishima Yukio, and the "critic," Kobayashi Hideo (1902–1983). One would imagine that Kurahashi would view Kobayashi, a representative modern Japanese critic renowned for his subjective, aestheticizing essays, negatively. But a radical change in Kurahashi's view of Mishima is suggested by his name being mentioned side by side with Kobayashi's, in a context in which outright hatred is expressed for both of them. Although the reason for this negative evaluation of Mishima is not specified in *Pleasure Exchange,* it is evident that Kurahashi is no longer fascinated with Mishima, given that no counterresponse to defend him is made in the novel. Mai's detachment from Kurahashi's one-time literary father in *Popoi* is reinforced here.

Conclusion:
Female Readership and Writing as Rereading

When Kurahashi writes her stories and novels as reader-response criticism, she calls attention to writing as an act of rereading, and reading as an act of rewriting. In other words, Kurahashi foregrounds the significance of the reader's participation in literary production. And she shows how differently she reads other writers' works from the ways they have been read—most significantly, by male critics in the literary establishment of Japan.

Early in her career, Kurahashi was criticized for the way in which her writing revealed what she had read. She was read not always according to the values she herself espoused but according to those of her male critics. Their reading of Kurahashi was not dialogic with the author but rather colonizing, imposing their own standards on her. Kurahashi maintained that the novelist is in no need of a critic. This literary daughter cried out to dispel fatherly control over her.

In later years, however, Kurahashi herself became a critic. Her references to earlier literary works, in fact, suggest that she was a critic before becoming a writer. She is a critic, however, who challenges the value of the literary establishment itself and canonizes neglected authors, while de-canonizing those who appear to her undeservedly glorified. This literary daughter thus questions the heritage of her literary fathers. The presence in her works of female and non-Japanese readers reveals negatively how biased the modern Japanese male reading of literature is and has been.

In Kurahashi's later works, the daughter not only decides who her fathers in literary production are—she is also empowered to name those "worth reading." It is no longer the case that "the daughter's art belongs to daddy." Instead, the fathers' art is recognized and re-established by the daughter's act of reading. The father does not determine the fate of his daughter as an author. Rather, it is the daughter, as reader, who judges the value of her fathers' works.

Kurahashi not only performs as the "fathers" whom she has chosen for herself, in the sense that she rewrites them, but also performs the role of Father in re-creating them. (Re)reading male authors' works as a woman, Kurahashi "fathers" them.

Notes

An earlier version of this chapter was orally presented as "My Art Belongs to Daddy? Kurahashi Performing Fathers" at the conference "(Un)Dutiful Daughters: Modern Japanese Female Writers and Their Cultural Fathers," sponsored by the Edwin O. Reischauer Institute of Japanese Studies, Harvard University, 4 May 1996. Translations are mine unless otherwise noted.

1. Hirano's review is reprinted in *Bungei jihyō*, p. 311. "Parutai" originally appeared in the *Meiji Daigaku shinbun* and was reprinted in a number of anthologies of the author's work. It was translated into English twice, by Grolmes and Yumiko and by Tanaka and Hanson.

2. Hirano, *Bungei jihyō*, p. 311.

3. Ibid., p. 312.

4. Hirano viewed Ōe's work positively, as "contemporaneous and artistic." Ibid., pp. 198–199.

5. Hirano, "Shin-sakka hitori," *Shinchō* (March 1960): 59–61.

6. Kurahashi, "Natsu no owari."

7. For a report on the selection process of the Akutagawa Prize, see "Akutagawa Ryūnosuke."

8. Kurahashi, "Hebi."

9. *Gunzō* 15.4 (April 1960): 193–197.

10. Etō's review of "Parutai" first appeared in *Shinchō* (May 1960) and is included in Etō, *Sakka ronshū*, pp. 224–226.

11. Kurahashi, "Kafuka to Watashi," p. 98.

12. Etō's review of "Hebi" first appeared in *Bungakukai* (July 1960) and is included in Etō, *Sakka ronshū*, pp. 265–266.

13. Itō, "Bundan."

14. Ibid., p. 47.

15. Ibid.

16. Nakamura, "Bungei jihyō," in *Zenshū*, pp. 550–551. Nakamura was not consistently negative toward Kurahashi's fiction; while acknowledging "the influence, or imitation, of Mr. Ōe Kenzaburō" in Kurahashi, Nakamura applauds her story "Kai no naka" (In the shell, 1960) for the "robust mentality and talent in satire and parody, which are missing in Mr. Ōe." Ibid., p. 538.

17. Nakamura's comments on "Mikkoku" are cited in Okuno Takeo, "Riari-zumu," and were originally published in the *Chūō kōron* (December 1960).

18. Okuno, "Kurahashi Yumiko," in *Bundan.*

19. Kurahashi, "Shōshetsu," p. 292.

20. Kurahashi, "Hihyō no kanashisa."

21. Kurahashi, "Shōsetsu," p. 290.

22. Fowler, *Rhetoric;* Hijiya-Kirschnereit, *Rituals;* and Suzuki, *Narrating the Self.*

23. Kurahashi, "Sakuhin nōto" (1975), pp. 244–245.

24. Haniya's comment on "Doko nimo nai basho" appeared in *Kindai bun-gaku* (February 1961) and is cited in Etō, *Sakka ronshū,* pp. 237–238.

25. Ibid., p. 237.

26. Ibid.

27. Hinuma, "Kandō no imēji."

28. The references in the text hereafter are to the 1969 reprint edition of *Kurai tabi.*

29. Okuno, "Kurahashi Yumiko cho *Kurai tabi.*"

30. See Butler, "Subjects," esp. pp. 24–25.

31. Kurahashi, "Dokuyaku," p. 299.

32. Okuno, "Etō Jun."

33. Kurahashi, *Kurai tabi,* p. 122.

34. Ibid., p. 128.

35. Ibid.

36. Etō, "Kaigai bungaku."

37. Kurahashi, "*Kurai tabi* no sakusha kara," pt. 2.

38. Etō, "Kaigai bungaku," pt. 1.

39. In "*Kurai tabi* no sakusha kara anata e," Kurahashi teases Etō for being tri-umphant in "enumerating superficial resemblances [of *Kurai tabi*] to *La Modifi-cation,* which are *obvious to anyone*" (emphasis added).

40. Okuno, "Etō Jun," p. 361.

41. Shimizu Tōru's article "Resonances butoriennes au Japon," written in French, published in a French journal, and intended for a French audience, described Butor's influence in Japan—including his influence on Kurahashi. To the best of my knowledge, this is the only link that has been established between Kurahashi and her French literary father. Kurahashi also claimed a wealth of other European fathers, whose styles she imitated. The most extensive list of such writers appears in her "Shōsetsu no meiro to hiteisei," which reads: "Sade, Dostoevsky, Thomas Mann, Robert Musil, Marcel Proust, James Joyce, Jean Genet, Henry Miller, Lawrence Durrell, Julien Gracq, André Breton, Maurice Blanchot, Michel Butor, Alain Robbe-Grillet. . . ." (p. 291), though again this literary pater-nity has not been acknowledged by her putative fathers.

42. Shimizu, "*Kurai tabi.*"

43. *Shunposhion* was first serialized in *Kaien,* from November 1983 through October 1985, and then published as a book the same year. Quotations are from the book edition.

44. Kurahashi, "*Kurai tabi* no sakusha," pt. 2.

45. Kurahashi, *Shunposhion,* p. 38.

46. See, for example, Mori, "Drag the Doctors into the Area of Metaphysics."

47. Kurahashi, "Nagai yumeji."

48. After being serialized in *Bungei, Han higeki* was published by Kawade shobō shinsha in 1971. The postscript, or *atogaki,* appears in pp. 329–332.

49. Hirano, "12–gatsu."

50. Yoshida, "Bungei jihyō," pp. 340–341.

51. For another important aspect of *Sumiyakisuto Kyū no bōken*—its absurdist and idea-oriented content, reminiscent of Kurahashi's earliest works, see Aoyama, "The Love That Poisons," esp. p. 38, in which she introduces Okuno Takeo's review of the Kurahashi novel, in *Kokubungaku kaishaku to kanshō.* Okuno humorously imagines how "the critic Mr M.N., the orthodox authority of our literary world" might think of this work, having criticized Kurahashi for not writing prose fiction in a proper way. Aoyama annotates the quotation, saying that the "M.N." "must be Nakamura Mitsuo," and I agree with her. I am grateful to Professor Howard Hibbett for informing me of the article.

52. *Yume no ukihashi* was first serialized in *Umi* from July through October 1970 and was published by Chūō kōronsha in May 1971.

53. Teika.

54. Saeki, "Kaisetsu," attached to a paperback edition of *Yume no ukihashi.* Yamamoto, "Kurahashi Yumiko."

55. Kurahashi, "Sakuhin nōto" (1976), p. 219.

56. Borges, "Kafka and His Precursors," p. 201. (Emphasis in original.)

57. Miura, "Kaikatsuna nihirisuto tachi"; Kawamura Minato, "Kaisetsu," attached to a paperback edition of *Sumiyakisuto Kyū no bōken;* Kanai Mieko, "Bungakuteki fūdo to sakuhin."

58. Kurahashi, "Eiyū no shi."

59. *Sei shōjo* was first published by Shinchōsha in 1965. An earlier version of a part of the novel, narrated by a secondary narrator (female), was published in *Shinchō* (February 1964).

60. In a published exchange of letters between Kurahashi and Nakamura, entitled "Bungei ōrai," Kurahashi writes of her struggle to shift from writing stories [*récit*] to novels [*roman*] and of her interest in Nakamura's novels and stories, while Nakamura expresses his interest in *Kurai tabi,* which he does not consider a novel, and encourages her to "imitate" more to transcend "the grammar [of literature] accepted by the current Japanese literary establishment."

61. "Himawari no ie" was published in *Bungei* (November 1968).

62. Nakamura, "Bungei jihyō."

63. Kurahashi, "Dokuyaku," p. 301.

64. *Popoi* first appeared in *Kaien* (August 1987) and was published by Fukutake shoten in September 1987.

65. For the ways Kurahashi parodies various works of literature and art, centering around the motif of a severed head—Keats's "Pot of Basil," Oscar Wilde's *Salomé,* Cranach's *Judith and Holofernes,* among others—see Sakaki, "Denaturalizing Nature." A shorter version of this article ("A Gallery of 'Severed Heads'") appeared in Sakaki, *Dramas of Desire.*

66. Kurahashi, *Popoi,* p. 57.

67. Ibid., p. 59.

68. Ibid.

69. *Kōkan* was first serialized in the *Shinchō* in 1988–1989.

70. Kurahashi, *Kōkan,* p. 31.

324   ATSUKO SAKAKI

Works Cited
Location of Japanese publishers is Tokyo unless otherwise noted.

"Akutagawa Ryūnosuke shō kettei happyō." *Bungei shunjū* (September 1960): 292–298, and (March 1961): 272–279.

Aoyama Tomoko, "The Love That Poisons: Japanese Parody and the New Literacy." *Japan Forum* 6.1 (April 1994): 35–46.

Borges, Jorge Luis. "Kafka and His Precursors." Trans. James E. Irby. In *Labyrinths: Selected Stories and Other Writings*, pp. 199–201. New York: New Directions, 1962.

Butler, Judith. "Subjects of Sex/Gender/Desire." In *Gender Trouble: Feminism and the Subversion of Identity*, pp. 1–34. New York: Routledge, 1990.

Etō Jun. "Kaigai bungaku to sono mozōhin." Part 1. *Tokyo shinbun* (9 December 1961, evening ed.), p. 8.

———. *Sakka ronshū.* Vol. 2 of *Etō Jun chosakushū.* Kōdansha, 1967.

Fowler, Edward. *The Rhetoric of Confession: Shishōsetsu in Early Twentieth-Century Japanese Fiction.* Berkeley and Los Angeles: University of California Press, 1988.

Fujiwara Teika. *Shin kokin waka shū* 1.38 (Spring 1). Hisamatsu Sen'ichi; Yamazaki Toshio and Gotō Shigeo, eds., *Shin kokin waka shū*, vol. 28 of *NKBT*, p. 45 (Iwanami shoten, 1958).

Hijiya-Kirschnereit, Irmela. *Rituals of Self-Revelation: Shishōsetsu as Literary Genre and Socio-Cultural Phenomenon.* Cambridge: Harvard University Press, 1996.

Hinuma Rintarō. "Kandō no imēji: 'Parutai' ronsō zehi." In *Hihyō* (Winter 1961).

Hirano Ken. *Bungei jihyō.* Kawade shobō shinsha, 1969.

———. "12–gatsu no shōsetsu." In *Bungei nenkan*, p. 66. Nihon bungeika kyōkai, 1969. Reprinted from *Mainichi shinbun* (29 November 1968, evening ed.).

———. "Shin-sakka hitori." *Shinchō* (March 1960): 59–61.

Itō Sei. "Bundan to bungaku 7: Ai no sekai towa nanika." *Shinchō* (July 1960): 43–47.

Kanai Mieko. "Bungakuteki fūdo to sakuhin: Kurahashi Yumiko ganzō no bigaku." *Nihon dokusho shinbun* (24 November 1975), p. 1.

Kawamura Minato. "Kaisetsu: *Sumiyakisuto Kyū no bōken* saidoku no tame no nōto." In *Sumiyakisuto Kyū no bōken*, pp. 456–463. Kōdansha bungei bunko, 1972.

Kowaleski-Wallace, Elizabeth. *Their Fathers' Daughters: Hannah More, Maria Edgeworth, and Patriarchal Complicity.* New York: Oxford University Press, 1991.

Kurahashi Yumiko. "Atogaki." In *Han higeki*, pp. 329–332. Kawade shobō shinsha, 1971.

———. "Dokuyaku to shite no bungaku." In *Watashi no naka no kare e*, pp. 299–304. Kōdansha, 1970. Reprinted from *Takahashi Kazumi, Kurahashi Yumiko, Shibata Shō shū*, in *Warera no bungaku*, vol. 2 (Kōdansha, 1966).

———. "Eiyū no shi." *Shinchō* (February 1971): 83–84.

———. *Han higeki.* Kawade shobō shinsha, 1971.

———. "Hebi." In *Kurahashi Yumiko zensakuhin*, vol. 1, pp. 79–121. Shinchōsha, 1975. Reprinted from *Bungakukai* (June 1960).

———. "Hihyō no kanashisa: Etō Jun san ni." *Shinchō* (August 1961): 204–209.

———. "Kafuka to watashi." In Kurahashi, *Jishaku no nai tabi*, pp. 64–99. Kōdansha, 1979. Reprinted from *Kafuka, Sekai bungaku zenshū*, vol. 33 (Gakushūkenkyūsha, 1978).

———. *Kōkan*. Shinchō bunko, 1993. Reprint (Shinchōsha, 1989).

———. *Kurai tabi*. With original and new postscripts. Gakugei shorin, 1969. Reprint (Tōto shobō, 1961).

———. "*Kurai tabi* no sakusha kara anata e." Part 1. *Tokyo shinbun* (8 February 1962, evening ed.), p. 8.

———. "*Kurai tabi* no sakusha kara anata e." Part 2. *Tokyo shinbun* (9 February 1962, evening ed.), p. 8.

———. "Mikkoku." In *Kurahashi Yumiko zensakuhin*, vol. 1, pp. 183–211. Shinchōsha, 1975. Reprinted from *Bungakukai* (August 1960).

———."Nagai yumeji." In *Vāzinia*, pp. 85–141. Shinchōsha, 1970 (reprinted from *Shinchō*, December 1968). Trans. Atsuko Sakaki, "The Long Passage of Dreams," in *The Woman with the Flying Head and Other Stories by Kurahashi Yumiko* (Armonk, N.Y.: M. E. Sharpe, 1998), pp. 105–155.

———."Natsu no owari" In *Kurahashi Yumiko zensakuhin*, vol. 2, pp. 5–18. Shinchōsha, 1975 (reprinted from *Shōsetsu Chūō kōron*, November 1960). Trans. Victoria V. Vernon, "The End of Summer," in *Daughters of the Moon: Wish, Will, and Social Constraint in Fiction by Modern Japanese Women* (Berkeley and Los Angeles: University of California Press, 1988), pp. 229–240.

———. "Parutai." *Kurahashi Yumiko zensakuhin* 1 (1960): 19–36 (reprinted from *Meiji Daigaku shinbun*, 14 January 1960). Trans. Samuel Grolmes and Yumiko Tsumura, "Partei," *New Directions in Prose and Poetry* 26 (1973): 8–22. Also trans. Yukiko Tanaka and Elizabeth Hanson, "Partei," in *This Kind of Woman: Ten Stories by Japanese Women Writers 1960–1976* (New York: Putnam, 1982), pp. 1–16.

———. *Popoi*. Shinchō bunko, 1991. Reprint (Fukutake shoten, 1987).

———. "Sakuhin nōto." In *Kurahashi Yumiko zensakuhin*, vol. 2, pp. 241–252. Shinchōsha, 1975.

———. "Sakuhin nōto." In *Kurahashi Yumiko zensakuhin*, vol. 8, pp. 213–228. Shinchōsha, 1976.

———. *Sei shōjo*. Shinchō bunko, 1981. Reprint (Shinchōsha, 1965).

———. "Shōsetsu no meiro to hiteisei" (1966). In *Watashi no naka no kare e*, pp. 285–296. Kōdansha, 1970. Partial trans. Dennis Keene, "The Labyrinth and Negativity of Fiction," in introduction to "To Die at the Estuary" (trans. of Kurahashi's "Kakō ni shisu," 1970), in *Contemporary Japanese Literature: An Anthology of Fiction, Film, and Other Writing since 1945*, ed. Howard Hibbett (New York: Knopf, 1977), p. 247.

———. *Shunposhion*. Shinchō bunko, 1988. Reprint (Fukutake shoten, 1985).

———. *Sumiyakisuto Kyū no bōken*. Kōdansha bungei bunko, 1988. Reprint (Kōdansha, 1969). Trans. Dennis Keene, *The Adventures of Sumiyakist Q* (St. Lucia, University of Queensland Press, 1979).

———."Watashi no kokoro wa papa no mono." *Shinchō* (February 1964): 6–42.

———. *Yume no ukihashi*. Chūō bunko, 1973. Reprint (Chūō kōronsha, 1971).

Kurahashi Yumiko and Nakamura Shin'ichirō. "Bungei ōrai: Roman wa kanō ka." *Bungei* (April 1962): 182–183.

Miura Masashi. "Kaikatsuna nihirisuto tachi." *Shinchō* (September 1989): 286–289.

Mori, Jōji. "Drag the Doctors into the Area of Metaphysics: An Introduction to Kurahashi Yumiko." *Literature East and West* 18 (1974): 76–89.

Nakamura Mitsuo. "Bungei jihyō." In *Nakamura Mitsuo zenshū*, vol. 6, pp. 550–551. Chikuma shobō, 1972. Reprinted from *Asahi shinbun* (19 July 1935).

Nakamura Shin'ichirō. "Bungei jihyō." In *Bungei nenkan*, pp. 64–65. Nihon bungeika kyōkai, 1969. Reprinted from *Sankei shinbun* (26 October 1968, evening ed.).

Okuno Takeo. "Etō Jun shi no Kurahashi Yumiko ron e." In *Bungakuteki seiha*, pp. 360–362. Shunjūsha, 1964. Reprinted from *Tōkyō shinbun* (15 December 1961).

———. "Kurahashi Yumiko." In *Bundan hakubutsushi: hito to sakuhin*, pp. 138–142. Yomiuri shinbun sha, 1967.

———. "Kurahashi Yumiko cho *Kurai tabi*." In *Bungakuteki seiha*, pp. 359–360. Shunjūsha, 1964. Reprinted from *Nihon keizai shinbun* (20 November 1961).

———. Review of Kurahashi's *Sumiyakisuto Kyū no bōken*. *Kokubungaku kaishaku to kanshō* (August 1971): 149.

———. "Riarizumu e no gimon: Nakamura Mitsuo hihan" (1960). In *Bungakuteki seiha*, pp. 16–33. Shunjūsha, 1964.

Saeki Shōichi. "Kaisetsu." In *Yume no ukihashi*, pp. 257–266. Chūkō bunko, 1973.

Sakaki, Atsuko. "Denaturalizing Nature, Dissolving the Self: An Analysis of Kurahashi Yumiko's *Popoi*." In *The Proceedings of Nature and Selfhood in Japanese Literature*, ed. Kin'ya Tsuruta, pp. 241–256. Vancouver, B.C.: Jōsai International University and the University of British Columbia, 1993.

———. "A Gallery of 'Severed Heads': A Comparative Study of Yumiko Kurahashi's *Popoi*." In *Dramas of Desire, Visions of Beauty*, ed. Ziva Ben-Porat, Hana Wirth-Nesher, Roseann Runte, and Hans R. Runte, pp. 386–393. International Comparative Literature Association, 1995.

———. Introduction. In *The Woman with the Flying Head and Other Stories by Kurahashi Yumiko*, pp. xiii–xxii. Armonk, N.Y.: M. E. Sharpe, 1998.

———. "(Re)Canonizing Kurahashi Yumiko: Toward Alternative Perspectives for 'Modern' 'Japanese' 'Literature.'" In *Oe and Beyond: Fiction in Contemporary Japan*, ed. Stephen Snyder and Philip Gabriel, pp. 153–176. Honolulu: University of Hawai'i Press, 1999.

Shimizu Tōru. "*Kurai tabi* ronsō no mondaiten: *Kokoro gawari* no yakusha kara." *Tokyo shinbun* (20 March 1962, evening ed.), p. 8.

———. "Resonances butoriennes au Japon." *Michel Butor: Regards critiques sur son oeuvre, Oeuvres and Critiques* 10.2 (1985): 99–109.

Suzuki, Tomi. *Narrating the Self: Fictions of Japanese Modernity.* Stanford, Calif.: Stanford University Press, 1996.

Yamamoto, Fumiko. "Kurahashi Yumiko: A Dream of the Present? A Bridge to the Past?" *Modern Asian Studies* 18.1 (1984): 137–152.

Yoshida Ken'ichi. "Bungei jihyō." In *Yoshida Ken'ichi chosaku shū, Hokan* (suppl. vol.) 2, pp. 340–341. Tarumi shobō, 1964. Reprinted from *Yomiuri shinbun* (21 November 1968, evening ed.).

Chapter 12
Ogino Anna's Gargantuan Play in *Tales of Peaches*

Midori McKeon

Mirth's my theme and tears are not,
For laughter is man's proper lot.

François Rabelais, "Advice to Readers,"
The Histories of Gargantua and Pantagruel

A very smart-looking professor in a well-tailored business suit smiles radiantly at the camera. In her arms, a live pig. This portrait of Ogino Anna (b. 1956) and the pig she named Oginome Tonko is printed on the penultimate page of her ambitious work of fiction *Momo monogatari* (Tales of peaches, 1994). The photograph was taken on the occasion of a visit to a pig farm in Mie Prefecture in 1993, during one of the twelve factory tours Kyōdō Tsūshinsha (Kyodo News) arranged for Ogino's reportage series entitled *Anna no kōjō kankō* (Anna's factory tours).[1] Ogino, a self-confessed pig lover *(butazuki)* and a well-known collector of pig artifacts, could not resist hugging the cute baby pig. "With a motherly sentiment" *(hahaoya no yōna kimochi de)* and the factory owner's permission, she gently cradled the piglet.[2] The picture was apparently special enough to her that she included it in *Tales of Peaches,* which she regards as her major work so far (figure 12.1).

The name Ogino assigned her beloved four-legged "baby," "Oginome Tonko," illustrates the author's craft and humor. "Tonko" signifies "a female pig"— *"ton"* means "pig," and *"ko,"* which literally means "a child," is a suffix frequently used in women's names. In addition, the pig's full name is a play on the names of the Oginome sisters, entertainers who were very popular in Japan from the mid-1980s to the mid-1990s:[3] But Ogino's wordplay does not stop there. In the photo, Ogino's eye (*"me"* in Japanese) has been superimposed over

Figure 12.1. Ogino Anna with Oginome Tonko. Reprinted with the author's permission.

the pig's left eye. Thus, the pig's name "Ogino-me Tonko" represents a female pig child with Ogino's eye. The "child," in this manner, has inherited not only the surname but also a physical trait of her human "mother."

Furthermore, this humorous picture of "mother" and "child" can

be construed as a madonna-and-child pastiche, one of the most adored
and enduring artistic subjects in Western civilization. This interpretation is enhanced by the fact that *Tales of Peaches* parodies the Biblical
creation myth and the history of human civilization. (The Virgin Mary
herself appears in the tale as the mother of Christ and as the adoptive
mother of the Japanese folktale hero Momotarō.) In this interpretation, the biblically wrong sex and wrong species of Ogino's "baby"
themselves become elements of travesty.[4] Regardless of whether
the picture is interpreted as an innocent expression of Ogino's love
of the pig or as an integral part of her parodic scheme, it demonstrates Ogino's characteristic playfulness. Who would imagine that a
Sorbonne-educated professor of the French Renaissance would publicly display such impishness?

This picture symbolizes the essence of Ogino Anna's oeuvre, a happy
combination of the seemingly incongruous—the beauty and the beast,
high culture and low culture, sophisticated sensibility and childlike
mischievousness, erudition and vulgarism, the serious and the hilarious—inseparably bonded to each other, creating a world empowered
by wit and laughter. In her works, Ogino challenges the conventions
of modern literature and undermines its "grammar" from every con-
ceivable angle.[5] She melts the form of the novel into her genre-less
creations, entangling, displacing, and complicating the narrative structure with calculated playfulness. She creates a carnival of diverse narrative voices to bring unique perspectives of unconventional speakers
—a cockroach, mitochondria, a quilt, and a dream-eating cactus mon-
ster—to the attention of a (human) audience.[6] She deprivileges the
authorial voice by crisscrossing the boundaries among author, narrator, and characters in a manner radically different from the intimate fusing of the three in which confessional autobiographical novelists of modern-day Japan indulge. Calling herself "the Destroyer of
Language" *(kotoba no desutoroiyā)*, she drags the literary language down
from its citadel, turns it upside down, and gives it a spin with the punch
of a gag.[7] Above all, she is fearless in speaking the unspeakable and
the unimaginable. Who else would write a parody of the Judeo-Christian creation myth in which cathedrals are piles of Eve's excreta?[8]
Who else would speak of a zombie whose favorite part-time job is
getting dissected in an anatomy class and then coming alive to surprise medical students?[9] With its refreshing oddity and entertaining
surprises, her literary imagination disarms readers, liberates them
from the confines of binary preconceptions (sacred-vulgar, high-low,

human-nonhuman, etc.), and expands the horizon of their percep-
tivity while they laugh their hearts out. Ogino says, "When I write, I
have no sense of shame, nor do I worry about my reputation; I cast
aside my pride as a human being."[10] What gave her the strength and
confidence to write so boldly?

The Patriarch's Porcine Gift

In the beginning was father's word. Had it not been for the word of
the father, Ogino Anna the writer, as we know her today, would not
have existed. Nor would her extensive pig-artifact collection have
come into being. Her unforgettable initial encounter with father's
word occurred in 1971. Anna, a fifteen-year-old ninth-grader at Ferris
Girls' Junior-Senior High School in Yokohama, stumbled on a partial
Japanese translation of *Gargantua et Pantagruel* (Gargantua and Pantagruel, 1532–1564), by François Rabelais (ca. 1490–1553) in the school
library and fell in love. The work became her *"shōgai no issatsu,"* the
book she would enjoy throughout her life, her lifetime companion.[11]
Few people, Japanese or otherwise, read Rabelais at such a young
age. Most never read him at all, although they probably come across
the author's name and the titles of his famous works at some point in
their lives. Anna was exceptional in this regard. She was utterly fascinated with the work's "unprincipled" *(musessōna)* quality. In her personal essay "Kore de jinsei kuruimashita" (This made my life go awry),
collected in *Anna-ryū genki ga naniyori* (Being high-spirited like Anna
can't be beat), Ogino recaptures the excitement of her first reading
of Rabelais:

> Right next to a humorous medieval tale appears an eloquent pas-
> sage in an exquisite Ciceronian style. While a bridge of parody spans
> the rough waters of garrulity, there lies a tranquil utopia constructed
> of lucid compositions. And a chapter can consist of 140 ludicrous
> titles of books, such *as The Tailpiece of Discipline.* Nonsense and sense
> intertwine there, and I was amazed at the supreme erudition [dis-
> played] and was entertained by the "worst" vulgarity [exhibited].[12]

Whether her life went "awry" or not is anyone's guess, but the course
her life was to take was indeed determined the moment the fifteen-
year-old "grew intoxicated" by Rabelais's rich text.[13] On none but her
own instinct, the girl adopted her cultural father from sixteenth-
century France. Thereafter, the energy and devotion she invested in

the establishment of this new relationship were without equal. She would spend the next fifteen years—that is, the entirety of her *seishun*, or her youthful years—growing acquainted with this long-deceased, foreign-born father and learning to understand his inscrutable language. Such passion would easily overshadow any real human relationships, even those with lovers.

And in the beginning was a pig. Of all the outrageous things she read in *Gargantua and Pantagruel*, one short passage caught her eyes in particular. It portrayed a multicolored flying pig-monster. In chapter 41, the Fourth Book, of *Pantagruel*, amid the battle between Giant King Pantagruel and a wild tribe called Andouilles (Chitterlings or sausage people), the pig made its brief but impressive appearance:

> From a northerly direction there flew toward us a great, huge, gross, gray swine, with wings as long and broad as the sails of a windmill, and plumage as crimson red as the feathers of a phoenicopter, which in Languedoc is called a flamingo. It had flashing red eyes like carbuncles and green ears the color of chrysolite. Its teeth were as yellow as a topaz. Its tail was long and as black as Lucullian marble. Its feet were [as] white, diaphanous, and transparent as a diamond, and broadly webbed like those of a goose, or as Queen Pedauque's were of old at Toulouse. It had a gold collar round its neck, inscribed with some Ionic lettering of which I could only make out two words: ΥΣ ΑΘΗΝΑΝ—the hog (instructs) Minerva. . . . Then, after flying several times up and down between the armies [which had now laid down their arms, awestruck], the monster threw more than twenty-seven pipes of mustard down on the ground, and disappeared, flying through the air and shrieking continuously: "Mardi Gras, Mardi Gras, Mardi Gras!"[14]

This fantastic pig made an immense impression upon young Anna. She loved it so much that she started collecting pig artifacts soon after, and her collection continues to grow even today.[15] Crystallized in the image of the flying pig was the quintessential Rabelais with his extraordinary imagination—wild, hyperbolic, ludicrous, erudite, jocular, and baffling. "If one were actually to witness something like this flying in the sky, one would have 80 percent uncanny and 20 percent comical feelings," says Ogino in "Tonderu buta" (A flying pig; *"ton"* is a pun on "pig" and "to fly"), published in her essay collection *Shūkan Ogino* (Weekly Ogino, 1993).[16] The "delight" of discovering that such "comical uncanniness" *(omoshiro-bukimi)* existed in the world of literature became her starting point.[17] Rabelais's pig (= father's word) thus initiated the daughter into the world of literature. She adopted it as her "baby," whom she would adore and nurture as she aspired to grow into a writer like the father.

This early awakening of Anna to her calling raises a series of questions. What made her so accepting of Rabelais at such a young age? What, more specifically, did he teach her? Has she become a competent heir to Rabelais's literary legacy? What contributions has she made to the world of literature through her efforts to become a daughter worthy of her paternity? In our attempt to find answers to these questions, we will first explore the sources of Ogino Anna's strength in her unique family background, which fortified her endeavors to become Rabelais's literary daughter. Second, we will examine prominent elements of Rabelais's art that significantly influenced Ogino's creative vision. Third, we will analyze *Tales of Peaches,* her most overtly Rabelaisian text written to date, to discuss the ways in which she succeeds to Rabelais's literary heritage and gives new life to it.[18]

A Father's Absence: Ogino's Family Heritage

Ogino Anna is, by birth, a product of both Japanese and Euro-American heritages. Born on 7 November 1956 as Anna Gaillard in Japan's largest port city of Yokohama, she was the only child of Henri Gaillard, a French-American sea captain, and Ogino Kinuko, a Japanese artist of Western painting known as Emi Kinuko. Until 1985, the Japanese nationality law had dictated that a child born to a Japanese mother and a father of foreign nationality would assume the father's nationality. Since Anna's father had entered Japan on his French passport, Anna was a French national until 1966, when her mother, having fallen gravely ill, took the legal procedures to naturalize Anna in order to spare her the difficulty of living in Japan as a motherless foreigner. In May of that year, at age nine, Anna Gaillard became a Japanese citizen and assumed her mother's family name, Ogino. Subsequently, her mother recovered her health. Anna later adopted her Japanese legal name as her pen name with a small but significant modification: in her pen name, "Anna" is rendered in *katakana,* the Japanese syllabary used to transcribe words of foreign (especially Western) origin. In contrast, her legal name, "Anna" is written in *kanji,* or Sino-Japanese ideographs, emphasizing the Japanese-ness of the naturalized name. By choosing to write her pen name in a mixture of *katakana* (for the given name) and *kanji* (for the family name), she restored the French-American identity in her given name and reaffirmed her dual heritage.

Ogino Anna is constantly reminded of her ethnic hybridity not only by her name but also by her distinctive physical appearance; when she rides a train in Tokyo, she receives compliments on her proficiency in Japanese from unknowing Japanese people who mistake her for a foreigner.[19] Ogino's awareness of her difference, in my view, sharpened her ability to perceive things objectively from across the border, so to speak—to "relativize" (her favorite expression) concepts, to engage in issues (to borrow Bakhtian terms) "dialogically," not "monologically."[20]

Anna's father, Henri, was born in Le Havre, France, in 1914, as the second son and the third of the four children of Joseph and Marianna Gaillard. Joseph, a Frenchman, was captain of a commercial ship. He died during World War I, when his ship was attacked by German warplanes and sank. Marianna, an American born in France, moved to California with her children after Joseph died.[21] Henri was nine. He studied briefly in the California Academy of Fine Arts but abandoned his dream of becoming an artist when he realized it would not lead to a secure livelihood. He became a sailor instead, following his father's path, and traveled the world.

Henri's love of art played the role of Cupid in bringing Anna's mother into his life. Kinuko also had a passion for art. Not easily deterred by her parents' reluctance, Kinuko eventually entered the Kobe Municipal Institute of Western Painting, where she studied for four years and succeeded in sending her works to exhibitions. It was at just such an exhibition that Henri Gaillard encountered Emi Kinuko's paintings. Visiting Kobe on one of his many voyages, Henri not only bought one of Kinuko's paintings but claimed Kinuko as his wife as well. They married in 1951.

Anna's relationship with her father was unusual in that it hardly existed for the first nineteen years of her life. As the captain of an oil tanker, he was seldom home. Although he usually stopped by two or three times a year, once he did not come home for two years (from 1960 to 1962). Anna's mother found her husband's absences convenient, because they allowed her the space to concentrate on her work. But for Anna, the long absences deprived her of any real paternal relationship. Henri Gaillard was at best "a gentleman who came to visit from time to time bringing gifts" (*omiyage o motte tokidoki kuru ojichan*).[22] This "communication by gifts" (*omiyage no komyunikēshon*) lasted until his retirement in 1975, by which time Anna was a college student and had already decided what to do with her life.[23]

The only male voice that infiltrated this all-female household in her father's prolonged absences was that of a *rakugoka,* a professional narrator of humorous stories on the radio.[24] In radio broadcasts of *rakugo,* the gestures and facial expressions of the artist are lost to the listeners whose interest is sustained solely by the storyteller's vocal narrative skills. After a short prologue, the narrator unfolds the plot of the main story through vivid dialogues, keeping his own intrusions to a minimum. Often portraying scenes of everyday life or presenting classical humorous pieces, the storyteller deftly personifies many different characters—men and women of every social class and age— mimicking their tones of voice, mannerisms, and other linguistic characteristics with perfect verisimilitude. Ogino Anna's polyphonic narrative style, in which plural voices with distinctly different speech converge to enfold their own lively dialogue with little or no moderation, reflects *rakugo*'s art of narration. It is noteworthy that *rakugo* is performed professionally by men only, although the audience includes both men and women. In this light, the *rakugo* master's voice, which in a way surrogated the voice of little Anna's absent father, was not strictly meant to be identified as that of a male. It was a phantasmagoria of various voices, male and female, produced through transgender vocal acrobatics. In her essay "Warau Nihon" (Laughing Japan), Ogino affirms that the *rakugo* narration she heard on the radio "christened" her as a baby held in her mother's arms and seeped into her mind long before she encountered "the medieval farce and the large-minded openhearted laughter" of Rabelais.[25] In sum, *rakugo* prepared Anna for Rabelais's laughter and his carnivalesque polyphony.

Before I bring this biographical portrayal of Ogino Anna and her family to a close, I would like to present a cursory chronology of dates and events pertinent to this present study. In 1963, at age six, Anna entered Yokohama Futaba Elementary School, a private missionary school near her family home. The Catholic education that she received there introduced her to the Bible and Christian doctrine and rites and thereby provided, in Ogino's words, "the provisions" for her later studies of Renaissance literature.[26] At age twelve, when she was a seventh-grader at Yokohama Futaba Middle School, she read the works of Giovanni Boccaccio (1313–1375). At age fourteen, she read works by the Marquis de Sade (1740–1814) and *Madame Bovary* (1857) by Gustave Flaubert (1821–1880).

In 1971, she transferred to the ninth-grade class at Ferris Girls' Junior-Senior High School, a highly reputed private school in Yokohama.[27] That was the year that Anna, in her biological father's absence, adopted a literary father from her father's native land, Rabelais. At high school, she expanded her reading to include picaresque novels—most notably, *Don Quixote* (1605, sequel 1615)—and works by Japanese poets such as Hagiwara Sakutarō (1886–1942) and Nishiwaki Junzaburō (1892–1982).

In 1975, Anna entered the Department of French Literature at Keiō University, one of the most prestigious private universities in Japan. It was her desire to read Rabelais in the original French that prompted her to major in French literature. In July 1978, Anna went to France to study at the University of Paris for a year as an exchange student. She received her bachelor of arts degree in French literature in March 1980 and her master of arts degree in the same field two years later, both from Keiō University. Both her B.A. graduation thesis and her M.A. thesis were on Rabelais. Anna entered the doctorate program at Keio in April 1982.[28] In November 1983, when she was twenty-seven, she left home to study at the Sorbonne as a recipient of a scholarship from the French government. Three years later, in 1986, she submitted her dissertation on Rabelais to the Sorbonne and earned her doctorate. In the spring of 1987, she returned from France to the doctoral program of Keiō University, completing her doctoral studies there in March 1989.

While in the midst of her studies, Ogino also demonstrated interest in becoming a creative writer. As a freshman, she had sent poems to *Yuriika,* an influential literary magazine, only to have her submissions rejected. She turned her attention to prose fiction instead. Although she had never written a single line of fiction, she confidently declared, "I will win the Akutagawa Prize by age thirty!"—an assertion that earned her the sobriquet "*Horafuki* Ogino" (Ogino the Braggart). There is a similar episode from the earliest days of Ogino's graduate study at Keiō. When she found that the school had no professor specializing in Rabelais, "Ogino the Braggart" announced: "*I* will be the one!" *(Watashi ga narimasu).*[29] Both of these assertions were made publicly to her professors, not privately to her friends or family members. If the first of these proclamations was made without any foundation except for her own determination, the latter had at least more believable ground; she assiduously and single-mindedly devoted her time to her study of Rabelais at school and at home. Anna was so busy pursuing Rabelais that even her father's final homecoming did not divert her attention. Interactions between Henri and Anna were limited to conversations at the dinner table.[30] Metaphorically speaking, Henri Gaillard had his daughter's heart and soul stolen by Rabelais.

The Cosmic, the Comic, and the Unboundedness of Laughter: A Rabelaisian Legacy

Ogino's love of Rabelais and the inspiration she derives from his works constitute the foundation of her life and art. It is not an easy task, therefore, to summarize the specific nature of his far-reaching influence. I shall limit the range of my discussion to the most formative aspects of that influence. In addition to fascinating her as a supreme magician of language, Rabelais taught Ogino the essential importance of laughter in literature. He showed her how the comic can cradle the cosmic and can function as a vessel for delivering serious content. And he illustrated to her the boundlessness of what constitutes literature and how a literary text can generate and maintain massive energy within itself.

The Importance of Laughter

Ogino Anna attaches central importance to "play" and "laughter" in her writing—a risky endeavor in a milieu where comic fiction does not enjoy high regard. Japanese critical discourse tends to be reticent about the subject.[31] And it was not until Joel Cohn's *Studies in the Comic Spirit in Modern Japanese Fiction* (1998) was published that a systematic study of the comic elements in modern Japanese prose literature was even available. In this book, Cohn discusses the works of Ibuse Masuji (1898–1993), Dazai Osamu (1909–1948), and Inoue Hisashi (b. 1934). He summarizes the adverse circumstances with which Japanese writers of comic literature, in classical and modern times, have had to cope as follows:

> Comedy has not generally been considered an independent literary category in Japan and has not been accorded its own place in the overall artistic scheme; rather, its existence has simply been identified by the presence of humor, or in distinction from the "serious," whether in individual works or in genres (*kyōgen* as vs. *Nō*, *haikai* as vs. *renga* and later *senryū* as vs. *haikai* verse). . . . In Japa-

nese high culture, the cult of seriousness—with its aversion to
dualities, its preference for the savoring of emotional states over
delight in complex intrigue, its discomfort with the pleasure that
arises from mirth, and its reluctance to admit works animated by a
comic spirit into the canon of high art—has persistently retained
such formidable power and prestige that comic artists have had a
great deal of trouble in presenting their work as a legitimate alternative. The power of the cult of seriousness is reflected not only in
the lack of critical discussion of comedy, but in the tendency either
to exclude comic works from that discussion or at best to relegate
them to a distinctly secondary artistic status, frequently coupled
with a tendency toward association with lower social status.[32]

Japan's modern fictional form, *shōsetsu* (prose fiction), "neither
arose as a comic countergenre nor gave rise to one, and there was no
comfortable place for comedy in it."[33] Furthermore, the dominance
and the enduring influence of the autobiographical *shishōsetsu* ("I"-
novel) in twentieth-century Japanese fiction (since the appearance
of Tayama Katai's *Futon* in 1907) created a literary ideal out of "truthful" public exposures of the author's own life and made the *shōsetsu*
genre inhospitable to playful "fabrications."[34] By giving comical elements an essential role in her writing, Ogino risks being labeled frivolous. She acknowledges this danger herself: "I tend to be playful in
my writing, which is sometimes regarded as a misunderstanding on
my part of what is supposed to be a serious genre called *shōsetsu*."[35]
She distinctly remembers her work's being called "trash of trash" by
the renowned Japanese (male) critic Asada Akira (b. 1957).[36] Nevertheless, she remains undaunted.

For example, in "Seishin no zeitaku to wa?" (What is the luxury
of the mind?), collected in *Being high-spirited like Anna can't be beat,*
she challenges what she terms "the vague preconception" underlying modern Japanese literature that "if it is not serious, it is not literature."[37] Her major weapon for assaulting Japan's bias for the serious
is Rabelais's *Gargantua and Pantagruel.* In order to elucidate the
powerful effects of laughter on literature and on the human mind,
Ogino refers particularly to chapter 13 of the First Book, entitled "How
Grandgousier realized Gargantua's marvelous intelligence by his
invention of an arse wipe." In the chapter, five-year-old Gargantua
conducts a "long and curious" experiment to find out what in all the
world is the best implement for wiping bottoms. He experiments
with everything imaginable—accessories (such as a lady's velvet mask,

earmuffs, and a bonnet), plants; household linens; interior goods; materials such as hay, straw, litter, wool, and paper; and birds and other animals. And after he has further tested items such as a lawyer's bag, a penitent's hood, and a coif, Gargantua proudly announces the conclusion of his study to his father: "There is no arse wiper like a well-downed goose."[38] In the middle of his jolly presentation, Gargantua even displays his distinctive literary talent by reciting two poems, complete with rhyme (one of which is a *rondeau*), on the subject of defecating.

How does one react to such a story? Ogino's analysis of this "most vulgar" chapter plainly manifests her philosophy of literature:

> "That's ridiculous," [you think, but] laughingly you read it and somehow feel the constipation in your head has been relieved. Here, everything—from plants and animals to inanimate objects —that is supposed to be mainly associated with the upper half of the body is used as toilet paper and serves the needs of the lower part of the body. The top and the bottom change places, overturning everyday rules. Momentarily the world is turned upside down. *Laughter is, and literature is, a hammer that knocks down hardened preconceived ideas. Mundane literature that draws forth tears is fine, but literature that can lend a charm even to excrement is more powerful. Perhaps the real luxury of the mind is learning to laugh through literature.*[39] (Emphasis added.)

The significance of this message, which she extracts from this particular chapter in *Gargantua,* is underlined by her repeated reference to the same chapter and reiteration of her view in *Raburē shuppan* (An embarkation on Rabelais, 1994), a scholarly volume in which she sets out her analysis of Rabelais's literature. It is important to note that the type of laughter she truly values is not simply therapeutic or entertaining; it is the type that creates a new consciousness by "overturn[ing]" established hierarchies within value systems" and "knock[ing] down" preconceptions. Such laughter is, in Mikhail Bakhtin's words, a "gay carnival bonfire in which the old world is burnt."[40] In this light, her self-appellation "the Destroyer of Language" assumes a new dimension beyond the linguistic plane; it signifies the deconstruction of hardened dichotomies as pursued thematically in works such as "Warau Bosshu" (Laughing Bosch, 1991), *Tales of Peaches,* and *Hanshi hanshō* (Half dead, half alive, 1996).[41] Extending the principle of deconstruction further to the form of literature, Ogino also attempts to obliterate the walls between established genres and to merge them into new creative categories such as found in her "fiction critiques" (literary criticism presented in the form of entertaining fiction), biographies presented under the pretense of tall tales, and articles of reportage appropriating the stylistic freedom and humor normally reserved for personal essays. Of course, turning the world topsy-turvy is not a literary technique peculiar to Rabelais.[42] What *is* unique about Rabelais, and what impresses Ogino, is his thorough, systematic treatment of the theme to the extent of creating "a ludicrous, and yet well-structured microcosm" of a universe rotating around its "gay core" (i.e., "excrement").[43] The deconstructive energy of Rabelais's laughter is generated in such a cosmic treatment of the comic.

The Comic and the Cosmic

Having learned from her encounter with Rabelais that mirth and seriousness can coexist and that such coexistence creates greater literary truth, Ogino gained the courage to venture against the grain of the Japanese modern literary establishment. Her mission: to present a serious message comically; her vehicle: parody. Rabelais fashions *Gargantua and Pantagruel* as a parody of the medieval knight's tale. Moreover, he uses parodic incidents throughout to achieve his satiric ends. Little Gargantua's experiment with the arse wipe, for example, mimics scientific inquiry, which in Rabelais's times had begun to usher in a new liberated, materialistic knowledge that challenged the hierarchical principles of the old theological view of the world.[44] Not surprisingly, therefore, Rabelais's literary daughter, along with Inoue Hisashi and Kurahashi Yumiko (1935–), has become one of the most notable parodists among contemporary Japanese writers.[45] I will not dwell on parody per se, or even on Ogino's extensive knowledge of the history of parody in European literature.[46] Suffice it to say that, through her repeated reading, she familiarized herself with every form of parody used in Rabelais's texts, such as comic travesties of literary works, mimicry of pidgin French, pastiches of pictures, and satires of social systems and procedures.

Ogino's dissertation, *Les Éloges paradoxaux dans le Tiers et le Quart Livres de Rabelais: Enquête sur le comique et le cosmique à la Renaissance* (The paradoxical eulogies in Rabelais's third and fourth books: a study on the comic and the cosmic in the Renaissance), was submitted to the Sorbonne in 1986 and published in 1989. In it, she explores her

insight into Rabelais as an artist who integrated the not-so-easily-
compatible dual qualities of the comic and the cosmic.[47] In particular,
she focuses on the "paradoxical eulogies" (praises of things that are
normally viewed negatively) that appear in Rabelais's later works and
analyzes the process by which comical subject matters assume cosmic
dimensions. The gist of her analyses of paradoxical eulogies in the
dissertation are re-presented for a broader Japanese audience in *An
Embarkation on Rabelais,* which we shall use as our reference here. For
example, in "Panurge's praise of debtors and borrowers" (chapter 3
of the Third Book), what starts as an amusing, sophistic defense of
debts incurred by Panurge (Pantagruel's retainer and friend) acquires
a universal dimension when he declares that debts are "the connect-
ing link between earth and Heaven, the unique mainstay of the
human race."[48] There follows an explication of the law of the universe in terms of the lending and borrowing of energy (i.e., energy
exchange in the macrocosm) and the metabolism of the human
body (i.e., energy exchange in the microcosm) that sustains life and
the human race.[49]

In addition to paradoxical eulogies, Rabelais employs another
peculiar method to transform the comic into the cosmic. An example
is found in chapter 7 of the Second Book, where 139 imaginary titles
of books, ostensibly housed in the Library of Saint-Victor, are listed.
The first eight titles read (in English translation): *The Props of Salvation; The Codpiece of the Law; The Slipper of the Decretals; The Pomegranate
of Vice; The Threadball of Theology; The Long Broom of Preachers, composed
by Turlupin; The Elephantic Testicle of the Valiant;* and *The Henbane of the
Bishops.*[50] In *An Embarkation on Rabelais,* Ogino points out that these
book titles not only satirize law and theology by combining those
most esteemed subjects with erotic imagery but also encompass in
just eight short phrases a small universe of considerable variety: an
animal (elephant), plants (pomegranate and henbane), clothing (codpiece and slipper), and other inanimate objects (prop, broom, and
threadball).[51] Subsequent book titles cited in the same chapter mix
scholasticism and law with, among other things, food and scatology.
In short, the list of books creates a microcosm embracing both the
spiritual and the material. The traditional worldview in the Renaissance would place theology and law at the top of a hierarchy, ordinary material objects of daily life such as food and clothing in the
middle stratum, and scatology and sex at the bottom. In contrast,
according to Ogino, the universe of the books of Saint-Victor Library

is a space where "everything is upside down; where things are stirred up and set afloat as matters of equal value in a vacuum."[52] In other words, comical twists of meaning, the semantic overlaying of word-play, and the unexpected fusing of incongruous words en masse—in sum, the emancipation of language from conventional syntax and normative functions—become an expression of a liberated philosophy.

Hilarious lists of unusual items also appear in Rabelais's Third Book, including 169 types of healthy "ballbags" (chapter 26), 171 unhealthy "ballbags" (chapter 28), and 208 kinds of fools (chapter 38). A defining characteristic of Rabelais's style, these lists differ significantly from the poetic *monozukushi* (an enumeration of names of things belonging to one category such as bridges and flowers) that have appeared in Japanese literature since the Heian period (794–1185).[53] *Monozukushi* include names of items that actually exist and are calculated to evoke aesthetic effects, not a parodic microcosm of the world. Rabelais's lists are highly charged, densely packed energy fields in which the alloy of the comic and cosmic is created by rhetorical alchemy.

The Boundlessness and the Durability of Literature

The combination of the comic and the cosmic, the sacred and the vulgar, the mundane and the enlightened, is not localized in paradoxical eulogies and extensive lists alone. It informs the whole of *Gargantua and Pantagruel,* the complexity of which caused Jean de La Bruyère (1645–1696), "the great moralist" of the seventeenth century, to utter the highest praise and the harshest criticism of Rabelais in his book, *Les caractères* (Characters, 1688; trans. 1963):

> Rabelais above all is incomprehensible: his book is a mystery, a mere chimera; it has a lovely woman's face, with the feet and tail of a serpent or of some more hideous animal; it is a monstrous jumble of delicate and ingenious morality and of filthy depravation. Where it is bad, it excels by far the worst, and is fit only to delight the rabble; and where it is good, it is exquisite and excellent, and may entertain the most delicate.[54]

From an inspiring lecture written in epistolary form, emphasizing the importance of learning, to descriptions of gluttony on a colossal scale; from an eloquent speech urging the enemy to choose a peaceful solution to conflicts, to satirical thrusts at religious establishments and mockery of the legal system; tall tales, fantasies, Greek philosophy, folk culture; an unreadable chapter written in "murdered" French language; the spectacle of 600,014 male dogs "pissing" on a beautiful lady: there is no limit to what finds its way into Rabelais's created world. La Bruyère was but one of the many who were bewildered, or worse, repelled by Rabelais's texts.[55] Ever since Rabelais's books were published, readers, overwhelmed by the sheer enormity and the diversity beyond their comprehension, have tended to only partial readings, a situation Ogino decries. "Morals, confessions of faith, satire, wordplays, and all the details" are integral parts of the work.[56] *Gargantua and Pantagruel* constitutes "a single whole" *(hitotsu no zentai),* "one thing" *(hitotsu no mono);* "it cannot be disassembled into parts just as this complex world of ours cannot."[57] Ogino asserts that what makes Rabelais's literature uniquely Rabelais is, more than anything else, its "awe-inspiring high level of energy,"[58] and she has discovered in her voyage through Rabelais's texts that the scientific principle of the conservation of energy *(e = mc²)* applies to Rabelais's literary world as well: Rabelais maintains the high energy level by manipulating the "mass" (enormous quantities of rhetorically highly charged matters presented as bulks, such as the long lists that we have seen) and the "velocity" (the fast movement of his imagination and the narrative speed).[59] Ogino has also discerned that Rabelais's language is durable because it is not "a helper [*suketto*] to explain or describe things" but "aims to be a body of energy [*enerugī-tai*] that turns into a 'thing' [*mono*], emancipating the signified in the very process."[60] Ogino attempts to apply the same principles to her *Tales of Peaches,* as we shall see.

At Play in a Paper Paradise

After returning from France, Ogino Anna launched her dual career as academician and writer in spring 1987, becoming an assistant *(joshu)* in the Department of Commercial Science at Keiō University in April and publishing her first work of literary criticism, "Ūtopia to shite no Kumano" (Kumano as Utopia), a review of Nakagami Kenji's *Himatsuri* (Fire festival, 1987), in the June 1987 issue of *Bungakukai.*[61] The success of the review brought requests for others. In time, Ogino's writing began to evolve from straightforward literary criticism to literary criticism written in the form of fiction ("fiction critique") and eventually to pure fiction (short stories), with notable success. Her first story, "Uchino okan ga ocha o nomu" (My mom drinks tea, 1989) was nominated for the prestigious Akutagawa Prize. She received successive nominations for her second story, "Doa o shimeruna" (Don't shut the door, 1989), and her third story, "Supein no shiro" (A Spanish castle, 1990)[62] before finally winning the Akutagawa Prize for her fourth novella, "Seoimizu" (A lease on the life of love), in 1991.[63] She was thirty-four years old—only a few years short of her bold prediction. Her first three Akutagawa-nominated works were republished in her first collection of short stories, titled *Yūkitai* (Wanna-play-organism, 1990).[64] "Seoimizu" is collected as the title piece in *Seoimizu* (1991), together with three other lighter and humorous tales.[65] As of April 2000, Ogino Anna has published thirty books in less than ten years since the appearance of *Wanna-Play-Organism*. *Tales of Peaches* is her tenth book and by far the longest.

Tales of Peaches, 445 pages long, is inspired both by Rabelais's *Gargantua and Pantagruel* and by the form of narrative farce advocated by novelist Sakaguchi Ango (1906–1955).[66] A parody of world history and storytelling, the narrative opens with the Judeo-Christian creation myth and proceeds to trace the adventures and encounters of a Gargantuan-cum–picaresque hero named Momotarō—all the while toying with the polysemous symbolism of the word *momo* ("peach," "one hundred," and "thigh[s]").[67] Momotarō is known to readers, of course, as Japan's beloved folktale hero the Peach Boy—so named because he was born from a huge peach—who conquered *oni* (ogres). Ogino saw in Momotarō a Japanese Gargantua because of their shared origins in folklore and their capacity as heroes of a knight's tale. Combining Japanese folklore with the Rabelaisian tale allowed Ogino a great amount of creative freedom in terms of content while simultaneously providing a sturdy framework to hold the work together as a single piece.[68]

The consistent theme of *Tales of Peaches* is the most profoundly cosmic of all possible subject matters: the principle of relativity or, to express the idea in more literary language, the relativity of truth.[69] The work demonstrates that dichotomies such as Momotarō-*oni*, hero-villain, good-evil, and true-false are products of a given, often prescribed perspective and that they are subject to change whenever the perspective shifts. Ogino reveals this fundamental ambiguity underlying human discourse (history, fiction, advertisement, everyday conversation, academic writing, etc.) and civilization. She conveys this serious message comically; she successfully prevents the narrative

from degenerating into a didactic, scholastic, or political discourse
and it remains thoroughly hilarious and absurd. Her playfulness is apparent, for example in the bridging of East and West by the use of a
bilingual pun that connects *sadō*, the Japanese traditional art of tea
ceremony, and "Sado," the Japanized pronunciation of (the Marquis
de) Sade, as well as in the crossing of the folk hero Momotarō with a
juvenile delinquent of contemporary Japan. Since "the moment a
perspective is fixed, the world is reduced to a two-dimensional good-
evil [paradigm]" and because "only perpetual movements that constantly keep shifting perspectives can guarantee a three-dimensional
worldview," Ogino keeps changing the roles (mythical, social, and alle-
gorical), the ethnicity, and even the gender of Momotarō throughout the work's seven chapters, which are further subdivided into one
hundred (= *momo*) segments.[70] A brief analysis of individual chapters
will illustrate this point.

In chapter 1, "Eden no momo" (The peach of Eden), "ano-hito"
(lit. that person) is busily engaging in the act of creating the world.
His "habitual" modus operandi is to run out of the breath of originality after making one or two decent creatures and then save trouble by creating parodies of His own works.[71] Thus by mentioning the
problems that apply to any act of creation, Ogino questions the very
making of civilization. "Ano-hito" ends up making His own parody:
Adam. To relieve *(ibu-suru)* Adam's ennui, "ano-hito" creates Eve (pronounced "ibu" in Japanese) by inserting Adam's rib into a peach
ripened on a branch of Eden's peach tree. Eve is identified as the ur-
Momotarō, and Jesus of Nazareth is another Momotarō who emerged
from a big peach that the Virgin Mary plucked from a stream, intend-
ing to make it her dinner. The Eve-Momotarō character has an insatiable appetite for food, which in Ogino's literary world often signifies knowledge; she eats everything in Eden (ingests an enormous
amount of knowledge) and with her own excreta (product of her
studies) creates lifelike sculptures of the things she has just consumed.
The epitome of humanity, Eve-Momotarō is an avid learner and artist,
an imitator of God's act of creation. When Adam and Eve are expelled
from Eden, "ano-hito" presents them with a bill for an astronomical
amount of debt that they have unknowingly incurred for food and
accommodation in the paradise. This notion of "the original debt,"
in lieu of "the original sin," defines the governing principle of the
world of *Tales of Peaches,* and it clearly echoes Rabelais's understanding of energy exchange (lending and borrowing of energy) as the fun-

damental law of the universe as well as that of human existence, social
and biological.

If chapter 1 casts Momotarō among the principal mythological and
religious figures of Western civilization, chapter 2 brings Momotarō
closer to the figure of Everyman. Entitled "Momo kuri sannen, oni
wa soto" (Peach and chestnut trees bear fruits in three years, out
with the devils), this chapter evolves from an innocent question that
a little boy named Momotarō puts to his mother:[72] "What is an *oni*?"
(the name for the "it" in a child's game of tag). Her tall-tale answer
parodies the biblical story of Cain and Abel as she explains that the
elder brother *(oniisan)*, having killed his younger brother, was disowned by God and lost the right to his father's inheritance *(isan)*,
thus becoming *oni*. The mother's bogus answer is edited, so to speak,
for her young audience and leaves the deleted adult-version truth
"under erasure" in Derridian terms—crossed out but not removed
so that the "truth" remains in plain view of a mature audience.[73] The
lesson that the young audience receives but does not see is that the
one who rebels against and displeases the authorities is subsequently
labeled *oni*. Little Momotarō receives a more straightforward but
puzzling answer from one of his ninety-eight elder brothers who are,
incidentally, all named Momotarō. He tells him, "We are all *oni*."[74]
Thus the text implies for the first time that Momotarō is himself an
oni. Furthermore, the mother of all these Momotarōs (one hundred
—i.e., *momo*—of them, including the one she is pregnant with) is
named Eve, from Eden. The implication, therefore, is that all human
beings are Momotarō-cum-*oni*. But these hints remain abstract notions
until the second half of the chapter, when the implied dual identification of Momotarō as *oni* is "clinically" proven by a peculiar psychoanalytical treatment called the know-your-previous-life therapy" *(zensei
chiryō)*, described as an application of hypnotherapy based on karmic
philosophy. Readers witness a particular man, who claims to suffer
from a recurring blood-colored nightmare, as he undergoes the treatment. While under therapy, he discovers that his soul was created
many centuries ago and that he has lived ever since in various times
and places throughout the history of humanity as either Momotarō,
the killer, or as his victim, the *oni*.

Chapter 3, "Be-Bop Osorezan," recounts Momotarō's conquest of
the *oni* but makes the conventional distinction between the hero and
the antihero difficult because the Momotarō in this chapter is the
leader of a band of juvenile gangsters who have been expelled from

high school. Momotarō is permitted to enter a very special high school named Lycée Osorezan, located near the hallowed Mt. Osore in northern Japan that is known to be a haven for spiritual mediums and wandering ghosts. This particular school accepts only the worst juvenile delinquents in the nation and only by recommendation. Turning society's standards upside down, the school is a veritable paradise for these young hoodlums, requiring them to do everything that normal mores prohibit. They are expected to consume unlimited amounts of alcohol, for example, and to smoke, have sex indiscriminately, shoplift, and wear the provocative fashion and hairstyles typical of delinquents. Momotarō soon uncovers the hellish truth belying this paradise: the Lycée's principal, the self-claimed "Sorbonne-educated philanthropist" known as "Monsieur," is in fact a Japanese Al Capone running a ring of illegal businesses with Lycée's graduates as his slave labor. Momotarō battles against and defeats "Monsieur" and his army of *yakuza* (Japanese gangsters) with the help of Momotarō's own cohorts, the author "Ogino" (who threatens to disclose all of Monsieur's criminal acts in her novel, *Tales of Peaches*), and Rabelais's flying pig, which appears at a critical moment. Unlike the folk hero Momotarō, whose bloody slaughtering of his enemies is hinted at but omitted in the Japanese folk tale, this Momotarō defeats his *oni* (Monsieur) with an onslaught of "love," as I shall explain below. And in contrast to the original Momotarō, who brings home heaps of the *oni*'s treasures, thus exercising the conqueror's "legitimate" right to plunder, this Momotarō and his gang *give* to the *oni* most generously. During the battle against Monsieur, the flying pig–Cupid hits Kyōko, Momotarō's comrade, with one of his arrows, and suddenly she is overwhelmed by a tremendous capacity for love. She wishes then and there that all humans be relieved of their excess body fat. Kyōko, it should be noted, is not really human herself but an extraterrestrial from a planet called Deconstruction, as is the Momotarō of this chapter. Since she has the ability to teleport materials, she instantaneously realizes her wish by removing all the excess body fat from all the human beings on earth and grafting it onto the body of Monsieur, making him a heap of fat higher than Mt. Everest. Ironically, however, Monsieur dies of starvation. In the "over-the-top" exaggeration of this chapter, which thoroughly deconstructs the Momotarō folk tale, one can easily see the imprint of Rabelais. This chapter, the longest in the book at 196 pages, is its centerpiece.

The brief fourth chapter, entitled "Momoyama banashi" (a pun on *yomoyama banashi,* which means "a talk on all sorts of things"), is another comical variation of Momotarō's victory over the *oni.* But this time the focus is on the subject of fiction writing. The chapter plays on a folk belief that liars are punished for their sin by having their tongues pulled out by an *oni.* In certain respects the chapter is comparable to the "Hotaru" (Fireflies) chapter of *The Tale of Genji* (ca. 1010), in that the art of prose fiction is discussed in terms of the issue of truthfulness, of "facts" and "fabrication." And yet, our interlocutors—far from the Shining Prince and his beautiful foster daughter, Tamakazura—are a variety of *oni* with bizarre skin colors and a "greasy-skinned, dandruff-covered, gum-eyed" Ogino.[75] Every morning, after sitting up all night working, Ogino, our intratextual author-character, is visited by different *oni* and hounded for having written falsehoods. Hilarious arguments unfold between her and the *oni* on the subject of literature. One *oni,* apparently an enthusiastic supporter of the autobiographical *shishōsetsu* (the canonical modern Japanese novel), specifically insists that the foundation of literature exists in the pure and sincere disclosure of the truth and the exultation of the pathos of life. Accordingly, he "punishes" Ogino in a fantastic-comical manner for writing nothing but lies. Interestingly, each *oni* who visits Ogino accuses her of fabricating all previous conversations with the other *oni.* Thus, the narrative assumes the structure of nesting boxes with falsehood nested within other layers of falsehood, until even the lecture on the "truthful" *shishōsetsu* is folded into the fabric of lies. At the end of the chapter, Ogino, the author-character within the text, recognizes her inherent nature as a Momotarō with the almighty power to annihilate the truth-advocating *oni* and triumphantly turns off her word processor.

Chapter 5, "Berusaiyu no momo" (The peaches of Versailles), expands its setting to include Europe and delivers the thematic message of the work in clear expository terms.[76] Ogino the slow-writing author-character has been confined to a Japanese inn in Tokyo by editors who would force her to write *Tales of Peaches* more efficiently. Suddenly, she is teleported to the Bastille, where it is 1789, shortly before the French Revolution. Here she meets the jailed Marquis de Sade, who is secretly training a guerrilla team called the Regiment of Peaches to rebel against the authorities. Here readers also encounter a Kansai dialect–speaking Momotarō who has been employed as a prison guard since 1784 and has taught Sade (pronounced "Sado" in Japanese) both the Kansai dialect and the tea ceremony *(sadō).*[77]

Apparently, this Momotarō, perhaps to be construed as a personification of Einstein's principle of relativity, is able to go anywhere in the
world at any chosen moment—the past, the present, and the future.
And the most profound lesson that this ageless sage of a Momotarō
has taught Sade and now teaches our intratextual Ogino (and by extension her readership) is the importance of changing the way one
thinks *(hassō no tenkan)*. Under his tutelage, for example, Ogino learns
that jail is actually paradise because jailed men are emancipated from
their nagging wives and other troublesome family issues. Moreover,
imprisonment leads to the creation of a rich culture in that it forces
the imprisoned to transcend the smallness of their physical space
through such creative expressions as that of the tea ceremony, which
is typically in a tiny room. Momotarō also describes the French Revolution as a kind of *oni taiji*, or subjugation of the fiends, thus incorporating a major historical event into the unfolding saga of Momotarō and the *oni*. Finally, Momotarō's definition of *oni* as the shifting
object of one's hate strikes the keynote in *Peaches*:

> Suppose there are two human beings. The moment their feelings
> turn in the opposite directions, B becomes an *oni* for A, and A for
> B. The one that emerges victorious after a battle is named Momo-
> tarō. This is called the principle of relativity in regard to the [issue
> of] *oni*.[78]

The Momotarō in chapter 6, "Yonigeru momo" (The peach's night
escape), is a man born into this world with an enormous amount of
debt incurred by speculative investments while still in the womb of
his peach (a contemporary manifestation of "the original debt" introduced in chapter 1). Thus, the first step he takes after birth is to run
away from loan sharks. Obviously, this Momotarō is a personification
of the bankrupt Japanese economy in the early 1990s.[79] At the same
time, his debt-dodging flight and his repeated attempts to make money
through innovative enterprises take him to many countries, allowing the narrative to incorporate world geography and cultures in
the portrait of Momotarō as a hero-cum-loser, defying the clear-cut
dichotomy displayed in the folktale version. Momotarō's travel around
the globe in this late chapter is clearly meant to parallel the Giant
King Pantagruel's voyage in search of a holy oracle in the Fourth
Book of *Pantagruel*. Momotarō is a king, all right, but he is a King of
Debtors. He ends up in France and stumbles into a power struggle
between the liberalist scholar Persicum ("Peach Boy" in Latin) and

the oppressive Professor Onimus (*oni* + mus) of the Theology Department of the Borsonne. Onimus is a devilish power-monger who burns his opponents at the stake, a practice reminiscent of what the Theology Department of the Sorbonne did in Rabelais's time. Nevertheless, the orthodox Momotarō-*oni* dichotomy does not work here. Momotarō switches sides between the two camps many times and finally decides to work for Onimus, not for any worthy cause but simply because Onimus pays more than Persicum. Although Momotarō eventually leads Onimus's camp to victory, Onimus, becoming apprehensive of Momotarō's gaining too much power, betrays him by informing his Japanese creditors of his whereabouts. In this manner, the strife among Momotarō, Persicum, and Onimus exposes the ugly, secular nature of power struggles occurring within academic and religious institutions. *Oni* (Onimus) triumphs over Momotarō by outwitting him, completely reversing their traditional roles. This is the culmination of Ogino's deconstruction of the Momotarō tale. At the end of the chapter, Momotarō's flight from his creditors (another kind of *oni* altogether) is once again imminent, as the *Momotarō ondo* (The song of Momotarō) sounds the ultimate theme of this story: "Momo-tarō-san, Oni-tarō-san, / Yesterday's Momotarō is today's *oni*."[80]

The short final chapter, "Yokubō no nigai momo," (The bitter peach of desire), is an epilogue. As if to reinforce the book's message to readers, the chapter retraces the history of civilization in quick brushwork, summarizing the historical evolution of Momotarō's identity—after leaving the Garden of Eden, from farmer to hunter, then barterer, merchant, thief, and, finally, soldier. In this manner, *Tales of Peaches* clearly presents itself as a parody of the history of mankind, including both the conqueror and the conquered, and reveals the dubious nature of history, which represents only the view of the conqueror while suppressing that of the conquered.

As seen above, structurally Ogino's work moves from the basic to the advanced. Historically, the narrative progresses from the origin of humanity to the contemporary world. Thematically, the narrative follows the chronology of educational growth, from a child learning at his mother's knees to an adult involved in doctoral studies. In terms of literary form, the narrative successively moves from the mythological to the folk narrative, from philosophical debates about truth and falsehood to a historical tale with a science fiction flavor. *Tales of Peaches* also proudly manifests its indebtedness to Rabelais in many narrative details. To Rabelais's Pantagruel, with his servant Panurge and other merry retainers, Ogino offers Momotarō and his trio of helpers (a dog, a monkey, and a pheasant). Rabelais's flying pig is met by Ogino's flying closet *(oshiire)*. Ogino's Momotarō rivals Rabelais's Gargantua in his colossal gluttony. And Mount Osore, where the voices of the dead can be heard through the mouths of mediums, serves as Ogino's version of Epistemon's descent to Hell. To describe each of the parallels between Ogino's work and that of her literary father would require an additional chapter, if not indeed an entire book. Because the presence of lists is such an integral and interesting aspect of both works, I will here confine my discussion of rhetorical parallels to an exploration of the longest and the most important list in *Tales of Peaches*— that devoted to the peaches themselves.

Undoubtedly inspired by Rabelais, Ogino generates a list of 122 kinds of peaches.[81] Only two *(koke-momo* and *suimitsutō),* it would seem, are recognizably real terms for peaches. The rest are fictitious. In each of them, Ogino creates a new compound noun by prefixing an existing noun, an adjective stem, or a verb stem to the Chinese character that signifies the peach (which can be pronounced in Japanese as either *momo* or *tō)*. This encyclopedic list of the nouns, adjectives, and verbs thus prefixed produces a microcosmic view of human society —food, clothing, animals, plants, and human activities, as well as various stages of human life (birth, youth, maturity, old age, death) and serves Ogino's narrative in a variety of ways. First and foremost, it provides humor. Ogino's wordplays (puns, tongue twisters, and so on) are hilarious, as are her intrusive comments; and the fabricated peach names are outrageous. Second, Ogino's list, like Rabelais's, is a sarcastic portrayal of contemporary society. Ogino looks askance at Japan's diet consciousness (sweets are "to be avoided" and dairy foods "clog arteries with cholesterol") and its children's all-study-and-no-play lifestyle; the core subjects taught at primary school appear on the list, but not a single child's toy or game is mentioned. The list also mirrors Japan's economic woes in the years immediately following the collapse in 1990 of its overinflated economic "bubble." "Stocks, [promissory] notes, securities" make the list as "dangerous investments," and retailers' desperate attempts at enticing consumers with "red-tagged, half-priced, and blemished" merchandise are there as well. A Rabelaisian list of this kind is not complete without sex and scatology, of course. An overtly erotic triplet on "the color pink" (a metaphor of eroticism in Japanese), "round [lit. 'peach'] breasts," and "round [also 'peach'] derriere" succinctly expresses Japanese men's erotic fixations. "Morning erection" (sex), "an afternoon nap" (unemployment), and "flight by night" (bankruptcy) constitute Ogino's satirical summary of the life of a Japanese man in the economically strained, sex-crazed Heisei era (1989–present). And the penultimate line, consisting of "eye mucus" (*me-kuso,* lit. 'eye-shit'), "nose dirt" (*hana-kuso,* lit. 'nose-shit'), and "grime," adds a scatological touch to the list.[82]

Tales of Peaches was published with the words *wake wakaran*—a Kansai-dialect version of *wake no wakaranai* (incomprehensible), a word reminiscent of La Bruyère's criticism of Rabelais—emblazoned in large print across its promotional wrapper-band on the cover. Unfortunately, the self-prediction seems to have been fulfilled, as Ogino's tour de force was largely disregarded by critics. The book garnered no written reviews, probably because it was difficult to appreciate as a whole, just as was Rabelais's *Gargantua and Pantagruel.* Another possible and paradoxical reason would be that Ogino Anna, the scholar, attached her own erudite explication of the basic schemata of the text at the end of the book.[83] She thus performed the role of critic herself by commenting on such matters as her use of Sakaguchi's narrative farce, her reasons for selecting Momotarō as her hero, and her interpretation of the main theme of the work. Although it was nominated for the Women's Literature Prize (*Joryū bungaku shō*) in November 1994, it lost the prize to Matsuura Rieko's *Oyayubi P no shugyō jidai* (The Big Toe P's years of apprenticeship, 1994) and received no comments from the judges at all.[84] Ironically, it was a fair success commercially, selling approximately 12,000 copies.

Conclusion

Tales of Peaches, a Gargantuan fiction, and *An Embarkation on Rabelais,* a scintillating study of *Gargantua and Pantagruel,* both published in 1994—the reputed five hundredth anniversary of Rabelais's birth—stand as tributes to this literary father.[85] In this context, the photograph of Ogino and the pig, appearing as it does at the end of *Peaches,* yields yet another symbolic meaning: it is Ogino's salutation to Rabelais. On one hand, it signals that Rabelais's literary heritage (his "pig") is alive and well in his daughter's tender care, and on the other, the photograph serves as a proud report on what this literary daughter has just accomplished *(Tales of Peaches)* in the father's tradition. Although *Tales of Peaches* earned the author no literary prize, the robust scholarship demonstrated in *An Embarkation on Rabelais* won Ogino the position of associate professor of the French Renaissance in the Department of French Literature at Keiō University in 1995.

As Rabelais's literary daughter, Ogino has contributed to modern Japanese literature in various ways. First, her radical reformism seeks to overturn the conventions of the novel and demonstrates that powerful works of fiction can emerge without adhering to these conventions. Second, Ogino's many hybrid creations, such as fiction-critique and narrative farce, have opened up new possibilities in Japanese literature. Underlying these activities to transcend the limitations of the novel is Ogino's concern over the modern novel's narcissism, its self-absorption, as manifest in the proliferation of metafiction (fiction about fiction) in the latter half of the twentieth century. She regards metafiction as a terminal stage in the novel's evolution and believes that it leads only to self-starvation and the novel's extinction (if it has not met its "death" already).

Not surprisingly, Ogino's concerns are packaged with humor. In the forty-fifth segment of *Tales of Peaches,* for example, which she titled "Tobi-buta" (A flying pig), she describes how in the beginning there were rainbow-colored flying pigs with superb language abilities who were wise enough to teach Minerva, the Greek goddess of wisdom (it should be recalled that the flight of one of their descendants was described in Rabelais's book), but at the last stage of their evolution they emerged as "metapigs" and became extinct in just one generation because they were too busy trying to define "What is a pig?" to procreate.[86] In this line of logic, the only way prose fiction might avoid a similar course of self-destruction would be to maintain its direct contact with "first-order" languages—that is, the everyday, ordinary languages that precede the construction of specialized "meta-languages."[87] In my view, what Ogino has attempted to do in *Peaches* (and many of her other works) is to rejuvenate literature, to imbue it with fresh life, by absorbing enormous amounts of lively first-order languages as they are spoken and used by people of all walks of life—from juvenile gang leaders to mothers and children, from tour guides to psychotherapists and magazine reporters, from Osaka merchants to the cabaret hostesses of northeastern Japan. We find the jargon of pop culture, advertising, and law, as well as proverbs, mythology, *rakugo, manzai* (comical dialogues performed by two comedians), and restaurant menus. Inspired by Rabelais, she has created a late-twentieth-century Japanese version of a carnivalesque festival of languages and, in so doing, has offered prose fiction a new lease on life. In this sense, Ogino's contribution to modern Japanese prose fiction is comparable to that of Walt Whitman (1819–1892) to American poetry and that of Tawara Machi (b. 1962) to modern Japanese *tanka* poetry.

One of Ogino's more important contributions to Japanese literature has been her rare comic spirit. Joel Cohn, in *Studies in the Comic Spirit in Modern Japanese Fiction,* acknowledges Natsume Sōseki (1867–1916), Uno Kōji (1891–1961), Tanizaki Jun'ichirō (1886–1965), Maruya Saiichi (b. 1925), Tsutsui Yasutaka (b. 1934), and Wada Makoto (b. 1936) as comic writers, in addition to highlighting Ibuse Masuji, Dazai Osamu, and Inoue Hisashi. No doubt because of the time lag between the writing and the publication of his book, Cohn makes no mention of more recent works by female writers such as Ogino's *Tales of Peaches* or *Nihyakkaiki* (The two hundredth memorial service, 1994), by Shōno Yoriko (b. 1956). Referring to Inoue's seeming retreat from the comic front in his recent fiction, Cohn suggests "the disconcerting possibility that the rising curve [of comic literature] has already reached its peak, and that the works under discussion in [his book] constitute a climactic moment rather than a stage in the development of something larger."[88] I would offer Ogino Anna as a challenge to this assumption. It is now clear that the climactic moment did not pass with Inoue. Rather, comedy is alive and well and cradled comfortably in Ogino Anna's arms. Her large-scale humor, including the kind openly made on scatology or procreation (though her expressions steer clear of being erotic or lewd), is the most prominent characteristic of Ogino as Rabelais's literary daughter. Her spirit can be seen nowhere else in the history of Japanese literature than in the primordial laughter of the "eight-hundred myriad deities" recorded in the ancient myths of the *Kojiki* (712), a type of large laughter that transcends the dichotomy between the sacred and the culturally created preconceptions of vulgarity and obscenity.[89]

Finally, there is Ogino's indisputable "uniqueness." Maruya Saiichi has defined Japanese literature as *"ren'ai chūshin"* (love-centered).[90] But Ogino clearly does not conform to this paradigm in her decision to eschew realistic portrayals of romance or entangled emotional issues related to man-woman relationships.[91] This is Ogino's distinct literary heritage from Rabelais and renders her particularly unique as a Japanese (woman) writer. In choosing not to deal with this most prominent theme of Japanese literature in the traditional (tearful, confessional, tormented) manner, Ogino cultivates subject areas for literature beyond domesticity. What Ogino treasures most is clearly the Rabelaisian capacity to laugh despite the harsh reality of the world. That is the kind of laughter that she thinks is "the most necessary thing for us today," and that is the kind of mirth that she tries to create in her texts.[92]

Ogino's fiction-critique piece "Kobayashi Hideo de gozaimasu: Minami Haruo to iu koto" (I am Kobayashi Hideo: the being of Minami Haruo, 1993) contains the following lyric for an *ondo* (folk song). It reflects Kobayashi Hideo's philosophical stance toward his life and literature, but I think that it can very well double as Ogino Anna's theme song as a writer. "Tsurezure ondo" (Song of idleness) is its title—obviously a parody of the famous opening lines of "Tsurezuregusa" (ca. 1330; trans. Sansom, "Essays in idleness," 1967), by Yoshida Kenkō (ca. 1283–ca. 1352)—and it is to be sung merrily à la Minami Haruo, Japan's popular *enka* ballad singer:

> Let's write to while away the idle hours, seated before
>   the inkslab,
> (*Chorus:* Yes, Let's!)
> By jotting down without order or purpose whatever tri-
>   fling thoughts occur,
> Verily this is a pleasurable thing to do![93]
> . . . .
> Coupling begets grudges and reproaches,
> That kind of life is no longer tolerable.
> If I imitate a fool, I am a fool. Imitate a wise man and
>   get wise.
> Haaaaa, an idle, idle, idle song (*Tsurezure tsurezure tsure-
>   zure ondo).*[94]

And so, imitating a wise man, Ogino goes on writing funny tales of wisdom and wise tales of nonsense. Seemingly a respectful and dutiful daughter of Rabelais, she has mined her adoptive father's works to storm the fortress of defensive self-absorption behind the walls of which the modern novel has sheltered itself. No mean Momotarō-cum-*oni* herself, she has given the flagging genre a new energy and spirit, another "hundred" leases on life.

Notes

An earlier version of this paper entitled "Ango, Rakugo, Rabelais: Ogino Anna's Literary Heritage" was presented at the literary workshop "(Un)Dutiful Daughters: Modern Japanese Female Writers and Their Cultural Fathers," sponsored by the Edwin O. Reischauer Institute and held at Harvard University on 4 May 1996.

No English translation of any of Ogino Anna's works has been published to date. All the English translations of the titles of her publications and of the passages cited from her works are mine. I am deeply obliged to Ms. Ogino Anna for answering my questions and providing me with bibliographical information not easily accessible. I am responsible, however, for any mistakes that might remain.

My biographical portrayal of Ogino Anna's family has been constructed mostly from my records of several telephone conversations with Ogino Anna and her mother, Emi Kinuko, in the past years, as well as a two-hour personal interview with the author conducted in Tokyo on 30 July 1996. They have my sincere appreciation of their cooperation and support for this project. Ogino Anna's recent biographical writing on her father, *Horafuki Anri no bōken* (The adventures of Henri the Braggart), serialized in *Bungakukai* for two years (1997–1999), presented additional information. I have also referred to the chronology *(ryaku nenpu)* of Ogino Anna prepared by Odaira Maiko.

I am grateful for Professor Rebecca Copeland's guidance and encouragement, without which this essay would not have been completed. My heartfelt thanks go to Mr. Gary Bottone and Ms. Anita Axt of San Francisco State University and Professor Chiyuki Kumakura of Kinjō Gakuin University for furnishing me with excellent suggestions for the essay. I also acknowledge the help of my father, Tomosaburō Niwa, a retired professor of Chinese history living in Japan, who did library research for me on several topics about which information was difficult to gather in the United States.

1. Serialized monthly from April 1993 to March 1994 in various Japanese newspapers; revised and published as a book in 1995.

2. Ogino, *Anna no kōjō kankō,* p. 271.

3. Oginome Yōko (b. 1968) became a very popular singer in the mid-1980s, winning the 1986 Japan Gold Disk Grand Prize, the 1986 Japan Popular Song Grand Prize, and the Japan Record Grand Prize for four successive years, 1986–1989. She also became a successful actress in the early 1990s. Oginome Keiko (b. 1964) debuted as an actress when she was a teenager and, after a hiatus, resumed her acting career in 1983. She became popular in the late 1980s and the early 1990s.

4. Ogino, *Anna no kōjō kankō,* p. 270. The effect of this parody is perhaps intended to be self-humbling and humorous as well as blasphemous. In Japanese, *"ton"* (pig) functions as a self-derogatory adjectival prefix when attached to the noun *"ji"* (child). "Ton-ji" (lit. "pig-child") therefore means "my stupid child" and is used in self-deprecating courtesy to refer exclusively to one's own child when addressing an outsider. After the picture was taken, Ogino jokingly called herself a *ton-bo.* Her neologism plays on its denotation (a pig mother)

and connotation (a stupid mother) simultaneously, meaning "a stupid mother of a pig."

5. The phrase "grammar of modern Japanese literature" appears in Odaira, "Ogino Anna," *Kokubungaku,* p. 42.

6. For Bakhtin's concepts of "carnival" and "carnivalization," see his *Rabelais and His World,* 1965. For a brief summary of the concepts, see Fowler, *Dictionary,* pp. 59–60.

7. Ogino took her appellation of *"kotoba no desutoroiyā"* from an American professional wrestler, "the Destroyer," who was popular in Japan. See Odaira Maiko, "Sakka gaido," p. 446, for further reference to this appellation.

8. Ogino, *Momo monogatari,* p. 67.

9. Ogino, *Hanshi hanshō.*

10. Ogino, *Shūkan Ogino,* p. 79.

11. Ogino, *Anna-ryū,* p. 124.

12. Ibid., pp. 124–125.

13. Ibid., p. 125.

14. François Rabelais, *Histories,* p. 578.

15. In 1999, Ogino published *Sora-tobu buta* (A flying pig), a photo album introducing her famous Rabelais-inspired pig-artifact collection. Moreover, she takes pleasure in drawing a pig when autographing her books, identifying herself with the creature.

16. Ogino, *Shūkan Ogino,* p. 159. The title of the essay is also a take-off from the popular phrase *"tonderu onna,"* or a successful career woman "soaring high in the sky," in a realm beyond domesticity.

17. Ibid.

18. No writer has a single literary precursor. Ogino has been the recipient of many influences, and a true list of her "literary fathers" would be daunting. A tentative list might include *rakugo* master Kokontei Shinshō V (1890–1973); novelist Sakaguchi Ango (1906–1955); Russian philosopher and literary critic Mihkail Bakhtin (1895–1975); Matsubara Shūji (b. 1930), professor emeritus of French medieval philology at Keiō University, Ogino's alma mater; Yōrō Takeshi (b. 1937), professor emeritus of anatomy at Tokyo University; literary critic Kobayashi Hideo (1902–1983); *enka* (ballad) singer Minami Haruo (b. 1923); and a host of literary giants such as Aristophanes (ca. 445–ca. 385 B.C.), Giovanni Boccaccio (1313–1375), François Villon (1431–ca. 1463), Desiderius Erasmus (ca. 1466–1536), Michel Eyquem de Montaigne (1533–1592), Miguel de Cervantes (1547–1616), Jonathan Swift (1667–1745), the Marquis de Sade (1740–1814), Franz Kafka (1883–1924), and James Joyce (1882–1941). The list could be extended to include Ogino's various Japanese editors, and so on. But of all those who have influenced her, none has been as instrumental as François Rabelais.

19. See her personal essay entitled (in pidgin Japanese) "Nihongo mutsukashi desu ne."

20. Dialogue and the dialogic process are central to Bakhtin's cultural, philosophical, linguistic, and literary theories presented in his works such as (in English translations) *The Dialogic Imagination* and *Problems of Dostoevsky's Poetics.* For succinct summaries of Bakhtin's concepts of dialogism and monologism, I

quote the following two passages: the first by Michael Holquist, and the second by Bakhtin. "A word, discourse, language or culture undergoes dialogization when it becomes relativized, de-privileged, aware of competing definitions for the same things" (from the glossary in Bakhtin, *Dialogic Imagination,* p. 427). "Monologism, at its extreme, denies the existence outside itself of another consciousness, with equal rights and equal responsibilities, another *I* with equal rights *(thou)*. . . . Monologue is finalized and deaf to the other's response, does not expect it and does not acknowledge in it any *decisive* force" (Bakhtin, "Toward a Reworking of the Dostoevsky Book," pp. 292–293).

21. Marianna Gaillard left for California partly because she did not like the climate of France but also because she wanted to free herself from the control of her mother's elder sister, with whom she had lived for economic reasons since her husband's death.

22. Interview with Ogino Anna, 30 July 1996.

23. Ogino Anna reported that Henri Gaillard's retirement year was 1976 (ibid.), but her father corrected it to 1975 (telephone conversation with Anna, 6 September 1999).

24. *Rakugo* is a popular form of comic monologue in which a storyteller creates an imaginary drama through episodic narration and skillful use of vocal and facial expressions to portray various characters. Its roots extend back at least to Buddhist preaching of the sixth century. Both the traditional art of humorous storytelling and the narrated story are called *rakugo*. Radio broadcasts of *rakugo* began soon after Tokyo Broadcasting Station (precursor to NHK) started its AM broadcast in March 1925. Anna's mother was a fan of the renowned *rakugo* master, Kokontei Shinshō V, whose art was considered unsurpassable. For more information on *rakugo*, see *Japan: An Illustrated Encyclopedia* as well as the study by Morioka and Sasaki.

25. Ogino, *Anna-ryū,* p. 26. *Rakugo* humor is not of one kind. For explanations of various kinds of humor in *rakugo*, see ibid., pp. 27–29, and Morioka and Sasaki, *Rakugo,* pp. 69–156.

26. Odaira, "Ryaku nenpu," p. 448.

27. Anna stood out at her high school. One of her classmates attests that Ferris students were convinced that if someone among them should became famous, that person would be Ogino Anna.

28. Tatsumi, in "Ogino Anna: yaminabe gengo no uwaki musume" (Ogino Anna: A fickle girl of hodgepodge-casserole language), mentions that in 1983 Ogino Anna, while pursuing her graduate studies at Keiō University, published in a book titled *Yojigen-han* (The fourth-and-a-half dimension) *contes* (short narratives) for cartoons by others that won the Yomiuri International Cartoon Award). The copyright page of the publication credits "Anna-chan" (Miss Anna). Tatsumi's article reveals that Ogino had developed her characteristic style that freely combines a miscellany of vernaculars before her formal debut as a writer in 1987.

29. Telephone conversation with Emi Kinuko, 16 December 1996.

30. Another twenty years would pass before Ogino Anna sat down with her father to listen to him and take notes of his incredible stories of adventures. She published her father's biography, "Horafuki Anri no bōken," in *Bungakukai* in

1997–1999. An abridged book version, *Horafuki Anri no bōken,* is forthcoming (Bunge shunjū, 2001).

31. For a cogent summary of (the paucity of) Japanese critical discourse on modern Japanese comic literature, including the theories presented by Natsume Sōseki, Yanagita Kunio, Nakamaura Mitsuo, see Cohn, *Studies,* pp. 9–11.

32. Ibid., pp. 186–187.

33. Ibid., p. 187.

34. During the "Junbungaku henshitsu ronsō" (Debate on the transformation of pure literature) in the early 1960s, Hirano Ken characterized "pure literature" *(junbungaku)* as *shishōsetsu* and considered the "actuality" of literature as the central notion of "pure literature." Hirano's view served to consolidate the privileging of the "factual" over the "fabricated" mode of literature, as well as to harden the dichotomy between what he regarded as pure literature and the mass-media–driven popular literature *(taishū bungaku).* Comic and parodic literatures, under Hirano's definition, do not fit in the "pure literature" (Hirano, "Saisetsu"). For a critical view of such dichotomous approaches to modern Japanese literature, see Suzuki, "Junbungaku." See also Ariga, "Text versus Commentary," p. 374, for a discussion of the dichotomy between the "pure literature" and the "popular literature" in Japanese literature.

35. Ogino, *Anna-ryū,* p. 26.

36. After learning of Asada's pronouncement in an interview with Ogino Anna on 30 July 1996, I called the critic for confirmation. He admitted using this phrase to characterize Ogino's work but could not recall when or where he had done so.

37. Ogino, *Anna-ryū,* p. 90.

38. Rabelais, *Histories.* p. 40.

39. Ogino, *Anna-ryū,* p. 91. Ogino's reading of the episode as an "upside-down world" is not unique in that she was almost certainly inspired by Mikhail Bakhtin's interpretation, as presented in "Images of the Material Bodily Lower Stratum" in his *Tvorchestvo Fransua Rable* (1965), the Japanese translation of which (1973) she read avidly in college (see Bakhtin, *Furansowa Raburē).* Even after she successfully weaned herself from her earlier absolute acceptance of Bakhtin's theory on Rabelais, the chapter in which Bakhtin closely analyzes the episode remained her favorite.

40. Bakhtin, *Rabelais,* p. 380.

41. "Warau Bosshu," published in 1991 in *Shinchō* and her book *Buryūgeru tonda* (Brueghel flew), is a fantasy amalgamating art criticism and fiction. In it, Ogino deconstructs many dichotomies (such as human-nonhuman, reality-dream, standard Japanese–dialects, high culture–low culture, etc.), but most prominently the male-female binarism. *Hanshi hanshō* thematizes the transgression of boundary between life and death.

42. In *Rabelais and His World,* Bakhtin mentions that such imageries are "inherent in all forms of popular-festive merriment and grotesque realism" (p. 370) and that "the swab is a traditional humorous theme of debasement" in world literature (p. 379).

43. Ogino, *Raburē shuppan,* p. 14.

44. Bakhtin, *Rabelais,* pp. 380–381.

45. See Aoyama, "Love That Poisons," on contemporary Japanese parody.

46. A partial display of this knowledge is found in her article, "Retorikku to shite no parodī; shijō no rakuen" (Parody as rhetoric: the paradise on paper), in *Parodī no seiki* (The century of parody, 1997).

47. Ogino received the Keiō University Award (Keiō Gijuku-shō) in November 1989 for her published dissertation. Rabelais died in 1553, one year after the publication of the Fourth Book. The authenticity of the Fifth Book, published in 1564, has not been established. For this reason, Ogino does not discuss the Fifth Book in her publications on Rabelais.

48. Rabelais, *Histories,* p. 300; Ogino, *Raburē shuppan,* p. 96.

49. Ogino, *Raburē shuppan,* p. 96.

50. Rabelais, *Histories,* p. 175.

51. Ogino, *Raburē shuppan,* pp. 56–57. One could add to Ogino's list the following constituent elements as well: human beings (preachers and bishop), a person's name (Turlupin), a human body part (testicle), human activities both intellectual and physical (to "compose" and other intellectual activities implied by the names of academic disciplines as well as sexual acts and production of artifacts), artifacts of human activities (decretals, slipper, threadball, etc.), and abstract concepts (salvation, long, variant).

52. Ibid., p. 60.

53. *Monozukushi* appear in *jōruri* (puppet theater) texts, noh plays, *nagauta* (songs for separate performance or *kabuki*) texts, *sōkyoku* (songs with *koto* accompaniment) pieces, as well as in the late Heian *imayō* (popular songs), such as those collected in the *Ryōjin hishō* (Songs to make the dust to dance on the beams, ca. 1169). Some regard Sei Shōnagon's lists (of "beautiful things," etc.) in *Makura no sōshi* (The pillow book) as *monozukushi.* I would like to express my gratitude to Professors Tom Hare, Robert Khan, Richard Bowring, Yoshiko Samuel, and Roger Thomas for generously sharing their knowledge of *monozukushi* with me. Gary Bottone brought my attention to the list of first names in Nabokov's *Lolita,* p. 51–52. All of these lists of existing items are fundamentally different from Rabelais's lists of fabricated or rhetorically welded items.

54. La Bruyère, *Characters,* p. 11. Ogino Anna quotes a slightly shorter passage in Japanese in *Raburē shuppan,* pp. 7, 9.

55. It should be noted that when Rabelais was alive, the Department of Theology at the Sorbonne banned his works for blasphemy. When Rabelais died, Pierre de Ronsard wrote a poem titled "Epitafe de François Rabelais" (1554), portraying Rabelais as a drunkard, apparently projecting the fictional characters' deeds onto Rabelais himself and reducing the theme of his works to Dionysian merrymaking (Ronsard, *Poems,* pp. 44–47). And Voltaire "had no stomach for Rabelais' obscenities and criticized them severely" (Torrey, *Spirit of Voltaire,* p. 32). In the opening line of *Tvorchestvo Fransua Rable,* Bakhtin deplored the general perception of Rabelais: "Of all great writers of world literature, Rabelais is the least popular, the least understood and appreciated" (*Rabelais,* p. 1). Creativity during Rabelais's lifetime was fraught with danger. Étienne Dolet (1509–1546), a humanist and free thinker who incurred the displeasure of the authorities, was condemned to the stake in the same year that Rabelais's Third Book was published. Under increasingly dangerous circumstances, Rabelais dared to

publish his Third and Fourth Books under his true name. I would like to thank my colleague Anita Axt, lecturer of French at San Francisco State University, for information regarding La Bruyère and his works and for information on Dolet. See also Ogino, *Raburē shuppan,* p. 6.

56. Ogino, *Raburē shuppan,* p. 15.

57. Ibid., p. 17.

58. Ibid., p. 131.

59. Ibid., pp. 132, 134.

60. Ibid., p. 136.

61. *Joshu* is the entry-level postdoctoral academic position for an in-house candidate, which, with appropriate scholarly accomplishments, eventually leads to a professorship. This first opportunity for Ogino to publish her work in a leading literary magazine presented itself through her mother's connection. An editor of the magazine visited Emi Kinuko to pick up the book cover designed by her for *Himatsuri.* Anna served him a cup of tea. Discovering her literary talent through an informal conversation, the editor asked her to write a short review of the book.

62. "Uchino okan ga ocha o nomu" appeared in the June 1989 issue of *Bungakukai;* "Doa o shimeruna" and "Supein no shiro" were published in the December 1989 and the June 1990 issues of *Bungakukai,* respectively.

63. My translation of the title as "A Lease on the Life of Love" represents not a literal translation of the unusual Japanese word *"seoimizu"* but a translation of the possible symbolic meaning of the title. "Seomizu" is derived from a certain legend that an individual was born with all the water he would need for a life-time hoisted on his back in an invisible container. Thus, the more literal translation would be "shouldering life's store of water." Kasai Kiyoshi's interpretation of the symbolic meaning of *"seoimizu"* is different. He says, "*Seoimizu* can be construed as being symbolic of the amount of the effort and perseverance with which a woman plays the role of a mother that is imposed on her, rather than the amount of her love or perseverance she has for a man" (quoted in Kanai Keiko, p. 47; my translation from Japanese). I do not see the female main character playing the role of a mother at all, either for her male lover or for her father (after his divorce from his wife). The text emphasizes her similarity to her lover, not their gender difference. I interpret the word as symbolizing a lease of love in a more general sense, which applies to other human relationships depicted in the work as well. Anna's essay "Seoimizu no haha" (The mother of "Seoimizu") explains how a colleague's casual remark—"I ran out of my *seoi-*truffles" (by which she meant that she ate so many truffles, a life's share of them, that she does not want any more of them)—taught her the meaning of this unusual word and inspired her to write a story (Ogino, *Anna-ryū,* p. 141).

64. "Yūkitai" is Ogino's playful neologism containing two puns. It is a play on a legitimate Japanese word, *yūkitai* (organism, or organic body). Ogino created her own homonym of this word by replacing its first Chinese character *yū,* which by itself means "to exist" or "to possess," with another character, which signifies "to play." In addition, she took advantage of the fact that the third syllable *tai* ("body") is also a homonym of an auxiliary verb that denotes one's desire (to do something). Hence, the title can be translated "Wanna-Play-Organism."

65. Even these early stories attest to Ogino's flexibility and resourcefulness as a storyteller; they are distinct stories written in different prose styles that use varied narrative modes, an analysis of which shall be my project in a separate study.

66. Sakaguchi Ango perhaps comes closest of all to a Japanese literary father for Ogino. She engaged in an intensive study of Sakaguchi at the outset of her career, which resulted in a book entitled *Ai rabu Ango* (I love Ango, 1992). Despite her love for Sakaguchi's writing, Ogino ultimately sees his literary vision as unfulfilled. In an essay entitled "Katayoku no pegasasu: Ango o meguru gesakuteki shihyōron no kokoromi" (One-winged Pegasus: an essay of playful, informal critique on Sakaguchi Ango), Ogino likens him to a one-winged Pegasus, a creature who has the desire to fly but lacks the resources. She argues that Sakaguchi's unorthodox, yet inspired concept of farces as an all-affirming literary ideal could have led him to the heights attained by Rabelais, Swift, Joyce, and other literary masters, had he possessed the uncompromising objectivity of a satirist, had he been capable of laughter as large as Rabelais's, and had he not obstinately clung to the idea of expressing his vision through the confining form of a novel. She sees Sakaguchi with the penetrating eye of a critic trained in European literature and yet with the warm compassion excited by her understanding of him as a fallen comrade, so to speak, who shares a literary vision akin to hers but has failed to give suitable expression to it. For Ogino, Sakaguchi remains a Japanese might-have-been-Rabelais. See Ogino, *Ai rabu Ango,* pp. 76–82. For Sakaguchi's notion of farce, see his essay "FARCE ni tsuite."

67. Note that the French word *histoire* means both "history" and "narrative." Ogino parodies both in *Momo monogatari.*

68. Ogino, *Momo monogatari,* p. 440.

69. *Momo monogatari*'s main theme, "the relativity of truth," is a concept that Ogino Anna speaks of often, and it appears in her writing as early as in her 1988 essay "Katayoku no pegasasu": "'The principle of the relativity of truth,' or the understanding that the truth seen from one side always contains a falsehood seen from another side, is a common sense of literature and its starting point or home. But is there any literature around us that is built according to such a 'theory'?" (Ogino, *Ai rabu Ango,* p. 64). Surveying modern Japanese literature, she identifies Sakaguchi Ango and Kobayashi Hideo as the "two great intellectuals" who were conscious of the issue. *Momo monogatari* is her attempt to express the theme in a form proposed by Sakaguchi but unattempted by either Sakaguchi or Kobayashi (and nobody else in Japan): a narrative farce.

70. Ogino, *Momo monogatari,* p. 442.

71. Ibid., p. 12.

72. The title of chapter 2 is an amalgamation of the first half of a proverb, "Momo kuri sannen kaki hachinen" (Peach and chestnut trees bear fruits in three years, and persimmon in eight) and the latter half of a phrase "Fuku wa uchi, oni wa soto" (Fortune in! Devils out!) that is shouted at the time of bean throwing, an exorcism or purification rite performed at *setsubun,* which marks the change of seasons from winter to spring. This semantically incongruous title reflects the nature of the chapter, which consists of two different segments: a tale of a mother and her children (the mother nurtures her children's mind with her narratives just as those who plant peach and chestnut trees nurture

them, looking forward to their bearing fruits) and a tale of psychotherapy (a kind of exorcism).

73. By leaving deleted words "under erasure" *(sous rature)* in his texts, Jacques Derrida signals both the inadequacy (for his purpose) and the indispensability of them.

74. Ogino, *Momo monogatari,* p. 56.

75. Ibid., p. 290.

76. The title of this chapter is a play on the title of a comic for girls called *Berusaiyu no bara* (The roses of Versailles), by Ikeda Riyoko, serialized in *Shūkan Māgaretto* (Weekly Margaret) from spring 1972 to fall 1973. A ten-volume book version of the comic was also published, one volume at a time, between 1972 and 1974. The work is based on Stefan Zweig's *Marie Antoinette* (1932). The enormous popularity of Ikeda's comic created a flowering of "Berubara" cultures, including successful musical performances by Takarazuka (Girls') Operetta Troupe and a TV drama.

77. Although born and raised in Yokohama, Ogino was intimately familiar with the Kansai dialect, because it is what her mother and grandmother spoke at home. More specifically, they spoke Banshū dialect, which was what was spoken in the area of Hyogo Prefecture, where they had been born.

78. Ogino, *Momo monogatari,* p. 333.

79. Japanese stocks, which reached the peak in December 1989, began a rapid fall thereafter. It is generally thought that the "bubble" of Japanese economy collapsed in the first half of 1990, around March.

80. Ogino, *Momo monogatari,* p. 424. Ogino often expresses the theme of her work at a climactic moment and in the form of an *ondo,* or traditional Japanese folk dance music. For example, in "Warau Bosshu" she expresses her main theme in an *ondo.* She did the same with the theme of "Kobayashi Hideo de gozaimasu," one of her fiction-critique pieces. Perhaps her love of folk culture is another Rabelaisian legacy.

81. Ibid., pp. 341–342.

82. This long list of peaches also functions as a condensed table of contents of *Tales of Peaches,* because every word prefixed to the noun "peach" appears elsewhere in the book.

83. Ibid., pp. 438–443.

84. See "Heisei roku-nendo," in which the winner of the literary prize was announced with the judges' comments. Although all other four nominated works, including Matsuura Rieko's winning piece, received judges' comments, Ogino's *Momo monogatari* elicited none.

85. Rabelais's year of birth has not yet been established by scholars. From various studies, two promising dates have emerged: 1483 and 1494. See Ogino, *Raburē shuppan,* p. 3.

86. Ogino, *Momo monogatari,* pp. 186–189.

87. Ogino's view on metafiction echoes Roland Barthes's remarks made on metalanguage (language about language; also called a second-order language that interprets and explains a first-order language). In his book *Éléments de Sémiologie* (Elements of semiology, 1964; trans. 1967), Barthes mentions that the history of the social sciences could be construed as "a diachrony of metalan-

guages, and each science . . . would contain the seeds of its own death, in the shape of the language destined to speak it" (p. 93). J. A. Cuddon interprets Barthes's words as indicating that the chain reaction of a metalanguage creating an even higher order of metalanguage, which is yet farther removed from a first-order language, "could lead to an indefinite regression or *aporia*, which would ultimately undermine and destroy all metalanguages" (*Penguin Dictionary*, p. 506).

88. Cohn, *Studies*, p. 203.

89. Japan's tradition of humor goes as far back as the nation's creation myth, recorded in its oldest extant book, *Kojiki* (712). The myth has it that when the sun goddess Amaterasu, terrified at the destruction and violence committed by her younger brother, secluded herself behind the heavenly rock-door and refused to emerge, a goddess called Uzume performed a vivacious dance, exposing her breasts and private parts. The laughter of the congregated "eight-hundred myriad deities" at this dance enticed Amaterasu out of her hiding place, thus ending the prolonged night. In this episode, laughter is closely tied to the themes of renewal of life and reproduction. The exposure of female genitals, a symbol of fertility, was a magic rite to invigorate a declining life force ("Kojiki," in *Kojiki, jōdai kayō*, p. 83, n. 14), and it is believed that the basic motif of this myth reflects religious rituals performed around the winter solstice to regenerate the diminished power of the sun and, by extension, of the emperor (ibid., p. 81, note). To be short, what might be regarded in modern society as an extremely obscene (and even criminal) act of exposing one's genitalia in public had one of the most sacred religious purposes. This also reminds us that in the Japanese creation myth, scatology and cosmology go hand in hand; gods are born from excrement, vomit, and decaying corpses, as well as myriad other things. Thus, the country's first laughter was a large-scale laughter (of eight million gods) born in the realm untouched by the dichotomy of the sacred and the vulgar as we know it today. The distinction was to develop in the subsequent cultural history of the country. I believe that this primordial laughter is Japan's closest kin to what Ogino Anna calls "the large-scale laughter of Rabelais," in which, as Bakhtin mentioned, the theme of rebirth constantly emerges from Rabelais's uninhibited treatment of what his critics regarded as the most "vulgar" and "obscene" materials. Or rather, the *Kojiki*'s mythical world is a realm even prior to Rabelais's laughter. Ogino's systematic, gay incorporation of the "vulgar" and the "obscene" (learned from Rabelais) makes it possible for her to recapture in her literature the vigor of a lost primordial world such as that in *Kojiki*. Translated as *Kojiki*, 1968; *Kojiki*, 1976 [1952]; and *The Kojiki: Records of Ancient Matters*, 1981.

90. Maruya, "Long interview," p. 127.

91. A notable exception is her Akutagawa Prize–winning "Seoimizu," which deals with a waning love relationship. Ogino says that "Seoimizu" is not her type of writing (telephone conversation with Ogino, 24 April 2000).

92. Ogino, *Raburē shuppan*, p. 3.

93. In translating the song from Japanese to English, I borrowed phrases from "Essays in Idleness," trans. Sansom, p. 231.

94. Ogino, *Madonna no henshin shikkaku*, pp. 43–44. I have removed some lines from the original to keep the quotation short.

Works Cited

Location of Japanese publishers is Tokyo unless otherwise noted.

Aoyama, Tomoko. "The Love That Poisons: Japanese Parody and the New Literacy." *Japan Forum* 6.1 (April 1994): 35–46.

Ariga, Chieko. "Text versus Commentary." In *The Woman's Hand: Gender and Theory in Japanese Women's Writing*, ed. Paul Gordon and Janet A. Walker, pp. 352–381. Stanford, Calif.: Stanford University Press, 1996.

Bakhtin, Mikhail. *The Dialogic Imagination: Four Essays.* Ed. Michael Holquist. Trans. Caryl Emerson and Michael Holquist. Austin: University of Texas Press, 1981.

———. *Furansowa Raburē no sakuhin to chūsei runessansu no minshūbunka.* Trans. Kawabata Kaori. Serika shobō, 1973. Originally published as *Tvorchestvo Fransua Rable* (Moscow: Khudozhestvnnia literatua, 1965).

———. *Problems of Dostoevsky's Poetics.* Ed. and trans. Caryl Emerson. Vol. 8 of *Theory and History of Literature.* Minneapolis: University of Minnesota Press, 1984. Originally published as *Problemy poetiki Dostoevskogo* (Moscow, 1963).

———. *Rabelais and His World.* Trans. Hélène Iswolsky. Bloomington: Indiana University Press, 1984. Originally published as *Tvorchestvo Fransua Rable* (Moscow: Khudozhestvnnia literatua, 1965).

———. "Toward a Reworking of the Dostoevsky Book." Appendix 2 of *Problems of Dostoevsky's Poetics,* vol. 8 of *Theory and History of Literature,* ed. and trans. Caryl Emerson, pp. 283–302. Minneapolis: University of Minnesota Press, 1984. Originally published as *Problemy poetiki Dostoevskogo* (Moscow, 1963).

Barthes, Roland. *Elements of Semiology.* Trans. Annette Lavers and Colin Smith. New York: Hill and Wang, 1967. Originally published as *Éléments de Sémiologie* (Paris: Seuil, 1964).

Cohn, Joel R. *Studies in the Comic Spirit in Modern Japanese Fiction.* Harvard-Yenching Institute Monograph Series 41. Cambridge: Harvard University Asia Center and Harvard University Press, 1998.

Cuddon, J. A. *The Penguin Dictionary of Literary Terms and Literary Theory.* 4th ed. Rev. C. E. Preston. London: Penguin Books, 1999.

Fowler, Roger, ed. *A Dictionary of Modern Critical Terms.* Rev. and enlarged ed. London: Routledge and Kegan Paul, 1987.

"Heisei roku-nendo joryū bungakushō happyō." *Fujin kōron* (November 1994): 340–343.

Hirano Ken. "Saisetsu: Junbungaku henshitsu," *Gunzō* 17.3 (March 1962): 154–163.

Ikeda Riyoko. "Berusaiyu no bara." Serialized in *Shūkan Māgaretto* (Spring 1972–Fall 1973).

———. *Berusaiyu no bara.* Margaret Comics. 10 vols. Shūeisha, 1972–1974.

Japan: An Illustrated Encyclopedia. 2 vols. Kōdansha, 1993.

Kanai Keiko. "Ogino Anna: *Seoimizu.*" *Kokubungaku: kaishaku to kyōzai no kenkyū* 37.11 (September 1992): 46–47.

Kasai Kiyoshi. "Haha to musuko shika inai jigoku." *Kaien* 10.12 (December 1991): 212–221.

"Kojiki." In *Kojiki, jōdai kayō, NKBZ* 1, pp. 41–367. Shōgakkan, 1973.

Kojiki. Trans. Donald L. Phillipi. University of Tokyo Press, 1968.

Kojiki. Trans. Post Wheeler. New York: H. Schuman, 1952. Reprint (Westport, Conn.: Greenwood Press, 1976).

The Kojiki: Records of Ancient Matters. Trans. Basil Hall Chamberlain. Rutland, Vt.: Charles E. Tuttle, 1981.

La Bruyère, Jean de. *Characters*. Trans. Henri Van Laun. London: Oxford University Press, 1963. Originally published as *Les caractères* (1688). Reprint (Paris: Hachette, 1950).

Maruya Saiichi. "Long Interview: Fushigina bungakushi o ikiru." *Bungakukai* 48.7 (July 1994): 108–155.

Morioka, Heinz, and Miyoko Sasaki. *Rakugo: The Popular Narrative Art of Japan*. Harvard East Asian Monographs 138. Cambridge: Council on East Asian Studies, Harvard University, and Harvard University Press, 1990.

Nabokov, Vladimir. *Lolita*. Paris: Olympia Press, 1955. Reprint (New York: Vintage International, 1997).

Odaira Maiko. "Ogino Anna." *Kokubungaku: kaishaku to kyōzai no kenkyū* 44.3 (February 1999): 42–43.

———. "Ogino Anna ryaku nenpu." In *Josei sakka sirīzu*, vol. 22, *Nakazawa Kei, Tawada Yōko, Ogino Anna, Ogawa Yōko*, ed. Kōno Taeko et al., pp. 448–449. Kadokawa shoten, 1998.

———. "Sakka gaido: Ogino Anna." In *Josei sakka sirīzu*, vol. 22, *Nakazawa Kei, Tawada Yōko, Ogino Anna, Ogawa Yōko*, ed. Kōno Taeko et al., pp. 446–447. Kadokawa shoten, 1998.

Ogino Anna. *Ai rabu Ango*. Asahi shinbunsha, 1992.

———. *Anna no kōjō kankō*. Kōdō tsūshinsha, 1995.

———. *Anna-ryū genki ga nani yori*. Kairyūsha, 1993.

———. "Bahuchin o meguru porifonī." In *Mihairu Bahuchin no jikū*, pp. 26–35. Serika Archives. Serika shobō, 1997.

———. *Buryūgeru tonda*. Shinchōsha, 1991.

———. "Doa o shimeruna." In *Yūkitai*, pp. 59–148. Bungei shunjū, 1990. Reprinted from *Bungakukai* 43.12 (December 1989): 192–238.

———. *Hanshi hanshō*. Kadokawa shoten, 1996.

———. "Horafuki Anri no bōken." 24 segments. *Bungakukai* 51.1 (January 1997)–53.2 (February 1999). Pagination varies.

———. *Horafuki Anri no bōken*. Bungei shunjū, 2000.

———. "Katayoku no pegasasu: Ango o meguru gesakuteki shihyōron no kokoromi." In *Ai rabu Ango*, pp. 11–82. Asahi shinbunsha, 1992. Reprinted from *Bungakukai* 42.5 (May 1988): 242–275.

———. "Kobayashi Hideo de gozaimasu: Minami Haruo to iu koto." In *Madonna no henshin shikkaku*, pp. 7–51. Fukutake shoten, 1993. Reprinted with revision from *Kaien* 12.10 (October 1993): 224–240.

———. *Les Éloges paradoxaux dans le Tiers et le Quart Livres de Rabelais: Enquête sur le comique et le cosmique à la Renaissance*. Furansu tosho, 1989.

———. *Madonna no henshin shikkaku*. Fukutake shoten, 1993.

———. *Momo monogatari*. Kōdansha, 1994.

———. "Nihongo mutsukashi desu ne." In *Warau shika nai!* Ōsama bunko, pp. 80–82. Mikasa shobō, 2000. Enlarged and rev. ed. of *Anna-ryū genki ga nani yori*.

———. *Raburē shuppan*. Iwanami shoten, 1994.

————. "Retorikku to shite no parodī: shijō no rakuen." In *Parodī no seiki, Shirīzu haiku sekai* no. 6, ed. Ogino Anna, Natsuishi Banya, and Fukumoto Ichirō, pp. 104–111. Yūzankaku shuppan, 1997.

————. *Seoimizu.* Bungei shunjū, 1991.

————. "Seoimizu." In *Seoimizu* (Bungei shunjū, 1991), pp. 6–87; and *Seoimizu*, Bunshun bunko (Bungei shunjū, 1994), pp. 8–97. Reprinted from *Bungakukai* 45.6 (June 1991): 54–96.

————. "Seoimizu no haha." In *Anna-ryū genki ga nani yori,* pp. 140–141. Kairyūsha, 1993.

————. *Shūkan Ogino.* Kadokawa bunko. Kadokawa shoten, 1993.

————. *Sora-tobu buta.* Kyōdō tsūshinsha, 1999.

————. "Supein no shiro." In *Yūkitai* pp. 149–229. Bungei shunjū, 1990. Reprinted from *Bungakukai* 44.6 (June 1990): 70–110.

————. "Tonderu buta." In *Shūkan Ogino,* Kadokawa bunko, pp. 156–160. Kadokawa shoten, 1993.

————. "Uchi no okan ga ocha o nomu." In *Josei sakka shirīzu,* vol. 22, *Nakazawa Kei, Tawada Yōko, Ogino Anna, Ogawa Yōko,* ed. Kōno Taeko et al. (Kadokawa shoten, 1998), pp. 205–242; and *Yūkitai* (Bungei shunjū, 1990), pp. 13–58. Reprinted from *Bungakukai* 43.6 (June 1989): 108–130.

————. "Warau Bosshu." In *Buryūgeru tonda* (Shinchōsha, 1991), pp. 5–63; and *Josei sakka shirīzu,* vol. 22, *Nakazawa Kei, Tawada Yōko, Ogino Anna, Ogawa Yōko,* ed. Kōno Taeko et al. (Kadokawa shoten, 1998), pp. 243–295. Reprinted from *Shinchō* 88.6 (June 1991): 152–182.

————. "Warau Nihon." In *Anna-ryū genki ga nani yori,* pp. 23–29. Kairyūsha, 1993.

————. *Warau shika nai!* Ōsama bunko. Mikasa shobō, 2000. Enlarged and rev. ed. of *Anna-ryū genki ga nani yori.*

————. *Watakushi no aidokusho.* Fukutake shoten, 1991.

————. "Yaketa totan-yane no ue no okonomi-yaki: arui wa shoku ni yoru jiko-hyōgen ni tsuite." In *New Feminism Review,* vol. 2, *Onna to hyōgen: feminizumu hiyō no genzai,* ed. Mizuta Noriko, pp. 236–245. Gakuyō shobō, 1991.

————. [Anna-chan]. *Yojigen-han.* Kawade shobō shinsha, 1983.

————. *Yūkitai.* Bungei shunjū, 1990.

Parodī no seiki. Ed. Ogino Anna, Natsuishi Banya, and Fukumoto Ichirō. *Shirīzu haiku sekai,* no. 6. Yūzankaku shuppan, 1997.

Rabelais, François. *Garuganchua monogatari.* Trans. Watanabe Kazuo. Iwanami bunko. Iwanami shoten, 1973.

————. *The Histories of Gargantua and Pantagruel.* Trans. John M. Cohen. London: Penguin Books, 1955. Reprint in limited ed. with special contents. Franklin Center, Pa.: Franklin Library, 1978.

————. *Pantaguryueru monogatari.* 4 vols. Trans. Watanabe Kazuo. Iwanami bunko. Iwanami shoten, 1973–1975.

Ronsard, Pierre de. *Poems of Pierre de Ronsard.* Trans. and ed. Nicholas Kilmer. Berkeley and Los Angeles: University of California Press, 1979.

Sakaguchi Ango. "FARCE ni tsuite." *Aoitori,* no. 5 (1932). Reprinted in *Sakaguchi Ango zenshū,* vol. 14 (1990), pp. 17–32.

————. *Sakaguchi Ango zenshū.* 18 vols. Chikuma bunko, 1989–1991.

Sansom, G. B., trans. "Essays in Idleness" (Tsurezuregusa), by Yoshida Kenkō. In *Anthology of Japanese Literature: From the Earliest Era to the Mid-nineteenth Century,* ed. Donald Keene, pp. 231–241. New York: Grove Press, 1955.

Shōno Yoriko. *Nihyakkaiki.* Shinchōsha, 1994.

Songs to Make the Dust Dance: The Ryōjin hishō of Twelfth-century Japan. Trans. Yung-Hee K. Kwon. Berkeley and Los Angeles: University of California Press, 1994.

Suzuki Sadami. "Junbungaku to taishūbungaku." Serialized in *Bungakukai* 47.10 (October 1993): 170–192; 47.11 (November 1993): 180–205; 47.12 (December 1993): 338–360; 48.1 (January 1994): 238–263.

Tatsumi Takayuki. "Ogino Anna: yaminabe-gengo no uwaki musume." In *Koku-bungaku: kaishaku to kanshō, bessatsu* (10 May 1991), pp. 175–180.

Torrey, Norman L. *The Spirit of Voltaire.* New York: Columbia University Press, 1938.

CONTRIBUTORS

TOMOKO AOYAMA is a lecturer in the Department of Asian Languages and Studies at the University of Queensland, Australia. She received a B.A. from Ochanomizu University, an M.A. from the Tokyo University of Foreign Studies, and a Ph.D. from the University of Queensland. Her publications include "The Love That Poisons: Japanese Parody and the New Literacy," *Japan Forum* 6.1 (April 1994); and "Japanese Literary Responses to the Russo-Japanese War," in *The Russo-Japanese War in Cultural Perspective, 1904–05*, ed. David Wells and Sandra Wilson (Macmillan Press, 1999). She is working on two projects: food in Japanese literature and the father-daughter relationship in Japanese women's writing.

SONJA ARNTZEN received her Ph.D. in Japanese Literature from the University of British Columbia and is currently professor of East Asian Studies at the University of Toronto, Canada. Her books include *The Crazy Cloud Anthology of Ikkyū Sōjun* (1986) and *The Kagerō Diary: A Woman's Autobiographical Text from the Tenth Century* (Center for Japanese Studies, University of Michigan Press, 1997).

JANICE BROWN is associate professor of Modern Japanese Literature in the Department of East Asian Studies, University of Alberta, Canada. Author of *Hayashi Fumiko's I Saw a Pale Horse and Selected Poems from Diary of a Vagabond* (Cornell East Asian Series, 1997) and numerous articles on Japanese women writers, her current research interests include Japanese women's writing of the 1920s and 1930s with an emphasis on *gendaishi* (modern free verse), modern and contemporary poetry by Japanese women writers, and feminist literary theory.

REBECCA L. COPELAND is associate professor of Japanese Language and Literature and director of the East Asian Studies Program at Washington University in St. Louis. Her publications include *The Sound of the Wind: The Life and Works of Uno Chiyo* (University of Hawai'i Press, 1992), *Lost Leaves: Women Writers of Meiji Japan* (University of Hawai'i Press, 2000), and various translations of and articles on modern Japanese women writers.

MIDORI MCKEON is assistant professor of Japanese at San Francisco State University. Her publications include "The Transformation of the Urashima Legend: The Influence of Religion on Gender," *U.S.-Japan Women's Journal* (1996). She is currently involved in research on modern Japanese women writers and on gender representation in Japanese folktales.

EILEEN B. MIKALS-ADACHI is associate professor of Japanese literature at her alma mater, Ochanomizu University in Tokyo, where she was one of the first non-Japanese to earn a Ph.D. in Japanese literature. Her dissertation dealt with classical literary influences on the writings of Enchi Fumiko. Presently she is involved in numerous translation and writing projects concerning this author and other modern Japanese women writers.

JOSHUA S. MOSTOW is associate professor of Asian Studies at the University of British Columbia, Canada. Publications include *Pictures of the Heart: The Hyakunin Isshu in Word and Image* (University of Hawai'i Press, 1996) and "'Picturing' in *The Tale of Genji*," *Journal of the Association of Teachers of Japanese* 33.1 (1999). He is presently completing a translation of Heian period poem-tales: *At the House of Gathered Leaves: Shorter Biographical and Autobiographical Narratives from Tenth-Century Japan*. His current theoretical research focuses on the construction and gendering of the Heian period in modern Japanese thought.

SHARALYN ORBAUGH is associate professor of Asian Studies and Women's Studies at the University of British Columbia, Canada. Publications include "The Body in Contemporary Japanese Women's Fiction," in *The Woman's Hand: Gender and Theory in Japanese Women's Writing,* ed. Paul Gordon Schalow and Janet Walker (Stanford University Press, 1996) and "Arguing with the Real: Kanai Mieko," in *Ōe and Beyond: Fiction in Contemporary Japan,* ed. Stephen Snyder and Philip Gabriel (University of Hawai'i Press, 1999). Her work engages theories of vision and the body as represented in various narrative media.

ESPERANZA RAMIREZ-CHRISTENSEN was the discussant at the Association for Asian Studies conference panel on "Japanese Literary Women and Their Fathers" that was the initial source for the papers. She organized the 1997 Midwest Association for Japanese Literary Studies conference on the new historicism and served as Visiting Professor at the Kokubungaku Shiryōkan in Tokyo in 1997 and Faculty Fellow at the Michigan Institute for the Humanities in 1999–2000. She has published articles on *The Tale of Genji* and Heian narrative as well as medieval linked poetry *(renga)*. The author of *Heart's Flower: The Life and Poetry of Shinkei* (Stanford University Press, 1994), she is presently completing a manuscript on medieval poetics, Buddhism, and deconstruction. Ramirez-Christensen is associate professor of Japanese Literature at the Department of Asian Languages and Cultures, University of Michigan.

ATSUKO SAKAKI is associate professor of Japanese Literature at the University of Toronto. Her publications include *The Woman with the Flying Head and Other Stories by Kurahashi Yumiko* (M. E. Sharpe, 1998) and *Recontextualizing Texts: Narrative Performance in Modern Japanese Literature* (Harvard East Asian Monographs, 1999). She is currently working on a book-length study of Kurahashi Yumiko and a study of the images of China in Japanese literature.

EDITH SARRA is associate professor of East Asian Languages and Cultures and adjunct associate professor of Gender Studies at Indiana University, Bloomington. Her current research centers on thematic and conceptual developments in the fictional tales of late classical and early medieval Japan. She is the author of *Fictions of Femininity: Literary Inventions of Gender in Japanese Court Women's Memoirs* (Stanford University Press, 1999), as well as articles on major female writers of the Heian period.

ANN SHERIF is associate professor of Japanese Literature at Oberlin College. She is the author of *Mirror: The Fiction and Essays of Kōda Aya* (University of Hawai'i Press, 1999) and the translator of a number of Yoshimoto Banana's works.

INDEX